Study Guide

TO ACCOMPANY

Lipsey / Purvis / Steiner

ECONOMICS

FIFTH EDITION

prepared by

Douglas A. L. Auld
UNIVERSITY OF GUELPH

E. Kenneth Grant
UNIVERSITY OF GUELPH

Richard G. Lipsey

Douglas D. Purvis
QUEEN'S UNIVERSITY

with the assistance of

Fredric C. Menz
CLARKSON UNIVERSITY

HARPER & ROW, PUBLISHERS, New York
Cambridge, Philadelphia, San Francisco,
London, Mexico City, São Paulo, Singapore, Sydney

Study Guide to accompany ECONOMICS, Fifth Edition

For information address Harper & Row, Publishers, Inc., 10 East 53d Street, New York, NY 10022.

ISBN: 0-06-040405-1

CONTENTS

To the Student v

Part One: The Nature of Economics

Chapter 1: The Economic Problem 1
2: Economics as a Social Science 7
3: An Overview of the Economy 13

Part Two: A General View of the Price System

4: Demand, Supply, and Price 17
5: Elasticity of Demand and Supply 25
6: Supply and Demand in Action: Price Controls and Agriculture 34

Part Three: Demand

7: Household Consumption Behavior. The Marginal Utility Approach 43
8: Household Consumption Behavior: The Indifference Curve Approach 48
9: The Role of the Firm 56
10: Production and Cost in the Short Run 61
11: Production and Cost in the Long and Very Long Run 71

Part Four: Markets and Pricing

12: Pricing in Competitive Markets 80
13: Pricing in Monopoly Markets 87
14: Industrial Organization and Theories of Imperfect Competition 93
15: Monopoly Versus Competition 98
16: Who Runs the Firm and for What Ends? 102

Part Five: The Distribution of Income

17: Factor Pricing 106
18: Factor Demand and Supply 111
19: The Labor Market 116
20: The Problem of Poverty 123

Part Six: International Trade

21: The Gains from Trade 126
22: Barriers to Free Trade 132
23: Growth in Less-Developed Countries 137

Part Seven: The Market Economy: Problems and Policies

24: Benefits and Costs of Government Intervention 141
25: Public Finance and Public Expenditure 147

Part Eight: National Income and Fiscal Policy

26: Inflation, Unemployment, and Growth: An Introduction to Macroeconomics 152
27: Measuring National Income 161
28: National Income and Aggregate Demand 178

29: Changes in National Income I: The Role of Aggregate Demand 178
30: Changes in National Income II: The Role of Aggregate Supply 190
31: Business Cycles: The Ebb and Flow of Economic Activity 196
32: Fiscal Policy 204

Part Nine: Money, Banking, and Monetary Policy

33: The Nature of Money and Monetary Institutions 210
34: The Role of Money in Macroeconomics 218
35: Monetary Policy 229

Part Ten: Macroeconomic Problems

36: Inflation 235
37: Employment and Unemployment 241
38: Economic Growth 245

Part Eleven: International Macroeconomics

39: Foreign Exchange, Exchange Rates, and the Balance of Payments 250
40: Alternative Exchange Rate Regimes 257
41: Macroeconomic Policy in an Open Economy 264

Part Twelve: Macroeconomic Controversies

42: Macroeconomic Controversies 272

Answers 279-342

TO THE STUDENT

The content of this Study Guide tests and reinforces the student's understanding of the concepts and analytical techniques stressed in each chapter of ECONOMICS, Fifth Edition, by Lipsey, Purvis, and Steiner. Our own teaching experience has led us to believe that students have the most trouble in understanding technical information and in applying theoretical concepts to particular situations. Consequently, we have expanded the number of multiple-choice questions and exercises in most chapters. The exercises tend to be technical and numerical in nature. We feel that policy issues and specific applications of theory to "real-world" examples are primarily the responsibility of the textbook. You will find excellent discussions of issues and applications in the body of the text, especially in the policy "boxes" that appear in each chapter.

Each chapter in this Study Guide corresponds to a text chapter and is divided into three basic sections. The Chapter Objectives briefly summarize the important concepts and analysis covered in the textbook and Study Guide. It might be useful for you to compare this section with the summary section appearing at the end of each text chapter.

The Multiple-Choice Questions test your comprehension of definitions, analytical concepts, and techniques. When you answer these questions, avoid the temptation to leap at the first answer that seems plausible. For each question there is one best answer. You should be able to explain why any other answer is not as satisfactory as the one you have chosen.

In some ways the greatest reinforcement to learning economics comes from working the Exercises. You are usually asked to demonstrate numerically and/or graphically the sense of what has been expressed verbally. In addition, you are often asked to explain your method of analysis and your results. The ability to solve problems and to communicate and interpret results are important goals in an introductory economics course.

Do not be discouraged if you have difficulties with certain questions. Some are quite challenging for the beginner, and a full appreciation of the points involved can be achieved only after you have participated in lectures and carefully read the text.

The Exercise answers found at the back of the guide are limited in detail. They are provided as a way to check your comprehension of the material involved. The Multiple-Choice answers are complete.

ACKNOWLEDGMENTS

We would like to express our gratitude to our colleagues at the University of Guelph and at other Canadian universities and colleges, who assisted with the preparation of the fifth edition through comments and criticisms on the fourth edition. We would particularly like to thank our research assistant Eveline van Sligtenhorst.

Certain materials in this Guide were adapted from Forbush and Menz, Study Guide to accompany ECONOMICS, Seventh Edition, by Lipsey, Steiner, and Purvis. We also acknowledge the editorial contributions of Fredric C. Menz, Chair, Department of Economics, Clarkson University.

Douglas Auld
E. Kenneth Grant

PART ONE

THE NATURE OF ECONOMICS

CHAPTER 1

THE ECONOMIC PROBLEM

CHAPTER OBJECTIVES

This chapter introduces the basic issues to be covered in an economics course, focusing on the ways in which society uses its resources and distributes its production. Several examples are provided to illustrate the concept of opportunity cost and how this concept relates to a society's production possibility boundary. You should understand how the production possibility boundary separates attainable combinations of goods from unattainable combinations, and how factor reallocation relates to movements along the boundary. You should also be able to identify those factors which cause a shift in the production possibility boundary.

MULTIPLE-CHOICE QUESTIONS

1. Scarcity is a problem that
   (a) proper use of resources could eliminate
   (b) will continue to exist as long as humanity finds new wants to be satisfied
   (c) population control would solve
   (d) is confined to poor countries

2. Which of the following is <u>not</u> classified as a factor of production?
   (a) food
   (b) labor services
   (c) land
   (d) capital equipment

3. The act of using commodities to satisfy wants is called
   (a) production
   (b) consumption
   (c) investment
   (d) the distribution of income

4. Which of the following did <u>not</u> occur in the Canadian economy in the late 1970s and early 1980s?
   (a) relatively high rates of inflation
   (b) high levels of unemployment
   (c) Canada became a net importer of natural gas and oil
   (d) productivity growth was high and sustained

5. Drawing a production possibility boundary for swords and medical care will help us to
   (a) estimate how much it is necessary to spend on defense (swords)
   (b) estimate the amount of unemployment that is likely to result from a given government expenditure on hospitals (medical care)
   (c) illustrate the cost of defense in terms of the expenditure on medical care that will have to be foregone
   (d) show the relative desires of the public for war or health care

6. Opportunity cost
   (a) is measured by how much of one commodity you have to forego in order to get some stated amount of another good
   (b) measures how many different opportunities you have to spend your money
   (c) measures opportunities in terms of their relative prices
   (d) is always the same as money costs

7. If tuition plus other direct costs of going to college come to $10,000 per year, and you could have earned $12,500 per year working instead, the opportunity cost of your college year is
   (a) $10,000
   (b) $12,500
   (c) $22,500
   (d) $ 2,500

8. If a 12 month subscription to a fitness club costs as much as tickets for 24 Toronto Blue Jay baseball games, then the opportunity cost of a baseball game is
   (a) a one-year subscription
   (b) 2 months of membership or 1/6 of a subscription
   (c) 1 month of membership or 1/12 of a subscription
   (d) ½ month of membership or 1/24 of a subscription

9. If a commodity can be obtained without sacrificing the production or consumption of anything else,
   (a) its opportunity cost is zero
   (b) the economy is on its production possibility boundary
   (c) the opportunity cost concept is irrelevant and meaningless
   (d) its opportunity cost equals its money cost

10. Points to the left of the current production possibility boundary
    (a) are currently unattainable and are expected to remain so
    (b) will be attainable only if there is economic growth
    (c) will result if some factors of production are unemployed or used inefficiently
    (d) have higher opportunity costs than points on the boundary itself

11. A country's production possibility boundary shows
    (a) what percentage of its resources is currently unemployed
    (b) what choices in production are currently available to it
    (c) what it is actually producing
    (d) the available methods of production

12. A shift outward in the production possibility boundary
    (a) would result if more of one product and less of another were chosen
    (b) could reflect the higher prices for goods
    (c) could reflect increased unemployment
    (d) could result from increased productivity of resources

13. With respect to who owns the resources in an economy, which one of the following statements does <u>not</u> reflect the points in the chapter?
    (a) All economies are neither completely free-market nor command.
    (b) There is, in the world, a wide spectrum with respect to the degree of free-market and command activity.
    (c) The command economy cannot achieve production goals that free-market economies can.
    (d) The degree of free-market and command elements in an economy has changed over time for a number of countries.

14. The choice by a society of an economic system over others often reflects
    (a) a strong preference with respect to future and current consumption
    (b) a preference for individual as contrasted to public choices
    (c) a desire for freedom as contrasted to coercion
    (d) all of the above

15. The assignment of scarce factors to the production of goods is referred to by the term
    (a) resource allocation
    (b) consumption
    (c) macroeconomics
    (d) income distribution

EXERCISES

1. The following data show what combinations of corn and beef can be produced annually from a given piece of land.

Corn (bushels)	Beef (pounds)
10,000	0
8,000	900
6,000	1,200
4,000	1,400
2,000	1,450
0	1,500

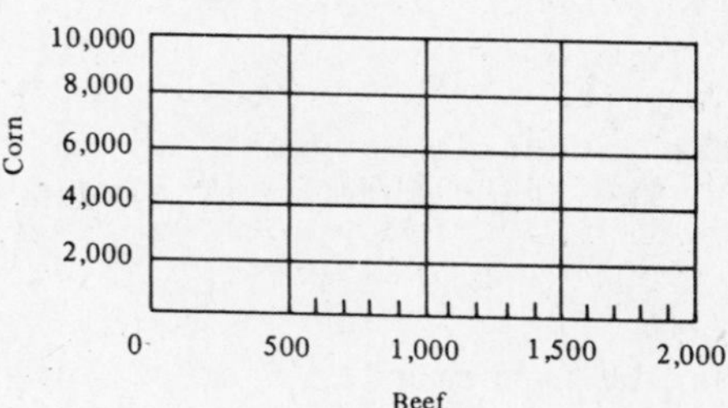

(a) On the graph above, draw the production-possibility boundary for this piece of land.

(b) Can this acreage produce 5,000 bushels of corn and 500 pounds of beef?

(c) Can this acreage produce 8,000 bushels of corn and 1,200 pounds of beef?

(d) What is the opportunity cost of expanding beef production from 900 to 1,200 pounds per annum?

(e) What would the production of 5,000 bushels of corn and 500 pounds of beef suggest about the use of this acreage?

(f) What happens to the opportunity cost of producing beef as this economy expands its production of beef?

2. A certain economy produces only two consumer goods, X and Y. Only labor is required to produce both goods and the economy's labor force is fixed at 100 workers. The table below indicates the amount of X and Y that can be produced daily with various quantities of labor.

Number of Workers	Daily X Production	Number of Workers	Daily Y Production
0	0	0	0
10	40	10	5
20	95	20	12
30	200	30	20
40	300	40	28
50	390	50	36
60	450	60	43
70	500	70	49
80	548	80	55
90	580	90	58
100	600	100	60

(a) Draw the production-possibility curve for this economy, using the grid on p. 5. (Hint: The labor force must always be employed.)

(b) What is the opportunity cost of increasing the output of X from 200 to 300 units? What is the opportunity cost of increasing the output of X from 500 to 600? What happens to the opportunity cost of producing more and more X?

(c) Suppose that actual production for a given period was 400 units of X and 20 units of Y. What can you infer from this information?

(d) A central planner in this economy calls for an output of X = 450 and Y = 48. Is this plan attainable? Explain.

(e) New technology is introduced in the production of X and each worker can now produce ½ units more per day. What happens to the production possibility curve? Draw the new curve on the graph. Can the planner's output plan be fulfilled now?

(f) If productivity in X remained as before (questions a to d), by how much would productivity in Y per worker have to increase for the planner's wishes to be fulfilled?

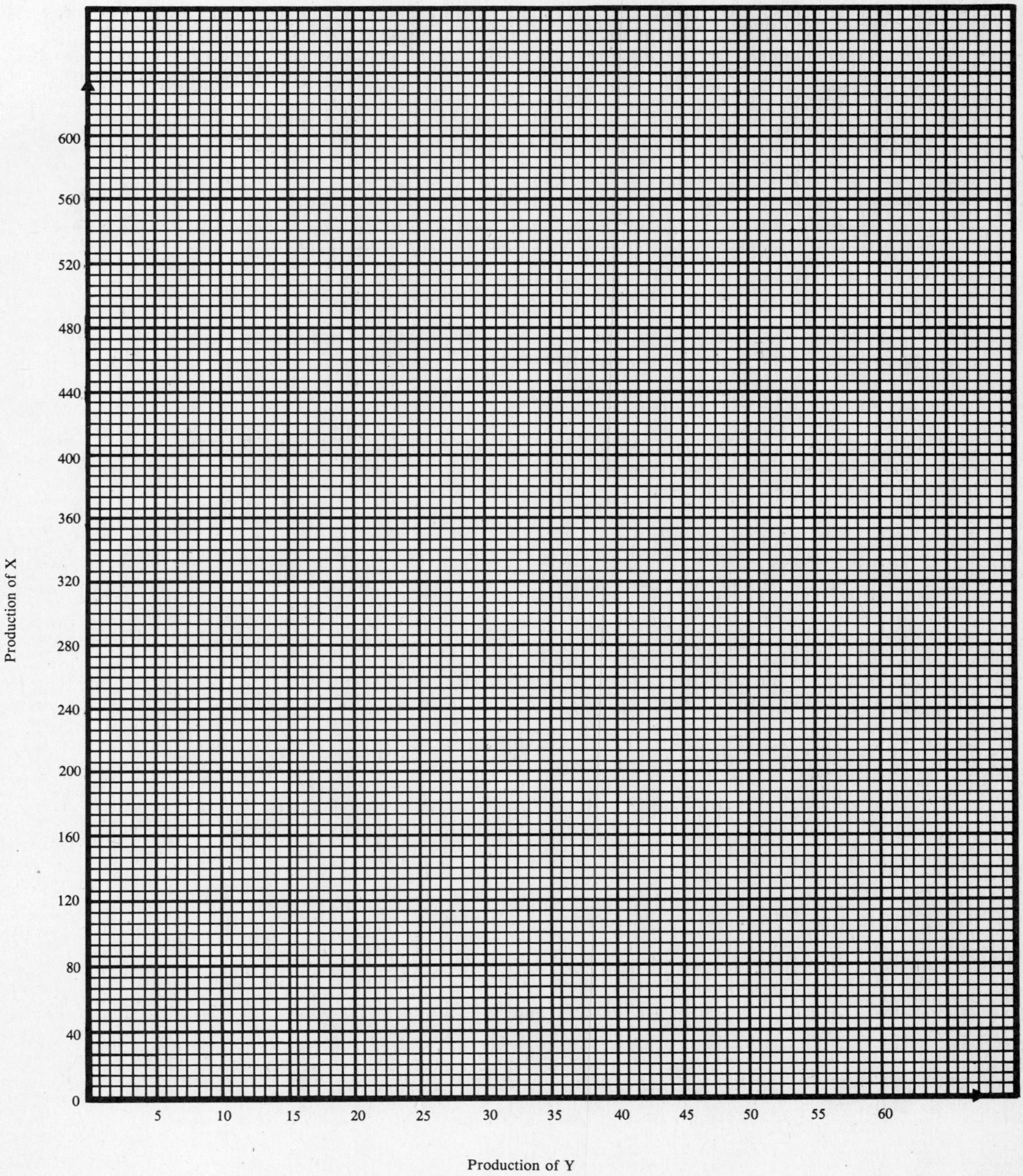

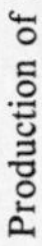
Production of X
600
560
520
480
440
400
360
320
280
240
200
160
120
80
40
0
5
10
15
20
25
30
35
40
45
50
55
60
Production of Y

3. An economy's production possibility boundary is given by the mathematical expression, $20 = 4A + B$, where A is the quantity of good "a" and B is the quantity of good "b."

(a) If all resources in the economy were allocated to producing good "a," what is the maximum level of production for this good? What is the maximum level of production for good "b"?

(b) Suppose that the production of "b" was increased from 12 to 16 units and that the economy is producing at a point on the production possibility boundary. What is the opportunity cost per unit of good "b"? What is the opportunity cost per unit of good "b" if the production of this good was increased from 16 to 20?

(c) In what way is this production possibility boundary different from those in questions 1 and 2 in terms of opportunity costs?

(d) In what way does the combination of 4 units of good "a" and 5 units of good "b" represent the problem of scarcity?

CHAPTER 2

ECONOMICS AS A SOCIAL SCIENCE

CHAPTER OBJECTIVES

This chapter expands on scientific aspects of economics, stressing the distinction between positive and normative propositions. You should recognize in a theory the choice of variables and assumptions and the hypotheses about the relation of variables that lead to testable predictions. The exercises emphasize the material in the appendix to this chapter such as functional forms, diagram drawings, slopes of curves, and shifts in curves.

MULTIPLE-CHOICE QUESTIONS

1. Positive statements concern what is; normative statements concern
   (a) what was
   (b) what is the normal situation
   (c) what will be
   (d) what ought to be

2. We do not want value judgments incorporated in scientific theories because
   (a) they are too complex
   (b) they are too unrealistic because they are generally idealistic
   (c) they cannot be tested by an appeal to evidence
   (d) they cannot be expressed mathematically

3. In economic theory, an exogeneous variable
   (a) is one that can be predicted with accuracy
   (b) has no influence on the theory
   (c) is not determined by other variables within the theoretical framework
   (d) is always constant

4. The significance of the normal curve of error for social scientists is that
   (a) all human behavior is rational and consistent
   (b) it shows that experimentation is not necessary
   (c) it shows how futile it is to bother measuring accurately
   (d) it aids in making predictions from a large number of observations

5. The "law" of large numbers asserts that
   (a) random actions of a large number of individuals tend to offset each other
   (b) what is true of large numbers is always true of a few individuals
   (c) too many observations result in an unacceptable number of errors
   (d) the range of errors of measurement increases with the number of observations

6. Which of the following statements is most appropriate for economic theories?
   (a) The most reliable test of a theory is the realism of its assumptions.
   (b) The best kind of theory is worded so that it can pass any test to which it could be put.
   (c) The most important thing about the scientific approach is that it uses mathematics and diagrams.
   (d) We expect our theories to hold only with some margin of error.

7. A theory may contain all but which of the following?
   (a) an unorganized collection of facts about the real world
   (b) predictions about behavior that are deduced from the assumptions
   (c) a set of assumptions defining the conditions under which the theory will be operative
   (d) one or more hypotheses about how the world behaves

8. A scientific prediction is a conditional statement because
   (a) it takes the form, "if one event occurs, then a particular result will follow"
   (b) it is impossible to test
   (c) it can never be based on enough observations
   (d) it is usually eventually shown to be false

9. If a time dimension is required to give a particular variable meaning, then that variable is considered
   (a) a stock variable
   (b) an endogenous variable
   (c) an exogeneous variable
   (d) a flow variable

10. Which of the following is the best example of a normative statement?
   (a) Unemployment has increased while inflation has decreased.
   (b) If government deficits increase, then unemployment will fall.
   (c) Oil price increases cause Canadians to use less oil.
   (d) The Canadian dollar should always be at par with the U.S. dollar.

11. Which of the following is the best example of a positive statement?
   (a) Equal distribution of national income is a desirable goal of society.
   (b) Foreign ownership is undesirable and therefore should be eliminated.
   (c) Inflation redistributes purchasing power away from those on fixed income to other members of the economy.
   (d) Public ownership of resources is preferable to private ownership.

EXERCISES

Note to the student: You may wish to refer to the Appendix to Chapter 2 before beginning some of the exercises to this chapter.

1. After each phrase below, write P or N to indicate whether a positive or normative statement is being described
   (a) a statement of fact that is actually wrong
   (b) a value judgment
   (c) a prediction that an event will happen
   (d) a statement about what the author thinks ought to be
   (e) a statement that can be tested by evidence

2. Indicate whether the following are flow variables (F) or stock variables (S).

(a) an economy's annual total output ____________

(b) the total value of factories and warehouses in Canada ____________

(c) monthly per capita milk consumption in Quebec ______________

(d) your bank balance at the end of the month _________________

(e) your 1984 income tax payments _______________

(f) the quarterly output of North American automobiles ________________

(g) the number of aircraft owned by Air Canada ___________________

3. <u>The Relationship Between Real Consumption (C) and Real Disposable Income (Y_d)</u>

Statistics Canada collected information concerning the expenditure of households on all goods and services and levels of household after-tax income, which is referred to as disposable income, over the period 1950-1970. These data are called <u>time-series</u> data. The agency then adjusted both Y_d and C in two ways; it divided each by the total Canadian population in each year to obtain <u>per capita</u> consumption and disposable income, and then it adjusted these figures for changes in prices in order to obtain <u>real</u> per capita, or <u>constant dollar</u> per capita, consumption and disposable income. The data are recorded below:

Year	Real per Capita Consumption C	Real per Capita Disposable Income Y_d
1950	$1,142	$1,216
1951	1,126	1,255
1952	1,168	1,303
1953	1,217	1,333
1954	1,224	1,300
1955	1,294	1,292
1956	1,358	1,360
1957	1,365	1,446
1958	1,375	1,462
1959	1,418	1,479
1960	1,435	1,496
1961	1,422	1,475
1962	1,457	1,557
1963	1,500	1,600
1964	1,561	1,644
1965	1,626	1,737
1966	1,680	1,818
1967	1,729	1,864
1968	1,786	1,914
1969	1,841	1,974
1970	1,858	1,994

(a) Plot the scatter diagram between the two variables.

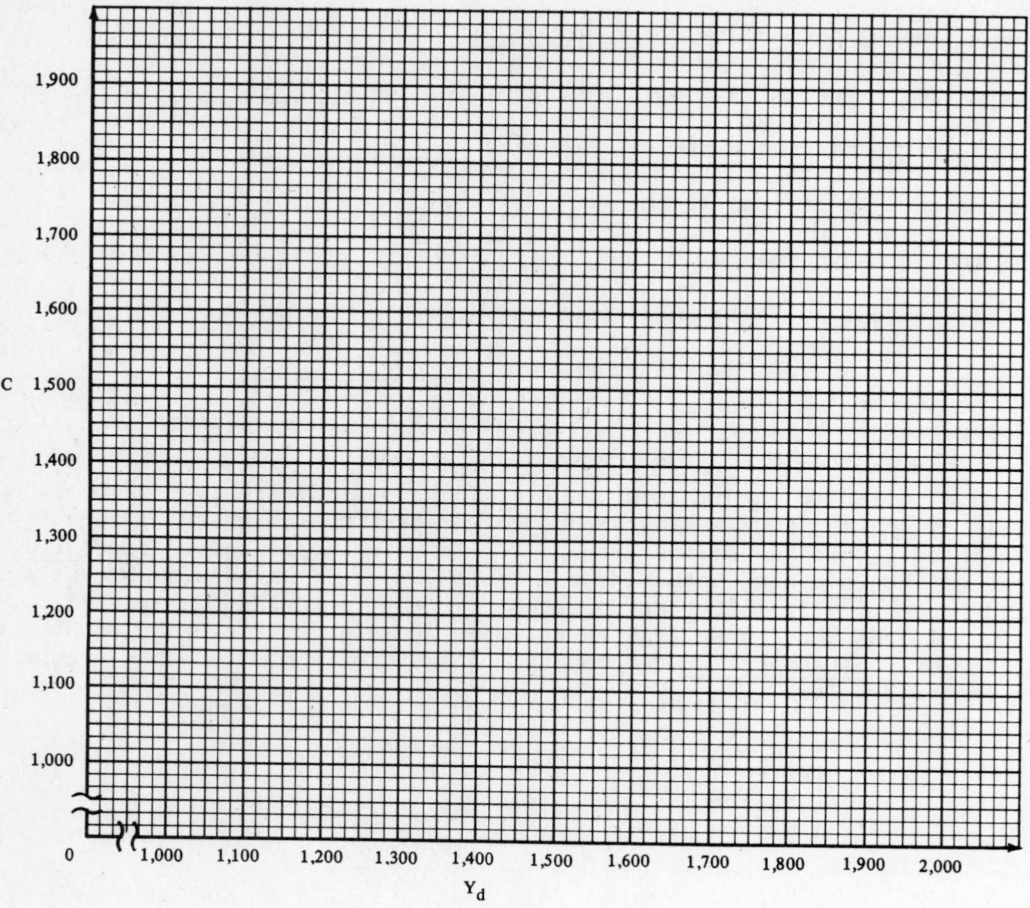

(b) Do the data suggest a positive or a negative relationship between C and Y_d?

(c) What was the increase in consumption between 1950 and 1960? Call this value ΔC, where the symbol Δ stands for "change in." Find ΔY_d between 1950 and 1960. Calculate the value $\Delta C/\Delta Y_d$. What is the meaning of this value? Calculate the value $\Delta C/\Delta Y_d$ for the period 1960 to 1970.

(d) Draw a 45° line in the graph starting at the coordinate (1,000, 1,000). Does the (C, Y_d) line lie above or below the 45° line? What do you think the distance between the two lines <u>at a given level</u> of Y_d represents?

(e) A statistician conducts a regression analysis of these data and obtains the expression $C = 5.16 + 0.93Y_d$. What does the value 0.93 represent? Why is the sign in front of the term $0.93Y_d$ positive?

4. Suppose that an economist hypothesizes that the quantity demanded of television sets (Q_d) over some time period is determined by the price of each television (P) and the average income of consumers (Y). The specific functional relationship among these three variables is hypothesized to be the expression $Q_d = 1Y - 4P$.

   (a) Which of these variables will be determined in the market for televisions? Are these variables considered endogenous or exogenous?

   (b) Which of these variables will be determined outside the market for televisions? Are these variables considered endogenous or exogenous?

   (c) What does the negative sign before the term 4P imply about the relationship between Q_d and P? What does the (implicit) positive sign before the term 1Y imply about the relationship between income and quantity demanded?

   (d) Which of the three variables are stock variables and which are flow variables? Explain.

   (e) Suppose for the moment that average income is constant at a level of 8,000. Write the expression for the demand relationship.

   (f) Assuming Y = 8,000, calculate the values of Q_d when P = 500, P = 1,000, P = 2,000, and P = 0.

(g) Plot the relation between P and Q_d (assuming Y = 8,000) on the graph below. Indicate the intercept values on both axes.

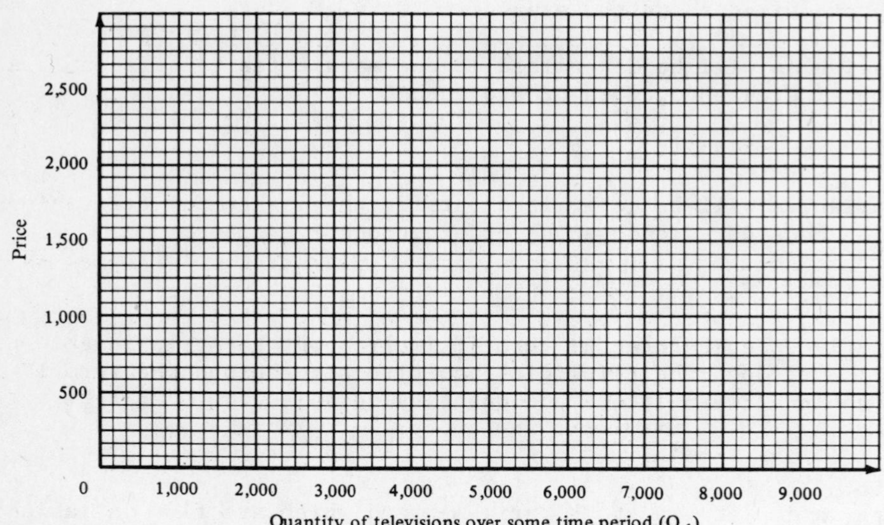

(h) Assuming Y = 8,000, calculate the change in the quantity demanded when the price increases from 1,000 to 2,000. Do the same for a price increase from 500 to 2,000. Call the change in the quantity demanded ΔQ_d and the change in the price ΔP. Form the ratio $\Delta Q_d/\Delta P$. Is this ratio constant?

(i) Suppose that the economist has additional evidence that the relationship in subsequent time periods has changed to $Q_d = 9{,}000 - 4P$. Plot the new relationship and indicate the intercept values on each axis. What has happened to the relation between the two variables? Why do you think the relationship changed over the two time periods?

CHAPTER 3

AN OVERVIEW OF THE ECONOMY

CHAPTER OBJECTIVES

This chapter discusses the nature of a market economy. Microeconomics emphasizes resource allocation within a coordinated set of factor and product markets in which changes in prices act as signals to households and firms to change their economic behavior. The questions test your understanding of the distinction between market and nonmarket activities and the distinction between the private and public sectors. Macroeconomics illustrates how national income is generated within a circular flow of goods and services and money payments among government, firms, and households.

MULTIPLE-CHOICE QUESTIONS

1. Specialization of labor
   (a) is generally less efficient than self-sufficiency in production
   (b) must be accompanied by trade to satisfy material desires
   (c) resulted in a shift of resources from industry to agriculture in early societies
   (d) was more common in nomadic societies than in modern economies

2. In a free-market economy, the allocation of resources is
   (a) determined by central authorities or other government agencies
   (b) possible only in a barter economy
   (c) determined only by producers who purchase factors of production
   (d) a result of decisions made by producers and consumers in various markets

3. A household, as defined in economics, is
   (a) assumed to own all factors of production except capital equipment
   (b) a homeowner rather than an apartment dweller
   (c) the principal user of the services of factors of production
   (d) assumed to make consistent decisions as if it were composed of a single individual

4. A firm can be described by all but which one of the following?
   (a) profit maximization
   (b) suppliers of most public goods
   (c) as though it were composed of a single individual making decisions
   (d) principal user of factors of production

5. The difference between a free-market economy and a command economy is
   (a) that large economies tend to be command economies and small ones tend to be free-market economies
   (b) primarily in terms of who makes the major decisions that influence resource allocation
   (c) that the free-market economy is a barter economy while the command economy is not
   (d) that the command economy is always in balance while surpluses and scarcities are trademarks of free-market economies

6. Which of the following is <u>not</u> usually a market sector activity?
   (a) the sale of automobiles
   (b) a fee-for-use public swimming pool
   (c) baby-sitting services through a private agency
   (d) the services of a fire department in a particular municipality

7. The price system in a free-market economy works in all <u>but</u> which one of the following ways:
   (a) price is a determinant of a firm's products and therefore encourages or discourages production
   (b) prices signal to consumers how much they must sacrifice to obtain a commodity
   (c) prices indicate relative scarcities and costs of production
   (d) prices allocate resources equally among different sectors of the economy

8. An increase in consumers' preference for chicken over pork may be predicted to lead to
   (a) a shift of resources into chicken farming
   (b) a rise in the price of pork
   (c) a fall in the price of chicken
   (d) a fall in the market value of existing chicken farms

9. Other things equal, an increase in the cost of producing coal may be predicted to lead to
   (a) a shift of resources into coal mining
   (b) a decrease in the price of oil
   (c) a greater quantity of coal demanded
   (d) a smaller quantity of coal demanded

10. The price system is effective in allocating resources because
   (a) nobody understands how it works
   (b) it is easy for central planners to manipulate consumer desires
   (c) it coordinates individual, and apparently unrelated, decisions.
   (d) shortages and surpluses tend to be eliminated automatically by prices falling and rising, respectively.

11. The circular flow refers to
   (a) the flow of goods and services from sellers to buyers
   (b) the flow of money in and out of the banking system
   (c) the flow of money incomes from buyers to sellers
   (d) both (a) and (c)

12. Which of the following is a <u>withdrawal</u> from the circular flow?
   (a) investment
   (b) taxes
   (c) government expenditure
   (d) consumption

13. Which of the following is an element of aggregate demand that arises directly from household spending?
   (a) government expenditure
   (b) exports
   (c) investment expenditures
   (d) consumption expenditures

14. Macroeconomics is concerned with aggregate flows within the entire economy, whereas microeconomics
    (a) looks at only the money flows in the aggregate economy
    (b) is concerned with the total flow of payments from households to firms
    (c) deals with the determination of relative prices and quantities in individual markets
    (d) concerns only commodity flows rather than money flows in the economy

EXERCISES

1. Indicate by checking which of the following events would likely occur in a market economy if there were a shift in interest from football to soccer.

    (a) Initially, a shortage of soccer equipment and a surplus of football equipment will develop.
    (b) Prices of footballs will be increased to eliminate the surplus.
    (c) Profits of soccer ball producers will rise.
    (d) Central authorities will order a shift of resources into production of soccer equipment.
    (e) Production of football equipment will be curtailed.
    (f) Sponsors would be prepared to pay higher rates for commercials during televised football games.
    (g) Labor and other resources will gradually transfer from football-related to soccer-related productive activity.
    (h) Resources particularly suited to football production will earn more, obtaining a higher share of national income.

2. Indicate by placing the Roman numeral of the statement in the right column how this statement has affected the market in the left column.

(a) price of beef falls ________	I. oil prices increase fourfold
(b) housing prices in Moncton decline ________	II. tastes change in favor of eating outdoors
(c) production of propane barbecues increases ________	III. beef producers have large excess stocks
(d) there is a shortage of loggers to cut firewood ________	IV. people move out of Moncton
(e) the price of coffee increases significantly ________	V. South America experiences heavy frosts and cold weather in late summer

3. Given the list of economic activities below, indicate whether they are attributable (in Canada) to the market economy (M), nonmarket economy (NM), private sector (R), or public sector (P). Any given activity may have more than one attribution.

    (a) the provision of national defense ________
    (b) repairs to the home by the owner ________
    (c) the sale of fresh produce at a market ________
    (d) government-operated toll bridge ________
    (e) lawyers' earnings from business real estate transactions ________
    (f) volunteer work for a provincial mental hospital ________

4. Assume there are four major decision-making groups in a particular economy; households (HH), firms (FM), government (GO), and banks (BA). The interaction between any two of the groups generates a flow of expenditure and income. These flows can be represented by a four-letter classification scheme. For example, the classification of HH-FM means a monetary flow originating from households and received by firms. Alternatively, it also means a receipt of income to firms from households.

   Using this scheme, classify the following transactions. Also indicate which of them is an example of an injection into the circular flow and which is an example of a withdrawal from the circular flow.

   (a) government pays the salaries of its civil servants ____________
   (b) households purchase automobiles ______________
   (c) government receives business tax payments ______________
   (d) firms receive loans for investment purposes from banks ____________
   (e) firms pay their workers ______________
   (f) banks receive deposits from the household sector ______________
   (g) government purchases goods from business firms ______________
   (h) firms retain some of their profits and deposit these in banks _________

PART TWO

A GENERAL VIEW OF THE PRICE SYSTEM

CHAPTER 4

DEMAND, SUPPLY, & PRICE

CHAPTER OBJECTIVES

The intersection of the demand and supply curves for a commodity establishes an equilibrium level of output and an equilibrium price. Shifts in either or both curves create disequilibrium--either excess supply or excess demand--at the original equilibrium price. The new intersection establishes a new equilibrium level of output and price. The exercises and questions in this chapter will help you to understand how disequilibria are resolved in the market-place. The notion of comparative statics is also reviewed.

MULTIPLE-CHOICE QUESTIONS

1. A survey shows that if new car prices are, on average, $11,000, consumers want to purchase 2 million new cars. Statistics for last year indicate that consumers actually bought 1.8 million cars.
   (a) The survey records quantity exchanged and the statistics record intended demand.
   (b) The survey records quantity demanded and the statistics record quantity exchanged.
   (c) The difference between the survey and the statistical report shows that a disequilibrium exists.
   (d) The survey and statistics both show what output is actually produced.

2. A large increase in the price of coffee will, other things equal,
   (a) cause a rightward shift in the demand curve for tea (a substitute)
   (b) cause a leftward shift in the demand curve for coffee
   (c) cause a downward movement along the demand curve for tea
   (d) cause both the demand curve for coffee and tea to shift right

3. A significant decline in the cost of home building materials will likely
   (a) cause the price of homes to rise
   (b) cause the demand curve for serviced building lots to shift right
   (c) cause the demand curve for serviced building lots to shift left
   (d) cause a movement along the demand curve for serviced building lots

4. An increase in the quantity demanded refers to
   (a) rightward shifts in the demand curve only
   (b) a movement down the demand curve
   (c) what consumers actually purchased at those prices
   (d) greater willingness to purchase at each possible market price

Use the table below to answer questions 5 and 6.

(1) (Case A) Quantity Offered for Sale	(2) Price	(3) (Case B) Quantity Offered for Sale
0	0	0
10	1	12
12	2	14
15	3	17
20	4	22
30	5	32

5. Columns (1) and (2) refer to
   (a) the supply curve
   (b) the revenue schedule for the firm
   (c) the supply schedule
   (d) a series of equilibrium price and output levels

6. If, given column (2), column (1) was replaced by column (3)
   (a) the corresponding graph would show a supply curve shift to the right
   (b) there would no longer exist a supply schedule
   (c) the corresponding graph would refute the basic hypothesis about supply
   (d) any firm would now be able to sell more at each price

7. The supply curve of houses would probably shift to the left if, other things equal
   (a) construction workers' wages increased
   (b) cheaper methods of prefabrication were developed
   (c) the demand for houses showed a marked decrease
   (d) the cost of building materials declined

8. If the cost of fertilizer falls significantly
   (a) the supply curve for corn will shift to the left
   (b) there will be a movement up the supply curve for corn
   (c) the supply curve for corn will shift to the right
   (d) the price of corn will rise

Use the diagram below to answer questions 9 to 11 (assume that price fluctuates freely)

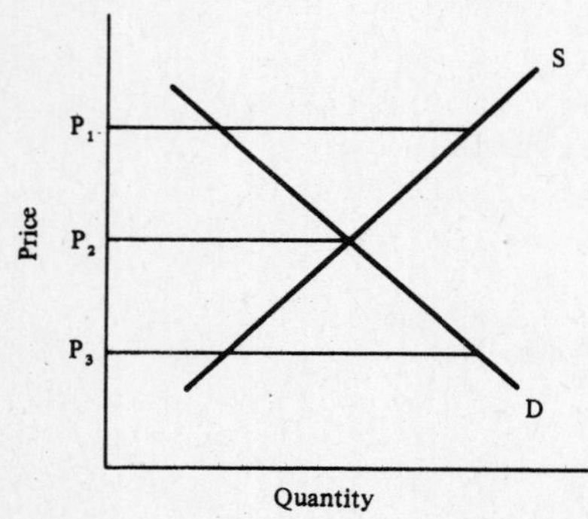

9. In the figure, at price P_1
   (a) quantity exchanged will exceed quantity supplied
   (b) the price will likely rise because demand is higher
   (c) there exists a disequilibrium
   (d) quantity demanded equals quantity supplied

10. At price P_3
   (a) there will be a tendency for the price to rise
   (b) there is excess supply
   (c) equilibrium can be restored only if the supply curve shifts
   (d) quantity exchanged equals quantity demanded

11. If the initial price is P_2 and the supply curve shifts to the right and at the same time consumer incomes fall,
   (a) price will remain constant
   (b) output will rise, price being constant
   (c) price will fall but output at the new equilibrium may not change
   (d) equilibrium output will definitely be less than initially

12. In the market for compact cars, permanently lower gasoline prices will most likely
   (a) cause a change in the demand for compact cars
   (b) result in an increase in the supply of compact cars
   (c) cause the price of compact cars to fall quickly in the short run
   (d) result in a movement along the demand curve for compact cars

13. The law of demand
   (a) allows us to predict accurately the change in the quantity demanded for any price change
   (b) explains all market behavior on the demand side
   (c) describes one aspect of market behavior which has stood up well to empirical testing
   (d) is immutable

14. Today the price of strawberries is \$.80 a quart and of raspberries, \$1.00. Tomorrow strawberries will be \$.60 and raspberries \$.75.
   (a) The relative price of raspberries is \$.75
   (b) The relative price of raspberries has fallen
   (c) Relative prices have not changed
   (d) Relative prices are now higher

15. If all prices are initially the same and the price of energy rises, the price of food declines and prices of all other commodities are unchanged,
   (a) energy has become relatively more expensive than all other commodities
   (b) there is overall inflation
   (c) energy has become relatively more expensive than food and relatively overall cheaper than other commodities
   (d) food has become relatively more expensive than all other commodities

16. Comparative statics
   (a) refers to unchanged prices and quantities
   (b) is the analysis of demand without reference to time
   (c) is the analysis of two market equilibria under two different sets of conditions
   (d) describes the time path of equilibrium prices

EXERCISES

1. The demand and supply schedules for good X are hypothesized to be as follows:

(1) Price per Unit	(2) Quantity Demanded (Units per Time Period)	(3) Quantity Supplied (Units Per Time Period)	(4) Excess Demand (+) Excess Supply (-) (Units per Time Period)
$1.00	1	25	______
.90	3	21	______
.80	5	19	______
.70	8	15	______
.60	12	12	______
.50	18	9	______
.40	26	6	______

(a) Using the grid below, plot the demand and supply curves (approximately). Indicate the equilibrium level of price and quantity of X by P_x and Q_x.

(b) Fill in column (4) for values of excess demand and excess supply. What is the value of excess demand (supply) at equilibrium? ______________

(c) Indicate and explain the likely direction of change in the price of X if excess demand exists. Do the same for excess supply.

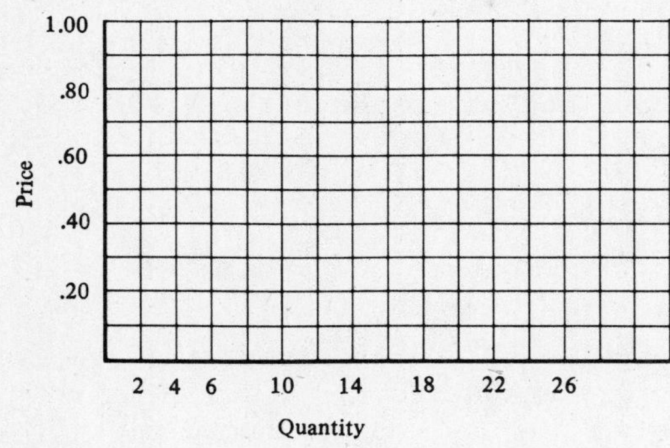

2. The hypothesis of demand and supply. Fill in the table on the next page. Draw new curves on the graphs to aid you. Show the initial effects predicted by the hypotheses of the indicated events on the markets. For shifts in the demand curve (D), shifts in the supply curve (S), equilibrium price (P), and equilibrium quantity Q, use + or - to show increase or decrease; for no change, use 0. (A rightward shift in the supply or demand curve is an increase). If the effect cannot be deduced from the information, use U.

Market	Event		D	S	P	Q
(a) Canadian wine	Early frost destroys a large percentage of the grape crop in British Columbia.	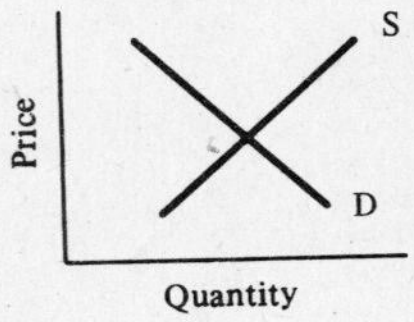 Price / Quantity graph (S, D)	___	___	___	___
(b) Copper wire	The Bell Telephone Co. greatly increases orders for wire to satisfy transmission needs.	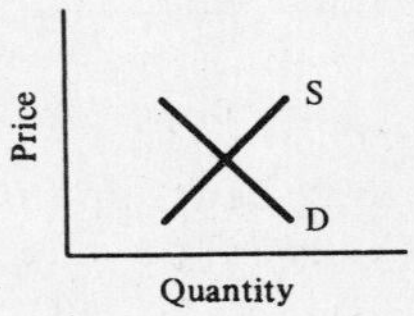 Price / Quantity graph (S, D)	___	___	___	___
(c) Pine antique furniture	"Antique hunting" becomes popular and Canadians attempt to furnish their homes with antique pine chairs and tables.	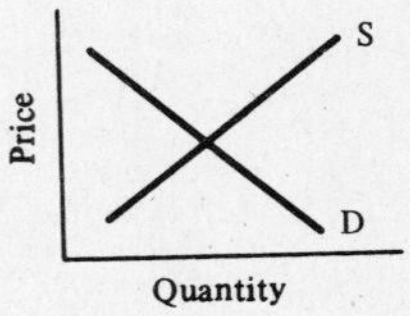 Price / Quantity graph (S, D)	___	___	___	___
(d) Auto tires	As incomes and population rise, the demand for autos rises; synthetic rubber, cheaper than natural rubber, is invented.	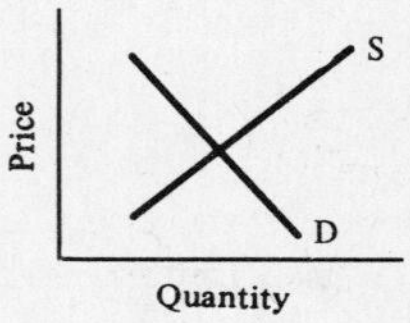 Price / Quantity graph (S, D)	___	___	___	___
(e) Cigarettes	A new law requires notice on each pack: "Warning: The Department of National Health and Welfare advises that danger to health increases with amount smoked."	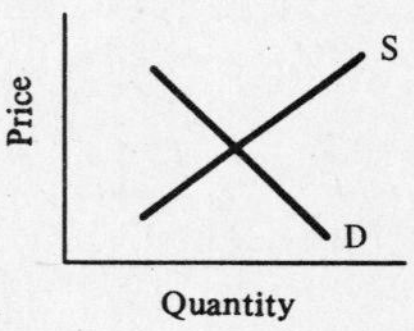 Price / Quantity graph (S, D)	___	___	___	___
(f) Automobile fuel	Middle East oil producers decrease the total amount of crude oil going to North America.	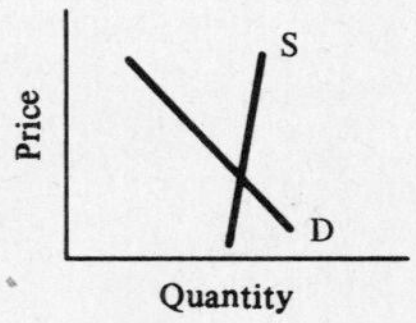 Price / Quantity graph (S, D)	___	___	___	___
(g) Heating gas	The National Energy Plan announces an \$800 subsidy for homeowners who convert to gas heating.	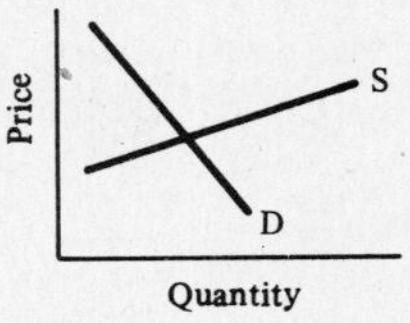 Price / Quantity graph (S, D)	___	___	___	___

3. The graph below describes a hypothetical market for beer in Nova Scotia.

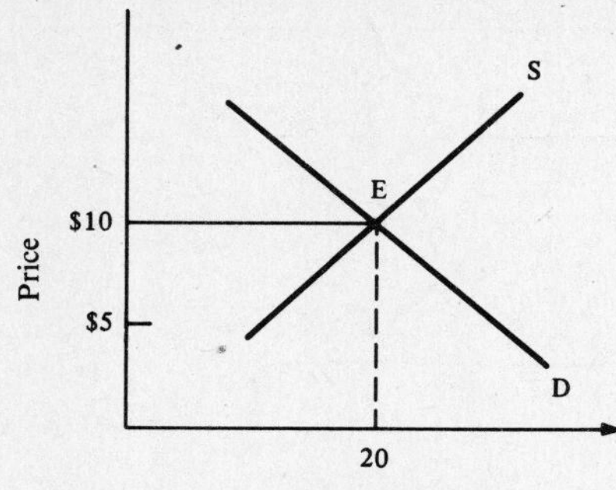

(a) In a prolonged heat spell, which curve would shift and in what direction? What would happen to the equilibrium price and output?

(b) Assume there is a constraint imposed on production such that 20,000 cases per week is the maximum. If demand shifts to the right, indicate this shift on the graph by D' and the initial excess demand by EZ. How would this excess demand be eliminated if price were set by market forces?

(c) Suppose the Provincial Legislature decided to impose a tax of $1 per case on beer producers. What would happen to the supply schedule, equilibrium price, and equilibrium output?

4. The demand for firewood (Q_d) and supply (Q_s) are given by

$$Q_d = 300 - 1.5P$$

$$Q_s = 1.0P$$

where P is price per unit.

(a) Plot the demand and supply schedules on the graph below.

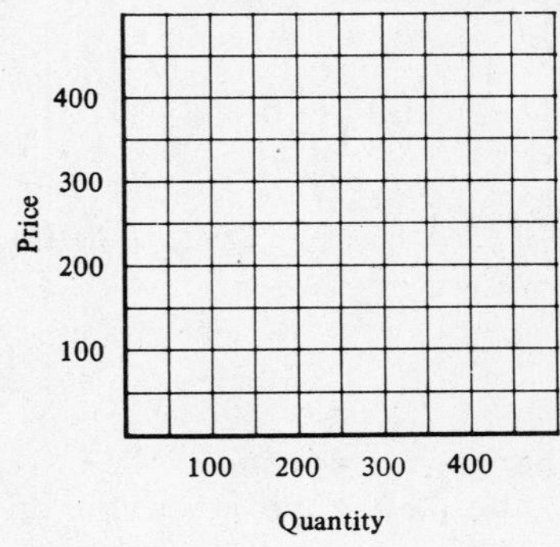

(b) What is the equilibrium price and output? (Equate Q_d and Q_s and solve.)

(c) If the demand schedule became $Q_d = 300 - .75P$, which way has the demand curve shifted? What happens to quantity exchanged and price? (Calculate the new values as in (b)). Show the new demand curve as D'.

5. Assume the following supply and demand functions:

$Q_d = 28 - 4p$ $\qquad\qquad$ $Q_s = 18 + p$

(a) Determine the equilibrium price and quantity.

(b) Plot the demand and supply curves on the graph and confirm your answer.

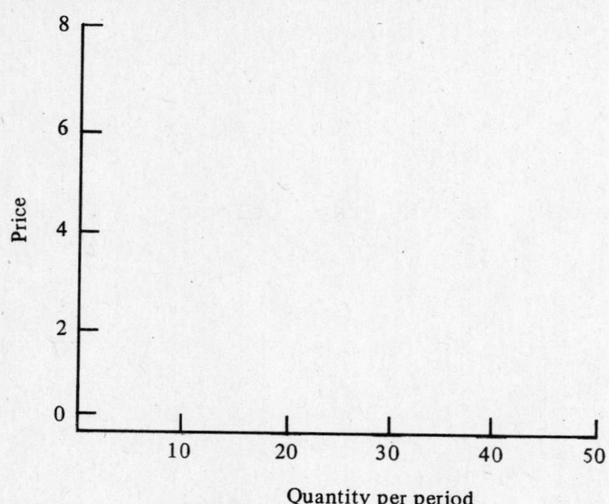

(c) Suppose supply changes to $Q_s = 8 + p$, with no change in demand. Calculate the new equilibrium price and quantity. Illustrate the new supply curve on the graph above.

(d) Suppose that price had been controlled by the government at the original equilibrium in (a). Predict the effects if supply shifts as in (c).

CHAPTER 5

ELASTICITY OF DEMAND & SUPPLY

CHAPTER OBJECTIVES

Price changes normally induce changes in quantities demanded and supplied. The degree of responsiveness, measured by the elasticity of demand and supply, is the focus of the questions and exercises in this chapter. Your understanding of such concepts as inelastic demand, perfectly elastic supply, and cross-elasticity are tested in this chapter. Changes in income will induce changes in some household expenditures. Such responses are measured by income elasticities which are also discussed in this chapter.

MULTIPLE-CHOICE QUESTIONS

1. The price elasticity of demand refers to
   (a) how the quantity demanded of a commodity changes when the price of that commodity changes, other things equal
   (b) the response of price to a supply change
   (c) how the quantity demanded of a commodity responds to a change in the price of a substitute commodity
   (d) how rapidly price changes when demand changes

2. Price elasticity of demand is measured by
   (a) the change in quantity demanded divided by the change in price
   (b) the change in price divided by the quantity demanded
   (c) the percentage change in quantity demanded divided by the percentage change in price
   (d) the percentage change in price times the percentage change in quantity demanded

3. To say that the demand for a commodity is <u>elastic</u> implies only
   (a) that the demand curve slopes downward to the right
   (b) that more is sold at a lower price
   (c) that a rise in price will increase total revenue
   (d) that the percentage change in quantity demanded is greater than the percentage change in price

4. Considering the element of time,
   (a) measured price elasticity of demand will usually rise as the time period is extended
   (b) short-run and long-run elasticity for demand tend to be the same for most commodities
   (c) the short-run elasticity of individual commodities in a group will be less than the short-run elasticity for a group of commodities
   (d) the long-run price elasticity of demand for most commodities is less than the short-run price elasticity of demand

Questions 5 through 7 refer to the figures below:

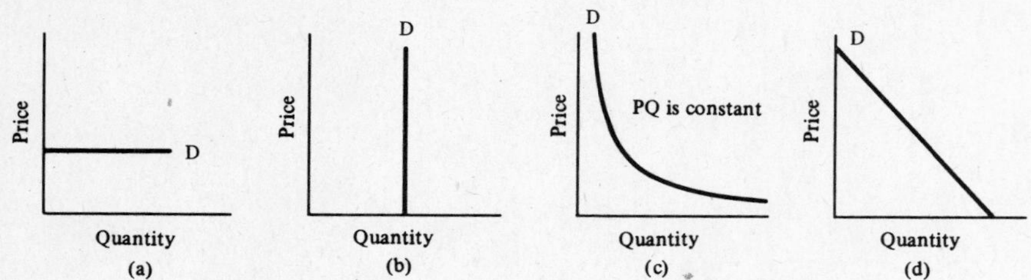

5. The demand curve with an elasticity of 0 is
   (a) a (c) c
   (b) b (d) d

6. The demand curve with an elasticity of 1 is
   (a) a (c) c
   (b) b (d) d

7. The demand curve with an elasticity of infinity is
   (a) a (c) c
   (b) b (d) d

8. When the demand is elastic
   (a) a fall in price is more than offset by an increase in quantity demanded, so that total revenue rises
   (b) the good is probably a necessity
   (c) a rise in price will increase total revenue, even though less is sold
   (d) buyers are not much influenced by prices of competing products

Questions 9 and 10 refer to the schedule below. (Consult Table 5-3 in text for the precise calculation of elasticity.)

Price/Unit	Quantity Offered for Sale
$10	400
8	350
6	300
4	200
2	50

9. The supply curve implied by the schedule is
   (a) elastic for all price ranges
   (b) inelastic for all price ranges
   (c) of zero elasticity for all price changes
   (d) variable, depending on initial price chosen

10. As price rises from $6 to $10 per unit, the supply response is
   (a) elastic (c) of zero elasticity
   (b) of unit elasticity (d) inelastic

11. If price elasticity of demand for a product is .5, this means that
    (a) a change in price changes demand by 50 percent
    (b) a 1 percent increase in quantity demanded is associated with a .5 percent fall in price
    (c) a 1 percent increase in quantity demanded is associated with a 2 percent fall in price
    (d) a .5 percent change in price will cause a .5 percent change in quantity sold

12. A demand curve is perfectly inelastic if
    (a) a rise in price causes a fall in quantity demanded
    (b) a fall in price causes a rise in sellers' total receipts
    (c) the commodity in question is highly perishable, like fresh strawberries
    (d) a change in price does not change quantity demanded

13. If a 100 percent rise in the membership fee of a club causes the number of members to decline from 600 to 450,
    (a) demand was inelastic
    (b) demand was infinitely elastic
    (c) demand was elastic
    (d) the price rise caused a shift in demand for membership, so it is impossible to say

14. Inferior commodities
    (a) have zero income elasticities of demand
    (b) have negative cross-elasticities of demand
    (c) have negative elasticities of supply
    (d) have negative income elasticities of demand

15. If, when incomes rise by 5 percent, the quantity demanded of a commodity rises by 10 percent, income elasticity is
    (a) -2
    (b) 2
    (c) -(1/2)
    (d) 1/2

16. Which of the following would you expect to have the highest income elasticity?
    (a) spaghetti
    (b) bus rides
    (c) personal computers
    (d) baby carriages

17. Margarine and butter probably have
    (a) the same income elasticities of demand
    (b) very low price elasticities of demand
    (c) negative cross-elasticities of demand with respect to each other
    (d) positive cross-elasticities of demand with respect to each other

18. If, when income rises from $10,000 to $12,000, expenditure on food rises from $1,000 to $1,100 and on entertainment from $500 to $600.
    (a) food expenditure is income inelastic and entertainment expenditure has unitary income elasticity
    (b) food expenditure is income inelastic and entertainment expenditure has unitary income elasticity.
    (c) both commodities have the same income elasticity
    (d) the income elasticity of entertainment is one-half that of food

19. The category of expenditures classed as meals purchased at restaurants
    (a) has been observed to have low income elasticity
    (b) has been observed to have high income elasticity
    (c) has been observed to have negative income elasticity
    (d) shows no consistent relationship with income

EXERCISES

(Note: Take elasticity calculations to two decimal places)

1. Per Capita Consumption.
The table below shows annual per capita consumption data on pork and eggs, along with the price change for each good in the years noted.

PER CAPITA CONSUMPTION AND PRICE CHANGE

Years	Pork (lb)	Price Change (%)	Years	Eggs (doz)	Price Change (%)
1964	51.8		1963	32.1	
1965	47.9	+ 11.4	1964	32.0	- 13.7
1970	58.7		1966	30.7	
1971	68.3	- 16.9	1967	31.2	- 15.6
1974	59.4		1972	30.8	
1975	50.9	+ 28.0	1973	29.2	+ 44.4

Source: Handbook of Food Expenditure, Price and Consumption, Agriculture Canada, 1977.

Note: The years were deliberately selected to ensure a substantial change in the price of the commodity.

(a) Assume that the change in per capita income from one year to the next has a negligible impact on per capita spending of selected food items and that the short-run response in per capita consumption is due to price fluctuations. Calculate the price elasticity of demand for each commodity for the pairs of years given. (In calculating percentage change in quantity, use the average volume of the quantities in the denominator. See the footnote to Table 5-3 in text.)

(b) What do these elasticities suggest about the importance of the two products in family consumption patterns?

(c) Do these elasticities confirm demand theory?

2. (a) Given the demand curve D_1 below, demonstrate that as price decreases the elasticity of demand goes from being elastic to becoming inelastic. (Hint: Use the reference points indicated by the arrows.)

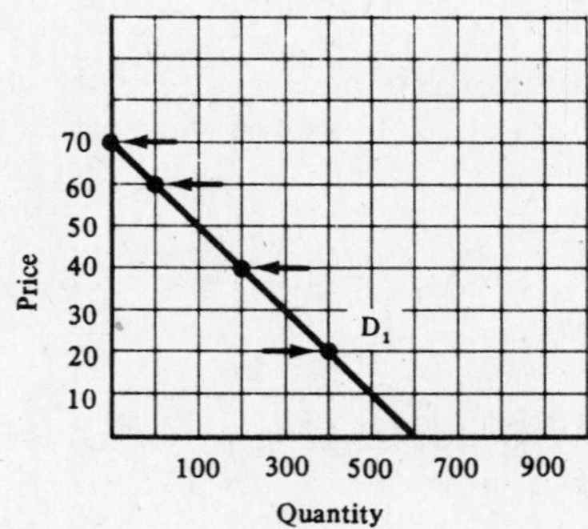

(b) What is the elasticity of demand for D_1 when the price falls from \$40 to \$30? What is happening to total revenue as the price falls further?

3. By mid-1977, Canadian lumber prices had risen substantially compared to those earlier in the year. It was stated at the time that the price rise was due to increased U.S. demand for housing and virtually fixed short-run supplies.
   (a) Illustrate on the graph below what occurred in the short run. What is the elasticity of supply in this instance?

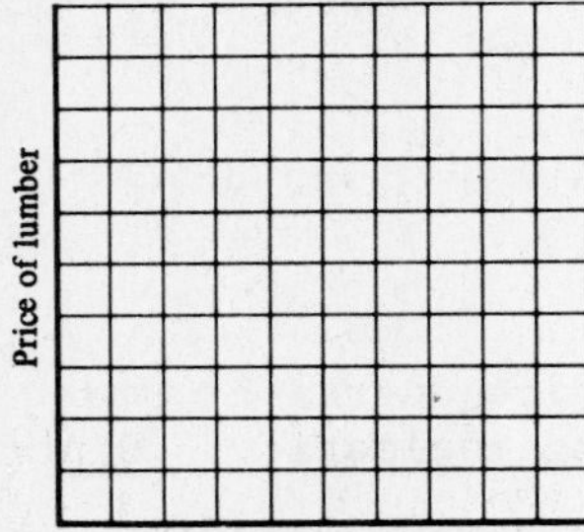

   (b) If builders in Canada were expecting housing demand to rise soon, and they believed supplies would continue to be restricted, what action would they take? What impact would this have on the market?

4. Given the information in the table below, calculate to two decimals the value of the price and income elasticities of commodity X in the three periods Year 1 to Year 2, Year 2 to Year 3, and Year 3 to Year 4. (Remember that you can only estimate price elasticity when income is unchanged and vice versa.)

Period	Per Household Annual Real Disposable Income	Per Household Real Consumption of X (annual)	Price for Unit of X
1	$15,000	$2,000	$100
2	16,000	2,100	100
3	16,000	2,150	95
4	17,000	2,150	105

(i) Year 1 to Year 2:

(ii) Year 2 to Year 3:

(iii) Year 3 to Year 4:

5. (a) The table below provides data on price, income, and quantity demanded. Calculate the elasticities that are underlined.

Income	Price of X	Quantity of X Demanded	Price of Y	Quantity of Y Demanded	Price Elasticity of Demand for X	Price Elasticity of Demand for Y	Income Elasticity of Demand for X	Income Elasticity of Demand for Y	Cross-Elasticity of Demand for X
$ 10,000	$ 25	10	$ 10	40					
10,000	28	9	10	40					
					___				
10,000	28	8	15	35					
						___			___
11,000	28	9	15	36					
							___	___	
11,500	30	7	14	34					

(b) As the quantity of X demanded falls from 9 to 7, why is it that we cannot "legitimately" calculate the price elasticity of demand for X?

6. DEMAND ELASTICITIES AND TOTAL REVENUE

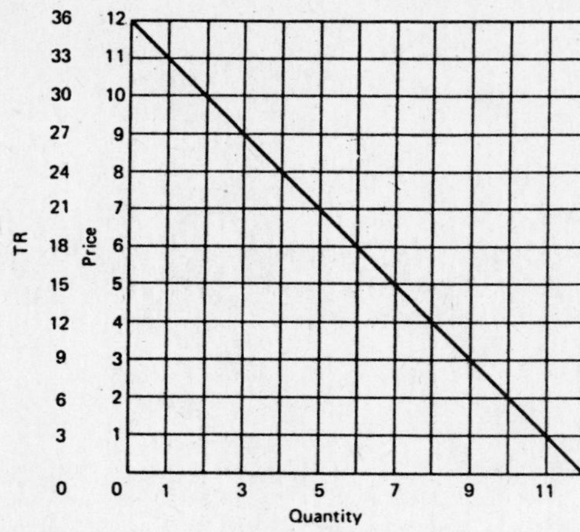

(a) You are given the demand curve in the diagram above, for which several points are contained in the table below. Its equation can be written Q = 12 - P. Note that $\Delta Q/\Delta P = -1$. Calculate the arc elasticities for the segments between the points, the point elasticities, and the total revenue. Draw in the total revenue curve on the diagram above (separate scale applies to total revenue curve), and enter the elasticities along the demand curve. For the arc elasticities use the proportion of ΔQ/ave.Q to ΔP/ave.P; for the point elasticities use $\Delta Q/\Delta P$ times P/Q. (Express elasticities as positive numbers as in the text)

P	Q	Arc Elasticity	Point Elasticity	TR
$11	1		_____	_____
		_____		
9	3		_____	_____
		_____		
7	5		_____	_____
		_____		
5	7		_____	_____
		_____		
3	9		_____	_____
		_____		
1	11		_____	_____

(b) What is the relationship between total revenue and price elasticity of demand?

7. The six diagrams below represent different situations with regard to the elasticity of demand and supply at the equilibrium price P_E. Complete the statements below by indicating which diagrams respond to the statement. (E_s refers to elasticity of supply and E_d refers to elasticity of demand.)

(a) E_d is greater than one and E_s is unity 

(b) E_d is unity and E_s is infinity ______________

(c) E_d is unity and E_s is unity ______________

(d) E_d is greater than one and E_s is zero ______________

(e) E_d is zero and E_s is unity ______________

(f) E_d is infinity and E_s is unity ______________

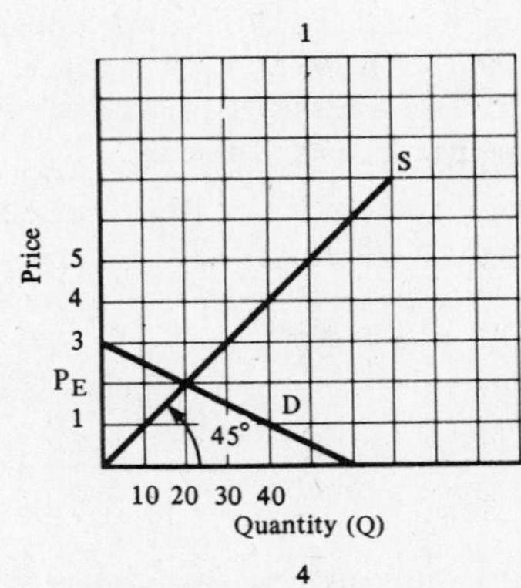

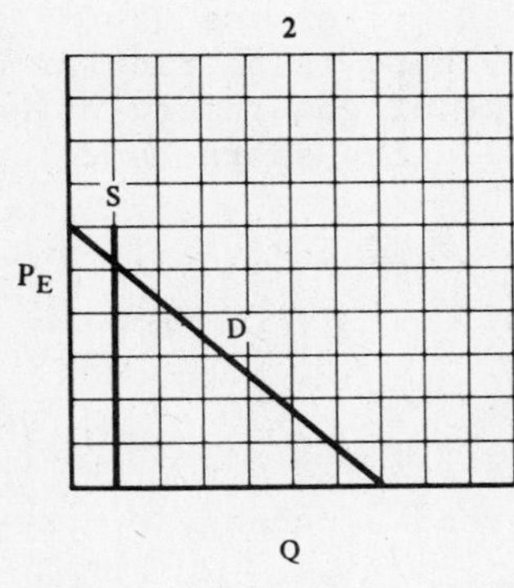

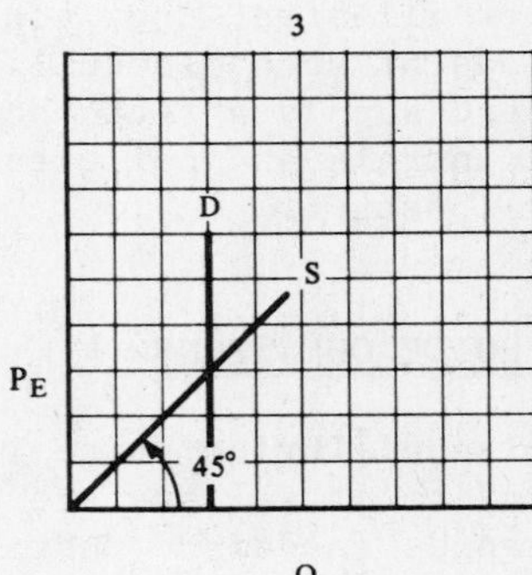

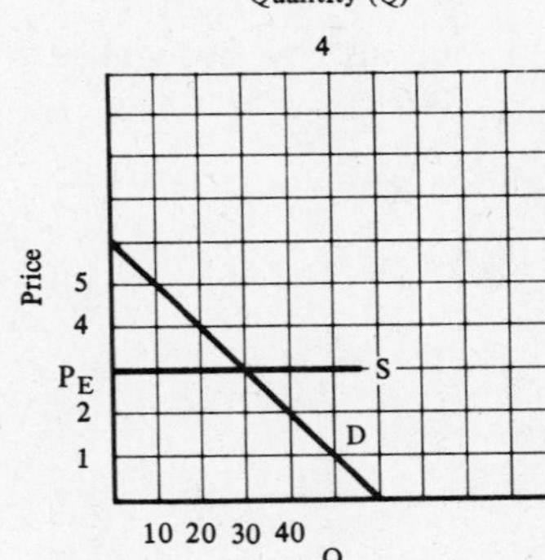

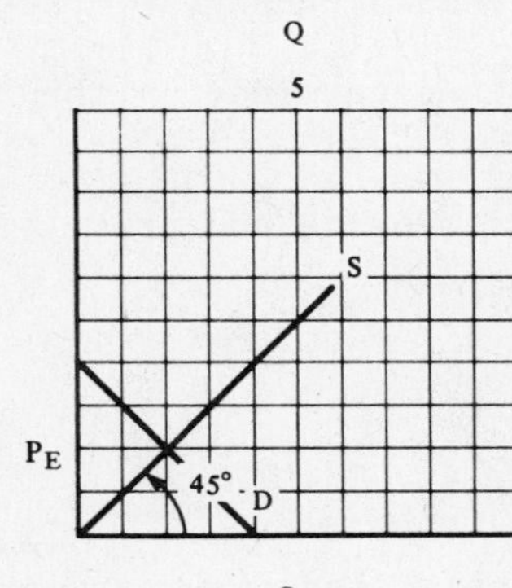

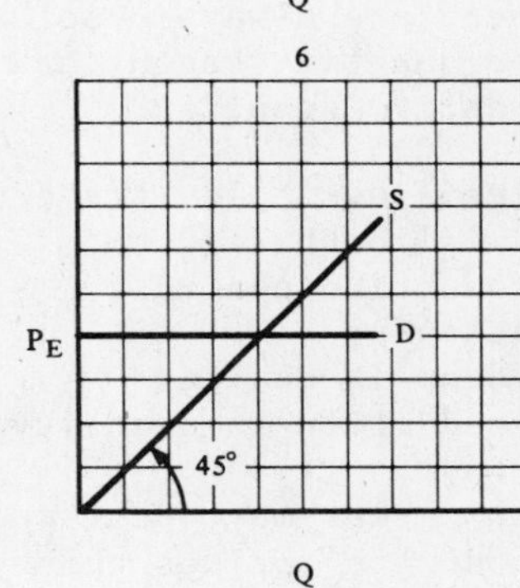

8. Given the two supply schedules S_1 and S_2 shown below, demonstrate that the elasticity of supply equals 1.0 throughout the ranges shown. (<u>Hint</u>: As intervals, use those price and quantity coordinates indicated by the arrows.)

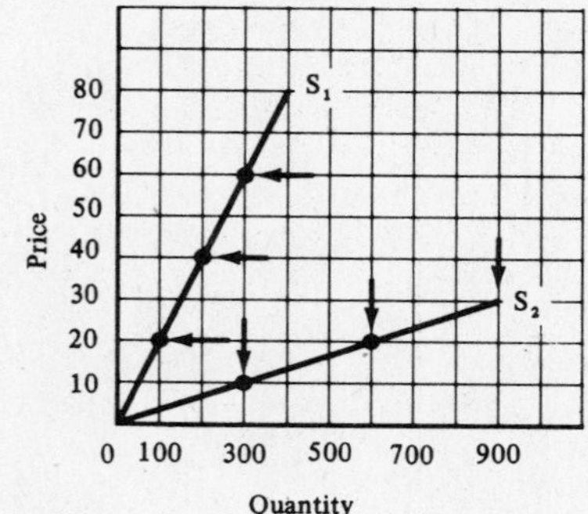

CHAPTER 6

SUPPLY & DEMAND IN ACTION: PRICE CONTROLS & AGRICULTURE

CHAPTER OBJECTIVES

In the everyday, real world, markets are not always permitted to operate freely; government controls on prices and/or output are not uncommon. The questions and exercises which follow illustrate how controls create excess demand or supply situations and the repercussions of such disequilibria. There is particular emphasis on how the elasticity of demand and supply affect the outcome of government price controls. Examples are drawn from rent controls and policies to alleviate short- and long-term problems in the agricultural sector.

MULTIPLE-CHOICE QUESTIONS

1. At a disequilibrium price
   (a) profits of sellers are eliminated
   (b) changes in demand must be matched by changes in supply
   (c) there are always unsold goods
   (d) the quantity bought and sold is determined by the lesser of quantity demanded or quantity supplied

2. Price ceilings below the equilibrium price and price floors above the equilibrium price will both lead to
   (a) production controls
   (b) rationing
   (c) a drop in quality
   (d) a reduction in quantity exchanged

3. A black market may occur whenever
   (a) producers' prices cannot be controlled but retailers' prices can be controlled
   (b) there is an excess supply of a commodity at the controlled price
   (c) consumers are prepared to pay more than the ceiling price and exchange between retailer and consumer cannot be enforced at the ceiling price
   (d) a floor price is maintained at too low a level

4. Allocation by sellers' preferences refers to which of the following?
   (a) giving all consumers the quantity they demand at the market price
   (b) government franchises to certain firms to sell goods
   (c) businesses selling only to regular customers
   (d) quotas on output

5. In a free-market economy, the rationing of scarce goods is done primarily by
   (a) the price mechanism
   (b) the government
   (c) business firms
   (d) consumers

Questions 6 and 7 refer to the figure below, which shows the demand for and supply of labor in the restaurant waiter/waitress industry.

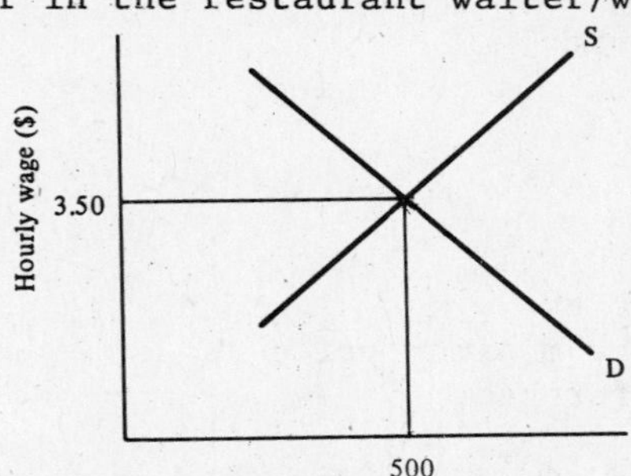

6. If a minimum wage (a form of price floor) was legislated at $4.00 per hour,
   (a) all those employed at $3.50 per hour would get a raise
   (b) fewer people would be willing to work in the industry
   (c) there would be unemployment in the industry
   (d) employers would tend to give "under the table" bonuses to attract labor

7. If a minimum wage was legislated at $3.00 per hour,
   (a) all those employed at $3.50 per hour would get the same; new workers would earn $3.00 per hour
   (b) employers would tend to give "under the table" bonuses to attract labor
   (c) fewer people would be employed
   (d) it would have no effect on the number employed

Questions 8 through 11 refer to the figure below.

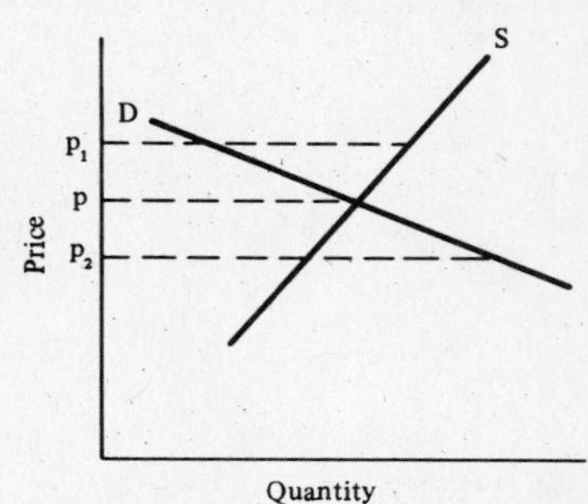

8. If p_1 were a price floor, it would
   (a) have no effect on equilibrium output
   (b) lead to shortages and probably to black-market activity
   (c) lead to surpluses and possibly to undercutting of the minimum price
   (d) cause excess demand

9. If p_2 were a price floor, it would
   (a) have no effect on equilibrium output
   (b) lead to shortages and probably to black-market activity
   (c) lead to surpluses and possibly to undercutting of the minimum price
   (d) require government rationing to be effective

10. If p_1 were a price ceiling, it would
   (a) have no effect on equilibrium output
   (b) lead to shortages and probably to black-market activity
   (c) lead to surpluses and possibly to undercutting of the minimum price
   (d) require government rationing to be effective

11. If p_2 were a price ceiling, it would
   (a) have no effect on equilibrium output
   (b) lead to shortages and probably to black-market activity
   (c) lead to surpluses and possibly to undercutting of the minimum price
   (d) tend to reduce allocation according to sellers' preferences

12. Rent controls are likely to produce all but which one of the following effects:
   (a) rental housing shortage in the long run
   (b) the development of a "black market"
   (c) rental housing supply increases in the short run
   (d) resource allocation away from rental housing industry

13. The rental housing market is characterized by
   (a) long- and short-run supply elasticities of equal magnitude
   (b) inelastic demand
   (c) short-run inelastic supply and long-run elastic supply
   (d) short-run elastic supply and long-run inelastic supply

Questions 14 & 15 refer to the figure below in which the demand for rental housing increases from D_0 to D_1 (SR and LR refer to short run and long run.)

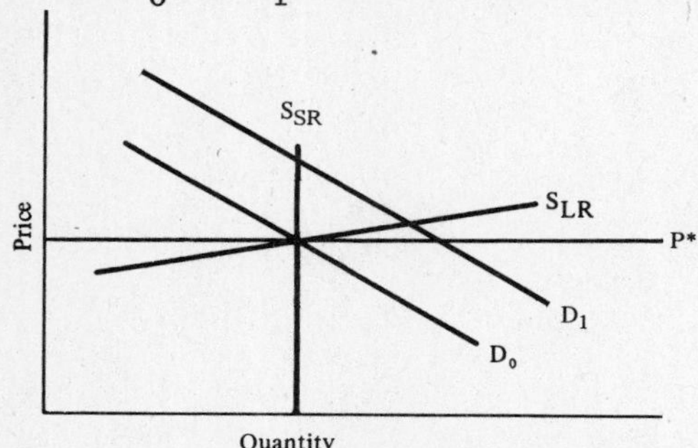

14. If demand increases from D_0 to D_1 and there are no rent controls,
   (a) there will be a greater quantity increase in the short run than in the long run
   (b) those renting will now be paying more
   (c) the amount of rental housing will not be affected in the long run
   (d) rents will rise more in the long run than in the short run

15. Assume rents are controlled at price p*. Which of the following best describes the likely events if demand increases from D_o to D_1?
   (a) There will be no shortage of rental units in either the short run or the long run.
   (b) Landlords will have less opportunity to discriminate among prospective tenants.
   (c) Landlords will tend to spend more on maintenance of apartments.
   (d) The apartment shortage will tend to worsen in the long run.

16. Agricultural output in Canada has increased substantially since World War II mainly because
    (a) many people are going back to farming
    (b) productivity and yields have risen
    (c) rising demand for farm output has kept prices steadily increasing
    (d) there has been good growing weather

17. Most farm receipts vary inversely with output levels
    (a) whenever buyers' preferences change
    (b) because most farm products have inelastic demands
    (c) because lower outputs means higher total costs
    (d) as long as supply is elastic

18. Price changes tend to be large given unexpected changes in agricultural output because
    (a) the demand for agricultural output is elastic
    (b) the demand for agricultural output is inelastic
    (c) the long-run and short-run supplies are the same
    (d) buyers' incomes change when output changes

19. The main reason for agricultural price supports is to
    (a) attempt to stabilize farm incomes
    (b) make certain there are always extra stocks of goods on hand
    (c) give the government control over agriculture
    (d) reduce competition

20. A price completely stabilized at the equilibrium level by a government buying surpluses and selling its stocks when there are shortages means that
    (a) poor farmers will benefit the most
    (b) government has imposed a perfectly inelastic demand curve on farms
    (c) farmers' revenues will be proportional to output
    (d) all farms will have satisfactory incomes and farm receipts will be stabilized

21. Assigning quotas to producers of agricultural goods
    (a) places a burden on new producers who wish to enter the industry
    (b) ensures an equitable distribution of farm income
    (c) maintains stable prices for food products
    (d) guarantees a fixed income to farmers

22. If markets are highly regulated and controlled,
    (a) costs can be lowered below those in unregulated markets
    (b) the signals required for the allocation of resources will not operate
    (c) relative prices will still change to reallocate resources
    (d) the distribution of income will be unchanged from that observed in an unregulated market

23. If the elasticity of demand for an agricultural product is 0.50 a decline in output from 100 tons to 80 tons will
    (a) increase the price of the product by exactly 20 percent
    (b) reduce total receipts
    (c) increase total receipts
    (d) increase the price by more than 50 percent

EXERCISES

1. Given the two market situations described below, answer the following questions.

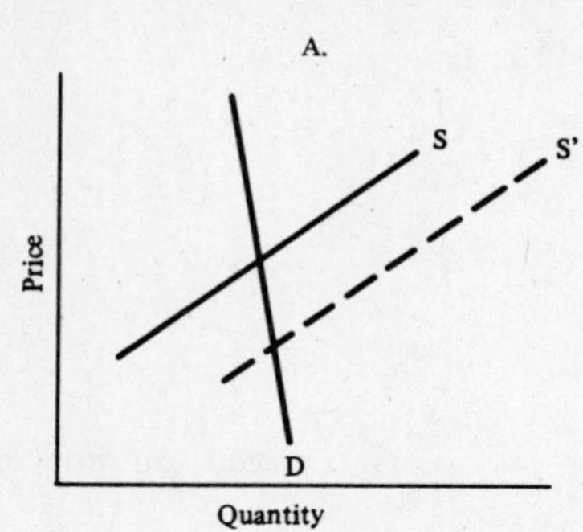

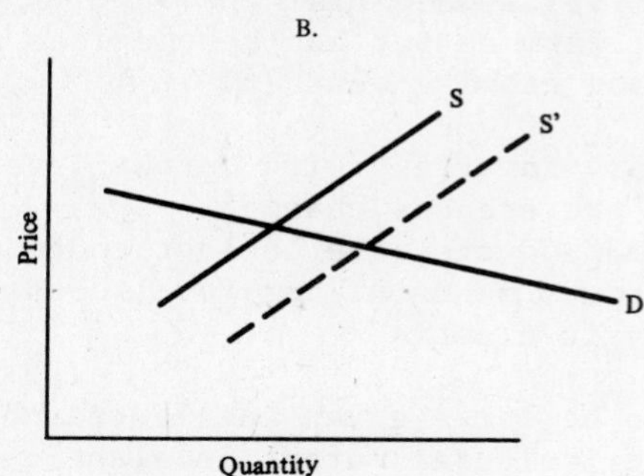

(a) If S and D denote the original supply and demand curves, indicate, by vertical hatching [vertical hatching], the total receipts in both markets.

(b) If the supply curve shifts to S' in both A and B, indicate the new receipts by horizontal hatching [horizontal hatching]

(c) Which market shows the largest loss in total receipts? What is the nature of the demand curve in that market?

(d) Suppose there was a price floor equal to the original equilibrium price (before the shift in supply) and the government was committed to purchasing unsold stocks at this price. Given the shift in supply in both A and B, would there be any difference in the quantity the government would have to purchase in the two cases? Explain.

2. Using the supply and demand curves below, demonstrate that, given a fixed quota in both markets A and B, the cost to the consumer when the demand curve shifts to the right by the same horizontal distance in both markets varies with the elasticity of demand. (The quota is the equilibrium quantity determined by the original supply and demand curve.)

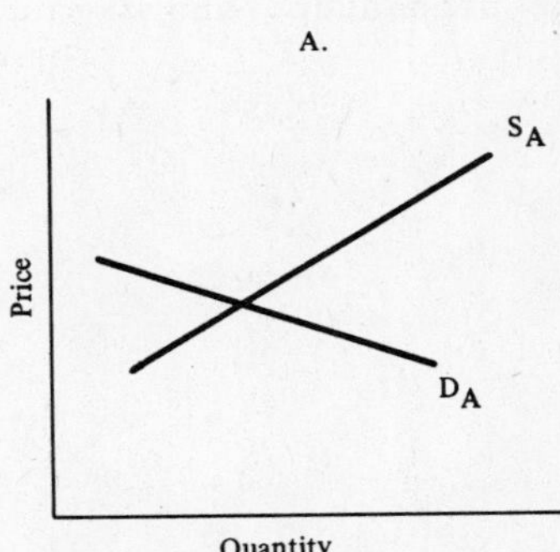

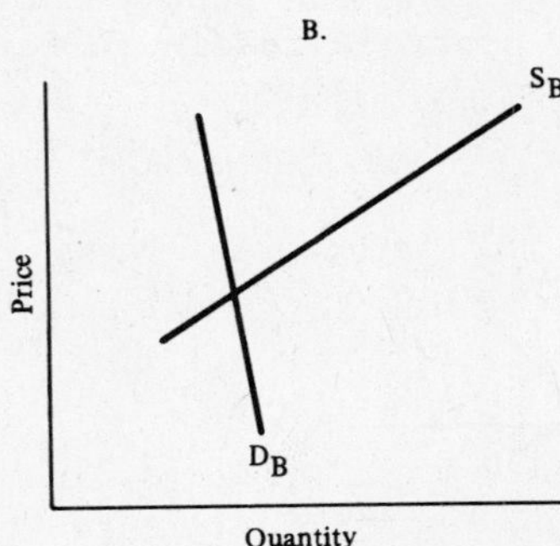

3. The graph below illustrates a short-run situation in the rental housing market. The subscripts for the demand and supply curves represent subsequent periods of time all within the short run. Price refers to rent per unit.

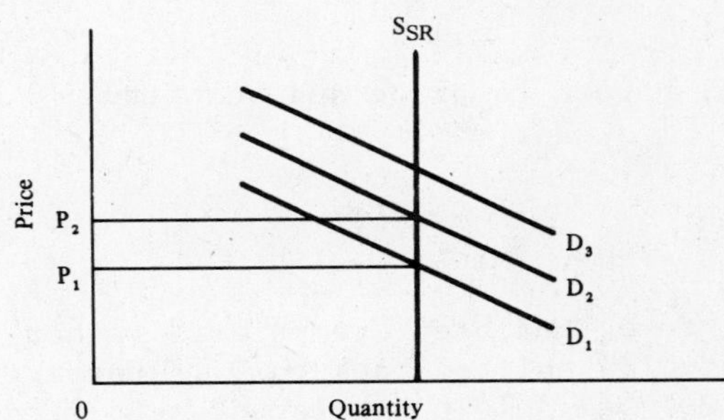

(a) From period one to period two (the short run), the demand curves shift from D_1 to D_2 and price rises. What would you expect to happen to the stock of rental housing in this time period? Why?

(b) Demand increases again, in the short run, to D_3 and rent controls are established, maintaining the price at P_2. Indicate the short-run supply necessary to clear the market (that is, the excess demand resulting from rent controls).

(c) In the diagram below, the long-run supply curve S_{LR} has been added and demand stabilizes at D_3. Rent controls remain in force at P_2.

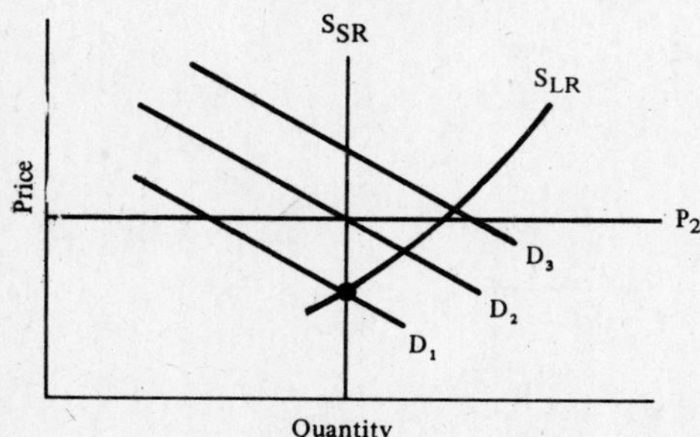

(i) Will the shortage persist in the long run? Explain.

(ii) If rent controls are removed, what will happen to price and quantity in the long run?

(iii) Suppose the demand curve shift from D_2 to D_3 had been "temporary" rather than "permanent," so that the demand curve eventually shifted back to D_2. Compare the effects with and without rent controls at P_2. (S_{SR} is the relevant supply curve).

4. The diagram that follows illustrates the rental housing market at a point in time. The government decides that the current "average" rent of $300 per month is socially desirable and fixes the rent at that price. Subsequently, the cost of supplying rental housing (fuel, maintenance, etc.) rises permanently by $50 per month.

(a) Draw the short- and new long-run supply curve (S_{SR} and S_{LR}').

(b) What happens in the long run (with controls) to the quantity of rental housing supplied? (Label it Q_{LR}'.)

(c) Indicate the price of rental housing (P_E) and quantity supplied (Q_E) if there were no controls.

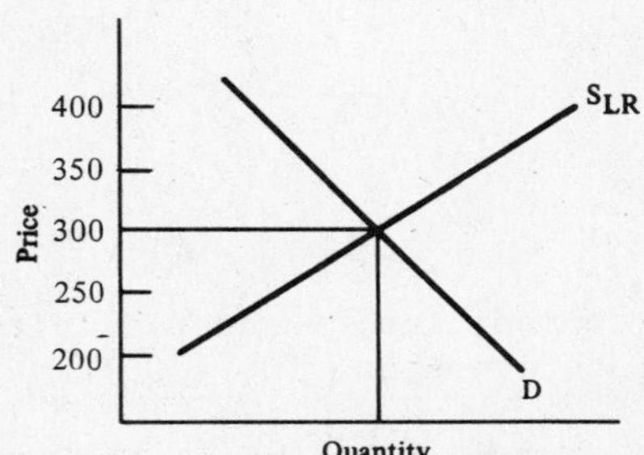

5. Given the agricultural market described in the figure below,

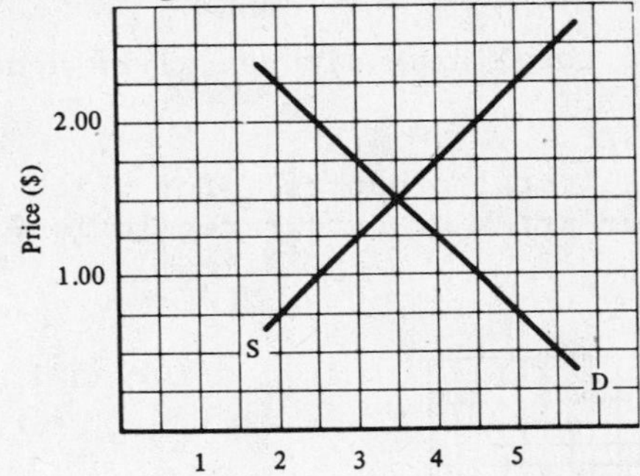

(a) What is the total revenue to producers at the equilibrium? ____________

(b) A price floor of $2 is set and any excess produce is purchased by the government. What is the producers' revenue now? ____________

(c) What change in quantity demanded will occur? ____________

(d) How many units of output will the government buy? ____________

(e) What will be the cost to consumers in terms of the taxes needed to purchase excess output? ____________

6. You are advising the Minister of Agriculture on whether to establish a quota, equal to current quantity produced and sold, or a price floor, equal to 50 percent above the current price. The Minister wants to maximize farm income but is not prepared to purchase any excess produce. You have calculated that the demand is likely to shift as shown by D' in the figure below. What do you advise the Minister? Explain your answer.

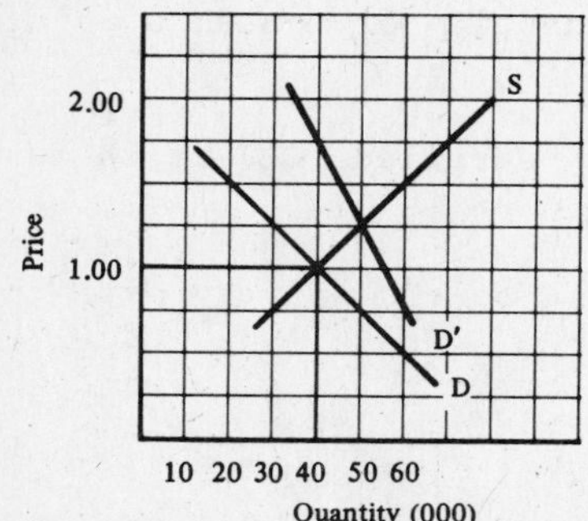

7. The diagram below illustrates demand curves for two commodities, A and B. Initially, the price of both is the same ($P_A = P_B$) and the outputs are equal ($Q_A = Q_B$).

(a) If output is increased to $Q_A' = Q_B'$, illustrate what will happen to the price of A and the price of B in the diagram and label the new prices P_A' and P_B'.

(b) Given the new prices, what has happened to the total expenditures given demand curve D_A? Given demand curve D_B?

(c) If output is unpredictable (such as with agricultural products), for which of these commodities are <u>producers</u> likely to favor price or output regulation? Why?

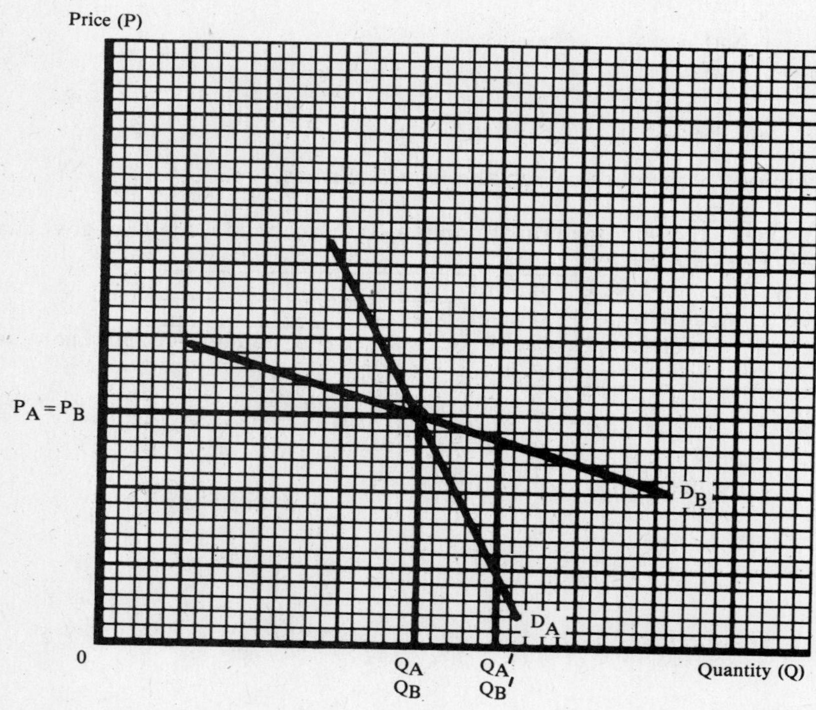

PART THREE

CONSUMPTION, PRODUCTION, AND COST

CHAPTER 7

HOUSEHOLD CONSUMPTION BEHAVIOR: THE MARGINAL UTILITY APPROACH

CHAPTER OBJECTIVES

Marginal utility theory helps to explain the negative slope of the demand curve and the relative market values of such items as diamonds and water. Given fixed market prices for commodities and services, each individual can gain the greatest personal satisfaction from his/her purchases by relating these prices to the marginal utility gained from purchasing additional units of the goods in question. Several of the exercises and multiple-choice questions demonstrate this important concept. The measurement of consumer surplus and the notion of a free good are also highlighted in this chapter.

MULTIPLE-CHOICE QUESTIONS

1. The "paradox of value" is that
   (a) people are irrational in consumption choices
   (b) the total utilities yielded by commodities do not directly relate to their market values
   (c) value has no relationship to utility schedules
   (d) free goods are goods that are essential to life

2. Marginal utility is most accurately defined as
   (a) total utility divided by the amount of a good consumed
   (b) what a consumer would pay for one more unit of a good
   (c) the change in satisfaction due to a change in the amount of a good consumed
   (d) a good that gives no more satisfaction if more is consumed

3. If a commodity gives less additional satisfaction for each additional unit consumed, that commodity
   (a) will not be purchased whatever the price
   (b) displays diminishing marginal utility
   (c) has zero marginal utility
   (d) will only be consumed if provided free of charge

4. The hypothesis of diminishing marginal utility states that
   (a) the less of a commodity one is consuming, the less the additional utility obtained by an increase in its consumption
   (b) the more of a commodity one is consuming, the more the additional utility obtained by an increase in its consumption
   (c) the more of a commodity one is consuming, the less the additional utility obtained by an increase in its consumption
   (d) marginal utility cannot be measured, but total utility can

5. For a free good, utility is maximized when
   (a) the consumption of an additional unit of it reduces total utility
   (b) utility begins to increase at a decreasing rate
   (c) it is no longer needed
   (d) marginal utility equals zero

6. According to utility theory, for a household which is maximizing total satisfaction, MU_a/MU_b
   (a) equals P_a/P_b
   (b) equals P_b/P_a
   (c) will not necessarily be related to relative prices
   (d) equals TU_a/TU_b

7. When the price of commodity X triples, all other prices and income remaining constant, then for an individual consuming X,
   (a) the quantity of X consumed must fall to one-third its previous level
   (b) the quantity of X consumed must fall until the marginal utility of X has tripled
   (c) the individual must increase his/her consumption of X
   (d) the consumption of all other commodities must fall

8. In maximizing utility, a household will allocate its budget among commodities
   (a) so that there is an equal amount of income allocated to each commodity
   (b) so that the utility of the last dollar spent on each commodity is equal
   (c) so that the marginal utility of each commodity is the same
   (d) so that the marginal utility of each dollar spent is zero

9. Given an initial equilibrium position for a household, a decline in the price of one good, X, given constant income and constant prices of other commodities,
   (a) requires a decrease in purchases of X to maintain equilibrium
   (b) implies that the marginal utility of X per dollar must fall to ensure equilibrium
   (c) results in an increase in the quantity demanded of all commodities except X
   (d) implies that the marginal utility of commodities other than X will be less at the new equilibrium

10. Consumer surplus derived from the consumption of a commodity
   (a) is the difference between the total value derived from that consumption and the total payment made to acquire the commodity
   (b) will always be less than the total amount paid for the commodity
   (c) is the extra amount received by the consumer because some units of the commodity are free
   (d) none of the above

11. If a utility-maximizing individual is prepared to pay $3 for the first unit of a commodity, $2 for the second unit, and $1 for the third unit, and the market price is $1 per unit,
   (a) consumer surplus will be $3
   (b) the demand schedule for the commodity is negatively sloped
   (c) the individual will purchase three units of the commodity
   (d) all of the above

12. Elasticity of demand
    (a) depends on total utility
    (b) will be greater if the marginal utility curve is relatively flat in the relevant range
    (c) will be greater for a steeply sloped marginal utility curve
    (d) is related to neither total nor marginal utility

13. The most important characteristic that distinguishes a free good from a scarce good is
    (a) that scarce goods are never provided free of charge by the government
    (b) that a free good will tend to be consumed up to where the marginal utility from consumption is zero
    (c) the difference in the total utility schedules of the two types of goods
    (d) the difference in the elasticity of demand

EXERCISES

1. The table below relates total utility and the number of milkshakes consumed per weekend.

Number of Milkshakes per Weekend	Total Utility
0	0
1	50
2	90
3	120
4	130
5	130
6	120

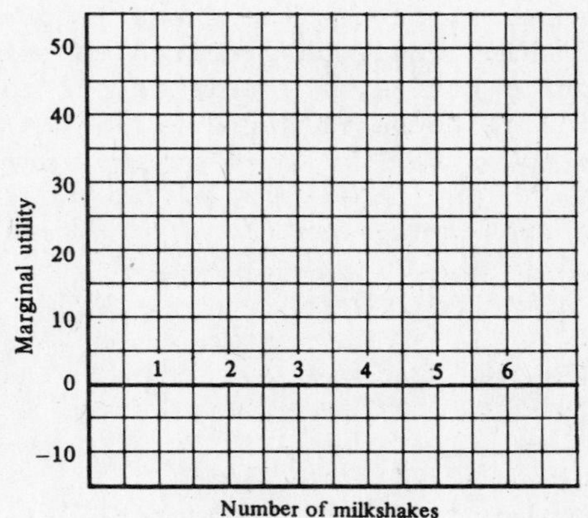

(a) In the diagram at the right of the table, plot the marginal utility schedule.
(b) At what point does the consumer experience disutility? (e.g., after how many milkshakes per weekend?)

2. Suppose a consumer spends recreation time and income on two leisure activities: tennis and fishing. The consumer has the basic equipment to pursue both activities. The costs associated with these activities are court fees (for tennis) and the expense of boat rental for fishing.

The marginal utility schedules for hours spent on these activities are shown below.

Number of Hours per Week Spent on ⟶	Marginal Utility Schedule	
	Fishing	Tennis
1	20	20
2	18	19
3	16	18
4	14	17
5	12	16
6	10	15
7	8	14
8	6	13

(a) If the cost per hour of each activity was $1 and the consumer spent 5 hours per week on recreation activity, how many hours would be spent on each activity in order to maximize total utility?

(b) Suppose the cost of tennis increased 19 percent. What change in the "mix" of tennis and fishing would be required to maximize utility? Explain, using marginal utility to price ratios, why this is the case. (Consider the initial cost of both activities in (a) to be $1 per hour.)

3. Goods X and Y display diminishing marginal utility. Given specific relative marginal utilities representing particular consumption bundles of X and Y, and the absolute prices shown below, what rearrangement in consumption is necessary to achieve utility maximization for each case? (Complete the last column of the table below.)

Case	Relative Marginal Utilities (MU_X/MU_Y)	Price of		Change: Increase (↑) or Decrease (↓) in Consumption of	
		X	Y	X	Y
1	4/3	$ 3.00	$6.00		
2	3/1	3.00	1.50		
3	2/3	1.00	1.00		
4	9/2	12.00	2.00		

4. The marginal utility curves for three commodities A, B, and C are given below. For each of these commodities, how responsive will the change in quantity be to a rise in its price? (I.e., will the elasticity of demand be high, low, or close to zero assuming price rises of equal magnitude in the three cases?) Explain.

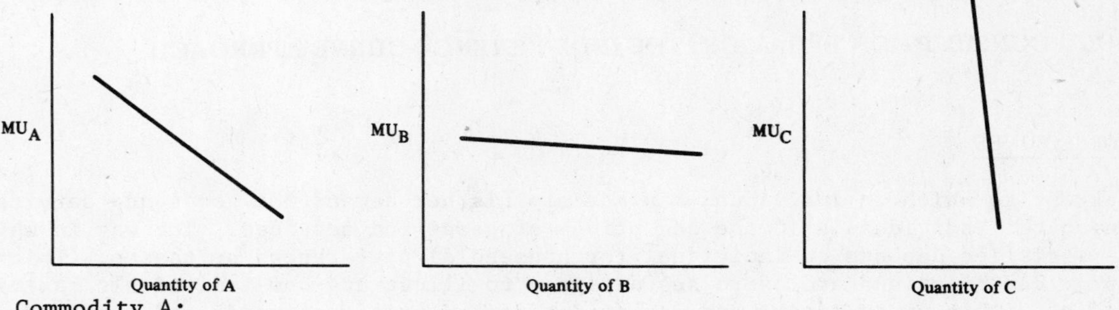

Commodity A:

Commodity B:

Commodity C:

5. Suppose an individual was prepared to pay for the first and subsequent large bottles of cola per week according to the following schedule.

Bottles of Cola per Week	Amount the Individual Is Prepared to Pay for Each Bottle
1st	$1.50
2nd	1.20
3rd	.90
4th	.60
5th	.50
6th	.40

(a) If the market price of large cola is $.50 per bottle, how many bottles per week will the individual consume? (Assume no budget constraint.)

(b) What is the total consumer surplus enjoyed by this individual?

(c) If the market price rises to $.90 per bottle, what effect does this have on the quantity demanded and consumer surplus?

CHAPTER 8

HOUSEHOLD CONSUMPTION BEHAVIOR: THE INDIFFERENCE CURVE APPROACH

CHAPTER OBJECTIVES

The extent to which an individual can satisfy his/her demand for goods and services depends upon the individual's income and prices of goods and services. The way in which wants are satisfied depends on individual (or household) preferences or tastes. This chapter provides questions and exercises designed to illustrate how individuals maximize their utility with a given income and market-determined prices of goods and services (budget constraint) and given tastes (their indifference map). Changes in relative prices and changes in income affect the budget constraint and how utility is maximized through the substitution effect and the income effect. Your understanding of Giffen goods and inferior goods is also tested.

MULTIPLE-CHOICE QUESTIONS

1. The budget line
   (a) represents combinations of commodities which use up the household's income
   (b) is also called an isocost line
   (c) has a negative slope
   (d) all of the above

2. The slope of the budget line with commodity Y on the vertical axis and commodity X on the horizontal axis is
   (a) $-(P_Y/P_X)$
   (b) $-(X/Y)$
   (c) $-(Y/X)$
   (d) $-(P_X/P_Y)$

3. A change in household money income will always shift the budget line parallel to itself if
   (a) money prices stay constant
   (b) relative prices stay constant with money prices changing in the same direction and by the same percentage as income
   (c) real income stays constant
   (d) money prices change in the same direction and proportion

4. Halving all absolute prices, other things constant, has the effect of
   (a) halving real income
   (b) halving money income
   (c) changing relative prices
   (d) doubling real income

5. A change in one absolute price, other things constant, will
   (a) shift the budget line parallel to itself
   (b) change money income
   (c) cause the budget line to change its slope
   (d) have no effect on real income

6. If household money income rises by 10 percent and all money prices rise by 5 percent,
   (a) household real purchases will increase by 10 percent
   (b) the household budget line will shift outward to the right
   (c) household real income has declined
   (d) the budget line shifts to the left and inward

7. An indifference curve shows
   (a) constant quantities of one good with varying quantities of another
   (b) the prices and quantities of two goods that can be purchased for a given sum of money
   (c) all combinations of two goods that will give the same level of satisfaction to the household or individual
   (d) combinations of goods whose marginal utilities are always equal

8. The hypothesis of diminishing marginal rate of substitution states that, for a given level of satisfaction,
   (a) the rate at which one commodity is substituted for another depends on the household income
   (b) the rate at which one commodity is substituted for another depends upon the amounts of the two commodities currently being consumed
   (c) indifference curves must have slopes which are positive
   (d) all of the above

9. Where the budget line is tangent to an indifference curve
   (a) equal amounts of goods give equal satisfaction
   (b) the ratio of prices of the goods must equal the marginal rate of substitution
   (c) the prices of the goods are equal
   (d) indicates that the household is not maximizing its satisfaction

10. Indifference curve theory assumes that
   (a) buyers can measure satisfaction in precise units
   (b) buyers can identify preferred combinations of goods without necessarily being able to measure their satisfaction precisely
   (c) buyers never behave consistently
   (d) all buyers have the same preference patterns

11. A Giffen good can be characterized as/by
   (a) an upward-sloping demand curve
   (b) a negative income effect which outweighs the substitution effect
   (c) one type of inferior good
   (d) all of the above

12. If the slope of the indifference curve for an individual consuming a specific combination of X and Y is -1.0, satisfaction will be maximized if
   (a) the budget line has a slope of -1.0
   (b) the budget line has a slope of +1.0
   (c) the marginal rate of substitution is -1.0
   (d) the relative price ratio of X to Y is greater than 1.0

13. For two commodities consumed by a household, the income-consumption line illustrates
    (a) how real and money income are related
    (b) how the relative prices of the two commodities change
    (c) how the household reacts in terms of purchasing the two commodities as income changes
    (d) that absolute prices determine the path of consumption

14. The price-consumption line, for two commodities consumed by a household, illustrates
    (a) an inverse relationship between relative prices and the demand for the two commodities
    (b) that absolute prices determine the path of consumption
    (c) the path of the consumption of two commodities as prices for both commodities and money income change
    (d) how a household responds in its purchase of two commodities when the price of one commodity changes and income and other prices are constant

15. The substitution effect
    (a) occurs when there is a change in the prices of all commodities
    (b) occurs when the price of one commodity changes, other things constant
    (c) leads to increased consumption of all commodities
    (d) is always accompanied by an equal income effect

16. The income effect
    (a) only occurs when real income is constant
    (b) occurs when a price change in one commodity, all other prices constant, effectively changes household income
    (c) leads to increased consumption of all commodities
    (d) relates only to changes in money income

17. An inferior good is best described as/by
    (a) an upward-sloping demand schedule
    (b) a commodity with a negative income effect
    (c) a commodity consumed by a few people
    (d) a commodity which has a negative marginal utility for all levels of consumption

EXERCISES

1. Assume that a household has a recreation budget of $800 per annum to be spent on two recreational activities: skiing (at $20 per unit of skiing) and movie-going (at $16 per unit of movie-going).
    (a) Using the graph below, draw the budget line for recreation expenditure for this household.
    (b) Can this household consume 30 units of skiing and 15 units of movie-going?

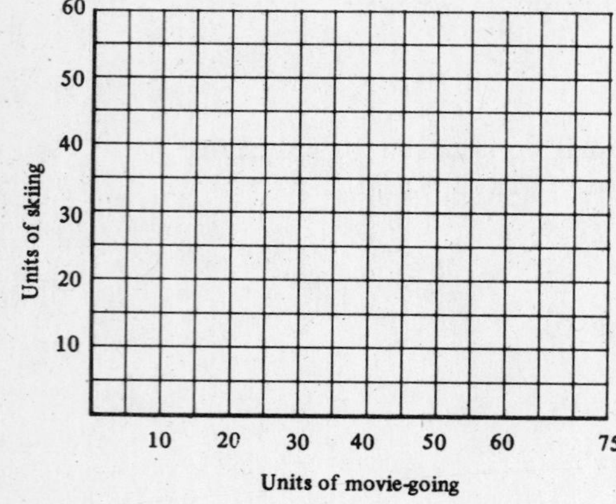

(c) If this household consumed 20 units of skiing, how many units of movie-going could it consume and keep within its budget?

(d) Suppose, because of an increase in family income, this household decides to allocate $1,200 to recreation. Draw in the new budget line.

2. Referring to the household recreation budget of $1,200 in Exercise 1, part (d), suppose now that the price of skiing has increased to $30 per unit.

(a) Draw the new budget line on the graph below.

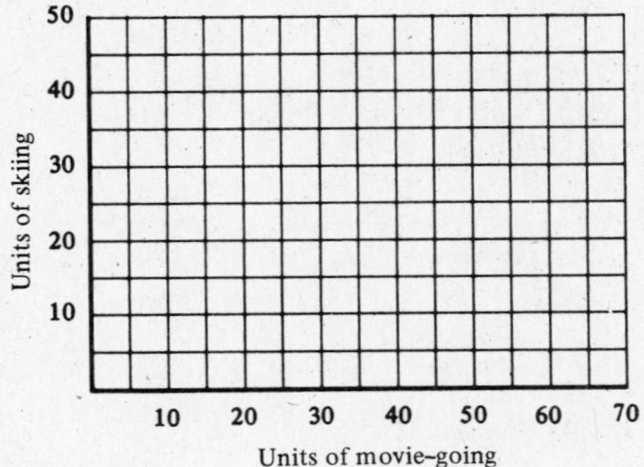

(b) If the family consumed 20 units of skiing, approximately how much movie-going is possible given the budget constraint?

(c) In addition to the increase in the price of skiing, suppose the price of movie-going increases to $24 per unit. With a budget of $1,200, draw in the new budget line. How does it compare with the budget line in Exercise 1, part (a)? Why?

3. (a) If all household income of $10,000 is spent on two goods, A and B, draw on the graph below the three budget lines possible for the pairs of prices shown below. Label the budget lines I, II, and III.

Commodity	Price Per Unit I	II	III
A	$100	200	80
B	50	150	100

A
125
100
75
50
25
50 100 150 200
B

(b) What is the slope of each budget line?
I:
II:
III:

(c) For budget line I, write the algebraic equation.

(d) If the cost of A relative to B is said to be 3:1, what is the opportunity cost of one unit of B?

4. If the following combinations of the monthly consumption of apples and oranges give equal satisfaction, an individual is said to be indifferent to each combination.

Apples/mo.	Oranges/mo.
30	10
24	12
19	15
15	19
12	24
10	35

(a) Plot the indifference curve on the graph below.

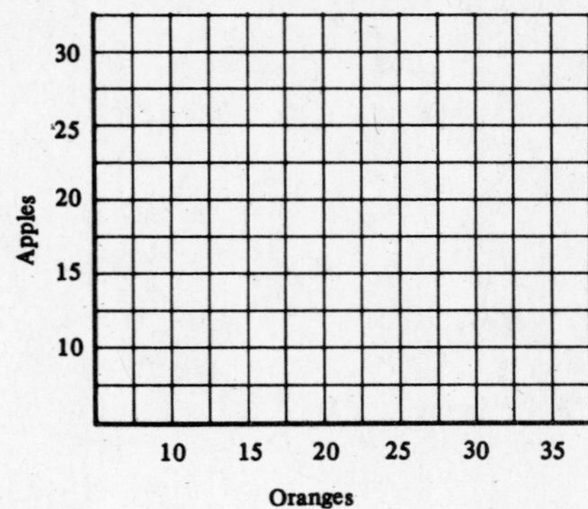

(b) Suppose that at the moment an individual is consuming 19 oranges and 15 apples per month. Would a combination of 15 oranges and 20 apples be preferred? Why?

(c) What (approximately) is the marginal rate of substitution at the point on the indifference curve where 15 apples are consumed? (Hint: Draw a line tangent to the indifference curve at this point and extend the tangent to both axes.)

5. Below you will find information on two indifference curves that are part of a household indifference map.

INDIFFERENCE CURVES

I		II	
Food	Shelter	Food	Shelter
50	10	54	13
35	15	39	18
30	18	34	21
25	25	29	28
21	37	25	40
18	46	22	49

(a) Draw these indifference curves on the graph below.

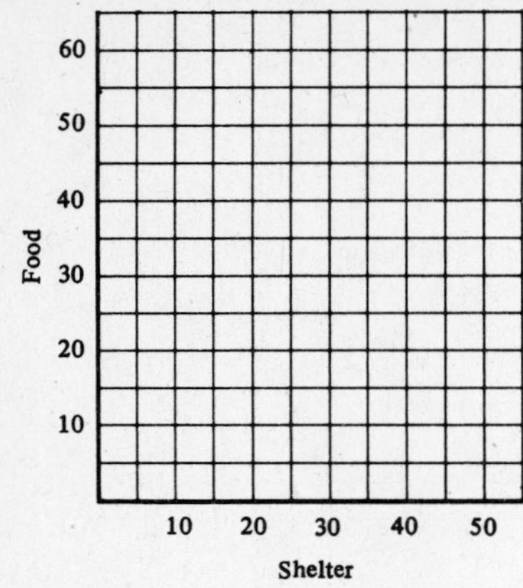

(b) If the household budget is $1,000 and food and shelter per unit cost $20 and $22.22, respectively, draw in the budget line on the graph.

(c) Given (a) and (b) above, what combination of food and shelter will maximize household utility? Explain.

6. Between 1969 and 1974, average after-tax family income and expenditure on specific goods changed as shown below.

	1969	1974	Percent Change in Prices in Same Period
Nominal After-tax Family Income	$7,761	$12,043	
Family Expenditure on			
Food	1,605	2,442	48.3
Clothing	727	988	21.9
Transportation	1,111	1,708	25.3
Alcohol/Tobacco	341	482	15.1
All Goods and Services			31.3

(a) What was the percentage change in real after-tax income between 1969 and 1974?

(b) What were the percentage increases in real expenditure on the following items?
Food:
Clothing:
Transportation:
Alcohol/Tobacco:

(c) During this five-year period, what change occurred in the relative prices of food and clothing? Of alcohol/tobacco and transportation? (Assume that the relative price ratio was unity in 1969.)

7. In the diagram below, a household moves from one equilibrium E_0 to a new equilibrium E_1, after a decline in the price of commodity X.

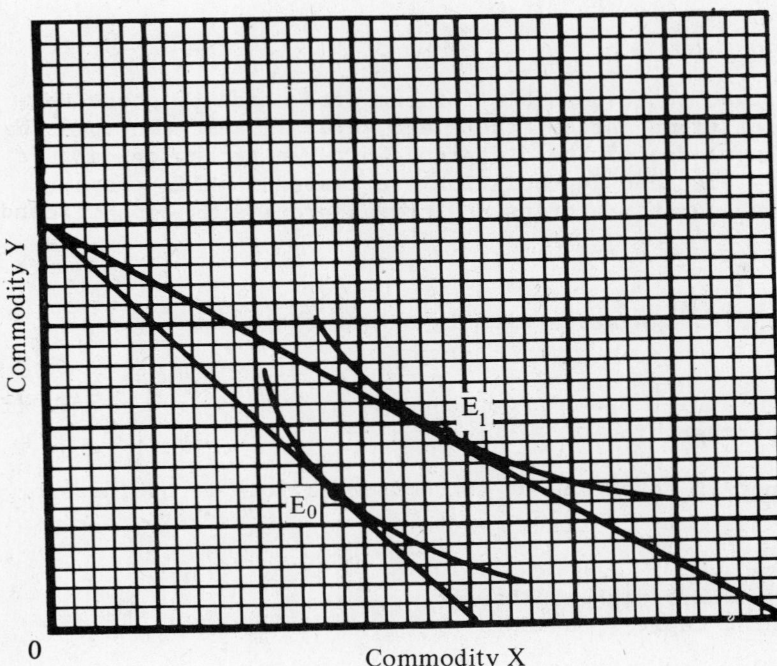

(a) Illustrate on the diagram the size of the substitution effect.
(b) Illustrate on the diagram the size of the income effect.
(c) Is commodity X an inferior good? Explain.

CHAPTER 9

THE ROLE OF THE FIRM

CHAPTER OBJECTIVES

The firm is the basic unit that is responsible for the production of goods and services. While the structure of firms varies, there are several basic concepts that apply to all producers. Your knowledge of the difference between technological and economic efficiency, opportunity cost and depreciation are tested in this chapter. In addition, the difference between economic profits and normal profits is emphasized.

MULTIPLE-CHOICE QUESTIONS

1. Limited liability for the claims against a firm is an advantage for
   (a) single proprietors
   (b) corporate shareholders
   (c) paid employees
   (d) general partners in a partnership

2. Which of the following is not an advantage of the corporate form of business organization?
   (a) limited liability
   (b) separate legal existence
   (c) close identification of owners with management
   (d) relative ease of obtaining capital funds

3. In the context of the operation of the firm, real capital is
   (a) financing which is provided by the owners
   (b) money borrowed from banks to run the firm
   (c) the outstanding obligations of the firm to others
   (d) comprised of plant, equipment, and inventories

4. Which of the following groups of claimants would be the last to have their claims honored in a bankruptcy?
   (a) bondholders
   (b) commercial creditors
   (c) common stockholders
   (d) employees owed back wages

5 Economic theory frequently assumes that firms try to maximize profits
   (a) because firms always maximize profits
   (b) because firms ought to maximize profits to be fair to their stockholders
   (c) because use of this simple assumption has frequently led to accurate predictions
   (d) because economists wish thus to criticize the greed of firms

6. Which statement is correct?
   (a) All technologically efficient methods are economically efficient.
   (b) All economically efficient methods are technologically efficient.
   (c) Some economically efficient methods are not technologically efficient.
   (d) Both (a) and (b) are true because economically efficient and technologically efficient methods must coincide.

7. Opportunity cost refers to
   (a) what must be given up to secure the next best alternative
   (b) unexpected profits or gain for the firm
   (c) the best rate of return possible on an investment
   (d) the return to using something in the most profitable way

8. If you give up a full-time job to go to the university, the major opportunity cost is
   (a) tuition and fees
   (b) room and board
   (c) the income you could have received from employment
   (d) social and miscellaneous expenses

9. Applying the concept of opportunity cost to the firm is difficult
   (a) because it requires imputing certain costs when a resource is not directly hired or purchased
   (b) because most of a firm's costs are monetary costs
   (c) to the extent that the modern firm borrows money from banks
   (d) all of the above

10. Depreciation is
   (a) a charge against a firm's revenue equal to the sunk cost of machinery and buildings, regardless of their current market value
   (b) equivalent to the value that a machine contributes to the value of output
   (c) a cost to the firm representing the "wear and tear" and obsolescence of capital goods used in the production process
   (d) always equal to the market value of second-hand items

11. Which of the following would most likely represent an imputed cost for a firm?
   (a) monetary payments to current employees
   (b) interest paid on borrowed funds
   (c) dividends paid to shareholders
   (d) interest that could have been received on money currently invested in inventory

12. The difference between economic profits and normal profits is that
   (a) normal profits are always smaller
   (b) normal profits are necessarily larger for all firms
   (c) normal profits are part of opportunity cost, whereas economic profits are revenues in excess of opportunity costs
   (d) normal profits take into account monopoly power; economic profits do not

13. Normal profits refer to
   (a) what all firms, on average, obtain as a return on investment
   (b) the base used by the tax authorities to levy business taxes
   (c) the imputed return to capital and risk-taking required to keep owners in the business
   (d) the level of profits necessary to ensure that the firm covers its day-to-day operating costs

EXERCISES

1. Assume that there are two methods of making 100 widgets per month with capital and labor as shown below.

	Method A	Method B
Capital	10 units	5 units
Labor	100 units	200 units

The cost of these factors of production are $5 per unit of labor and $20 per unit of capital.

(a) Can you distinguish which method (A or B) is the most technologically efficient? Explain.

(b) Can you distinguish the most economically efficient method? Explain.

(c) If labor cost dropped to $1 per unit, would your answer to (b) change? Why?

2. Arrange the following items and use the information below to obtain (a) net profit before income taxes, (b) economic profit before taxes, and (c) economic profit after income taxes (Hint: See Table 9-1 in the text)
   1. Revenue from sale of goods = $5 million
   2. Tax rate = 50 percent of net profit before tax
   3. Depreciation = $500,000
   4. Salaries, cost of raw materials = $3 million
   5. Return to capital and risk-taking = $500,000

(a) Net profit before income tax ________________
(b) Economic profit before tax ________________
(c) Economic profit after tax ________________

3. Assume that there are two basic methods of producing vegetables for sale from a garden plot, and that the grower can sell all output at a given price. One method involves hand tools and labor; the other, power tools and labor. The following information gives an idea of the production processes involved. (Output from the garden is proportional to the size of the lot.)

Garden Size (square feet)	Man-hours to Produce Output	
	Hand Tools	Power Tools
200	50	20
500	125	50
1000	250	100
2000	500	200

Note: (1) The hand tools are depreciated at $10 per year; (2) the power tools are depreciated at $300 per year; (3) labor cost is $4 per hour.

(a) At what garden size does it become economically efficient to use power tools?

(b) If the price of labor declined to $2 per hour, would this affect the answer in (a)? How?

4. (This is a true story: only the numbers have changed to protect the business.) In the early 1970s, an enterprising student decided to enter the paper and glass recycling business. He left the university, where he had been studying economics, and set about establishing a business, using his meager savings, to collect and deliver used paper and glass to paper mills and glass-using firms. His (hypothetical) monthly costs and revenues were:

Costs		Revenue	
Rent for old warehouse	$250	12 tons of paper at $50 per ton	$600
Depreciation of truck	100	1000 pounds of glass at $.40 per pound	$400
Labor (other than his own)	300		
Miscellaneous	100		

Shortly after being in business, large province-wide companies in the scrap business entered the recycling business. The buyers of used paper and glass were flooded with material, and the price of used paper plummeted to $30 per ton. Large companies simply intensified the use of capital in the recycling business to cut costs.

Our young entrepreneur sought to increase the capital intensity of his firm and upgrade the quality of his capital but was unable to find anyone who would lend him the money to do so at less than an exorbitant rate of interest. He closed his business and returned to complete his degree in economics.

(a) Why did this business feel the need to enter depreciation of the truck as a cost?

(b) What was the level of monthly accounting profits for the business before the price declined? What is inappropriate about using this figure as a profit figure?

(c) Given that the owner of the business worked 40 hours per week, do you think there were any "economic profits" in the firm?

(d) What was the opportunity cost of going back to the university?

CHAPTER 10

PRODUCTION & COST IN THE SHORT RUN

CHAPTER OBJECTIVES

The first part of this chapter tests your understanding of the relationship between inputs and outputs in the short run; the short-run production function. The concepts of total, average, and marginal product are stressed along with their relationship to diminishing marginal productivity. The second part deals with the short-run costs of firms. Given the cost of inputs, the production function can be used to derive a system of short-run cost curves for the firm. You are asked to undertake several calculations of average fixed cost, average variable cost, average total cost, and marginal cost for hypothetical firms in order to reinforce your comprehension of these important concepts.

MULTIPLE-CHOICE QUESTIONS

1. Decision making for the firm in the short run involves
   (a) having access to only a few additional fixed factors
   (b) being able to vary only some factors
   (c) no additional variable or fixed factors
   (d) no opportunity to change prices or output

2. Which of the following is an example of a production decision in the short run?
   (a) A contractor buys two additional trucks and hires two new drivers for them.
   (b) A contractor decides to work his crew overtime to finish a job.
   (c) A railroad decides to eliminate all passenger service.
   (d) A paper company installs antipollution equipment

3. Long-run decisions
   (a) do not affect short-run decisions
   (b) can consider all factors variable
   (c) are not very important because the long run is a succession of short runs
   (d) are taken with fewer alternatives open than in the case of short-run decisions

4. In the very long-run planning horizon
   (a) technology is allowed to change
   (b) the ratio of variable to fixed factors is given
   (c) technology is unchanging, but all inputs can be varied
   (d) firms cannot reduce their output

5. The production function relates
   (a) cost to inputs
   (b) cost to output
   (c) wages to profits
   (d) outputs to inputs

Use the table below, which describes a hypothetical firm, to answer questions 6 through 8.

Variable Factor	Fixed Factor	Output
0	20	0
1	20	50
2	20	120
3	20	220
4	20	300
5	20	360
6	20	410
7	20	450
8	20	470
9	20	480

6. The firm is
   (a) operating in the long run
   (b) operating in the short run
   (c) experiencing constant average product
   (d) altering its technology to increase its output

7. For additional units of the variable factor,
   (a) the average product is rising for all levels of output
   (b) marginal product is constant
   (c) the point of diminishing average productivity occurs when employment of the variable factor increases from four to five
   (d) average product falls when employment of the variable factor goes from two to three

8. For the firm,
   (a) the marginal product is defined as the change in total output divided by the amount of the variable factor
   (b) the point of diminishing marginal productivity for the variable factor occurs when output goes from 50 to 120
   (c) the point of diminishing marginal productivity for the variable factor occurs when output goes from 220 to 300
   (d) marginal product of the variable factor becomes negative at output level of 360

9. The hypothesis of eventually diminishing returns applies to production functions
   (a) having at least one fixed factor
   (b) in the long run only
   (c) in the very long run preferably
   (d) in which inputs are applied in fixed proportions

10. The law of diminishing average returns
   (a) implies that the average product of a variable factor will eventually decrease as units of the variable factor are added to a fixed factor
   (b) states that as a variable factor is added to a fixed factor output continuously declines at an increasing rate
   (c) applies only when labor is combined with capital to produce an output
   (d) states that marginal productivity declines as output increases

11. Average total cost is
    (a) total fixed cost plus total variable cost divided by the number of units of output produced
    (b) total fixed cost minus total variable cost
    (c) total cost divided by the number of units of the fixed factor
    (d) always constant if fixed cost is constant

12. Which of the following necessarily declines continuously as output increases?
    (a) marginal cost
    (b) average fixed cost
    (c) average variable cost
    (d) total fixed cost

13. When average total cost is declining,
    (a) marginal cost must be declining
    (b) marginal cost must be above average total cost
    (c) marginal cost must be below average total cost
    (d) marginal cost must be rising

14. The marginal or incremental cost associated with adding one more person to an airline flight
    (a) is always the same as the average cost
    (b) is always equal to zero once the flight is scheduled to go
    (c) is small but positive, due to additional variable costs associated with the last passenger
    (d) declines continuously, due to "spreading" the overhead costs

15. Diminishing average productivity
    (a) occurs over all ranges of output
    (b) is due to low-skilled workers
    (c) only occurs in the long run
    (d) implies that average variable costs will eventually rise

16. The marginal product of a factor may rise before declining
    (a) if the variable factor is cheaper than the fixed one
    (b) when land is the fixed factor
    (c) due to the division of labor
    (d) none of the above

17. Plant capacity is
    (a) the output at which short-run average total costs are a minimum
    (b) the maximum output possible for a firm
    (c) where short-run average costs are a maximum
    (d) where marginal costs begin to rise

EXERCISES

1. (a) The relationship between a variable input and output for a firm is shown in the first and second columns in the table. Calculate the average and marginal productivity.

Variable Input	Output	Average Product	Marginal Product
1	20	______	
2	60	______	______
3	120	______	______
4	200	______	______
5	270	______	______
6	324	______	______
7	364	______	______
8	384	______	______
9	396	______	______
10	404	______	______

(b) Graph the average and marginal product. (Remember to plot marginal product at the interval--see Table 10-1 in the text)

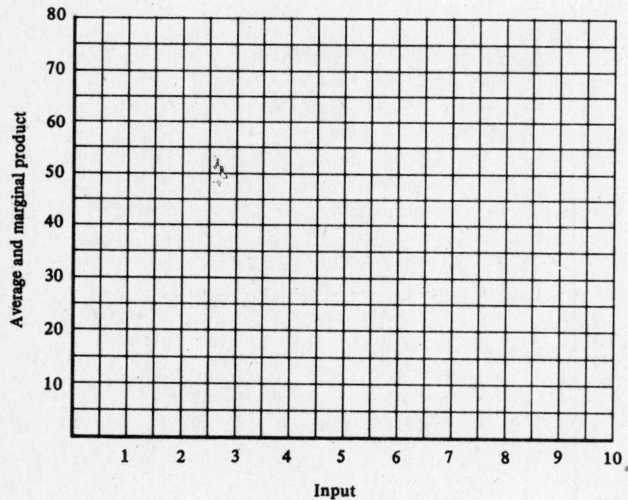

(c) The cost structure for the same firm is shown in the first and second columns in the table below. Complete the columns in the table.

Output	Total Fixed Cost	Total Variable Cost	Total Cost	Average Fixed Cost	Average Variable Cost	Average Total Cost	Marginal Cost
20	168	80	____	____	____	____	
60	168	160	____	____	____	____	____
120	168	240	____	____	____	____	____
200	168	320	____	____	____	____	____
270	168	400	____	____	____	____	____
324	168	480	____	____	____	____	____
364	168	560	____	____	____	____	____
384	168	640	____	____	____	____	____
396	168	720	____	____	____	____	____
404	168	800	____	____	____	____	____

(d) Graph approximately the average total cost curve and the marginal cost curve.

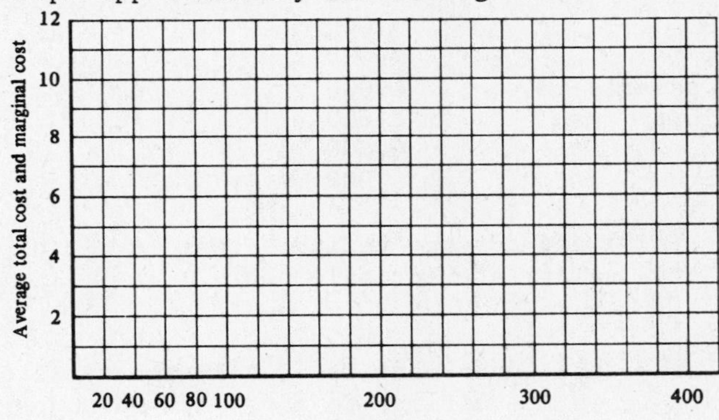

2. The marginal cost curve of a firm producing good X is shown in the graph below. (Assume that fixed costs = zero.)
   (a) Complete the table below. Note that the marginal cost from the graph applies to output level at the next highest whole number (e.g., MC of $3.50 applies to output of 1 unit).

Output	Total Cost	Average Total Cost
1	____	____
2	____	____
3	____	____
4	____	____
5	____	____
6	____	____

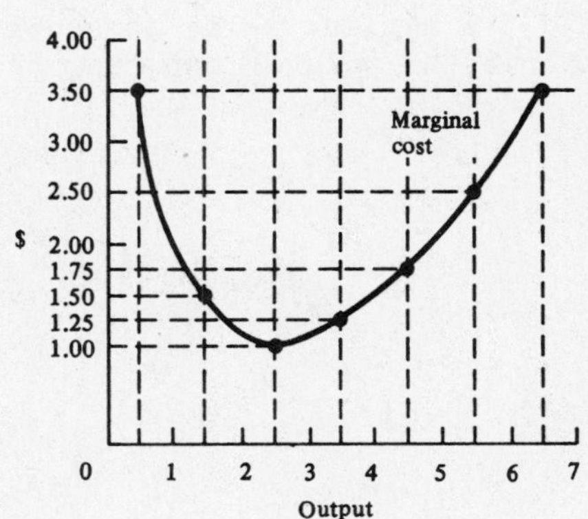

(b) Plot the average total cost schedule (approximately) on the graph below.

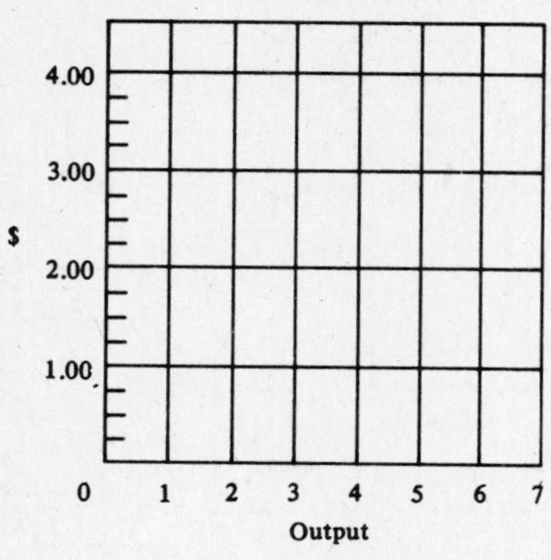

(c) What is the capacity level of output?

3. Suppose the following costs apply to a single flight from Toronto to Vancouver on a Boeing 727 with 180 seats.

Depreciation	$2,400
Fuel	6,000
Salary for crew	7,000
Administration salaries	4,000
Sales and publicity	2,000
Office rent	4,000
Interest on debt	6,000

(a) What are the average fixed cost (AFC) and average variable cost (AVC) for this flight? (Assume that fuel and crew salary are variable costs.)

(b) Suppose that, in establishing fares, the government regulatory agency sets the price per seat at the level that allows the airline to cover AFC when operating at 50 percent of capacity. What will be the regular fare per person on this run?

(c) Given this price, what is the marginal cost to the airline of carrying the ninety-first passenger on the flight?

(d) Should the airline agree to supply a charter flight for a group that offers to guarantee the sale of 140 tickets at $120 per seat? Explain.

4. A producer of a particular commodity finds that the total-cost curve can be described by the equation: $TC = 50 + 3Q + Q^2$.

(a) Complete the columns below. (Hint: The term $(3Q + Q^2)$ represents the variable costs, and 50 the total fixed cost.)

Q	TFC	TVC	TC	MC	AFC	AVC	ATC
0							
1							
2							
3							
4							
5							
6							
7							
8							
9							
10							
.							
.							
.							
20							

(b) At what output are average total costs (ATC) at a minimum?

(c) What is the marginal cost at this output?

(d) If there were only variable costs and no fixed costs, would MC be affected?

(e) By examining the table above, explain why ATC decreases to a minimum value and then starts to rise.

5. Given the cost curves of a hypothetical firm shown below, answer the following questions.
   (a) The capacity of the firm occurs at an output of ____________________.
   (b) The effect of eventually diminishing average productivity occurs after an output level of ________________________ (approximately).
   (c) ATC = MC at an output level of ______________.

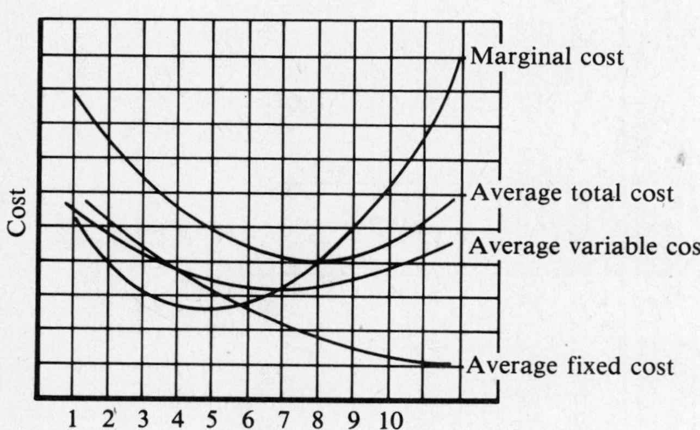

6. Mr. Gill has recently constructed, at a capital cost of $250,000, a large pond facility in order to raise trout for commercial sale. The more "fingerlings" and feed he adds to the pond, the greater is the output, in kilograms of marketable fish, as shown below.

Units of Fingerlings and Feed	Output (thousands of kg)	Cost of Fingerlings and Feed ($000)	Total Cost ($000)	Average Total Cost	Marginal Cost
0	0	0	_____	_____	
					_____
1	200	100	_____	_____	
					_____
2	375	200	_____	_____	
					_____
3	525	300	_____	_____	
					_____
4	650	400	_____	_____	
					_____
5	720	500	_____	_____	
					_____
6	780	600	_____	_____	

(a) Complete the table above
(b) Plot the average total cost and marginal cost curves in the graph below

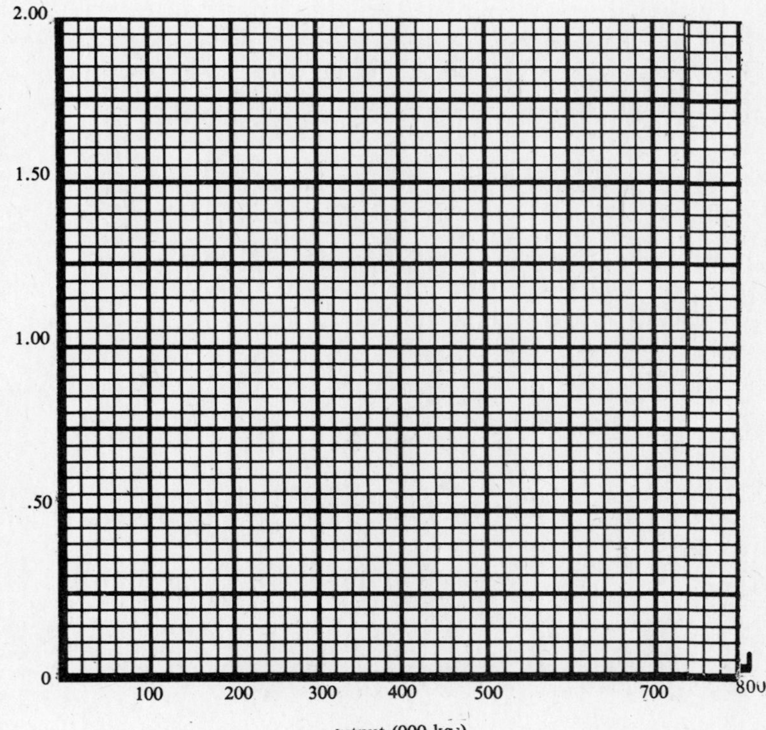

(c) What is the output associated with minimum average total cost?

(d) What is the relationship between the marginal cost curve and the average total cost curve?

CHAPTER 11

PRODUCTION AND COST IN THE LONG & VERY LONG RUN

CHAPTER OBJECTIVES

In moving from consideration of only the short-run production function and cost curves of the firm, the quantities of both labor and capital are allowed to vary in the long run. The substitution of capital for labor and vice versa depends on the marginal product of each factor and their prices. Several questions and exercises are designed to illustrate when and why it is optimal to make substitutions when relative factor prices change or relative marginal products of the factors change. From the knowledge of long-run production, long-run cost curves can be derived. Emphasis is given to the relationship between long-run decreasing costs and long-run increasing returns. This chapter also tests your understanding of the optional material relating to isoquants and isocost curves and how they are used to derive the optimal factor mix for the firm.

MULTIPLE-CHOICE QUESTIONS

1. The primary difference between short-run and long-run decision making for the firm
   (a) involves the accuracy of forecasts of future demand
   (b) is that in the long run all productive factors can be varied in quantity
   (c) is highlighted by the inability to alter fixed factors in the long run
   (d) is a matter of how quickly output can respond to changes in demand

2. For cost minimization where both capital and labor inputs can vary,
   (a) both factors are used until their marginal productivity is zero
   (b) the factors are used such that the marginal productivity per dollar expended on each factor is equalized
   (c) the factors are used such that the ratio of the amounts of the factors used equals the ratio of their marginal productivities
   (d) marginal productivity varies indirectly with price

3. If for a given combination of labor and capital, the ratio of their marginal productivities is 2:1, then for cost minimization
   (a) the ratio of their prices must be 2:1
   (b) two units of labor are combined with one unit of capital
   (c) the ratio of their prices must be 1/2
   (d) there is more capital being used than labor

4. If a firm expands its use of capital and reduces the amount of labor it uses to produce a given output
   (a) the marginal product of labor will rise and the marginal product of capital will fall
   (b) the ratio of the marginal products of capital to labor will be constant
   (c) the marginal product of capital will rise and the marginal product of labor will fall
   (d) the ratio of the marginal products of capital to labor must increase.

5. If the marginal product of capital is six times that of labor, and the price of capital is three times that of labor, for costs to be minimized,
   (a) capital should be substituted for labor
   (b) labor should be substituted for capital
   (c) the price of capital will fall, or the price of labor will rise
   (d) twice as much capital as labor should be employed

6. A rise in labor cost relative to capital costs in an industry, other things equal, will
   (a) lead to replacement of some workers by machines where possible
   (b) cause the industry to be unprofitable
   (c) necessarily increase long-run costs
   (d) always be offset by rising labor productivity

7. The principle of substitution implies that
   (a) as output expands, more of both factors of production must be used
   (b) labor will be substituted for capital as the price of labor rises
   (c) if the price of one factor decreases relative to another, more of the cheaper factor will be used
   (d) capital will always be substituted for labor as output expands

8. The long-run average cost curve
   (a) shows total output related to total input levels
   (b) assumes constant factor proportions throughout
   (c) reflects the least-cost production method for each output level when all factors are variable
   (d) rises because of the "law" of diminishing returns

9. Constant long-run average costs for a firm mean that
   (a) there are greater advantages to small- rather than large-scale plants
   (b) an unlimited amount will be produced
   (c) any scale of production is as cheap per unit as any other
   (d) no additional factors are being utilized

10. Decreasing long-run average costs for a firm as it expands plant size and output
   (a) result from decreasing returns to scale
   (b) result usually from the effects of increased automation and specialization
   (c) result from the increased complexity and confusion of rapid expansion
   (d) are rare and only are caused by exogeneous events

11. The long-run average cost curve is determined by
   (a) long-run demand
   (b) long-run supply
   (c) population growth and inflation
   (d) technology and input prices

12. Long-run decreasing returns may be the result of
   (a) rising factor prices
   (b) replication
   (c) "spreading the overhead"
   (d) management problems or other diseconomies of scale

13. A firm experiencing long-run increasing returns is
   (a) likely to be substituting labor for capital
   (b) likely to be using plants with greater capacities
   (c) characterized by increasing costs
   (d) none of the above

14. The short-run average total cost curve (SRAC) cannot fall below the long-run average cost curve (LRAC)
   (a) because factor prices are fixed
   (b) unless marginal productivities change
   (c) because the LRAC represents the lowest attainable costs for each output level
   (d) unless relative prices are changed

15. The family of SRAC curves will shift down for all but which one of the following?
   (a) lower prices for labor, capital, and other inputs
   (b) lower cost methods of production
   (c) technological advances
   (d) lower demand and reduced product prices

16. An isoquant
   (a) illustrates equal factor costs for a given output level
   (b) shows how output changes when one factor is substituted for another factor
   (c) shows how a given output can be produced with a fixed factor while changing the quantity of another factor
   (d) shows the set of technologically efficient possibilities for producing a given output.

17. In terms of combining factors of production, the marginal rate of substitution
   (a) measures relative prices as output changes over time
   (b) refers to the equivalence between the ratio of marginal productivities and prices
   (c) is always positive
   (d) measures the rate at which one factor is substituted for another with output held constant

18. If the marginal rate of substitution is -2 at a point on an isoquant involving two factors,
   (a) the ratio of factor prices is +1/2
   (b) the ratio of marginal productivities is -1/2
   (c) the ratio of marginal productivities is -2
   (d) one factor of production has negative marginal productivity

19. An isocost line for two factors C and L (their respective prices are P_C and P_L) could have which of the following equations?
   (a) LC = \$100

   (b) $\$100 = P_C + P_L C$

   (c) $\$100 = P_L L + P_C C$

   (d) $\$100 = P_L P_C$

20. If two factors C and L are graphed in the same unit scale with C on the vertical axis, and an isocost line has a slope = -2, then

   (a) $P_L = 2P_C$

   (b) $P_C/P_L = 2$

   (c) C = L

   (d) L = 2C

21. At the point of tangency of the isocost line in question 20 with an isoquant,
   (a) the desired factor combination has 2C for each L
   (b) the marginal product of labor is twice that of capital
   (c) the desired factor combination has 2L for each C
   (d) the marginal product of capital is twice that of labor

22. Which of the following statements is valid for costs and production in the very long run?
   (a) All factors of production can vary.
   (b) Production techniques are allowed to change.
   (c) The quality of labor services may change.
   (d) All of the above.

EXERCISES

1. In the table that follows, three different firms are able to combine capital (K) and labor (L) in various ways resulting in pairs of marginal productivities as shown. (Note that higher number combinations substitute capital for labor, which decreases MP_K and increases MP_L.) For all firms, the price of a unit of capital is $10.00 and the price of labor is $5.00.

Combination Number	FIRM A MP_K	FIRM A MP_L	FIRM B MP_K	FIRM B MP_L	FIRM C MP_K	FIRM C MP_L
1	10	1	6	3	25	2
2	8	2	5	4	20	4
3	6	3	4	6	14	7
4	4	4	3	8	10	8
5	2	5	2	10	5	10

   (a) Firm A is currently using combination 3, Firm B is using combination 2, and Firm C is using combination 4. Which firm is minimizing its costs? Explain.

   (b) How would the firms which are not minimizing their costs have to alter their use of capital and labor to do so?

2. The graph below shows the short-run average cost curve (SRAC) and the long-run average cost curve (LRAC) for a firm. Currently, the firm is producing output q_0.

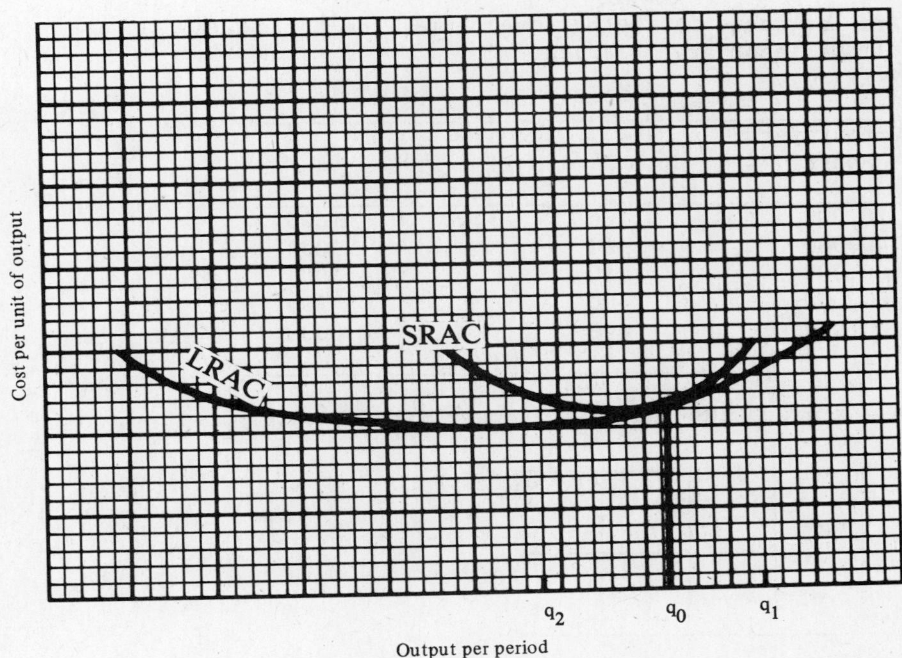

(a) If the firm expects a rise in demand and an increase in output to q_1 and this rise is expected to be only temporary, which cost curve should the firm use to expand its production? Why?

(b) If output decreased to q_2 and it is believed that this will be the output level in the foreseeable future, on what cost curve should the firm operate and why?

3. At the beginning of some time period, it is observed that a firm is producing 10,000 bottles of wine per month using 50 units of capital (K) and 1000 units of labor (L). The price of capital per unit is $20, and for labor the price is $4 per unit.

As the firm increases its output over time, the following changes in the use of capital and labor are observed:

Output per Month	K	L
20,000	100	1800
40,000	180	3000
60,000	250	4000
80,000	400	7200
100,000	600	10000

(a) Calculate and graph the long-run average cost curve.

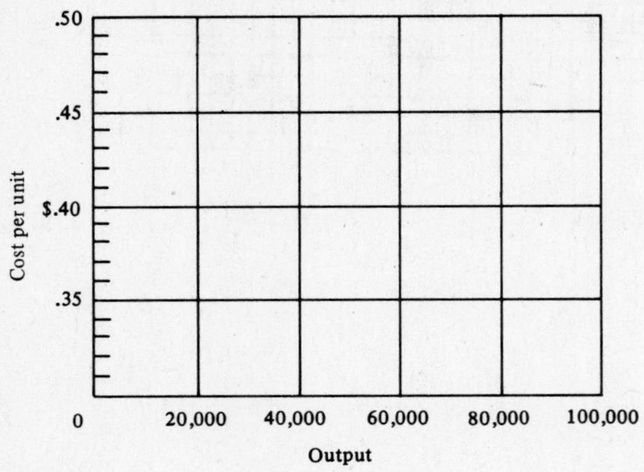

(b) At what output do increasing returns come to an end?

(c) What happens to the ratio of capital to labor as output expands?

4. The table below shows six methods of producing 100 widgets per month using capital and labor.

Method	Units of Capital	Units of Labor	Δ Capital	Δ Labor	Marginal Rate of Substitution
A	10	80	+5	-22	-4.40
B	15	58			
C	25	40			
D	40	24			
E	58	15			
F	80	9			

(a) Complete the last three columns.

(b) On the graph below, plot the isoquant indicated by the data above.

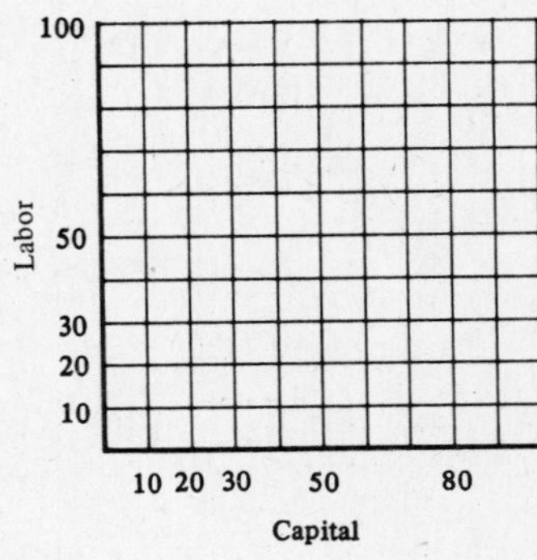

5. Suppose the input-output data for a firm are as shown in the table below.

	Labor Inputs				
	1	2	3	4	5
1			100	100	
2		100*		150	150
3	100		150		
4	100	150			
5		150			

*Units of output.

(a) Draw the isoquant map for the two levels of output.

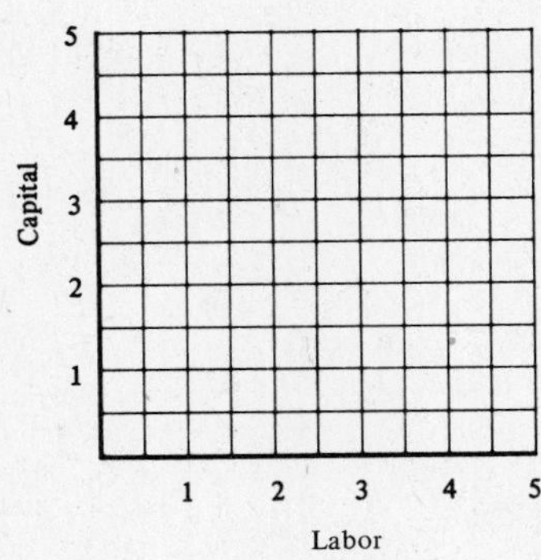

(b) Suppose that the firm was producing 100 units of output, and the isocost line had a slope of approximately -.40. How much capital and labor would the firm use to minimize cost?

(c) If the relative prices of capital and labor were to become unity, would this alter the nature of the production process for this firm? Explain.

6. The diagram that follows illustrates how various levels of output can be produced by different combinations of capital and labor.

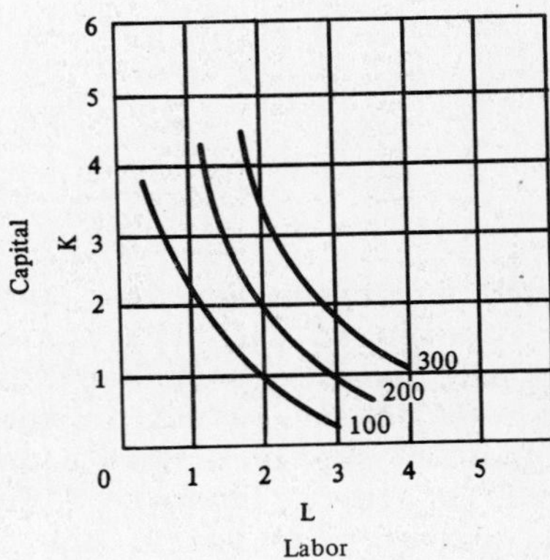

(a) If the ratio of the price of capital to that of labor was $P_K/P_L = 1/1$, how many units of capital and labor will the firm use to produce 100 units of output (at minimum cost)?

(b) If the price of capital per unit was to become one-half the original price, and the firm wished to produce 200 units of output, approximately how much capital and labor would it employ? Explain.

PART FOUR

MARKETS AND PRICING

CHAPTER 12

PRICING IN COMPETITIVE MARKETS

CHAPTER OBJECTIVES

The exercises and questions in this chapter are designed to strengthen your knowledge and comprehension of several important theoretical issues related to the behavior of the firm in a world of perfect competition. Most important is the relationship between marginal cost and marginal revenue and the determination of price and output in the market and by the individual firm. The derivation of firm and industry supply curves using the marginal cost schedule of the firm is also examined. Problems are designed to illustrate the relationship between a firm's elasticity of demand and market elasticity, how changes in market prices affect output decisions in the firm and the relationship between profits and perfect competition. The chapter includes questions on the concept of Pareto efficiency.

MULTIPLE-CHOICE QUESTIONS

1. Which of the following best characterizes a competitive market structure?
   (a) Each firm advertises unique attributes of the product.
   (b) Individual firms set price so as to maximize profits.
   (c) Existing firms restrict entry of new firms into the market.
   (d) Firms are price takers.

2. Marginal revenue
   (a) refers to a firm about to go bankrupt
   (b) is the additional output necessary to lower price
   (c) is the additional revenue when output expands by one unit
   (d) is the ratio of average revenue to total revenue

3. If total revenue for a firm is less than total variable costs
   (a) the firm must change technology
   (b) the firm could improve its net revenue position by ceasing production
   (c) the firm is breaking even
   (d) all of the above

4. If output occurs where marginal cost equals marginal revenue, then
   (a) the last unit produced adds the same amount to costs as it does to revenue
   (b) the firm is maximizing profits
   (c) there is no reason to reduce or expand output, so long as TR $\geq$ TVC
   (d) all of the above

5. Which is not a required characteristic of a perfectly competitive industry?
   (a) Consumers have no reason to prefer one firm's product to another.
   (b) There are enough firms so none can influence market price.
   (c) Any firm can enter or leave the industry.
   (d) Industry demand is highly elastic.

6. For a perfectly competitive firm
   (a) marginal revenue equals price at all output levels
   (b) price must be lowered to sell additional output
   (c) marginal revenue is less than price at every level of output
   (d) none of the above

7. A perfectly competitive firm does not try to sell more of its product by lowering its price below the market price because
   (a) this would be considered unethical price chiseling
   (b) its competitors will not permit it
   (c) its demand curve is inelastic, so total revenue will decline
   (d) it can sell all it wants to at the market price

8. If the market demand for wheat has an elasticity of .25
   (a) an individual wheat farmer can increase his revenue by reducing output
   (b) nothing can be said about the elasticity of demand for a wheat farmer
   (c) total revenue from wheat sales will rise with an increase of industry production
   (d) each wheat farmer, nevertheless, faces a highly elastic demand

Questions 9 through 11 refer to the diagram below, which applies to a firm in a perfectly competitive market:

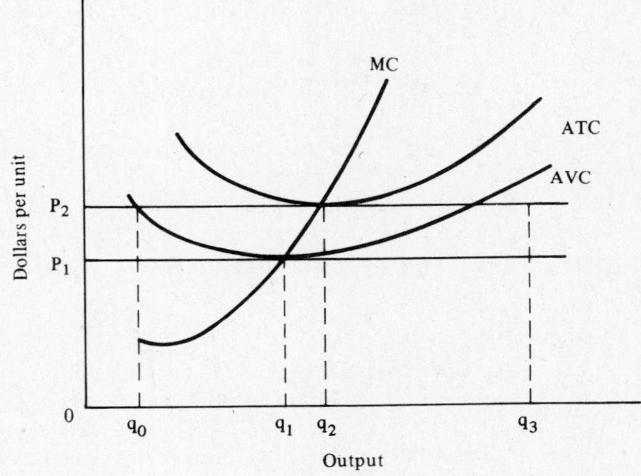

9. Assuming market price is P_2, which output maximizes the firm's profits?
   (a) q_o
   (b) q_1
   (c) q_2
   (d) q_3

10. If market price fell to P_1, what should the profit-maximizing firm do in the short run?
   (a) cease production entirely
   (b) continue to produce q_2
   (c) reduce output level to q_1
   (d) none of the above

11. Which of the following best describes the behavior of a profit-maximizing competitive firm in the short run?
   (a) produce q_3 regardless of price since P AVC for all units up to q_3
   (b) do not produce at all unless market price exceeds P_2
   (c) produce output q_1 at price P_2
   (d) produce output levels where $P = MC$ (as long as $P > P_1$)

12. In perfect competition, the short-run supply curve of the firm is
   (a) the marginal cost curve above average variable cost
   (b) the marginal cost curve above average total cost
   (c) the marginal cost curve above average fixed cost
   (d) the entire marginal cost curve

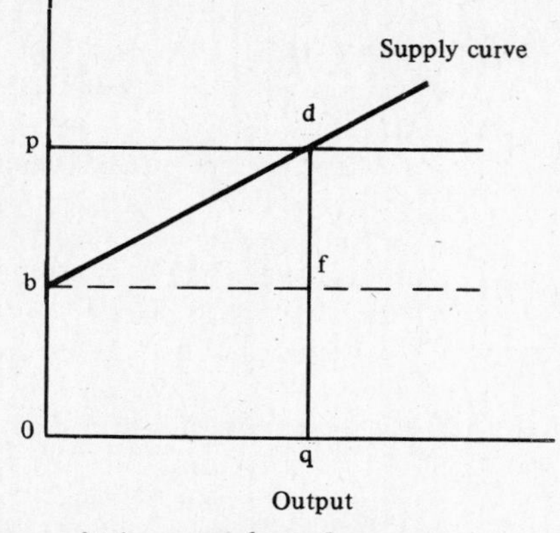

13. With reference to the diagram at the right, p is market price and q is quantity supplied. Producer's surplus is
   (a) the area 0pdq   (c) the area bdf
   (b) the area 0bdq   (d) the area bpd

14. Long-run economic profits will not exist in a perfectly competitive market because
   (a) new firms will enter the industry and eliminate them
   (b) corporate income taxes eliminate such excess profits
   (c) competitive industries are too inefficient to be profitable
   (d) long-run increasing costs eliminate profits

15. The conditions for long-run competitive equilibrium include all but which one of the following for all firms?
   (a) P = AVC   (c) P = MR
   (b) P = MC   (d) P = LRATC

16. If there were a steady decrease in demand for a product produced in a competitive market, we would predict that
   (a) firms will gradually leave the industry and capacity will shrink
   (b) firms will modernize capital equipment in order to increase efficiency
   (c) existing firms will increase output levels to recover losses
   (d) the industry will expand as new, more efficient firms enter.

17. Resources are said to be used efficiently when
   (a) changes in resource allocation will cause costs to rise
   (b) using resources in a different manner can only be done at the expense of making at least someone worse off
   (c) commodities are produced in sufficient quantities so that their marginal utility is zero
   (d) the allocation of resources among industries is fixed in the long run

18. Productive efficiency refers to
   (a) producing at the minimum average cost of production
   (b) producing what is demanded
   (c) using resources to ensure that at least some demand for all products is satisfied
   (d) producing the appropriate mix of products

19. Allocative efficiency is shown graphically as being equal to
   (a) the sum of producers' and consumers' surplus
   (b) the difference between producers' and consumers' surplus
   (c) the maximum amount of consumers' surplus
   (d) the maximum amount of producers' surplus

EXERCISES

1. World output of peanuts, it is assumed, is 2,000 tons in a given year. One of the many producers, Mr. Shell, has experienced a doubling of his output over his previous year's output of 4 tons. All other firms report no change in their output. The market elasticity of demand is estimated to be 0.20.

   (a) What is the effect on the world price of peanuts of Mr. Shell's increase in output (in percentage terms)?

   (b) Calculate the elasticity of demand facing Mr. Shell's firm.

2. The diagram below illustrates a firm that produces in a perfectly competitive market. Complete the questions below with a reference to the diagram.

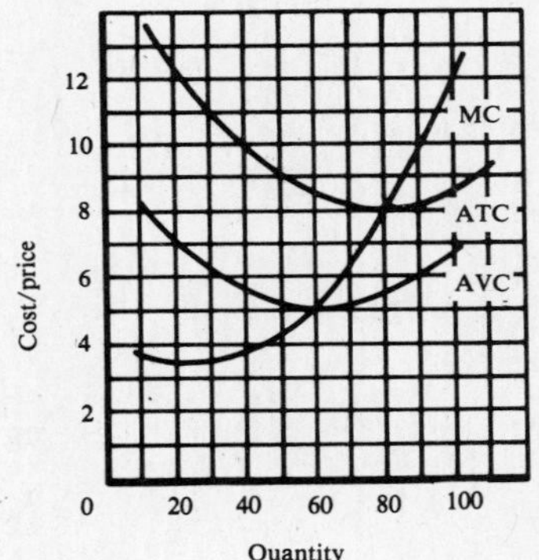

Note: MC = marginal cost
AVC = average variable cost
ATC = average total cost

If the market price is ⟶	$ 12	$ 8	$ 5
(a) equilibrium output will be	____	____	____
At this output			
(b) total revenue is	____	____	____
(c) total cost is	____	____	____
(d) total profit is (+) or (-)	____	____	____
(e) profit per unit of output is	____	____	____

3. The basic cost schedules for a firm producing in a perfectly competitive market are shown below.

Output/Month	Total Fixed Cost	Variable Cost (TVC)	Total Cost (TC)	AVC	ATC	MC
0	20	--				
1	20	15	____	____	____	
2	20	24	____	____	____	____
3	20	30	____	____	____	____
4	20	48	____	____	____	____
5	20	75	____	____	____	____
6	20	120	____	____	____	____

(a) Complete the table.

(b) If the firm is producing an output where ATC is a minimum and the market price is $8.00, should the firm continue production or shutdown? Explain.

(c) If the market price were $16.67, what output should this firm produce, if any at all? Explain.

(d) If the market price rose to $20.00, what would the firm experience? How would the industry respond in the long run?

4. At present output levels, a competitive firm finds itself with the following:

Output:	5,000 units
Market price:	$1.00
Fixed costs:	$2,000
Variable costs:	$2,500
Marginal cost:	$1.25 and rising for increases in output

(a) Is it maximizing profits? Why?

(b) Should it produce more, produce less, or stay the same? Explain.

5. The diagram below illustrates the cost position of firms operating in a perfectly competitive market immediately following the introduction of a cost-saving innovation.

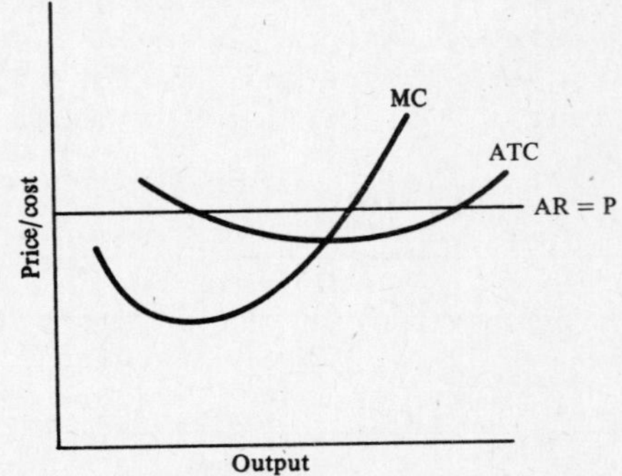

(a) What initial advantage are the firms enjoying?

(b) Can this advantage remain? Justify your answer by noting what will be taking place in the market as a whole in the long run.

6. The supply (S) and demand (D) curves for a competitive market are shown below in the figure on the left. The cost curve for one firm in this industry is shown in the figure on the right.

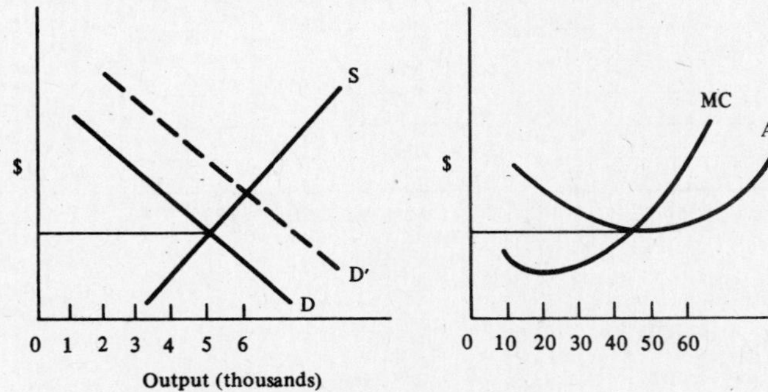

(a) If the market demand schedule were to shift to D', what is the initial impact on the price and output in this industry and on the economic profits of this firm?

(b) What change in the diagrams would be necessary so as to put this firm in a longrun equilibrium position? How would this firm respond?

7. In the table below are basic data on three firms that we are assuming comprise a perfectly competitive market. Complete the table. Then on the graph, plot at the intervals of output the short-run supply curve for each firm and a portion of the industry supply schedule. Note that the industry supply schedule will be a "rough" approximation given the format of the data. Recall that only after its intersection with the minimum point on the AVC is the MC a supply curve. Assume that all costs are variable and they are the minimum. Average variable costs are as follows for the three firms: A, $4 at output q = 30; B, $2.71 at output q = 35; C, $4.15 at output q = 40.

Firm A			Firm B			Firm C		
Output	Total Cost	Marginal Cost	Output	Total Cost	Marginal Cost	Output	Total Cost	Marginal Cost
30	120		25	80		36	150	
		___			___			___
40	160		30	82.5		40	166	
		___			___			___
50	210		35	95		44	186	
		___			___			___
60	280		40	135		48	214	
		___			___			___
70	380		45	195		52	254	
		___			___			___
80	520		55	335		56	310	

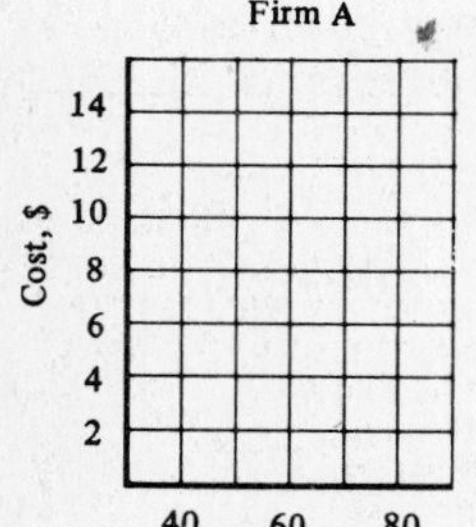

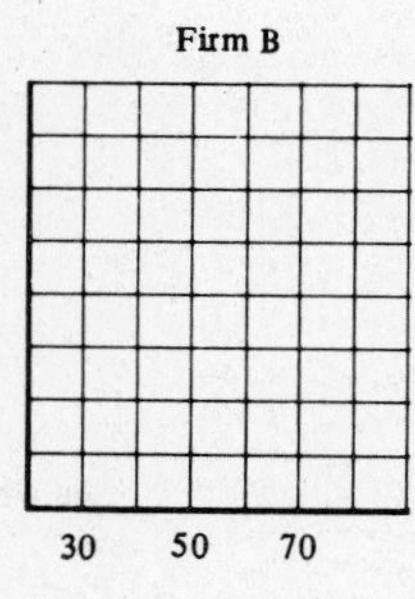

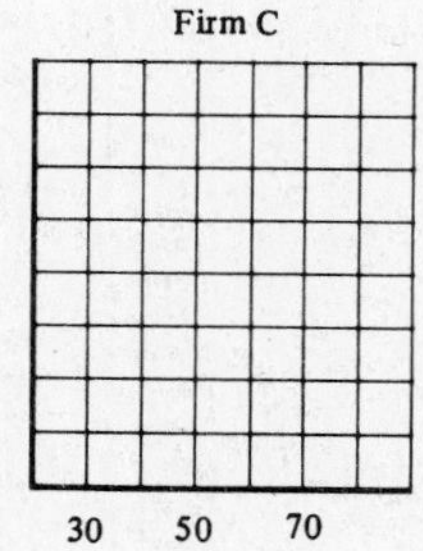

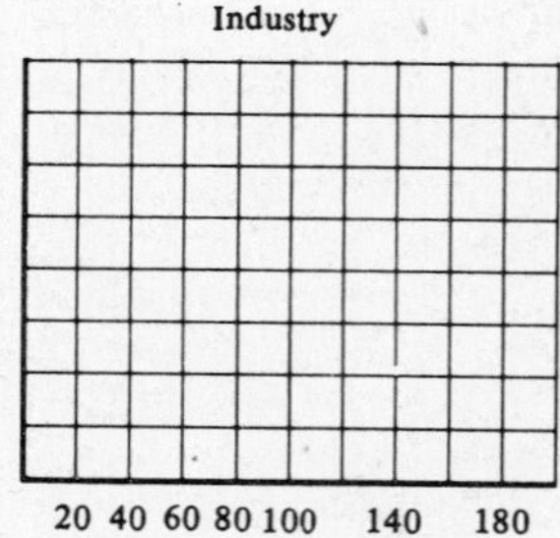

CHAPTER 13

PRICING IN MONOPOLY MARKETS

CHAPTER OBJECTIVES

At the opposite end of the market spectrum from perfect competition is monopoly. The fact that the firm's demand curve and the market demand curve are one and the same is examined in detail along with the optimizing behavior of the monopolist in terms of price and output decisions. Questions and problems dealing with the allocative inefficiency of monopolists (their failure to produce the rate of output where price equals marginal cost) and how monopolists can profit through price discrimination are also included in this chapter.

MULTIPLE-CHOICE QUESTIONS

Questions 1 through 4 refer to the diagram below.

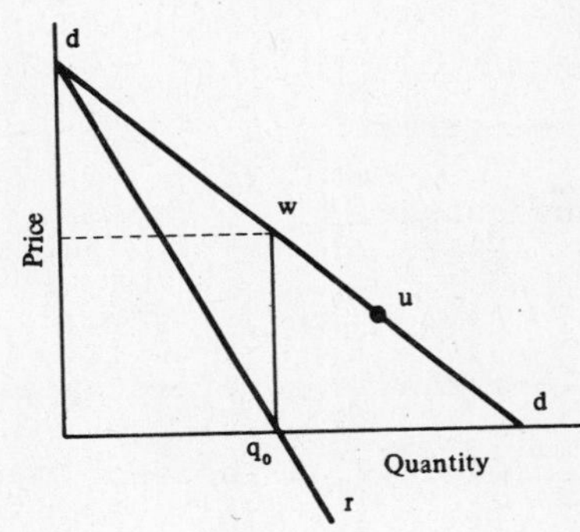

1. The curve labeled dd is
   (a) the monopolist's average fixed cost curve
   (b) the monopolist's average revenue curve
   (c) where marginal cost = marginal revenue
   (d) an elastic demand curve of unity

2. The curve labeled dr is the monopolist's
   (a) monopolist's demand curve
   (b) monopolist's total revenue curve
   (c) monopolist's marginal revenue curve
   (d) long-run supply curve for a decreasing cost industry

3. If a monopolist sets price at u, then it follows that
   (a) it is maximizing profits
   (b) demand is elastic at u
   (c) it should raise price and reduce output in order to increase profits
   (d) the marginal cost curve goes through u

4. Profit maximization for a monopolist will occur when
   (a) output is equal to or less than q_0
   (b) price equals w, regardless of marginal costs
   (c) price equals marginal revenue
   (d) output is to the right of q_0

5. If profits are to be maximized by a firm, whether monopolistic or perfectly competitive,
   (a) output should be increased whenever marginal cost is below average cost
   (b) output should be increased whenever marginal revenue is less than marginal cost
   (c) output should be set where unit costs are at a minimum
   (d) output should be increased whenever marginal revenue exceeds marginal cost

6. A monopolist has a downward-sloping demand curve because
   (a) it has an inelastic demand
   (b) typically, it sells only to a few large buyers
   (c) its demand curve is the same as the industry's demand curve
   (d) consumers prefer that product

7. Barriers to entry, which sustain monopoly, may be due to all but which one of the following?
   (a) patent laws
   (b) economies of scale
   (c) long-run constant costs
   (d) franchises

8. For a monopoly firm, all but which one of the following is correct?
   (a) The demand curve for the firm is downward sloping.
   (b) Price equals marginal revenue at the profit-maximizing output.
   (c) Price exceeds marginal cost at the profit-maximizing output.
   (d) Marginal revenue and average revenue do not coincide.

9. The degree of monopoly power a firm may exercise in the long run is governed by all but which one of the following?
   (a) the extent to which the firm's demand curve shifts leftward as an indirect result of the firm raising its price
   (b) the shape of the marginal cost curve
   (c) the price reactions of producers of substitute products
   (d) the ability of new firms to enter in response to this firm's short-run profits.

10. Concentration ratios have been found
    (a) to have considerable correlation with profit rates
    (b) to have little usefulness where there are more than two firms
    (c) to have little relevance in measuring the degree of monopoly power in an industry
    (d) to be very low in the great majority of manufacturing industries

11. Monopoly power
    (a) can be measured quite precisely by economists
    (b) is a term that applies only to sole suppliers in a given market
    (c) will always vary negatively with the concentration ratio
    (d) exists to the extent that a firm is insulated from loss of customers to other sellers

12. Price discrimination is possible
    (a) in all cases where firms have complete monopoly power
    (b) if firms keep it a secret
    (c) only if firms conspire with competitors
    (d) if buyers of the commodity can be prevented from reselling the commodity to others

Questions 13 through 15 refer to the diagram below.

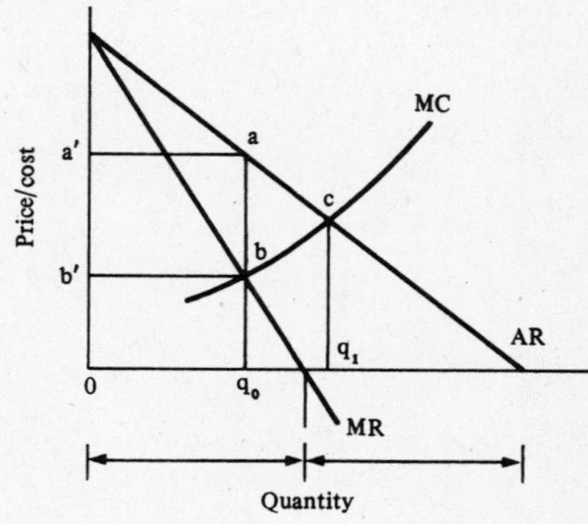

13. Allocative efficiency would be achieved in this market if the profit-maximizing output were
    (a) q_0
    (b) where MR = 0
    (c) q_1
    (d) none of the above

14. The profit-maximizing monopolist will establish price and output at
    (a) a' and q_1
    (b) b' and q_0
    (c) a' and q_0
    (d) c and q_1

15. Profit-maximizing monopoly profits per unit of output are shown by
    (a) ab
    (b) ca'/aq_0
    (c) 0q_0/a'b'
    (d) not possible to determine with the information provided

16. Price discrimination will produce the same output as perfect competition when
    (a) both situations result in price equal to average cost
    (b) the price of the last unit of output sold equals marginal cost
    (c) price or average revenue equals marginal revenue
    (d) there are no monopoly profits

EXERCISES

1. In the diagram below, the basic cost and revenue curves of a hypothetical monopoly firm are given.

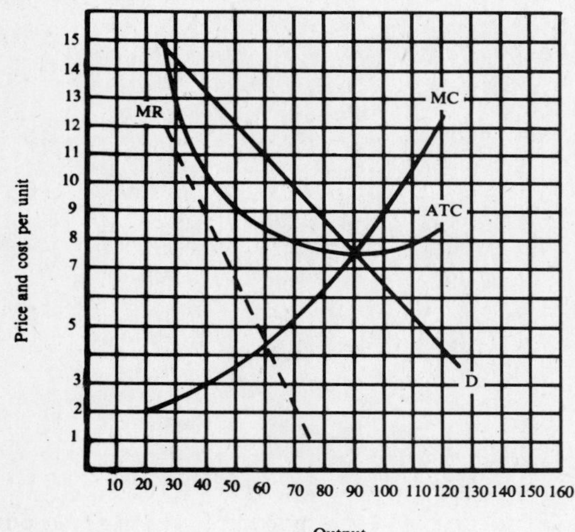

(a) What is the output where the firm's profits will be at a maximum? ______________

(b) What will be the price at this output? ______________

(c) What will be the total revenue (at this output)? ______________

(d) What will be the total costs? ______________

(e) What will be the total profit? ______________

(f) Within what range of output and price will the firm also make at least some profit, though not maximum? ______________

(g) What price would limit the monopolist to competitive long-run profits? ______________

2. The data below relate to a pure monopolist and the product that it produces.

Output	Total Cost	Price	Quantity Demanded	MC	MR	TR	Profit
0	$20	$20	0				
1	24	18	1				
2	27	16	2				
3	32	14	3				
4	39	12	4				
5	48	10	5				
6	59	8	6				

(a) Calculate MC, MR, and TR. Plot them (and TC) below.

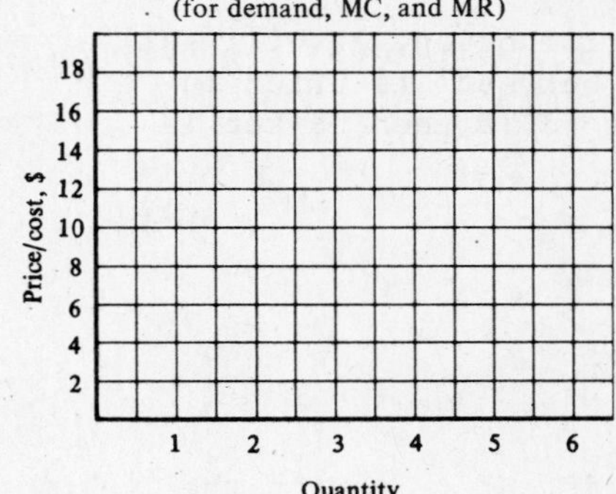

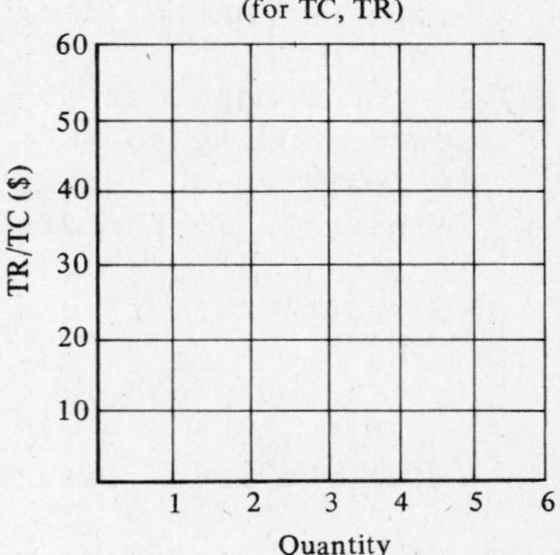

(b) What is the profit-maximizing output (whole units)?
(c) At what price will the monopolist sell the product?
(d) What are the monopolist's profits?

3. The diagram below shows the cost and revenue schedules for a monopolist.

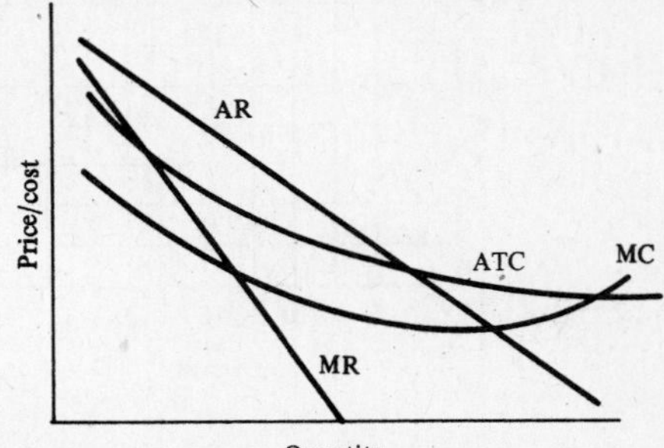

(a) Illustrate on the diagram the price the profit-maximizing monopolist will set and the quantity sold. (Label these P_M and Q_M.)

(b) Indicate by vertical hatching, ▥, monopoly profits.

(c) Suppose the monopolist, to be allocatively efficient, set price (AR) equal to marginal cost. Label the price P_E and the output Q_E. Would this output be sustainable in the long run? Explain with reference to the costs the monopolist faces in the diagram.

4. Two demand curves for the same product are shown below in diagrams A and B. These demand curves represent buyers that can be separated by a monopolist. The basic cost curve for the monopolist producing this product is shown in diagram C.

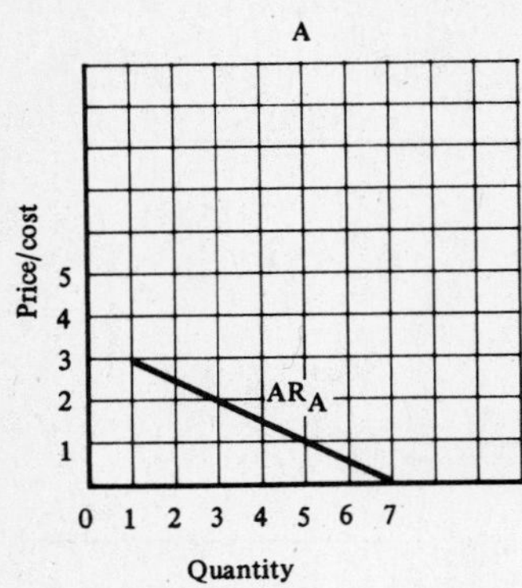

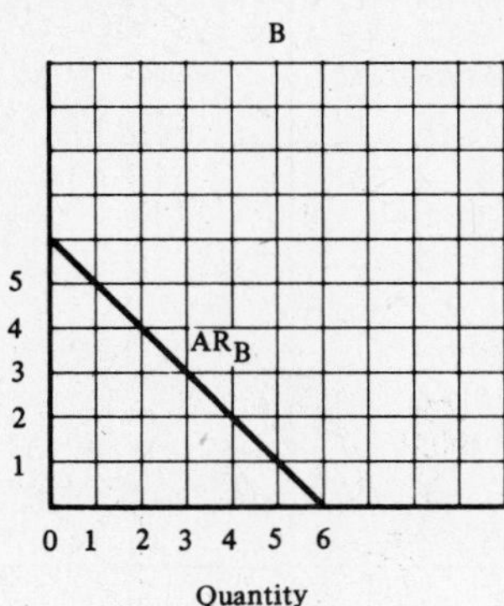

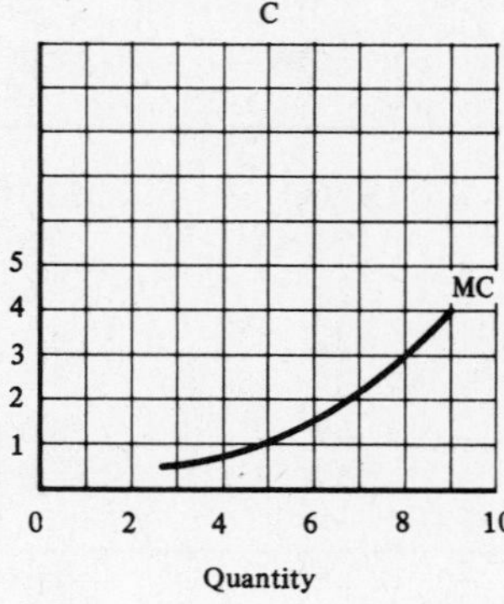

(a) Graph the market demand curve (AR curve) in diagram C.

(b) If the monopolist practices perfect price discrimination, it will sell an output corresponding to MC = MR for the total market, but set its price in each of the two markets such that the MR of the last unit sold in each market is the same. Illustrate in the diagrams above:

(i) total output sold ($Q_A + Q_B$)

(ii) output sold in market A and B (Q_A and Q_B)

(iii) the price charged in each market (P_A and P_B).

5. Some of the basic short-run cost data for a monopolist are given in the following table. Complete the table and answer the questions.

Output	Total Cost (TC)	Average Total Cost (ATC)	Marginal Cost (MC)
0	40		
5	50		
10	65		
15	90		
20	130		
25	190		
30	275		

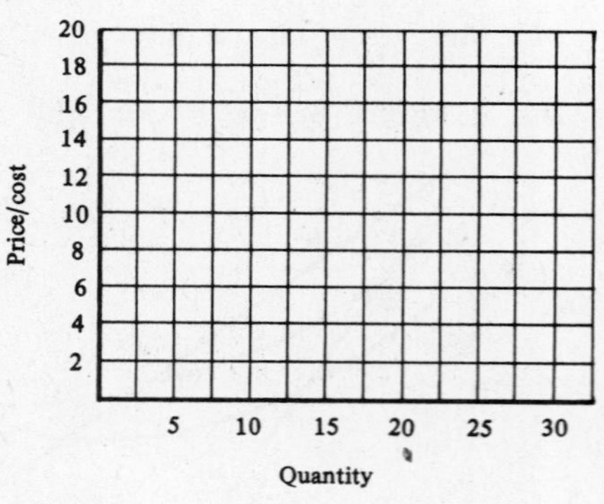

The demand or average revenue schedule is given by Q_d = 20 - 1.0AR, where Q_d is quantity demanded and AR is average revenue or price.

(a) Graph the average cost, marginal cost, average and marginal revenue schedules. (Note: Because the scales for the axes are not the same, the slope of the AR curve will not appear to be that which is given in the equation. Also, consult Chapter 13 for discussion of the relationship between average and marginal revenue.)

(b) What approximately is the profit-maximizing monopolist's profits? Show this by shading the area in the diagram you have completed.

(c) If the government imposed a tax equal to $4.00 per unit of output, would the monopolist change its price and output? Why and in what way?

CHAPTER 14

INDUSTRIAL ORGANIZATION AND THEORIES OF IMPERFECT COMPETITION

CHAPTER OBJECTIVES

The Canadian economy is not dominated by firms operating in perfectly competitive markets nor do they all act as monopolists. To a large extent, firms operate in a framework described by either monopolistic competition, where product differentiation is a distinguishing feature, or oligopoly, competition among the few with the knowledge that they are interdependent. These market structures are generally allocatively inefficient even though economic profits may not persist in the long-run. Many of the multiple-choice questions will test your knowledge of the characteristics of these market structures. Theories that have been advanced to explain modern industrial behavior sometimes utilize such terms as administered prices, minimum efficient scale, and Nash equilibrium. These are also examined in this chapter.

MULTIPLE-CHOICE QUESTIONS

1. The Canadian manufacturing sector is characterized by
   (a) government-controlled single-firm industries
   (b) perfect competition in all but one or two industries
   (c) monopoly in the key industries and perfect competition in the others
   (d) industries having a few large and dominant firms

2. In the sense used in this chapter, administered prices are
   (a) prices set by government agencies
   (b) prices determined by international forces
   (c) prices that incorporate costs of administration in price-setting agencies
   (d) set by individual firms, rather than in reaction to market forces.

3. Product differentiation refers to
   (a) the fact that consumers often do not have many choices in the types of products available
   (b) a situation whereby firms have some control over price because they are not selling a homogeneous product
   (c) an industry that produces more than one commodity group
   (d) the degree by which a firm can change its output from one product to another

4. The excess capacity theorem refers to
   (a) a lack of aggregate demand leading to less than full use of resources
   (b) the zero-profit long-run equilibrium of a monopolistic competitor
   (c) less than full employment in some industries
   (d) a situation where the firm's demand curve is tangent to the minimum point of the long-run average total cost curve

5. An important prediction of monopolistic competition is that the long-run equilibrium output of the firm occurs at an output
   (a) where price exceeds average cost
   (b) less than the one at which average cost is at a minimum
   (c) less than the one at which average cost equals average revenue
   (d) less than the one at which marginal cost equals marginal revenue

6. Short-run economic profits of a monopolistic competitor tend to be eliminated primarily by
   (a) production where average costs are at the minimum level
   (b) nonprice competition
   (c) entry of new firms
   (d) price reductions to meet new competition

Answer 7 and 8 referring to the diagram below:

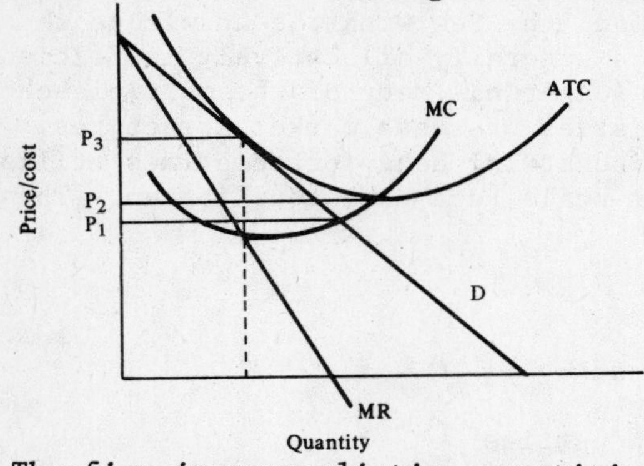

7. The firm in monopolistic competition will set its price equal to
   (a) P_1
   (b) P_2
   (c) P_3
   (d) minimum MC

8. The situation described by price P_3 and output q is
   (a) identical to perfect competition since there are no economic profits
   (b) a long-run equilibrium in monopolistic competition
   (c) unstable; new firms will enter the industry to eliminate economic profits
   (d) Pareto efficient

9. Which one of the following statements concerning monopolistic competition is correct?
   (a) Prices and unit costs will tend to be less than they would be in a perfectly competitive market.
   (b) Monopolistic competitors rarely find it useful to advertise.
   (c) A wider range of products is produced, but less cheaply than with perfect competition.
   (d) Monopolistic competitors usually engage in price competition rather than nonprice competition.

10. An oligopoly is characterized by
    (a) a single dominant firm in the industry
    (b) a formal agreement among firms on how much to produce and at what price
    (c) relatively few firms, each with limited market power due to intense rivalry
    (d) ease of entry by new firms

11. Short-run average variable cost curves which are "saucer-shaped" (flat) rather than "u-shaped," arise
(a) if a fixed factor (capital) is divisible in the short run
(b) only in situations where minimum efficient scale is large
(c) when the cost of variable factors of production decline
(d) only if there are no fixed factors

12. "Sticky prices" in oligopoly can be explained by
(a) flat short-run average cost curves
(b) kinked demand curves
(c) high costs of changing administered prices
(d) all of the above

13. With a Cournot-Nash equilibrium for an oligopoly,
(a) prices will be higher and output less than under perfect competition, other things equal
(b) firms will increase price and output when costs rise
(c) firms comprising the industry are likely to be selling markedly different products
(d) each firm assumes all other firms will change their output constantly in response to other firms' actions

14. A decision-making process referred to as conjectural variations
(a) guarantees a constant price across all firms in an oligopoly
(b) applies only to duopoly
(c) involves consideration of how rivals will respond to price changes
(d) is used only in monopolistic competition

15. In an oligopolistic industry, joint profit maximizing by setting prices through tacit agreement is
(a) more likely the fewer the number of firms
(b) more likely the less similar the products
(c) more likely when prices are falling than when they are rising
(d) invariably illegal under the anti-combines law

16. All but which one of the following characterizes oligopolistic behavior?
(a) Joint profit maximization is likely to be enhanced, the smaller the number of firms.
(b) In the long run, entry will eliminate profits.
(c) The more similar the product, the more likely there will be joint profit maximization.
(d) If barriers to entry are high, there is a greater tendency for joint profit maximization.

17. Minimum efficient scale (MES) refers to
(a) the short-run average cost of an oligopolist
(b) the marginal cost curve
(c) the size of the industry
(d) the smallest-sized firm which can take advantage of all available economies of scale

18. Economic profits can exist in an oligopolistic industry in the long run because of:
(a) natural barriers to entry
(b) barriers created by existing firms
(c) barriers created by government policy
(d) all of the above

19. Cartels tend to be unstable because
(a) losses to producing firms will occur whenever demand for the product is elastic
(b) individual firms have strong incentives to violate output quotas
(c) individual firms in a competitive industry will never find it profitable to restrict output and raise prices
(d) all of the above

EXERCISES

1. The figure below describes a firm in a monopolistically competitive industry.

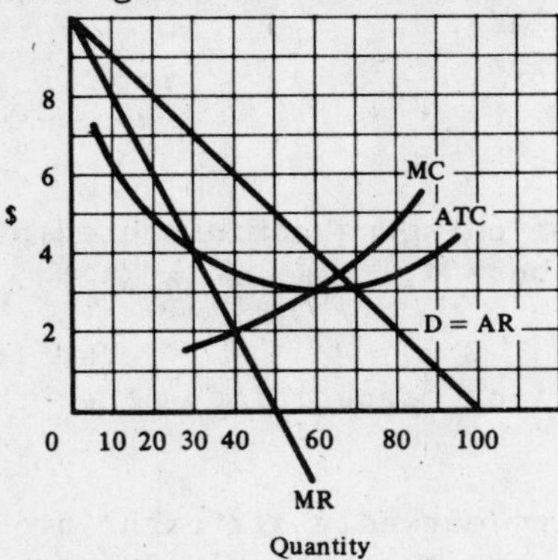

(a) What price will the firm set? ________

(b) What total economic profit will this firm receive? ________

(c) Given that entry is relatively easy, is this a long-run equilibrium situation? Explain.

(d) Which curves will be affected and in which direction, if the firm now increases its advertising expenditures by a given amount, causing increased sales?

(e) If new firms were attracted to this industry, what curves in the figure would be affected the most? Why? What would be the <u>main</u> consequence for this firm?

(f) Explain how the result in (e) illustrates the excess capacity theorem.

2. (Before proceeding with this question, you should refer to Box 14-1 in the text.) The diagram below illustrates two kinked demand curves.

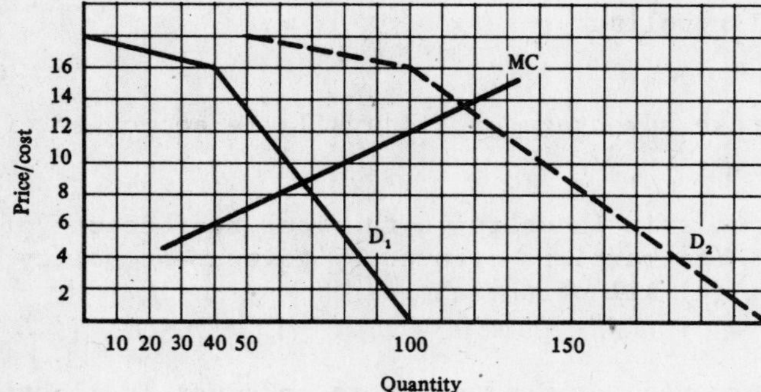

(a) Draw the MR (marginal revenue) curves and label them MR_1 and MR_2.

(b) Given the marginal cost curve above, the price when demand is D_1 will be ________; when it is D_2, the price will be ________.

(c) If the marginal cost became slightly lower, then for D_1, price would ________; for D_2, it would ________.

(d) If the marginal cost became slightly higher, then for D_1, price would ________; for D_2, it would ________.

(e) Demand curves of the type shown above are likely to be associated with what type of market structure? ______________________________

3. The saucer-shaped (flat) average cost curve discussed in the text can be estimated for the relevant range of output (where AVC is approximately equal to MC) by a total cost function in the form TC = a + bq, where a = TFC, q = output, and b = MC = AVC.
   (a) Assume a firm's "normal" demand curve is estimated as P = 50 - .01q, so that TR = $50q - .01q^2$, MR = 50 - .02q, and TC = \$25,000 + 10q. What is the profit-maximizing price and quantity?

   (b) According to the "sticky price" hypothesis of oligopoly theory, what changes in price and quantity are likely as demand varies over this range. Explain.

   (c) Assume demand increases to P = 60 - .01q. Compare the profit consequences of maintaining a constant price versus altering price (and output) in response to the demand curve shift.

4. A firm has the choice of constructing a plant with either of the long-run average cost curves shown in the figure below.
   (a) If there was considerable uncertainty about demand for the product, which plant would the firm choose to build? Why?

   (b) What does the shape of ATC_1 suggest about the nature of the fixed factors in this plant?

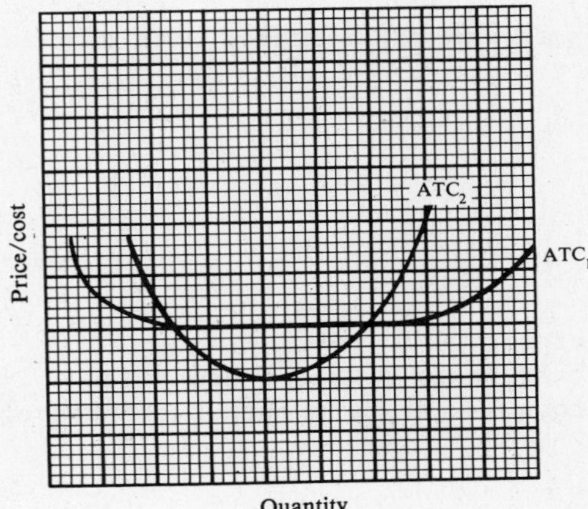

CHAPTER 15

MONOPOLY VERSUS COMPETITION

CHAPTER OBJECTIVES

Several of the questions and exercises in this chapter demonstrate the ways in which a monopoly is less efficient than an industry characterized by competitive behavior. There are cases, however, where a monopoly with some government control may be preferred to perfect competition. The advantages of monopoly power in terms of lower per unit costs of production and innovation are explored in this chapter. The chapter highlights the role government plays in terms of both curbing monopoly power and attempting to set an environment within which an industry of a few large firms can operate.

MULTIPLE-CHOICE QUESTIONS

1. In a monopoly, price and output response to marginal cost changes will be less than in competition because
   (a) the monopolist is guided by the average revenue schedule, which is more elastic than marginal revenue
   (b) monopoly firms tend to be large and adjustment to cost changes is slow
   (c) the monopolist is guided by marginal revenue, which is less elastic than the demand curve to which a competitive firm must respond
   (d) the monopolist will not change price in the elastic portion of the average revenue curve

2. A major difference between equilibrium in a competitive industry and monopoly is that
   (a) at competitive, but not monopolistic, equilibrium, MR = MC, thus achieving productive efficiency
   (b) when minimum efficient scale (MES) is large, competitive behavior will lead to lower average costs
   (c) at competitive, but not monopolistic, equilibrium, P = MC, thus achieving allocative efficiency
   (d) costs will almost always be less with competitive behavior

3. Assuming that cost curves would be the same in an industry under either monopoly or competition, a monopolist will produce at a point where, compared with the competitive equilibrium,
   (a) output is larger but price is higher
   (b) output is less but price is higher
   (c) output is less but price is the same
   (d) output is the same but price is higher

4. A natural monopoly
   (a) can occur only in the resources industry
   (b) evolves over time through conglomerate mergers
   (c) will tend to arise in industries with either scale or scope economies
   (d) leads to higher costs and higher prices than large-group market structures

5. The larger the minimum efficient scale of firms, other things equal,
   (a) the more likely a concentrated market structure will improve productive efficiency
   (b) the greater the tendency toward a natural monopoly
   (c) the greater the advantages of large-scale production
   (d) all of the above

6. The incentive to introduce cost-saving innovations
   (a) is not affected at all by either market structure, barriers to entry, or difficulty of copying the innovation
   (b) is less in monopoly than in competition because the monopolist has no incentive to reduce its costs
   (c) is likely to be greater in monopoly than in competition because the monopolist innovator can maintain economic profits in the long run
   (d) is greater in competition than in monopoly, according to economist Joseph A. Schumpeter

7. A patent law
   (a) guarantees exclusive use of an innovation in perpetuity
   (b) covers only innovations that occur in competitive industries
   (c) is generally regarded as the most important factor in stimulating innovation
   (d) lengthens the time a firm can reap excess profits by granting exclusive use of an innovation for a period of time

8. In comparison with the United States, Canada's competition policy
   (a) has stressed "trustbusting" activities
   (b) has effectively prevented mergers through civil legislation
   (c) has been less aggressively pursued
   (d) does not deal with misleading advertising

9. All but which one of the following is a problem for public utility regulation?
   (a) definition of costs
   (b) determining the allowable rate base
   (c) setting a fair return
   (d) obtaining control over price and level of service provided by a natural monopoly

10. "Protectionist" policies by regulatory commissions
   (a) are aimed at protecting the consumer
   (b) reflect concern of existing firms about potential competitors
   (c) concern the trade-offs between domestic and foreign trade policy
   (d) deal with work safety and environmental issues

11. The most significant feature of the 1975 Stage I amendments to the competition law in Canada was
   (a) increasing the staff of the RTPC
   (b) allowing economic evidence as admissible in court cases
   (c) giving the RTPC power to order the cessation of certain activities
   (d) the transfer to civil courts of certain matters dealing with competition policy

12. The usual argument in favor of accepting a "natural" monopoly, if it is regulated, is that
   (a) regulation guarantees fair, low prices
   (b) more than one company would be obviously wasteful
   (c) it gives the same results as public ownership
   (d) regulation keeps it out of politics

13. From the public's standpoint, a "fair rate of return" on utility investment
(a) should mean approximately the current rate on alternatives of similar risk
(b) should be determined by historical costs
(c) can always be earned, provided prices are set high enough
(d) means what the stockholders think is fair

EXERCISES

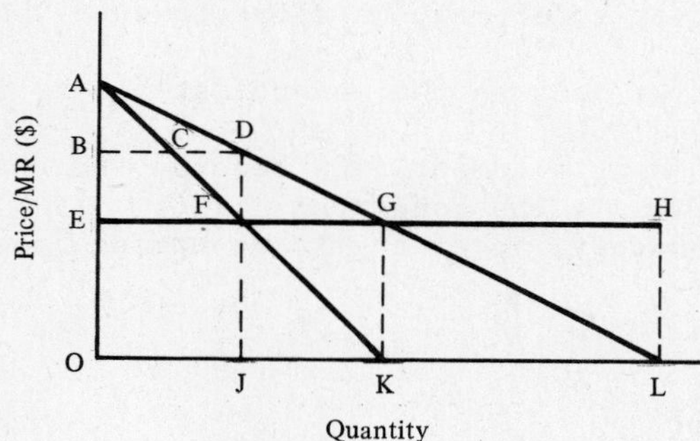

1. The above diagram is for a competitive industry that has been monopolized. AL is the market demand curve, and AK the marginal revenue curve. EH is the long-run supply curve for the industry and also the LRAC = LRMC for the monopolist. (There are no significant economies of scale or scope. It is a constant cost industry, and to change output the monopolist would simply shut down--or open--plants that had each previously been competitive firms.) Predict the following:
(a) the competitive price _____ and output _____
(b) the amount of consumer surplus under competition _____
(c) the amount of economic profits under competition _____
(d) the monopolistic price _____ and output _____
(e) the amount of consumer surplus under monopoly _____
(f) the amount of economic profits under monopoly _____
(g) the deadweight allocative loss under monopoly _____

2. The diagrams below illustrate a perfectly competitive situation and a monopoly situation in a market. If marginal costs were to rise by one dollar per unit of output, illustrate that the price would rise by less and output would fall by less in the case of monopoly.

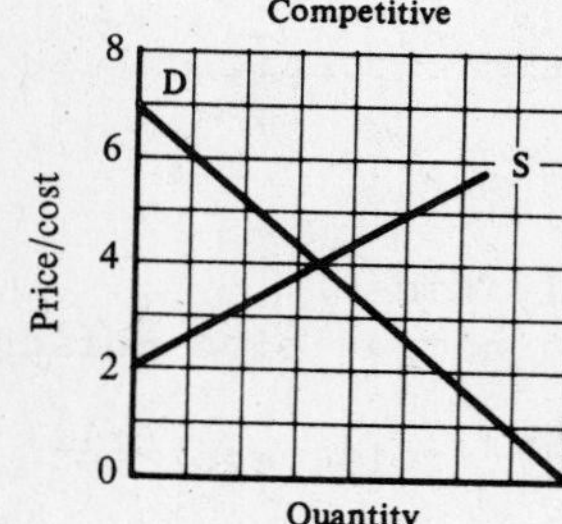

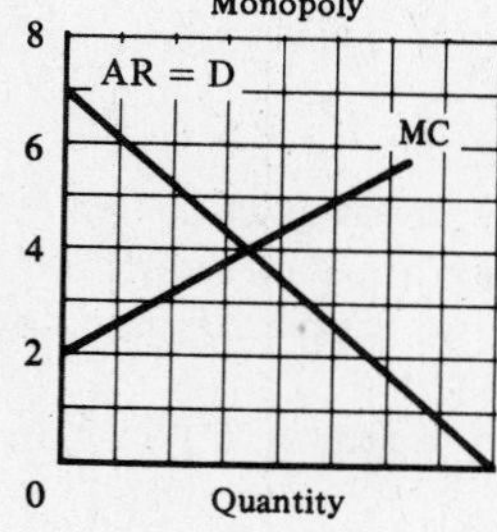

3. The diagram below illustrates a natural monopoly:

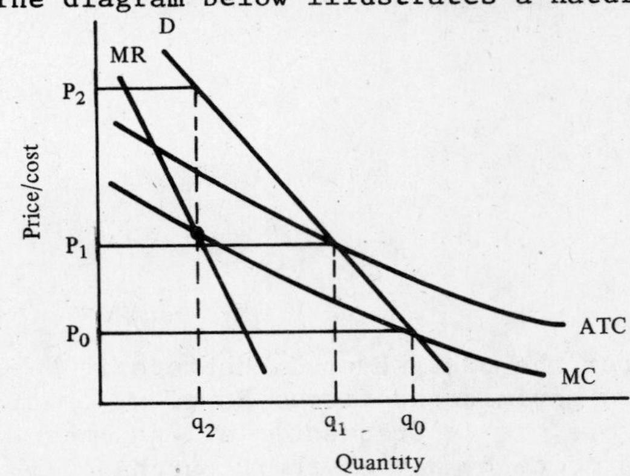

(a) Referring to the diagram above, explain what is meant by the term <u>natural monopoly</u>.

(b) An unregulated monopoly would produce output ____________ and charge price ____________.

(c) Assume a regulatory commission attempted to force this firm to obtain the equivalent of a perfectly competitive outcome. What price and output would this correspond to? Is this a realistic goal in this case? Explain.

(d) Average cost pricing is often the goal of regulatory commissions. In the diagram, what price and output would represent this goal?

(e) Compare the average cost pricing result in (d) with your answer to (c). Consider relative prices, outputs, profits, and efficiency.

4.

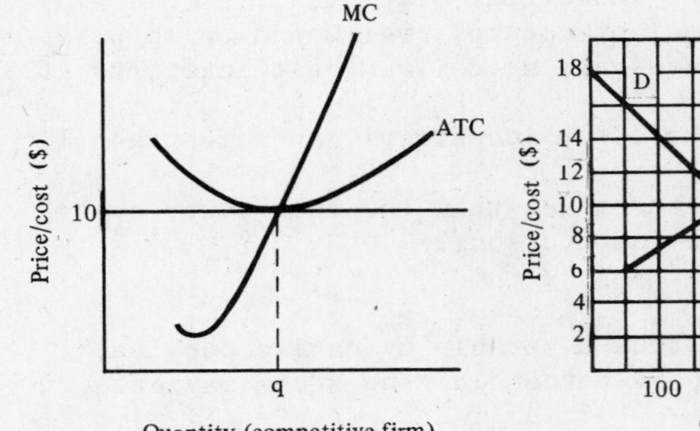

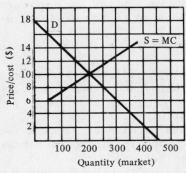

(a) In the market described above, if there are many buyers and sellers, the price will be ____________ and quantity exchanged will be ____________.

(b) If there is a profit-maximizing monopolist in this market, price will be approximately ____________ and output will be approximately ____________.

(c) In the case of the monopolist, by how much will price be in excess of minimum average total cost, assuming that the cost curves are the same in (a) and (b) and that $10 represents a long-run zero-profit competitive equilibrium?

CHAPTER 16

WHO RUNS THE FIRM AND FOR WHAT ENDS?

CHAPTER OBJECTIVES

The theory of the firm we have been examining for the past several chapters is based on the assumption that firms make decisions so as to maximize profits. However, critics suggest that this is not always the case. Furthermore, it is frequently alleged that consumers, instead of dictating what firms should produce by way of their purchases in the market, are manipulated by firms to buy what is produce. This chapter examines your knowledge of consumerism, the notion of the "new industrial state," full-cost pricing, and theories of nonprofit maximizing behavior. The exercises are designed to illustrate both profit and nonprofit maximization theories in the context of basic cost and demand theory.

1. Which of the following appears to be inconsistent with Galbraith's hypothesis of the "new industrial state"?
   (a) large advertising budgets for large corporations
   (b) interlocking directorships among large corporations
   (c) constraint of large firms by government policies
   (d) subversion of public institutions by corporate managers

2. One thing generally agreed upon even by opponents of Galbraith is that advertising
   (a) is essential to ensure the existence of corporations
   (b) shifts demands among similar products
   (c) causes major changes in peoples' values
   (d) must be limited by government to only informing consumers

3. What statement best describes Galbraith's "new industrial state"?
   (a) The federal government now has a great deal of control over Canadian corporations.
   (b) Corporations are very responsive to the desires, needs, and best interests of the buying public.
   (c) Because of the power of unions and shareholders, industrial management has little real control.
   (d) The size and influence of large corporations gives them too much power over government, consumers, markets, and other institutions.

4. The hypothesis of minority control
   (a) refers to programs that have encouraged stock ownership by native peoples.
   (b) recognizes that holders of much less than 51 percent of the stock may effectively select directors and managers.
   (c) holds that a minority of employees, the top managers, run the firm.
   (d) is seldom applicable.

5. The hypothesis of the separation of ownership from control
   (a) implies that the chief executive officer seldom is a stockholder.
   (b) implies that self-perpetuating management controls firms.
   (c) stresses the important role of government regulation in influencing management decisions.
   (d) is seldom applicable.

6. The sales-maximizing hypothesis implies that
   (a) a firm will sell as many units as it can at a fixed price, regardless of resulting profits
   (b) firms have no interest in profits, only in growth of sales
   (c) a firm will sell additional units by reducing price to the point where MR = MC
   (d) firms will seek to maximize their sales revenue, subject to a profit constraint

7. In Canada, the hypothesis of intercorporate control groups
   (a) is completely refuted by the evidence
   (b) exists particularly with respect to the links between chartered banks and corporations
   (c) cannot hold true due to the degree of foreign ownership
   (d) is verified for only the resource sector of the economy

8. The full-cost pricing hypothesis
   (a) predicts market behavior and results better than the profit-maximizing hypothesis
   (b) means that the firm can never maximize profits
   (c) holds that the firm's pricing adjustments respond only to substantial changes in costs
   (d) implies that firms will always be able to cover all their costs

9. Full-cost pricing
   (a) can never be consistent with profit maximizing, even when it is costly to change prices
   (b) is consistent with the slow response, in terms of price, to any change in cost or demand
   (c) if followed by a firm, leads to more frequent price changes than with profit maximizing, other things equal
   (d) implies that firms, when setting prices, just cover average total costs

10. Recent "evolutionary" theories of firm behavior
   (a) stress tradition and routine in firms' decisions
   (b) incorporate profit-maximizing assumptions
   (c) emphasize dynamic and innovative elements
   (d) suggest that firms react quickly to changing economic conditions

11. The central prediction of organization theory is that
   (a) the economy is becoming more centralized
   (b) different decisions will result from different kinds of organization
   (c) corporations should decentralize decision making
   (d) large organizations are more efficient than small ones

EXERCISES

1. The diagram below represents demand and cost conditions for a firm.

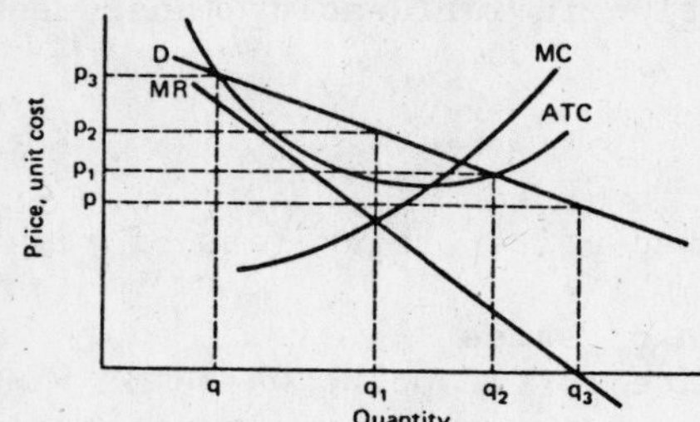

(a) What would be the choice of price and output for a profit maximizer? ______

(b) What would be the range of price and output for a profit satisficer who is content to cover opportunity costs as a minimum? ______

(c) What could be the price and output of a sales maximizer who is willing to accept losses for short periods (assume sufficient economies of scale so that LRAC will be less than p at q_3)? ______

2. The cost/revenue structure and initial price and output of three firms are given below. Indicate the change in price and output in response to tax changes that would need to be made in order that the firm meet the objectives outlined. You need not indicate the precise change in price; rather, indicate how price changes in response to the tax per unit or total tax. The initial position chosen is P_E in each case.

Policy Change	(1) Profit Maximizer	(2) Full-cost Pricing (markup = 0)	(3) Sales Maximizer (min. profit, net of tax = $4000)
(a) Tax equal to $.50 per unit of output			
(b) Excess profits tax equal to 50% of economic profits			

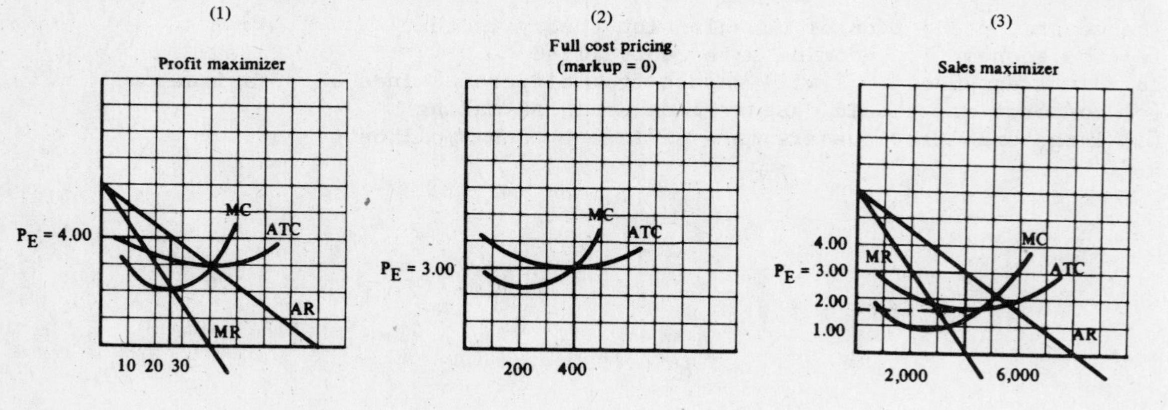

3. Assume that a firm is capable of making a reasonable projection of its profits as it expands output and sales and that this relationship is

$$\pi = 7Q - Q^2 - 6$$

where π is total profits and Q is output.

(a) For values of Q = 0, 1, 2, 3, 3½, 4, 5, and 6 plot the profits function below.

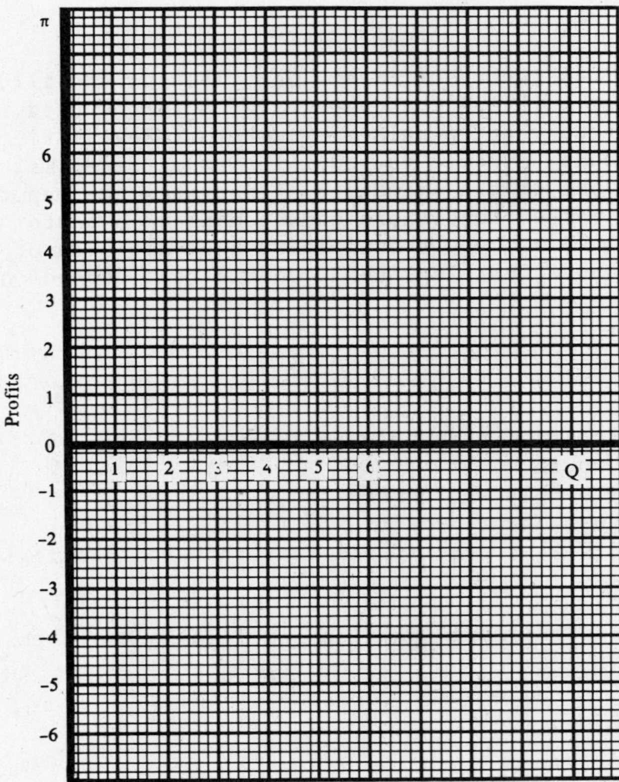

(b) If a "satisficing" firm has a profit target of 4, what level of output will that firm accept?

(c) What level of output is consistent with profit maximization?

(d) If the firm is a sales maximizer and the only constraint was to have profits of at least 1.0, what output will it attempt to achieve? (approximately)

PART FIVE

THE DISTRIBUTION OF INCOME

CHAPTER 17

FACTOR PRICING

CHAPTER OBJECTIVES

This chapter develops the neoclassical theory of income distribution and illustrates how this theory determines the price per unit and the quantity of a factor used in competitive factor markets. Moreover, the chapter raises a number of key distinctions: functional vs. size distribution of income, dynamic vs. equilibrium differentials, and transfer earnings vs. economic rents. One of the exercises illustrates the hypothesis of equal net advantage and how changes in market conditions cause changes in factor earnings and movements in factors of production. Also, you should learn that division of the actual earnings of a factor between transfer earnings and economic rent depends on the elasticity of the supply of the factor.

MULTIPLE-CHOICE QUESTIONS

1. The theory of factor prices in competitive markets says that
   (a) factors are paid what they are worth
   (b) factor prices are determined by supply and demand
   (c) factor prices depend on their cost of production
   (d) equilibrium factor prices would differ even if all factors were identical and all benefits were monetary

2. Data concerning the inequality of income among Canadian families indicate that the Lorenz curve for Canada
   (a) is above the diagonal line
   (b) is below the diagonal line
   (c) is equal to the diagonal line
   (d) has shifted substantially over the past 20 years

3. Economic rent is
   (a) the income of a landlord
   (b) earned only by factors in completely inelastic supply
   (c) the excess of income over transfer earnings
   (d) usually taxable under the income tax law, whereas transfer earnings are not

4. A dynamic differential in factor earnings
   (a) can exist in equilibrium
   (b) will be more quickly eliminated if factor supply is inelastic rather than elastic
   (c) will tend to cause movements of factors
   (d) is greater, the greater is the mobility of the factor

5. The division of income among the three basic factors of production is called the
   (a) functional distribution of income
   (b) Lorenz distribution of income
   (c) size distribution of income
   (d) average productivity of income

6. Economic rents will <u>not</u> exist if the supply curve of a factor is
   (a) perfectly inelastic
   (b) upward sloping
   (c) perfectly elastic
   (d) flatter than the demand curve for labor

7. Assume that Wayne Gretzky is willing to continue playing in the NHL as long as he earns $250,000 a year. If in a particular year his earnings are $1,000,000, his transfer earnings and economic rent are respectively,
   (a) $250,000 and $750,000
   (b) $1,000,000 and zero
   (c) $750,000 and $250,000
   (d) zero and $1,000,000

8. In a free-market economy, teachers would get paid more than truck drivers
   (a) only if teachers were scarcer relative to demand
   (b) only if teachers were smarter
   (c) because they paid more for their education
   (d) because of the nonmonetary advantages of driving trucks

9. Assuming all units of labor are identical, all benefits are monetary, and labor is mobile, a rise in the demand for goods in industry X relative to Y will cause
   (a) an equilibrium differential in wages
   (b) a permanent dynamic differential in wages
   (c) a short-run dynamic differential in wages
   (d) no short-run or long-run effects on wages.

10. The hypothesis of equal net advantage states that
   (a) factor mobility serves to equalize the net advantage earned by factors in different markets
   (b) a change in the relative rate of pay of a factor between two uses will not change the net advantages of the uses
   (c) net advantages of factors are only possible if an equilibrium differential exists
   (d) none of the above

11. Factor payments which are quasi-rents are those which are
   (a) economic rents in the short run and transfer earnings in the long run
   (b) transfer earnings in the short run and economic rents in the long run
   (c) half transfer earnings and half economic rents
   (d) economic rents in the short run and long run

12. A government policy designed to increase the supply of engineers by subsidizing engineers' salaries will in the short run
   (a) cause the supply curve of engineers to shift leftward
   (b) tend to increase the economic rents of those who already have engineering qualifications
   (c) reduce the economic rents of those who have engineering qualifications, regardless of supply curve elasticity
   (d) avoids payments of economic rents if the supply curve of engineers is highly inelastic

EXERCISES

1. Economic Rents and Transfer Earnings

(i) Suppose there is a labor market for a specific type of worker. The demand for labor is given by the expression $L_D = 95 - .25\ W$. (W is the wage rate and L is the quantity of labor.) There are two possible labor supply curves. Case A: $L_S = .5W - 10$. Case B: $L_S = 60$.

(a) Draw the labor demand curve and the two labor supply curves in the diagram below.

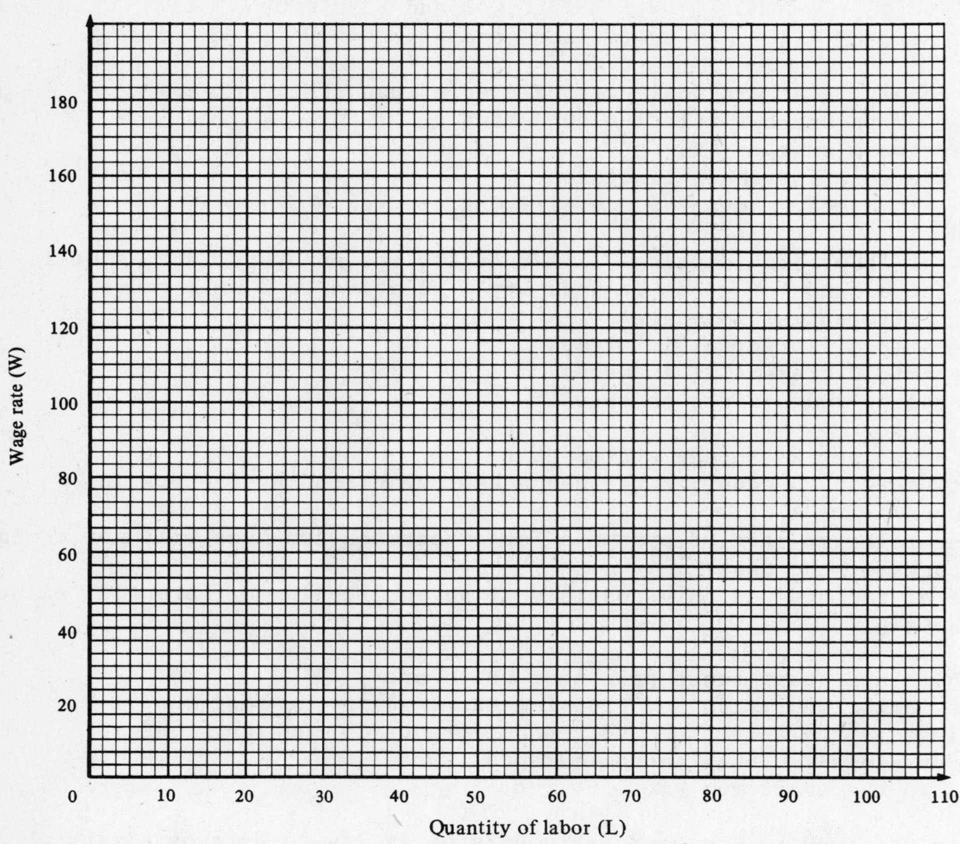

(b) What are the equilibrium values of W and L for both cases?

(c) Illustrate in the diagram the amount of economic rents for Case A. For Case B. What amount of transfer earnings is the sixtieth worker receiving in Case A?

(ii) Suppose the government is considering two options designed to increase the supply of workers in this market. Assume that <u>only</u> the supply curve $L_S = .5W - 10$ applies.

<u>Option 1</u>: Increase the demand for labor from $L_D = 95 - .25W$ to $L_D = 110 - .25W$ <u>and</u> keep the labor supply curve constant.

<u>Option 2</u>: Increase the supply curve from $L_S = .5W - 10$ to $L_S = .5W + 5$ and the demand curve from $L_D = 95 - .25W$ to $L_D = 110 - .25W$.

(d) If Option 1 is adopted, what are the new equilibrium values of W and L? What is the total magnitude of the economic rents earned by those workers who were in this market before the policy change?

(e) If Option 2 is adopted, what are the new equilibrium values of W and L? Have economic rents been created for those workers who were in this market before the policy change?

2. Construct the Lorenz curve for Canada, 1979, in the diagram below using the information in the following schedule.

Family Income Rank	Percentage Share of Aggregate Income
Lowest fifth	5.8
Second fifth	12.9
Middle fifth	18.6
Fourth fifth	24.5
Highest fifth	38.2

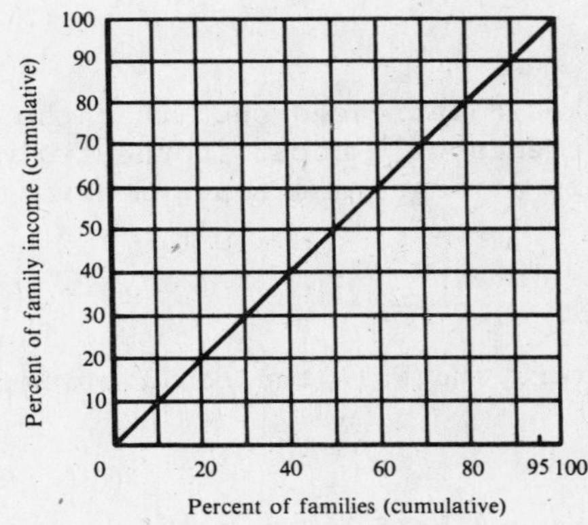

3. There are two competitive labor markets in a particular economy. The labor force, which is always fully employed, is equal to the value OK in the diagram below. A downward-sloping demand curve for labor in market A (D_A) is drawn such that the quantity of employment increases from left to right on the horizontal axis as the wage rate in that market falls. Moreover, a downward-sloping labor demand curve for market B (D_B) is drawn such that a decrease in the wage in that market causes an increase in the quantity demanded which in this case means a movement from right to left along the horizontal axis. Labor is assumed to be fully mobile between the two markets.

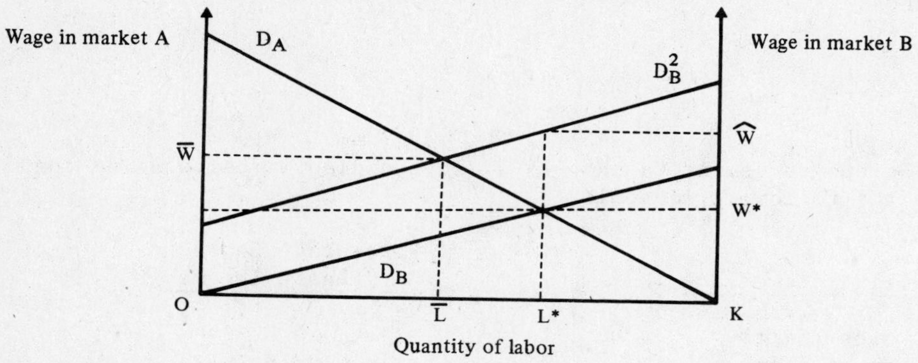

(a) What will be the equilibrium values of wages and employment in each market given demand curves D_A and D_B? Explain.

(b) Suppose that the demand for labor in market B increased such that the labor demand curve shifts from D_B to D_B^2. What adjustments will occur in the two markets and what will happen to the equilibrium levels of wages and employment in the two markets?

4. Given that DD is the demand curve for carpenters and W is the equilibrium monthly salary, draw in supply curves consistent with
(a) all wages paid being transfer earnings
(b) all wages paid being economic rents
(c) half of wages paid being transfer earnings and half being economic rent

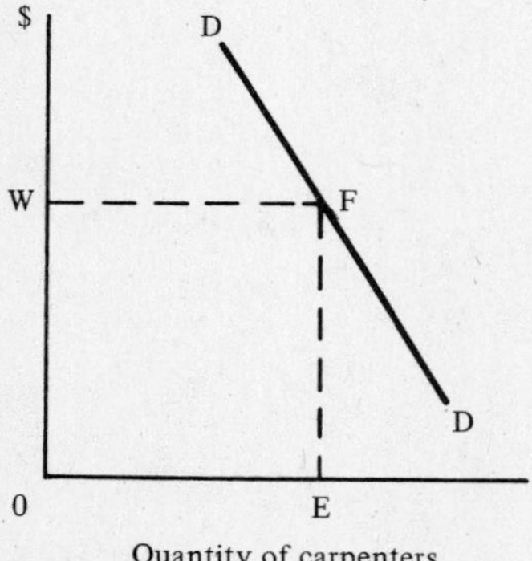

CHAPTER 18

FACTOR DEMAND AND SUPPLY

CHAPTER OBJECTIVES

This chapter extends the analysis of Chapter 17 by discussing in detail the economic factors that determine the demand and supply of a factor of production. The demand for factors is a derived demand--a profit-maximizing firm will hire a variable factor up to the point where its marginal cost (the price per unit in competitive factor markets) equals its marginal revenue product. Several questions are provided to improve your understanding of (1) why demand curves for factors are downward sloping, (2) what economic forces determine the elasticity of factor demand, and (3) the effects of shifts in the demand curve for a factor.

The chapter also distinguishes between the total supply of a factor and a particular use of a factor. The total supply of a factor tends to be variable over time while the supply of a factor to a particular use is discussed in terms of the hypothesis of equal net advantage and factor mobility.

MULTIPLE-CHOICE QUESTIONS

1. Which one of the following statements is not true about the demand for a factor of production?
   (a) It is more elastic the more elastic the demand is for the final product.
   (b) It is more elastic in cases where technology dictates its use in fixed proportions.
   (c) It is less elastic the smaller its contribution to the total cost of the product.
   (d) It is more elastic the more substitutes for its use are available.

2. The marginal revenue product of a factor is
   (a) the cost of employing additional units of a variable factor
   (b) the additional output produced by the last unit of a factor
   (c) the change in revenue as product sales are increased by one unit
   (d) additional revenue resulting from the sale of output produced by the last unit of a factor

3. The quantity demanded of a factor, other things equal, will vary negatively with
   (a) income
   (b) the price of the factor
   (c) the prices of other factors
   (d) changes in demand for the product

4. Profit-maximizing firms that employ additional units of a factor up to the point where MRP equals its price will
   (a) employ additional units of the factor if its price falls, other things equal
   (b) hire fewer units of the factor whose price rises, other things equal
   (c) vary quantity demanded negatively with a factor's price
   (d) all of the above

5. A profit-maximizing firm that is a price taker in factor markets hires a factor up to the point at which
   (a) the factor's price is equal to the amount of output it produces
   (b) the product's price is equal to the marginal revenue product
   (c) the factor's price minus the marginal revenue it produces is maximized
   (d) the price of the factor is equal to its marginal revenue product

6. The supply of effort is considered to be
   (a) the total population in an economy
   (b) the number of employed workers in the economy
   (c) the total number of hours of work that the population is willing to supply
   (d) none of the above

7. A factor of production that shifts easily between uses in response to small changes in incentives is said to be
   (a) highly mobile
   (b) in inelastic supply
   (c) highly mobile but in inelastic supply
   (d) immobile

8. For the marginal productivity theory of distribution to be a satisfactory explanation of factor allocation, it is necessary that
   (a) market conditions of demand and supply play important roles in determining earnings
   (b) factors move in response to changes in factor earnings
   (c) barriers to entry exist in factor markets
   (d) both (a) and (b)

9. Because of the need for physical presence, nonmonetary considerations are much more important for the allocation of
   (a) labor
   (b) capital
   (c) land
   (d) natural resources

10. The marginal productivity theory of distribution predicts that a decline in the demand for product X will cause
   (a) a decline in the derived demand for factors used to produce X
   (b) a fall in income for factors who produce X
   (c) both (a) and (b)
   (d) none of the above

11. Empirical evidence overwhelmingly supports the hypothesis that market conditions determine factor earnings
   (a) in all factor markets
   (b) in markets for nonhuman factors
   (c) in markets for labor, particularly when nonmonetary earnings are important
   (d) only in the short run and only for labor

12. Which one of the following statements regarding factor mobility is correct?
   (a) In spite of its geographical immobility, land can be highly mobile between particular uses
   (b) Labor mobility does not vary with respect to time, other things equal.
   (c) The durability of capital has no influence on its mobility.
   (d) All factors tend to be less mobile among particular uses than in total supply.

13. Which of the following explains why the demand curve for labor by a typical profit-maximizing firm is downward sloping? As the quantity of labor employed rises,
   (a) the market wage rate rises
   (b) the marginal product of labor rises
   (c) the marginal revenue product of labor falls
   (d) both (a) and (b)

14. Which one of the following is likely to shift the demand curve for carpenters rightward?
   (a) a decrease in demand for residential construction
   (b) an increase in benefits for unemployed carpenters
   (c) an increase in demand for residential construction
   (d) a decrease in carpenter productivity

EXERCISES

1. Assume that production and sales increase substantially for the following goods and services:
   (i) medical care services
   (ii) personal computers
   (iii) outdoor recreation activities (fishing, camping)
   (a) In each case, list several factors of production whose derived demand will increase.

   (b) Where will the additional factors of production be drawn from? Predict the effects on short-run and long-run earnings.

2. Shifts in the Demand for Labor: Changes in Marginal Revenue

This exercise asks you to actually show why the demand curve for a factor is downward sloping. The table below is partially completed to assist you. [If you have difficulty, consult the text appendix to Chapter 18].

(a) Complete the table and plot both MRP curves in the diagram below. What do you observe happens to the MRP values as additional units of labor are employed? Why does this occur?

Total number of Workers	Units of Output per Week	MPP	Case A MR	Case A MRP	Case B MR	Case B MRP
0	0	0	0	0	0	0
1	11	11	30	330	27	297
2	23	12	30	360	27	324
3	36	13	30	390	27	351
4	50	14	30	420	27	378
5	63	--	30	--	27	--
6	74	--	30	--	27	--
7	84	--	30	--	27	--
8	93	--	30	--	27	--
9	98	--	30	--	27	--

(b) What happens to the MRP curve as the product's price falls from $30 to $27?

(c) If the wage rate were $270 per week, how many workers would the firm hire to maximize profits? Case A ________________; Case B ____________.
[Remember: equilibrium for a profit-maximizing firm is to hire additional units until MRP = Factor price.]

(d) If the wage rate were to rise, what would happen to the number of workers hired? Explain.

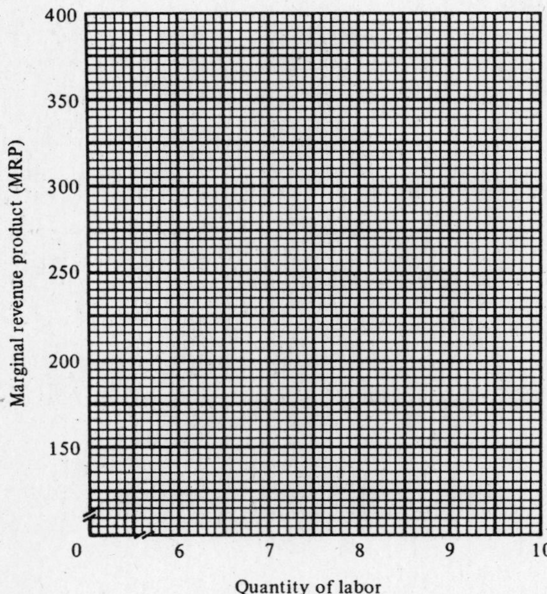

3. Shifts in the Demand Curve for Labor: Changes in the Production Function

Suppose that a firm is a perfect competitor and the price/unit of its product is $30. Technological changes occur such that the firm's production function changes from production function #1 to #2. Production function #1 is identical to that in question 2. Calculate the new MRP values for production function #2, and plot the MRP curve in the diagram for question 2 for quantities of labor greater than and equal to 7. What have you observed happens to the firm's MRP curve when the production function changes? What happens to the firm's employment if the wage rate per week is $300?

Production Function #1			Production Function #2		
Number of Workers	Units of Output/Week	MRP	Number of Workers	Units of Output/Week	MRP
7	84	300	7	91	330
8	93	270	8	101	--
9	98	150	9	107	--

4. Suppose there are three adult persons in a hypothetical economy, each with different preferences for working and leisure. We have portrayed the labor supply curve of each person below. The labor supply curve depicts the number of hours per time period that the individual is willing to offer to the labor market at various wage rates.

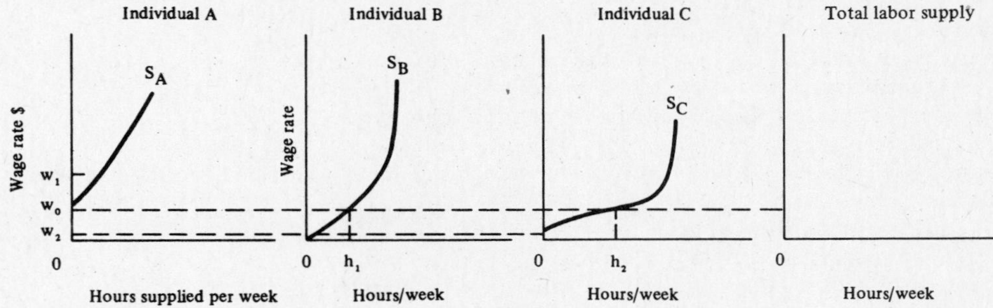

At wage rate w_0, A is not prepared to offer any hours per week, B is prepared to offer Oh_1 hours per week, and C is willing to offer Oh_2 hours per week. Therefore, we can say that the total number of hours offered to the labor market is $Oh_1 + Oh_2$. Furthermore, two of the three members of the population are willing to participate in the labor market. We say that the participation rate is two-thirds.

(a) Plot the total number of hours supplied per week at a wage rate of w_0. At w_1.

(b) Taking the higher wage rate of w_1, determine the effect of the higher wage on hours supplied to the labor market. Has the number of hours increased? Why?

(c) What are your predictions regarding the participation rate at wage rate w_2?

CHAPTER 19

THE LABOR MARKET

CHAPTER OBJECTIVES

This chapter discusses the operation of labor markets and the determination of wages. The analysis demonstrates that a firm exercising monopsony power would raise wages (and marginal labor costs) by hiring additional workers, has marginal labor costs which are higher than the wage, causes unemployment, and creates extra profits compared to the result under competitive conditions.

Several problems are designed to improve your understanding of the consequences of union practices or minimum wage legislation which result in setting a wage in an industry above that which would prevail in a free market.

MULTIPLE-CHOICE QUESTIONS

1. If a union sets wages above the competitive level in a competitive industry, all but which one of the following will occur?
   (a) Employment in the industry will fall.
   (b) Those employed will earn higher wages than before.
   (c) A pool of unemployed workers will be created.
   (d) The number of workers employed will remain the same.

2. Where the supply curve of labor is upward sloping, the marginal cost curve of labor to a monopsonist
   (a) is the supply curve of labor
   (b) lies above the supply curve of labor
   (c) lies below and exactly parallel to the supply curve of labor
   (d) lies above and exactly parallel to the supply curve of labor

3. A monopsonistic labor market without a union will generate
   (a) lower wages and employment compared with a competitive labor market
   (b) higher wages but lower employment compared with a competitive labor market
   (c) lower wages but higher employment compared with a competitive labor market
   (d) identical wage and employment values compared with a competitive labor market

4. In Canada, minimum-wage legislation is principally a responsibility of the
   (a) municipal governments
   (b) federal government
   (c) provincial governments
   (d) Canadian Labor Congress

5. A minimum wage is said to be "binding" in a labor market if
   (a) it has been set by a union
   (b) the minimum wage is below the market wage that would otherwise prevail
   (c) the minimum wage is above the market wage that would otherwise prevail
   (d) none of the above

6. Extensive evidence supports the belief that much of the incidence of unemployment caused by minimum-wage legislation is borne by
   (a) young and inexperienced workers
   (b) workers in the automobile industry
   (c) members of craft unions
   (d) college graduates

7. Which one of the following statements concerning the likely consequences of a comprehensive minimum wage is correct?
   (a) In competitive labor markets, an effective minimum wage has no adverse employment effects.
   (b) In monopsonistic labor markets, a minimum wage set equal to the competitive wage will increase wages but not employment.
   (c) The employment effects of minimum wages in competitive labor markets will be the same as in monopsonistic labor markets.
   (d) In competitive labor markets, an effective minimum wage raises the wages of those who remain employed, but also creates some unemployment.

8. Which of the following is not a requirement of a successful union?
   (a) difficulty of substituting other factors of production for union members
   (b) labor costs that are a relatively small contribution to total costs
   (c) relatively inelastic demand curve for labor
   (d) relatively elastic supply curve for labor

9. A union's ability to restrict the supply of a particular occupation and thereby to increase wages is greater if, other things equal,
   (a) the demand curve for labor is perfectly elastic
   (b) the occupation requires a specific and hard-to-acquire set of skills
   (c) the occupation requires general and easily obtained skills
   (d) the supply curve for labor is inelastic

10. Pension rights for workers may help employers keep total costs down because
   (a) they are a form of incentive pay
   (b) many workers choose not to accept them
   (c) employers have ways of avoiding providing them
   (d) they may reduce labor turnover

11. The recession of the early 1980s combined with the growing competition to North American manufacturing goods from foreign producers led to a recognition among major industrial unions that
   (a) higher wages did not imply high levels of layoffs and unemployment
   (b) automation and mechanization must be resisted at all costs
   (c) firms would allow profits to fall in order to retain their workers
   (d) significant reductions in wages and benefits were needed to prevent further layoffs and plant closings

12. Persistent involuntary unemployment can occur if
   (a) the wage rate is free to vary
   (b) the labor supply curve is vertical
   (c) workers choose not to work at the competitive wage rate
   (d) the real wage is held above its competitive equilibrium level

13. Which one of the following is not a feature of the new theory of labor markets?
   (a) Profits, not wages, fluctuate to absorb the effects of temporary increases and decreases in demand.
   (b) Any market clearing that occurs from short-term fluctuations in demand is through fluctuations in volume of employment.
   (c) Involuntary unemployment can only be explained by union practices and monopsonistic elements in labor markets.
   (d) The pay-by-age tradition combined with the practice of laying off least-senior employees allows for the payment of a steady wage in the face of fluctuating economic conditions.

Questions 14 through 20 refer to the diagram below. The labor market is assumed to be characterized by low-skilled workers.

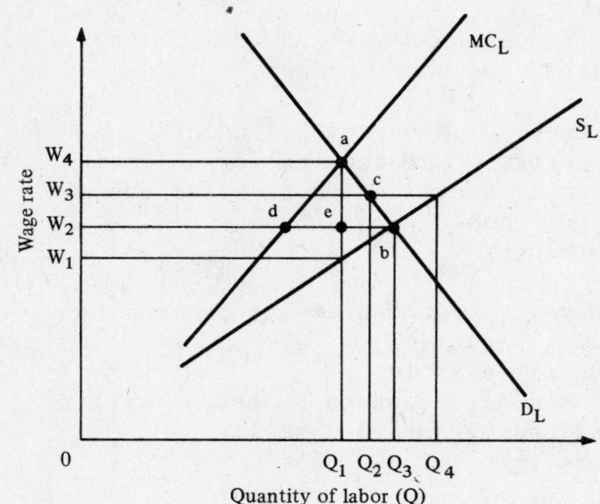

14. If perfect competition existed in this market, the values for the wage rate and the quantity of employment would be
   (a) W_4 and Q_1
   (b) W_1 and Q_1
   (c) W_3 and Q_2
   (d) W_2 and Q_3

15. Under conditions of a monopsonistic labor market, a firm would hire
   (a) Q_1 workers
   (b) Q_2 workers
   (c) Q_3 workers
   (d) Q_4 workers

16. Under conditions of a monopsonistic labor market, a firm would pay wages of
   (a) W_4
   (b) W_1
   (c) W_3
   (d) W_2

17. If a minimum wage of W_2 is imposed in this market, the supply curve of labor becomes
   (a) $MC_L - S_L$ (c) acb
   (b) W_2bS_L (d) W_2daMC_L

18. In this case a minimum wage of W_2 would generate employment of
   (a) Q_2 (c) Q_3
   (b) Q_1 (d) Q_4

19. If a minimum wage of W_3 is imposed in this market, the firm would hire
   (a) Q_2
   (b) more than Q_3 since the marginal cost of labor has fallen
   (c) Q_4 because the demand for labor shifts to the right
   (d) Q_1

20. With a minimum wage of W_3, total unemployment in this market is
   (a) $Q_3 - Q_2$ (c) $Q_4 - Q_3$
   (b) $Q_4 - Q_2$ (d) $Q_4 - Q_1$

EXERCISES

1. Columns 1 and 2 represent the supply-of-labor relationship for a monopsonistic employer. Fill in the values for total cost in Column 3 and then calculate the marginal cost values in Column 4. This exercise should demonstrate to you that the marginal cost of labor lies above the supply curve of labor in a nonparallel fashion.

(1) Quantity of Labor	(2) Wage Rate	(3) Total Cost	(4) Marginal Cost
8	$10.00	$80.00	
9	10.50		
10	11.00		
11	11.50		
12	12.00		
13	12.50		
14	13.00		

2. Referring to the diagram below, which represents the labor market in an industry, answer the following questions.

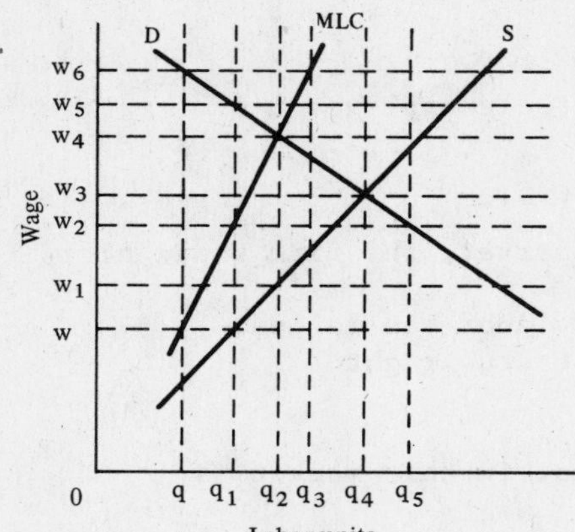

(a) If a competitive market prevailed, the equilibrium wage would be _______________, and the amount of employment would be __________________.

(b) If a wage-setting union enters this (competitive) market and tries to establish a higher wage at, for example, w_4, the amount of employment would be _____________, and the amount of surplus labor unemployed would be ____________________. How would the labor supply curve look?

(c) Assume that this market consists of a single large firm hiring labor in a local market. If the firm hired q_1 workers, it would have to pay all workers the wage ________________________, but the marginal labor cost of the last person hired would be ________________. Because the marginal revenue product of the last person (q_1) hired is equal to the amount _______________, there is an incentive for the firm to continue hiring up to the amount _______________, at which the wage will be __________________, the marginal labor cost will be _____________, and the marginal revenue product will be ___________________. Compare this with the result in (a).

(d) Suppose a union now organizes in the monopsonist market and sets a wage at w_3. The amount of employment will be __________________.

(e) Draw a new labor supply curve showing what happens when a union organizes this labor market but, instead of setting a high wage, excludes workers by stiff apprenticeship rules. Predict the effects.

3. There are two competitive labor markets in the economy of Saskatchewan. Market X has a labor demand function given by W = 360 - 3Q and a labor supply function W = 40 + 2Q. The wage rate is denoted as W and the quantity of labor is Q. Market Z has the same labor demand function as in X but a labor supply function W = 20 + 2Q.

(a) Calculate the competitive equilibrium levels of W and Q in each labor market.

(b) Suppose that a minimum wage of 162 had been imposed in market Z. At the minimum wage, what is the quantity of labor demanded? The quantity of labor supplied? How many workers are displaced in this market?

(c) If all of the unemployed persons in (b) entered labor market X, the supply curve of labor in X becomes W = 30 + 2Q. How many will obtain employment in market X? What will happen to the wage in market X?

CHAPTER 20

THE PROBLEM OF POVERTY

CHAPTER OBJECTIVES

This chapter discusses the nature and incidence of poverty in Canada. Using a Statistics Canada definition of poverty, the chapter describes the incidence of poverty according to certain characteristics of families whose income is below a poverty line. Canada's social insurance provisions are described, and the costs and benefits of antipoverty programs are discussed.

MULTIPLE-CHOICE QUESTIONS

1. According to a Statistics Canada definition, the poverty level (the low-income cutoff) is that annual level of income at which the family unit
   (a) has less than 20 percent of the Canadian median family income
   (b) spends 100 percent of its income
   (c) is in the last decile of the income distribution
   (d) spends more than 58.5 percent of its income on food, shelter, and clothing

2. The incidence of poverty tends to be highest for those persons (families) who
   (a) live in urban areas
   (b) have few children
   (c) are not in the labor force
   (d) have a male head of the family

3. The highest incidence of poverty occurs in which one of the following regions?
   (a) the Atlantic provinces
   (b) Quebec
   (c) the Prairie Provinces
   (d) British Columbia

4. An economic downturn is likely to
   (a) increase the number of occasionally poor families
   (b) decrease the number of occasionally poor families since members of the family opt out of the labor force
   (c) decrease unemployment insurance benefits to unemployed workers
   (d) have no effect on poverty since unions protect their members' incomes

5. Opponents of an all-out war on poverty argue all but which one of the following?
   (a) Welfare payments often reduce the incentive to work.
   (b) Given competing public expenditures, the opportunity costs of welfare payments are high.
   (c) All of those defined as poor are unwilling to work because of current welfare provisions.
   (d) Tax rates will rise as more people go on welfare.

6. Which of the following is <u>not</u> a component of existing social insurance provisions in Canada?
   (a) guarantees to ensure recipients at least a poverty level income
   (b) Canada Pension Plan
   (c) unemployment insurance benefits
   (d) Guaranteed Income Supplements

7. Welfare payments and provisions in Canada are
   (a) designed to ensure that each recipient receives income which is at least at the poverty line
   (b) completely uniform across all provinces
   (c) administered solely by the Department of Health and Welfare in Ottawa
   (d) different according to the family's province of residence

8. Between 1969 and 1981, the proportion of Canadians below the poverty level
   (a) nearly doubled, to 25%
   (b) remained fairly constant at 15%
   (c) decreased by nearly one-half, to 15%
   (d) remained fairly constant at 25%

EXERCISE

1. The Incidence of Poverty According to Occupations in Canada

   Table 20-1 in the text illustrates some of the major characteristics of families whose 1982 income was below some cutoff point called the poverty level. We now consider an additional characteristic: the main occupation of the head of the family. In the table below we have shown the incidence of low income according to the main occupation of the head of the family in 1967. For this year, the proportion of Canadian families who were below the poverty level was 18 percent. The figures in the table give rough indications of the chances, or "probabilities," of poverty according to various occupations. For example, we can say that there is about a 3 percent probability of being poor if you have a professional or technical occupation.

INCIDENCE OF LOW INCOME, CANADA, 1967*

Occupation of Head	Percentage
Managerial	6.7
Professional and technical	3.3
Clerical	5.6
Sales	7.2
Service and recreation	16.7
Transportation and communication	14.9
Farmers and farm workers	52.8
Loggers and fishermen	42.3
Miners	8.9
Craftsmen	9.6
Laborers	21.4

*Source: Statistics on Low Income in Canada, 1967, Statistics Canada, 1971.

(a) Academic and vocational education along with apprenticeship programs are examples of investments in human capital that improve individual skills and crafts. In turn, higher income is obtained for the improvement in skills. By inspecting the table above, select those occupations most likely to involve the greatest investments in human capital. Are the probabilities of poverty relatively high or low for these occupations?

(b) Individuals who find themselves continually unemployed and/or hired only for seasonal work will find their income is likely to be low. In your opinion, which of the above occupations tend to have the highest levels of unemployment and/or seasonality? Give reasons for your choices. What relationship exists between your choices and the incidence of poverty?

PART SIX

INTERNATIONAL TRADE

CHAPTER 21

THE GAINS FROM TRADE

CHAPTER OBJECTIVES

The foundations of trade theory are the concepts of absolute and comparative advantage. The existence of either or both allows a country to consume at a level beyond its production possibility frontier by specialization. Several questions and exercises require you to determine if absolute or comparative advantage exist between two countries for two commodities and calculate the gains from trade that can be realized through specialization. Gains from trade can also be identified using the concept of opportunity cost which is also examined in this chapter. Calculating the terms of trade for Canada in the 1970s and commenting on whether or not they were favorable in particular years is also covered in the exercises.

MULTIPLE-CHOICE QUESTIONS

1. Gains from specialization and international trade can result whenever
   (a) countries produce and consume different commodities
   (b) a country has an absolute advantage in producing a product
   (c) countries are producing the same commodities, but opportunity costs differ
   (d) opportunity costs are the same in all countries

2. Absolute advantage
   (a) occurs when one country can produce a greater quantity of all goods than another country
   (b) refers to the cost of factors of production
   (c) is a synonym for gains from trade
   (d) occurs if one country, using a given bundle of resources, can produce more of any good than another country using the same bundle of resources

3. Country A has a comparative advantage over country B
   (a) if, for two goods, A produces more of both commodities than does B
   (b) when the opportunity cost of production in country A is lower
   (c) if A's output of one commodity exceeds that of B for the same commodity
   (d) all of the above

Questions 4 through 7 refer to the following table.

	One Unit of Resources Can Produce	
	Lumber (bd. m)	Aluminum (kg)
Australia	4	9
Canada	9	3
Brazil	3	2

4. In the situation described above, considering just Australia and Canada,
   (a) Australia has an absolute advantage in lumber
   (b) Australia has an absolute advantage in aluminum
   (c) there are no gains from trade to be realized through specialization and trade
   (d) Canada should specialize in aluminum production

5. Considering just Canada and Brazil,
   (a) Brazil has an absolute advantage in lumber
   (b) Brazil has a comparative advantage in aluminum
   (c) Canada has an absolute advantage in only one commodity
   (d) there are no gains from trade due to specialization

6. In Australia, the opportunity cost of 1 board meter of lumber is
   (a) 2.25 kg of aluminum
   (b) 0.44 kg of aluminum
   (c) 0.36 kg of aluminum
   (d) 3.60 kg of aluminum

7. In Canada, the opportunity cost of 1 kg of aluminum is
   (a) 0.33 bd.m of lumber
   (b) 2.70 bd.m of lumber
   (c) 3.0 bd.m of lumber
   (d) 3.33 bd.m of lumber

8. Which one of the following statements is <u>not</u> true about opportunity cost?
   (a) Equal opportunity costs for pairs of commodities between two countries leads to gains from trade.
   (b) Opportunity costs depend on relative production costs.
   (c) Differences in opportunity costs between two countries for similar commodities can enhance total output of both commodities with specialization and trade.
   (d) Comparative advantage can be expressed by differences in opportunity costs.

9. Suppose an equal quantity of resources could produce in Japan two radios and four cameras and in the United States one radio and two cameras.
   (a) The United States should export cameras to Japan and import radios.
   (b) The United States should export radios and import cameras.
   (c) Japan will be able to undersell the United States in both commodities, whatever the exchange rate.
   (d) There is no basis for mutually advantageous trade between the United States and Japan in cameras and radios.

10. Nations through trade
   (a) may consume at levels beyond their production possibility frontiers
   (b) will be limited in their consumption to points on the production possibility frontiers
   (c) will not alter their previous production patterns
   (d) are more likely to be confined to choices inside their production possibility frontiers

11. The terms of trade refer to
    (a) specific trade agreements between two countries
    (b) the ratio of opportunity costs within a country
    (c) the quantity of domestic goods that must be exported to get a unit of imported goods
    (d) the inverse of the opportunity costs between two products in a given country

12. A country would welcome a favorable change in its terms of trade because
    (a) it can now import less per unit of goods exported than previously
    (b) it must now export more to pay for any given amount of imports
    (c) a given amount of exports will now buy more imports than before
    (d) import prices relative to export prices are now greater than before

EXERCISES

1. For each of the situations below, determine which commodity each country should specialize in and export:

(a) One unit of resources can produce:

	Wheat (100 bushels)	Beef (hundredweight)
Canada	2	4
Argentina	3	1

The opportunity costs are:

	Wheat/100 bushels	Beef/hundredweight
Canada	________	________
Argentina	________	________

Canada should specialize in the production of ____________.
Argentina should specialize in the production of ____________.

(b) One unit of resources can produce:

	Wheat (100 bushels)	Beef (hundredweight)
Canada	2	4
Argentina	1	3

The opportunity costs are:

	Wheat/100 bushels	Beef/hundredweight
Canada	________	________
Argentina	________	________

Canada should specialize in the production of ____________.
Argentina should specialize in the production of ____________.

(c) One unit of resources can produce:

	Wheat (100 bushels)	Beef (hundredweight)
Canada	2	4
Argentina	1	2

The opportunity costs are:

	Wheat/100 bushels	Beef/hundredweight
Canada	________	________
Argentina	________	________

Canada should specialize in the production of ____________.
Argentina should specialize in the production of ____________.

2. Below are the production patterns with respect to wheat and wool for Canada and Australia.

	One Unit of Resources Will Produce	
	Wheat (bu)	Wool (kg)
Canada	10	2
Australia	12	6

(a) What is the opportunity cost of wheat, in terms of wool, for both countries?

(b) Do these data suggest the existence of absolute advantage, comparative advantage, or both?

(c) Is a gain from trade possible? Why?

(d) Assuming opportunity costs remained constant, if Canada moved 1/2 unit of resources from wool to wheat and Australia moved 1/4 unit of resources from wheat to wool, complete the table below. What has happened to world output of both products?

PATTERN OF CHANGES IN WHEAT AND WOOL PRODUCTION

	After Resource Transfer	
	Wheat	Wool
Canada	______	______
Australia	______	______
World	______	______

(e) Will trade take place if the world price for wheat is \$3 and that for wool is \$8? Explain.

3. (a) The table below provides data on the index of merchandise import prices and the index of merchandise export prices for Canada. Using the definition of the terms of trade that involves indexes, complete the fourth column and plot the terms of trade.

Year	Index of Export Prices	Index of Import Prices	Terms of Trade
1970	100.6	98.6	______
1971	100.0	100.0	______
1972	103.3	102.3	______
1973	118.1	110.0	______
1974	157.1	135.6	______
1975	173.2	156.6	______
1976	176.6	157.9	______
1977	189.4	177.0	______
1978	205.4	200.7	______
1979	248.4	229.0	______

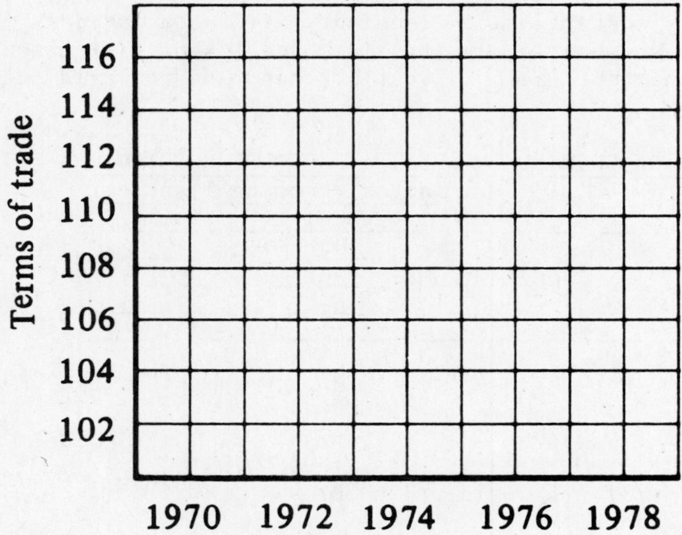

(b) For the periods listed, indicate if the change in the terms of trade was favorable (F) or unfavorable (U).

1970–1975	______
1972–1973	______
1975–1979	______
1971–1979	______
1974–1978	______

(c) If in 1971 the export of 50 units of pulp and paper was required to import 10 units of automobiles, how many units of pulp and paper were needed in 1972 to buy the same quantity of imported automobiles? (Assume the terms of trade in (a) can be applied here.)

4. Suppose that in a particular country the rate at which wool and lumber could be exchanged in international markets was 2:1. Initially, production and consumption are at R, with W_0 and L_0 being the amounts of wool and lumber produced and consumed.

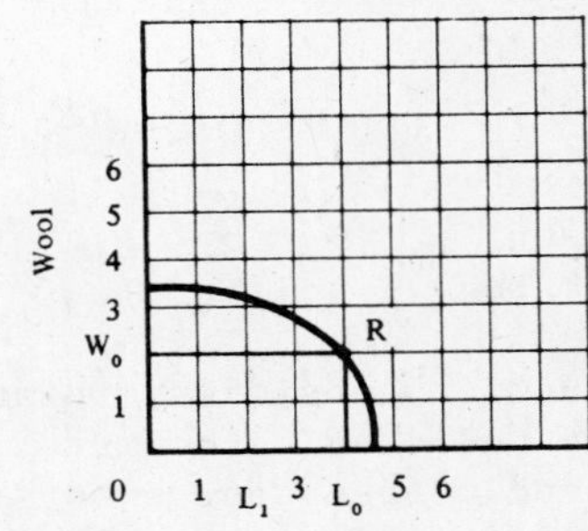

(a) If, in a "no trade" situation, only L_1 of lumber was desired, what change in the production of wool would be required? Indicate the new point on the graph.

(b) Exploiting the opportunity of trade, what consumption point could this country reach while maintaining production at R and consuming L_1 of lumber? Indicate the exports and imports on the graph.

CHAPTER 22

BARRIERS TO FREE TRADE

CHAPTER OBJECTIVES

Free trade versus protectionism, tariffs, quotas, production subsidies, infant industry arguments; these are all part of the modern debate surrounding commercial policy. The Foreign Investment Review Agency, extraterritoriality and nonresident ownership are all related to the debate in Canada on the optimal degree of foreign ownership. Questions in this chapter test your understanding of these and other matters related to the debate. The exercises are designed to help you understand how protectionist policies alter prices and the level of imports and domestic output for commodities which compete in the world market.

MULTIPLE-CHOICE QUESTIONS

1. Commercial policy in international trade refers to
   (a) the government's policy with respect to exports and imports
   (b) how international banks cooperate
   (c) the relationship between domestic and international currencies
   (d) central bank control over domestic financial policy

2. Which one of the following would not be a protectionist policy?
   (a) a tariff on imported lumber products
   (b) an import quota on Italian shoes
   (c) foreign exchange restrictions on importers
   (d) a sales tax on hotel rooms rented by foreigners

3. The difference between an ad valorem tariff and a specific tariff is that
   (a) the first applies only to agricultural products
   (b) the former is always greater than the latter as a percentage of the commodity's price
   (c) the latter is a percentage of the price of the imported commodity
   (d) the former is a percentage of the price of the imported commodity while the latter is a fixed sum per unit of the commodity

4. An important economic difference between import quotas and tariffs is that, other things equal,
   (a) tariffs result in a higher price whereas quotas have no effect on price
   (b) tariffs will not cause higher prices whereas quotas will
   (c) quotas result in extra market value to the goods' suppliers whereas revenue from tariffs is appropriated by governments
   (d) quotas restrict imports whereas tariffs do not

5. Which of the following is a valid statement concerning free trade?
   (a) Free trade always benefits all countries.
   (b) A greater degree of specialization will occur with free trade than without it.
   (c) The introduction of free trade in Canada would be easily accomplished at no cost.
   (d) With free trade, one trading partner gains while the other loses.

6. Which of the following is <u>not</u> a valid reason for protectionism?
   (a) Protectionism in the short run is useful to stimulate new industry.
   (b) A protectionist policy encourages domestic spending and keeps the money at home.
   (c) Protectionist policies may be needed to diversify an economy away from one or relatively few specialized industries.
   (d) Cultural traditions may require protectionist policies.

7. Protection against low-wage foreign labor is a fallacious protectionist argument because
   (a) free trade always benefits all countries
   (b) the gains from trade depend on comparative, but not absolute, advantage
   (c) if the foreign country attempts to sell too much, its wages will rise
   (d) terms of trade will eventually be equal for low- and high-wage countries

8. Canadian exports tend to be comprised primarily of
   (a) relatively labor-intensive products
   (b) natural-resource-intensive products
   (c) services provided by foreign visitors
   (d) relatively capital-intensive products

9. The staples thesis is based on the idea that
   (a) Canada is basically self-sufficient
   (b) Canadian production should be concentrated in the areas of wheat and lumber
   (c) Canada has an absolute advantage when it comes to exporting raw materials and natural resources
   (d) economic growth in Canada has traditionally been related to the comparative advantage the country has enjoyed in several primary products

10. A common market refers to
   (a) a group of countries where there is centralized planning related to exports and imports
   (b) an arrangement among some countries to have free trade among themselves and a common commercial policy toward the rest of the world
   (c) completely free trade with respect to a given commodity
   (d) all of the above

11. Which of the following is <u>not</u> a nontariff barrier to trade?
   (a) subsidies to domestic producers who export
   (b) quotas on imports
   (c) a 10 percent tax on imported wine
   (d) rules requiring minimum levels of "domestic content" in commodities purchased by government.

12. Nonresident ownership in Canada
   (a) is concentrated in the service sector, such as restaurants
   (b) is highest in the petroleum, mining, and manufacturing sectors.
   (c) is not more than 25 percent in any sector
   (d) has been of little concern to policymakers

13. Problems associated with extraterritoriality
   (a) are not in evidence in Canada
   (b) involve Canadian ownership in the United States
   (c) are associated with countries where trade is minimal
   (d) involve the application of one country's laws and government regulations to activities carried on within another country

14. The Foreign Investment Review Act
    (a) sets limits on the degree of foreign ownership in Canada
    (b) has been in effect since the 1930s
    (c) established a screening device to evaluate potential foreign ownership
    (d) limits foreign investment to only a few sectors of the economy

EXERCISES

1. (a) The three diagrams below illustrate the demand for and supply of an imported commodity Z, given free trade. Revise these diagrams according to the protectionist policy outlined below each diagram and indicate what the new price (P*) and quantity exchanged (Q*) will be.

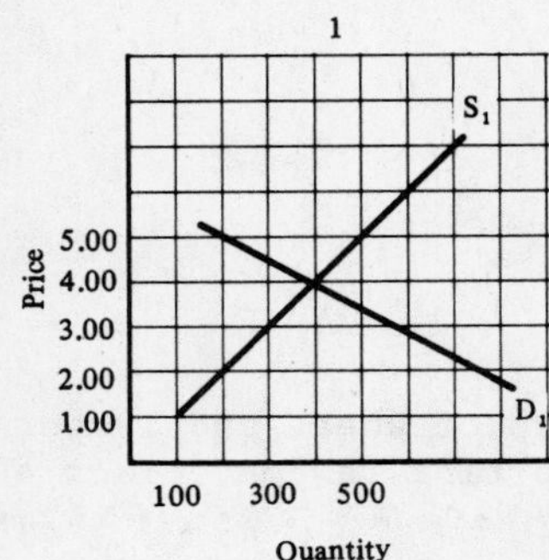

The government restricts importers to purchasing only 1/2 of what they previously purchased, at any new price.

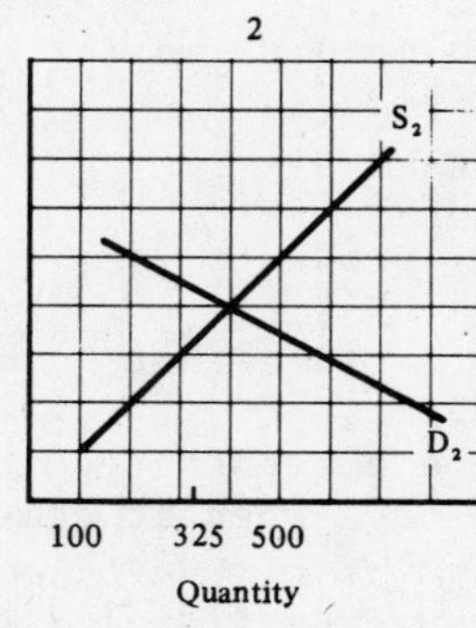

The government imposes a quota of 325 units of Z that can be imported.

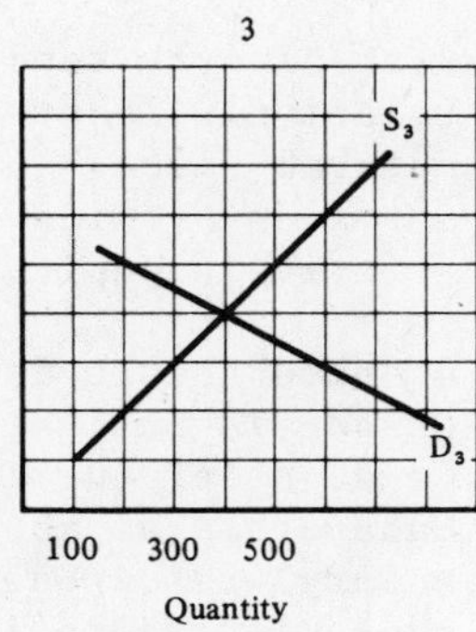

The government imposes a tariff at $1.00 per unit on the foreign good.

(b) If the demand for Z was highly inelastic, which policy would government likely <u>not</u> choose if it wanted to maximize its restriction on the amount of the import purchased? Why?

(c) Which policy would the government likely choose if it was concerned that restricted or protectionist policies might be inflationary? Why?

2. The diagram below illustrates the domestic supply of steel (S_D), the foreign supply of steel (S_F) and the domestic demand (D).

(a) Draw the total supply curve for steel and establish the domestic output (Q_D) and overall price (P_0).

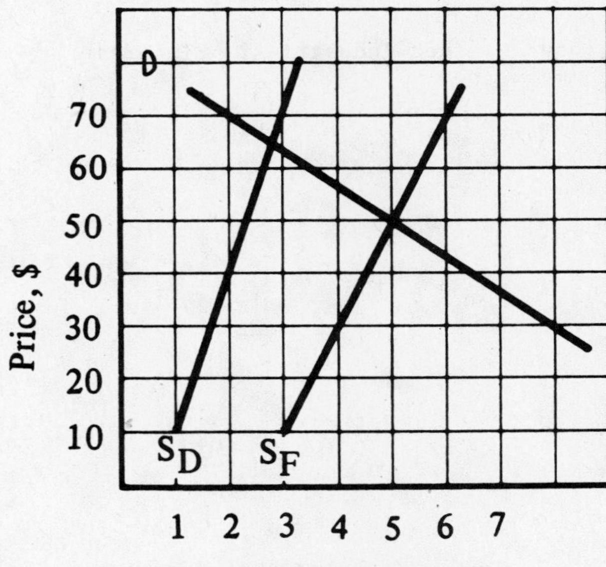

(b) The "domestic" government now levies a tariff of $20 per ton of steel on foreign suppliers. Using a broken line, draw the "after-tariff" supply curve for foreigners and the new total supply curve, labeling them S_F' and S_{D+F}'. Label the new price P_1.

3. The following hypothetical quotation is from a union official:

We are not opposed to competition from imports so long as it does not destroy jobs. It seems nonsensical to me, however, that last year, when the overall unemployment rate was 11.5 percent, we destroyed another 100,000 jobs by allowing the importation of cheap goods from abroad.

(a) Would a higher tariff on a particular imported product reduce the overall unemployment rate? Explain.

(b) Would such a tariff reduce the unemployment rate in the domestic industry that competes with the imported product?

(c) Would such a tariff "destroy" jobs in other industries? Elaborate.

CHAPTER 23

GROWTH IN THE LESS-DEVELOPED COUNTRIES

CHAPTER OBJECTIVES

The questions and exercises in this chapter reinforce your understanding of the features of less-developed countries (LDC), some of which inhibit real per capita economic growth. The multiple-choice questions examine such issues as the vicious circle of poverty, agricultural dependency, and the New International Economic Order while the exercises test your understanding of growth and compounding and production efficiency.

MULTIPLE-CHOICE QUESTIONS

1. A Lorenz curve showing the world's distribution of income as compared to the Lorenz curve showing the distribution of income in Canada would be:
   (a) closer to the diagonal line
   (b) farther from the diagonal line
   (c) at the diagonal line
   (d) in approximately the same position

2. Increases in real GNP in LDCs do not necessarily lead to economic advancement
   (a) if prices rise faster than GNP growth
   (b) if population growth exceeds real GNP growth
   (c) if capital cannot be accumulated at the same time
   (d) all of the above

3. In a LDC, X-inefficiency might well be caused by
   (a) the economy being on the wrong place on the production possibility boundary
   (b) unemployment
   (c) malnutrition of the labor force
   (d) market imperfections preventing resources from moving to their most valuable uses

4. Which one of the following would NOT be among the barriers to economic development?
   (a) an inadequate financial system
   (b) population growth
   (c) inefficient use of resources
   (d) international trade

5. A strong reason for government intervention to raise economic growth in LDCs is
   (a) the need to control prices of exports
   (b) the desirability to force people to save
   (c) the need to control wages and other costs
   (d) the need to expand agricultural production

6. The vicious circle of poverty
   (a) describes an income-consumption process which cannot generate sufficient savings to raise the capital stock
   (b) applies to countries which borrow from abroad and spend the proceeds on consumer goods
   (c) is a result of failure of policies in LDCs to hold population growth to 0 percent
   (d) describes a situation where any savings out of domestic income is invested abroad, lowering the domestic rate of capital accumulation.

7. Heavy reliance on expanding agricultural production in LDCs is to be avoided, according to some experts, because
   (a) such reliance would suggest little need to educate the population
   (b) it would be difficult to sell the surplus at any price
   (c) expanded agricultural output would depress prices and worsen the terms of trade for LDCs
   (d) per dollar of factor input, the value of manufacturing output is greater than agricultural output

8. The New International Economic Order proposals
   (a) seek to achieve a redistribution of world wealth toward LDCs
   (b) concern primarily economic development in LDCs rather than transfers of existing wealth
   (c) rely extensively on the market mechanism to stimulate growth in LDCs
   (d) concern all of the above

9. In raising capital for development, an LDC would be inclined to prefer foreign borrowing over domestic saving because:
   (a) there is less reduction in living standards in the future
   (b) of the political disadvantages of foreign ownership of business firms
   (c) less current consumption must be foregone
   (d) of the interest which must be paid

10. The "green revolution" refers to:
   (a) recent inflows of U.S. dollars to various Asian countries
   (b) the dramatic growth in food exports from certain underdeveloped countries
   (c) recent increases in agricultural productivity in certain underdeveloped countries, resulting from advances in technology
   (d) the policy of changing the emphasis in underdeveloped countries from agriculture to manufacturing

EXERCISES

1. Why may the gap between the rich and poor countries grow larger, even if both have the same rate of growth? Consider the following example. Use the "rule of 72," recognizing that for continuous compounding, as in population growth, the doubling time is the number 72 divided by the annual percentage rate.

	Country A	Country B	Difference
Year X, GNP per capita	$2,000	$100	______
Annual rate of per capita growth	3%	3%	______
Year X + 1, real GNP per capita	______	______	______
Year X + 24, real GNP per capita	______	______	______

2. Use the "rule of 72" for the following (assume annual compounding):
   (a) If real GNP is rising at a steady rate of 4 percent, it will be doubled in how many years? ____________
   If the population is rising steadily at 3 percent per year, it will double itself in how many years? __________
   In how many years, then, will real GNP per capita be doubled in this example?
   __________.

   (b) It was predicted in 1971 that at current rates of increase the population of the less-developed countries (the "third world") would double itself by the year 1996. What would have been the approximate annual rate of increase in population in these countries? ________________

   (c) In the early 1980s, the population growth rate in the LDCs was 2.4 percent annually. At this rate, population of the LDCs will double in __________ years.

3. Production Possibilities, Efficiency, and Development
   Suppose that there are two countries, A and B, both of which are less developed in terms of advanced country standards. Both countries have x units of working labor and y units of land, but very little capital. Country A has a population of 8 and country B has a population of 10. Assume that either country produces and consumes only wheat and peanuts. The production possibilities are given in the schedules below.

Country A		Country B	
Wheat (bu.)	Peanuts (bu.)	Wheat (bu.)	Peanuts (bu.)
100	0	200	0
90	10	180	18
80	19	160	35
70	27	140	51
60	34	120	66
50	40	100	80
40	45	80	93
30	49	60	105
20	52	40	116
10	54	20	126
0	55	0	135

(a) Plot the production possibility boundaries on the diagram provided. To obtain successive increases in wheat production, what is happening to the rate of loss in peanut production in country A? Country B? What can be said about the change in opportunity costs?

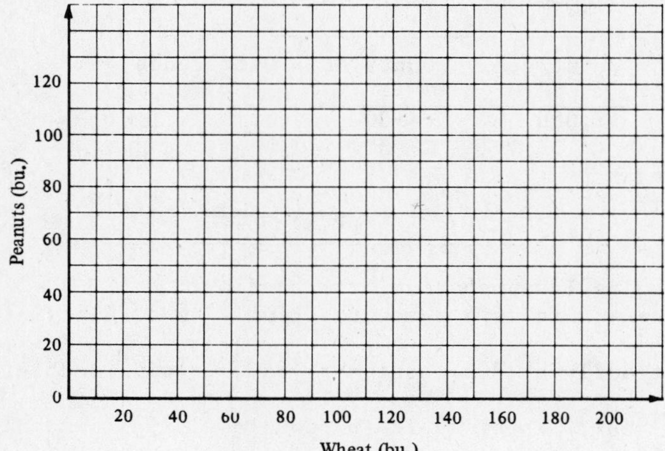

(b) Suppose that production and consumption in country A are 16 bushels of peanuts and 80 bushels of wheat and in country B are 160 bushels of wheat and 35 bushels of peanuts. Does inefficiency in the use of resources exist in either country? What type?

(c) Assume production as in (b). If wheat is worth in U.S. dollars $2 per bushel and peanuts are worth $.50 per bushel, what is the value of GNP in each country in terms of U.S. dollars? What is the per capita level of GNP in each country?

(d) Assuming production as in (b), give possible reasons why country B is using its resources more efficiently than country A.

(e) What type of foreign aid could Canada give to country A to increase its per capita income? How would this affect the production possibility boundary?

PART SEVEN

THE MARKET ECONOMY: PROBLEMS AND POLICIES

CHAPTER 24

BENEFITS AND COSTS OF GOVERNMENT INTERVENTION

CHAPTER OBJECTIVES

The market economy, left to its own devices and under certain conditions, is highly responsive to changes in consumer preferences and costs, and it coordinates economic activity automatically. However, markets do not always work satisfactorily, such as in situations where transactions in the market affect individuals who are not directly part of the transaction. These are referred to as externalities. Your knowledge of these and related causes of social and private cost differences are examined in this chapter. Government intervention may be required to reduce negative externalities but, unless carefully devised and administered, such intervention may impose additional costs on individuals and society.

MULTIPLE-CHOICE QUESTIONS

1. An increase in the demand for wood-burning stoves will likely
   (a) cause the price of fuels other than wood to rise
   (b) increase the production of certain types of steel
   (c) lower the price of stoves
   (d) leave unchanged the price of firewood

2. The likely result in a market system if government taxed away all windfall profits would be
   (a) a quicker shift of resources from declining to expanding markets
   (b) the removal of the most important driving force for allocating resources
   (c) improved market signals and responses
   (d) increased information about temporary shortages and surpluses

3. Which one of the following is not an argument for increased reliance on markets for allocating resources?
   (a) The market system coordinates economic activity automatically.
   (b) With competitive markets, price will tend to equal minimum average total costs of production.
   (c) Markets function best when external costs are associated with consumption or production of a commodity.
   (d) Market forces tend to correct disequilibrium situations.

4. The appearance of windfall profits in one industry in a market economy indicates
   (a) unexpected changes in supply and/or demand in the industry
   (b) a disequilibrium phenomenon
   (c) an unanticipated benefit to producers in that industry
   (d) all of the above

5. One of the most important features of the price system is
   (a) long-term stability of prices and output
   (b) the ability to respond to change, thereby correcting or at least reducing disequilibrium conditions
   (c) the assurance that there can never be excess profits, even in the short run
   (d) the need to have detailed information in order to establish prices

6. If a ton of newspaper costs $350 to produce and in the process causes $10 worth of pollution damage to the environment,
   (a) the private cost is $360 per ton
   (b) the social cost is $10 per ton and the private cost is $350 per ton
   (c) the private cost is $350 per ton and the social cost is $340 per ton
   (d) the social and private costs per ton are $360 and $350, respectively

7. An individual who decides to drive to work by car rather than take the subway
   (a) is maximizing private utility
   (b) is likely to be creating an externality
   (c) creates a situation in which social cost is likely to exceed private cost
   (d) all of the above

8. Which of the following is the best example of a collective consumption good?
   (a) a home's solar heat collector
   (b) a pencil
   (c) a television broadcast
   (d) a fire extinguisher in a rural home

9. Moral hazard refers to a situation where
   (a) managers of firms pursue their own goals and not those of the firm
   (b) values differ among sellers of products and services
   (c) government intervention is required to internalize an externality
   (d) in a two-person transaction, one person has information not available to the other leading to an increase in aggregate risk

10. If there are negative externalities associated with an economic activity and that activity is carried out until net private benefits equal zero,
   (a) that activity should be subsidized
   (b) net social benefits for the last unit will still be positive
   (c) output should be restricted
   (d) private costs exceed social costs

11. The presence of external costs implies that
   (a) private output exceeds the socially optimal output
   (b) private output is less than the socially optimal output
   (c) private output corresponds with the socially optimal output
   (d) none of the above

12. An effluent tax or charge based on pollution damages would
   (a) provide an incentive to expand output and increase external costs
   (b) be inequitable to consumers of the product
   (c) encourage the polluter to reduce pollutant emissions
   (d) always entirely eliminate pollution

13. All <u>but</u> which one of the following are causes of government "failure" to achieve its potential with respect to intervention?
   (a) transactions costs
   (b) imperfect knowledge
   (c) bureaucratic rigidities in government
   (d) political constraints

14. In order to achieve the optimal level of government intervention,
   (a) enforcement costs must be subtracted from direct costs to estimate total costs
   (b) expected gains from government intervention should be compared with expected costs
   (c) ideal government performance should be compared with ideal market performance
   (d) government intervention should proceed until negative externalities are entirely eliminated

15. If pollution abatement becomes increasingly expensive with increasing levels of abatement,
   (a) the optimal level of pollution is not likely to be the minimum attainable
   (b) the optimal level of pollution reduction will depend on the benefits from pollution abatement as well as the costs
   (c) optimal pollution will not be zero pollution
   (d) all of the above

<u>EXERCISES</u>

1. Assume that Mr. Maple has access to his wooded retreat by way of a 2-km road that he and another individual, Mr. Oak, must maintain. The demand for the quality of the road on the part of Mr. Oak and Mr. Maple is shown below, where Q* is some "maximum" quality of the road. The cost of increasing the quality is shown as S = MC. (We assume that "zero" quality implies the road is passable.)

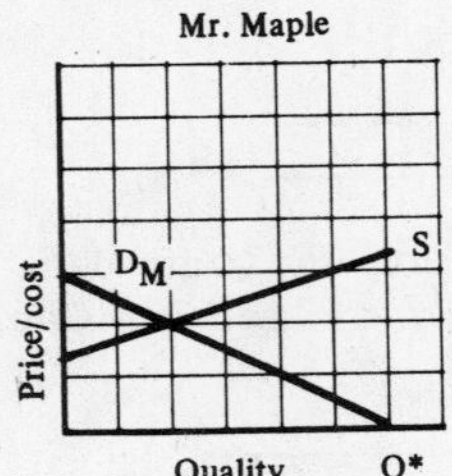

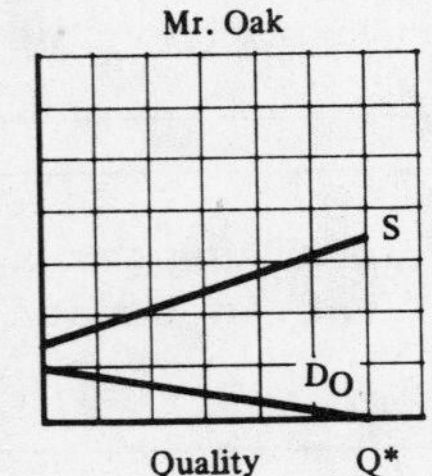

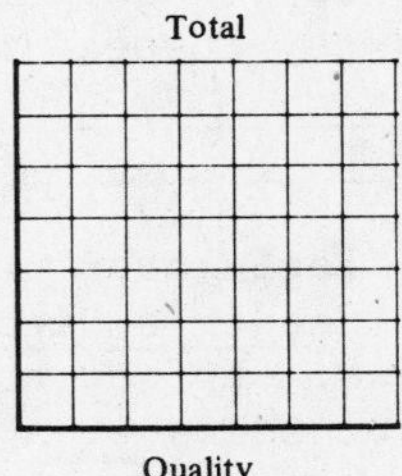

   (a) What quality level will Mr. Maple maintain without considering Mr. Oak?

   (b) How would you illustrate the social demand for road quality? Use graph 3. (<u>Hint</u>: Recall the discussions in the text on external benefits and collective consumption goods.)

(c) Given the costs of quality improvements as shown, would the socially desirable quality result in an improvement in the quality of the road compared to the quality maintained by Mr. Maple alone?

(d) If the level of road quality given by (c) was produced, and the costs shared, would Mr. Maple pay more or less than in (a)?

2. The following are examples of possible government intervention in the economy. In a word or two, predict the effect on relative profitability of the indicated industries.
(a) The Province of Ontario passes new laws reducing allowed length and weight of trucks on provincial highways. Effect on:
trucking ______________________________
railroads ______________________________

(b) The government of Canada imposes a tax on gasoline that applies only to individuals who use gasoline for noncommercial purposes. Effect on:
private gasoline consumption ______________________________
trucking ______________________________

(c) The Federal Department of Transport announces a new policy of letting aviation pay its own way; federal aid to airport construction and air traffic control will henceforth be financed from higher taxes on airline fares, aviation gasoline, and airport taxes, instead of from general tax revenues. Effect on:
airlines ______________________________
railroads ______________________________

(d) Parliament legislates new laws that disallow tax advantages that various U.S. magazines (*Reader's Digest* and *Time*) had in Canada and gives subsidies to Canadian publications. Effect on:
foreign publishers ______________________________
Canadian publishers ______________________________

3. The following schedule shows (a) how the cost of production increases as a pulp and paper firm expands output and (b) the effect of pollution from the firm on commercial fishing in the area.

Output (tons/wk)	Total Private Cost $	Dollar Value of Fishing Loss Due to Pollution $
0	0	0
1	500	100
2	550	225
3	620	365
4	710	515
5	820	675
6	1050	845
7	1350	1025

(a) Complete the table and graph your results below.

Average Private Cost (APC)	Marginal Private Cost (MPC)	Average Social Cost (ASC)	Marginal Social Cost (MSC)

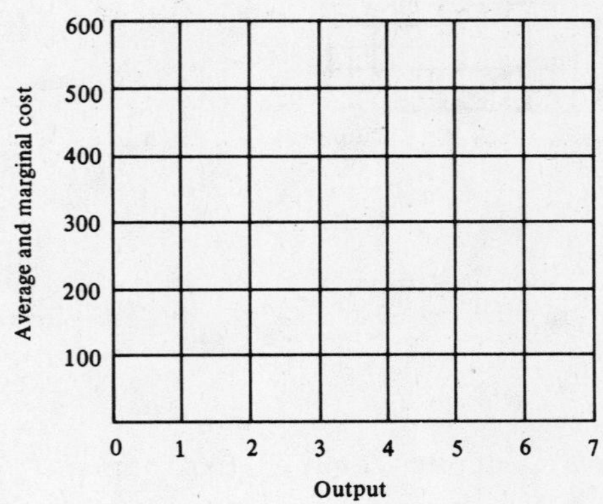

(b) If the firm was producing four tons of output per week, what price would it require to cover the private cost? What price would be required to cover the social cost?

(c) Assume a perfectly competitive market for this firm's product (paper) and that this firm's private costs of production are typical for the industry. Predict the long-run equilibrium price and the output for this firm. (Assume no pollution controls.)

(d) Assume now that firms in this industry are required either to pay compensation for the negative externalities or incur abatement costs to eliminate them. The industry price would be (higher, the same, lower) and the output (less, same, greater). This firm's ability to survive would depend on the long-run equilibrium price for paper being at least ____________, or upon it being able to keep the total of negative externalities and costs of abatement at levels as (low, high) as those of its competitors.

4. In the diagram below the marginal social damage schedule (MSD) refers to pollution costs on society associated with a production activity. The marginal net private benefit schedule (MNPB) is the net private gain (MR - MC) to the producer as output is increased.

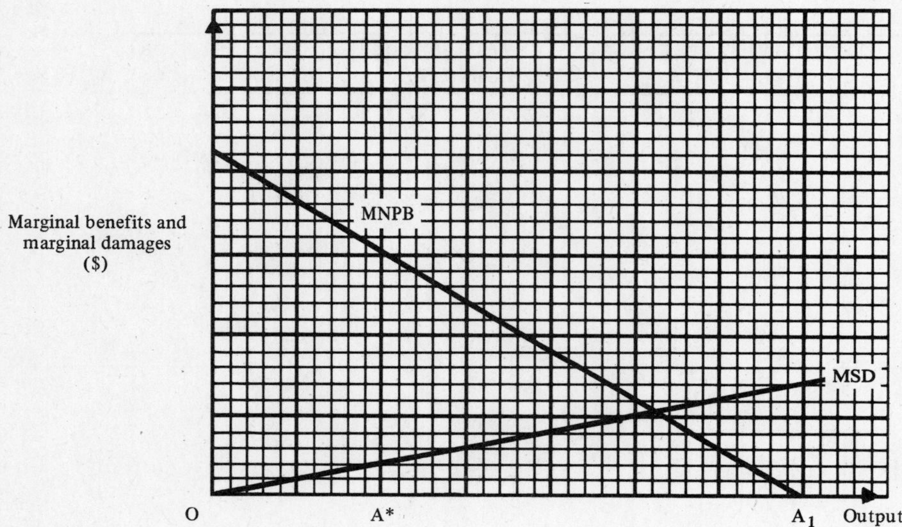

(a) With no government intervention, what level of output would the producer choose? Why?

(b) From society's point of view, what is the optimal output level? Explain.

(c) Suppose the government, unaware of the precise shape of the MSD schedule, limits the producer to OA* of output. At A*, is society better off or worse off than in a "no intervention" situation? Explain.

CHAPTER 25

PUBLIC FINANCE & PUBLIC EXPENDITURE

CHAPTER OBJECTIVES

The public sector represents a large share of total economic activity in Canada. The emphasis in this chapter is on understanding the structure of the tax system and the effects of various taxes and tax systems on the economy. The scope of federal-provincial transfers is also highlighted. Taxes on commodities affect prices and output levels in different ways, depending on the elasticities of demand and supply. The significance of this is illustrated in one of the exercises.

MULTIPLE-CHOICE QUESTIONS

1. If as income rises, the amount of tax paid increases,
   (a) the tax is proportional
   (b) the tax is progressive
   (c) the tax is regressive
   (d) one cannot say with certainty what pattern it exhibits

2. Which one of the following statements concerning the distributional effects of taxes in Canada is correct?
   (a) The sales and excise taxes used in Canada today are as a whole proportional.
   (b) There is consensus among economists that the property tax is progressive.
   (c) The personal income tax is progressive in effect as well as in structure.
   (d) The corporate income tax must be proportional in its effect because it is a flat-rate tax.

3. The marginal rate of taxation of a progressive income tax is necessarily
   (a) the same as the average rate
   (b) less than the average rate
   (c) more than the average rate
   (d) higher the lower the income

4. The marginal rate of tax of 50 percent at an income level of $40,000 means
   (a) all $40,000 of assessed income is taxed at 50 percent
   (b) total tax paid will be $20,000
   (c) assessed income above $40,000 will be taxed at a minimum rate of 50 percent
   (d) the average tax rate is constant for incomes equal to and above $40,000

5. Comprehensive income taxation
   (a) refers to the taxation of all income
   (b) requires that there be many different taxes
   (c) means a fixed proportional tax rate
   (d) refers to reducing the difference between the tax base and total income

6. A negative income tax of the type described in the text would have the advantage of
   (a) reducing the progressivity of the tax structure
   (b) guaranteeing a minimum income to the poor with less red tape and with increased work incentives
   (c) penalizing those with large families
   (d) keeping recipients out of the labor force where they would cause unemployment

7. Tax "incidence" indicates
   (a) who actually bears the final burden of the tax
   (b) who pays the tax to the federal government
   (c) the progressivity of the tax
   (d) whether or not the tax is fair

8. The more elastic the demand for a commodity on which a specific excise was levied, other things equal,
   (a) the greater the after-tax price increase
   (b) the less the reduction in the quantity produced
   (c) the more elastic the associated supply curve
   (d) the less the after-tax price increase

Questions 9 and 10 refer to the diagram below.

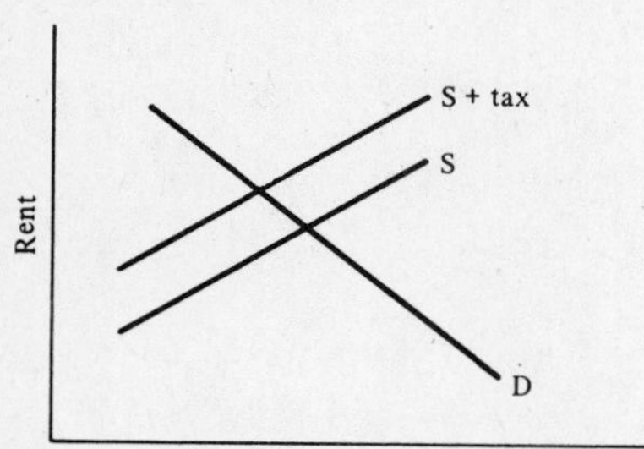

9. A tax on landlords in the market described in the diagram
   (a) would be paid entirely by landlords
   (b) would be paid entirely by renters
   (c) would be shared by landlords and tenants
   (d) would produce a leftward shift in the demand schedule

10. In the situation described by the diagram,
   (a) the amount of rental housing demanded remains the same before and after the tax
   (b) the quality of rental housing would improve
   (c) the quantity of rental housing demanded would fall
   (d) the quantity of rental housing that landlords would be willing to supply does not change

11. The largest component of federal expenditures in 1982 was
   (a) interest on public debt
   (b) transfers to persons
   (c) purchases of goods and services
   (d) transfers to provincial governments

12. Transfer payments in Canada have grown rapidly in recent years for all <u>but</u> which one of the following reasons?
   (a) changes in regulations regarding eligible recipients
   (b) taxes used to pay for transfer payments have risen rapidly
   (c) more concern in society for low-income families
   (d) unemployment compensation has increased due to higher rates of unemployment

13. Equalization payments
   (a) redistribute income from wealthy individuals to poorer individuals directly
   (b) involve a federal-provincial agreement over the sharing of tax fields
   (c) are payments from Ottawa to provinces with below-average tax capacity
   (d) have declined during the past ten years due to increasing wealth in Alberta

14. Decentralization of government economic activity can be justified by all but which one of the following?
   (a) regional preferences
   (b) income redistribution efforts by government
   (c) particular local needs for public expenditure
   (d) cultural differences within the country

15. Increasing amounts of tax revenue have been transferred to the provincial and municipal governments for all but which one of the following reasons?
   (a) Expenditure needs of urban areas are rapidly growing.
   (b) Municipal revenue sources have been growing slowly.
   (c) Provincial and municipal governments do not collect tax revenue.
   (d) The federal government has greater access to the high-growth tax sources.

EXERCISES

1. The three diagrams below represent three different market situations with respect to the supply and demand for rental accommodation in the short run. Assume that a property tax of equal yield is imposed in all three situations.

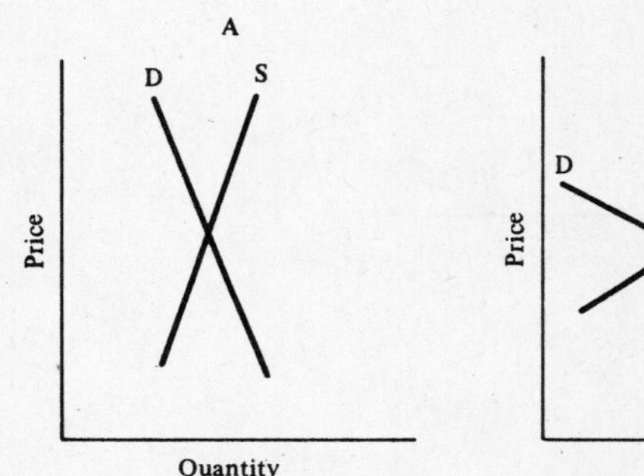

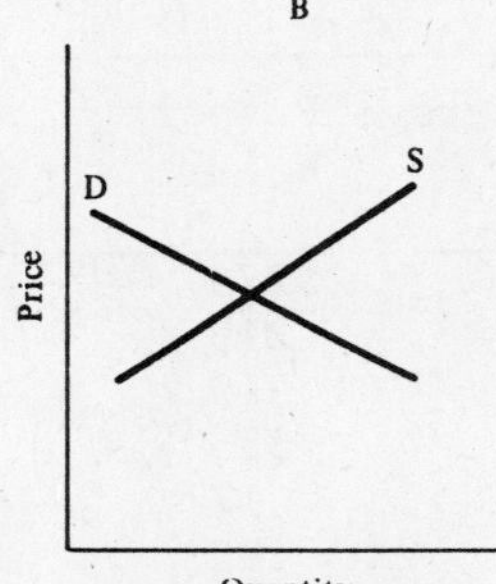

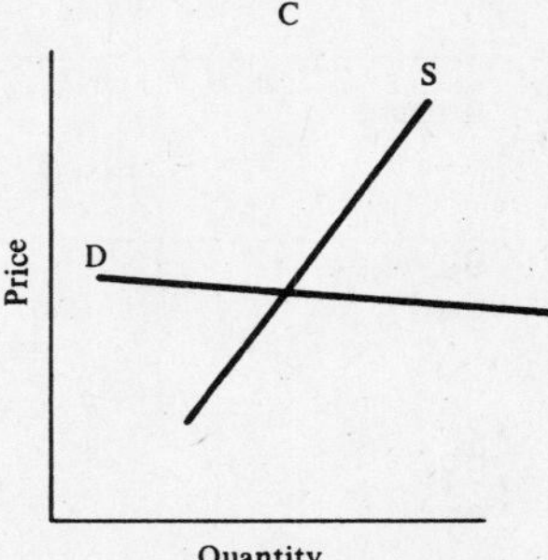

   (a) In which market situation will the landlord bear most of the tax burden? Explain.

   (b) In which market situation is there the smallest change in the quantity of rental accommodations? Why is this the case?

   (c) Suppose that in Case B rent controls had "fixed" rent or price at the original equilibrium, pretax rate. Is the tax burden shouldered by the landlord in Case B altered because of the existence of rent control?

2. (a) The table below provides information on the taxes paid by four individuals in different income categories. For each of the three taxes, A, B, and C, indicate whether the tax is proportional, regressive, or progressive.

Tax	Income Category and Tax Paid			
	$5,000	10,000	20,000	30,000
A	500	1,000	2,000	3,000
B	400	700	1,300	1,800
C	200	600	1,500	2,500

Tax A is ______________.
Tax B is ______________.
Tax C is ______________.

(b) Taking all taxes together (A + B + C), is the tax system progressive, regressive, or proportional? ____________________

3. A study by the Province of Ontario produced data (which are summarized in the following table) illustrating the relationship between household income and property taxes in Guelph, Ontario.

Household Income (class)	Average Property Tax Paid
$ 2,500-4,999	$275
5,000-6,999	279
7,000-9,999	319
10,000-11,999	355
12,000-14,999	417
15,000-19,999	495
20,000-24,999	581
25,000-49,999	650
50,000-99,999	836

Source: Ministry of Treasury, Economics and Intergovernmental Relations; Analysis of Property Taxes in Guelph, October 1972.

(a) Given these data, does the property tax appear to be regressive, proportional, or progressive? Why? (To make your calculations, use the midpoint of the income range.)

(b) If the tax were proportional at a tax rate roughly equal to 4 percent, how would the average property tax paid compare with that shown in the table?

4. Classify each of the following into one of these categories; government expenditure on goods and services (G); transfer payments (R); intergovernmental transfer (IR); none of the above (N)
   (a) provincial share of the cost of municipal recreational facilities ______________
   (b) expenditure on police protection ______________
   (c) profit-sharing bonuses to employees of private firms ______________
   (d) subsidies from provincial government to firms to hire young workers ______________
   (e) construction of a university building financed by a corporation ______________
   (f) federal government purchases of aircraft ______________
   (g) provincial government scholarships ______________

PART EIGHT

NATIONAL INCOME & FISCAL POLICY

CHAPTER 26

INFLATION, UNEMPLOYMENT, AND GROWTH: AN INTRODUCTION TO MACROECONOMICS

CHAPTER OBJECTIVES

The first part of this chapter discusses the definition and measurement of various macroeconomic variables such as national income, price indices, inflation rates, and unemployment rates. Several problems are designed to enhance your understanding of how to derive a price index and how to calculate rates of inflation over certain time periods. Moreover, you are expected to learn the distinction between real and nominal national income.

The concepts of aggregate demand and short-run aggregate supply are introduced. The intersection of a downward-sloping aggregate demand curve and an upward-sloping SRAS curve represents equilibrium levels of real national income and the price level. The difference between equilibrium national income and potential national income is defined as the GNP gap. Several exercises are provided to improve your skills at drawing these curves and to illustrate the effects of shifts in both curves on short-run real national income, the price level, and the GNP gap.

MULTIPLE-CHOICE QUESTIONS

1. If the price index increases from x to y from one year to the next, then the rate of inflation is
   (a) $y - x$
   (b) $(y - x)/x$
   (c) (y/x) times 100 percent
   (d) $[(y - x)/x]$ times 100 percent

2. If the prices of food items in the Consumer Price Index increase by 8 percent over a year, all other prices remaining constant, then the total CPI will
   (a) increase by more than 8 percent
   (b) increase by less than 8 percent
   (c) increase by 8 percent
   (d) remain constant since food items are not included in the CPI

3. If nominal GNP rises from $100 billion to $115 billion and the GNP deflator rises from 125 to 150,
   (a) real GNP has risen
   (b) real GNP has fallen
   (c) real GNP is unchanged
   (d) it is impossible to tell the change in real GNP

4. National income in nominal terms refers to
   (a) the total purchasing power of the household
   (b) the total market values in current prices of goods and services produced in the economy
   (c) the physical output of all goods and services produced in the economy
   (d) the total market value in current prices of goods and services consumed by the households in the economy

5. Decreases in real GNP reflect
   (a) price level decreases
   (b) output decreases
   (c) output increases and price decreases
   (d) none of the above

6. A GNP gap exists when
   (a) actual GNP and potential GNP differ
   (b) actual GNP and potential GNP are equal
   (c) there are no unemployed resources
   (d) current dollar GNP is greater than real GNP

7. The labor force is defined as the
   (a) total adult population in an economy
   (b) number of civilian, adult workers who are employed
   (c) number of civilian, adult employed workers minus the number of unemployed workers
   (d) number of civilian adults who are employed plus those actively seeking employment

8. The domestic labor force will increase by 10 if
   (a) ten unemployed workers become employed
   (b) ten unemployed workers leave the country
   (c) ten twenty-year-old females leave school and obtain employment
   (d) all of the above

9. The unemployment rate is defined as
   (a) the percentage of the labor force who are unemployed
   (b) the total number of unemployed workers
   (c) the ratio of unemployed to employed workers
   (d) the percentage of the adult population who are unemployed

10. The AD curve is usually depicted as
    (a) a positive relationship between the total amount of real output (Y) that will be demanded by purchasers and the price level (P)
    (b) a positive relationship between nominal GNP that will be demanded by purchasers and P
    (c) a negative relationship between current dollar GNP that will be demanded and P
    (d) a negative relationship between real GNP that will be demanded and P

11. The Canadian AD curve is likely to be downward sloping because Canadians will buy more imported goods and foreigners will purchase fewer Canadian-produced goods if, other things equal,
    (a) the Canadian price level falls and the foreign price level remains constant
    (b) the Canadian price level rises and the foreign price level remains constant
    (c) the Canadian inflation rate is equal to the foreign inflation rate
    (d) the Canadian inflation rate is less than the foreign inflation rate

12. The short-run aggregate supply (SRAS) curve relates
    (a) potential GNP and price levels
    (b) the level of nominal GNP that will be supplied as all prices change
    (c) the level of total real output that will be produced and the price level
    (d) employment levels and output levels

13. An upward-sloping SRAS curve indicates that
   (a) increased output is associated with increased input prices
   (b) potential GNP increases with higher prices of goods and services
   (c) increased output is associated with higher prices due to rising unit costs of factors of production
   (d) unit costs are constant but prices and real output are positively related

14. With a given upward-sloping SRAS curve, a shift in the aggregate demand curve to the right (demand shock) will cause
   (a) an increase in real national income and the price level in the short run
   (b) an increase in real national income but a decrease in the price level
   (c) an increase in the price level but a decline in real national income
   (d) decreases in real national income and the price level in the short run

15. With a given aggregate demand curve, a shift in the SRAS curve to the left will cause
   (a) increases in real national income and the price level in the short run
   (b) an increase in the price level but a decrease in real national income in the short run
   (c) a decrease in the price level but an increase in real national income
   (d) a decrease in the GNP gap

Questions 16 to 21 refer to the diagram below

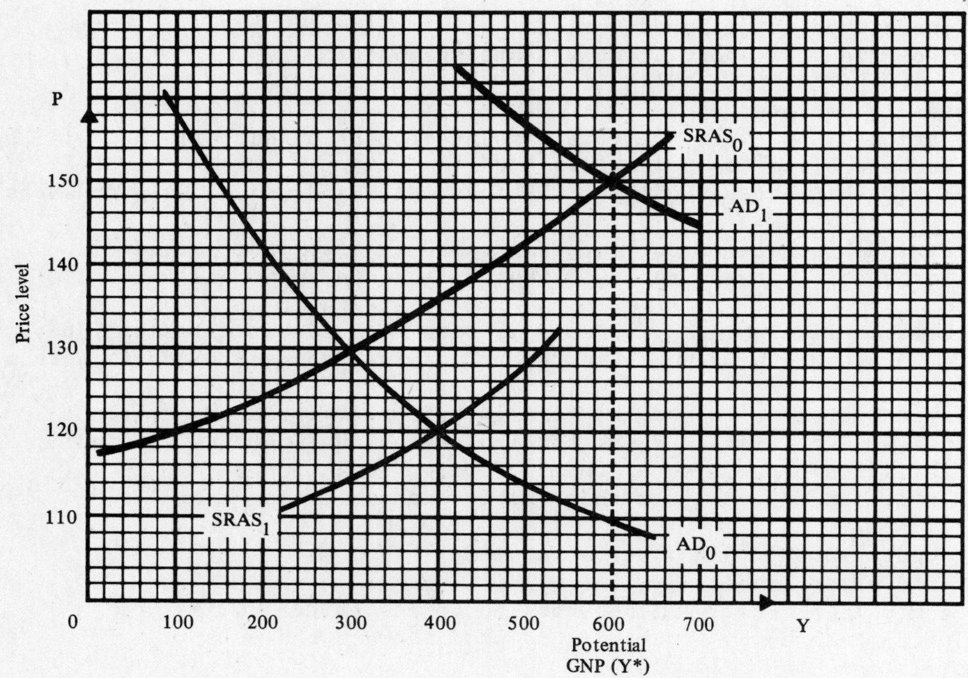

16. Assuming that AD_0 and $SRAS_0$ apply, the equilibrium levels of real national income and the price level will be
(a) P = 120, Y = 100
(b) P = 130, Y = 300
(c) P = 150, Y = 600
(d) P = 120, Y = 400

17. For the curves AD_0 and $SRAS_0$ the size of the GNP gap is
(a) 600
(b) 100
(c) 300
(d) 0

18. For the curves AD_0 and $SRAS_0$, when P = 120, the quantity of real output produced is
(a) greater than the amount purchasers wish to buy
(b) equal to the aggregate quantity demanded
(c) equal to potential real national income
(d) less than the aggregate quantity demanded at that price level

19. If the curves labeled $SRAS_0$ and AD_1 apply,
(a) the economy attains potential real national income
(b) the equilibrium price level is 150
(c) the GNP gap is zero
(d) all of the above

20. If the curves labeled $SRAS_1$ and AD_0 apply,
(a) the GNP gap is 200
(b) the equilibrium price level is 120
(c) equilibrium real income is 400
(d) all of the above

21. With a given aggregate demand curve (say, AD_0), as the short-run aggregate supply curve shifts farther and farther to the left,
(a) prices continually fall
(b) real income increases
(c) the GNP gap grows in magnitude
(d) potential GNP increases

EXERCISES

1. Construction of a Price Index

Suppose that the government's data collection agency has determined that on average consumers spend in the following proportions:

Shelter	30%
Food	25
Transportation	15
Clothing	10
Entertainment	10
Other	10

The average prices of these consumer items for two years are:

	Base Year	Next Year
Shelter	$3,000	$3,300
Food	2,500	2,500
Transportation	5,000	5,000
Clothing	100	110
Entertainment	60	60
Other	300	330

(a) Compute the average price level in the base year and in the next year. You must assume the proportions do not change.

(b) The price index for the base year, by definition, is 1.00 or 100. Compute the price index for the next year.

(c) You may have noticed that the price of shelter, clothing, and other goods increased by 10 percent each. Does your answer in part (b) indicate a 10 percent increase in the price index from the base year? Why or why not?

(d) Suppose that a group of households in this country consume the products listed above according to the following proportions: Shelter 40 percent; Food 30 percent; Transportation 5 percent; Clothing 15 percent; Entertainment 0 percent; Other 10 percent. Does the increase in the overall price index [in part (b)] underestimate or overestimate the cost of living increase for this particular group of households?

(e) If the oil-producing countries substantially increased the prices of heating fuel oil and gasoline, what commodity prices would be most seriously affected? If the oil price increase was a permanent one, what might happen to overall consumer spending proportions?

2. <u>Nominal and Real Output and the GNP Deflator</u>
There are two industries in an economy. Output and unit price for each industry are shown for three years. Year 1 is the base year.

	Quantity of Industry A (tons)	Quantity of Industry B (meters)	Prices Industry A (per ton)	Prices Industry B (per meter)
Year 1	4,000	20,000	20	5
Year 2	6,000	21,000	22	4
Year 3	6,000	18,000	24	6

(a) Calculate the nominal value of output in Industry A in each of the three years. Do the same for Industry B. Find national output in nominal terms for each of the three years by adding the two output values for A and B.

(b) Assuming that year 1 is the base year, calculate the real value of output in Industry A for each of the three years. Do the same for Industry B. What is the value of real output in the economy for each of the three years? [Use base-year prices.]

(c) Calculate the value of the implicit national income deflator for each of the three years.

3. You are given the following price indices for various years. The base year has an index of 100.

Year	Price Index	Annual Inflation Rate (%)
7	118.1	NA
8	121.9	____
9	125.1	____
10	______	1.1

(a) Calculate the annual inflation rate (to one decimal) for years 8 and 9 and fill in the blanks in the third column.

(b) What was the inflation rate over the period from the base year through year 9?

(c) Calculate (to one decimal) the price index for year 10.

4. (a) Complete the following table using the figures given to fill in the missing values.

Year	Canadian GNP in Current Dollars (billions)	Canadian GNP in Constant Dollars (billions)	GNP Deflator
1971	94.45	____	100
1972	105.23	100.25	____
1974	147.53	____	132.1
1975	____	113.13	146.2
1976	191.49	119.39	160.4

(b) What was the base year? Constant dollars refer to what year?

(c) What was the percentage increase in current dollar GNP between 1971 and 1976? What was the percentage increase in constant dollar (real) GNP in the same period?

5. The following table provides information about the Canadian economy for seven years.

(a) Fill in the underlined missing values in the table.

Date	Constant $GNP (billions)	Labor Force (000)	Unemployed (000)	Employed (000)	Unemployment Rate (%)
1976	119.1	10,206	____	9,479	7.123
1977	121.9	____	850	____	8.097
1978	126.1	10,882	____	____	8.362
1979	129.8	11,207	838	____	____
1980	130.5	11,522	867	10,655	7.525
1981	134.5	____	898	10,933	7.590
1982	128.0	11,879	1,305	10,574	____

(b) Calculate the percentage change in real (constant dollar) GNP between 1978 and 1979. Compare this value with the percentage change in employment in this time period. Do the same analysis for the two-year period 1981-1982.

(c) Does there appear to be a positive or negative relationship between real GNP and employment for these two time periods?

(d) Between 1977 and 1978 the unemployment rate increased while employment increased. How is this possible?

(e) Calculate the values of the real national income per member of the labor force for 1979 and 1982.

(f) The potential GNP in 1976 was $121.4 billion. Calculate the value of the GNP gap in 1976.

6. You are given the following schedules for AD and SRAS. Assume that potential real national income is 800. P is the price level; Y is the real output.

Aggregate demand (AD)		Short-run Aggregate Supply (SRAS)		
P	Y	P	Y	
			Case A	Case B
10	850	10	400	250
20	800	20	800	500
30	750	30	1,200	750
70	550	70	2,800	1,750
90	450	90	3,600	2,250

(a) Inspecting the relationship between P and Y for the aggregate demand schedule, is there a negative relationship between the two variables? Provide three theoretical justifications for your answer.

(b) There is a positive relation between P and Y for both cases (A and B) of the short-run aggregate supply schedule. Explain why real output increases are associated with increases in the price level.

(c) Using the values described in Case A for short-run aggregate supply combined with those for aggregate demand, what are the equilibrium values of P and Y? What is the size and sign of the GNP gap?

(d) "If the short-run aggregate supply curve shifts upward and to the left, the price level will rise, real national income will fall, and the size of the GNP gap will increase." Demonstrate this statement in two parts. First, demonstrate that Case B represents an aggregate supply curve which is to the left of that depicted by Case A. Second, demonstrate that the equilibrium values of P and Y for Case B (in combination with the aggregate demand curve) differ from those you derived in part (c). Moreover, you should be able to prove that the size of the GNP gap has increased.

7. The aggregate demand function is given by $P = 40 - 2Y$ and the short-run aggregate supply function is given by $P = 10 + Y$, where Y refers to real national income and P is the price level. Potential real national income is equal to 40.

(a) Plot the AD curve in the diagram below and indicate both of the intercept values.

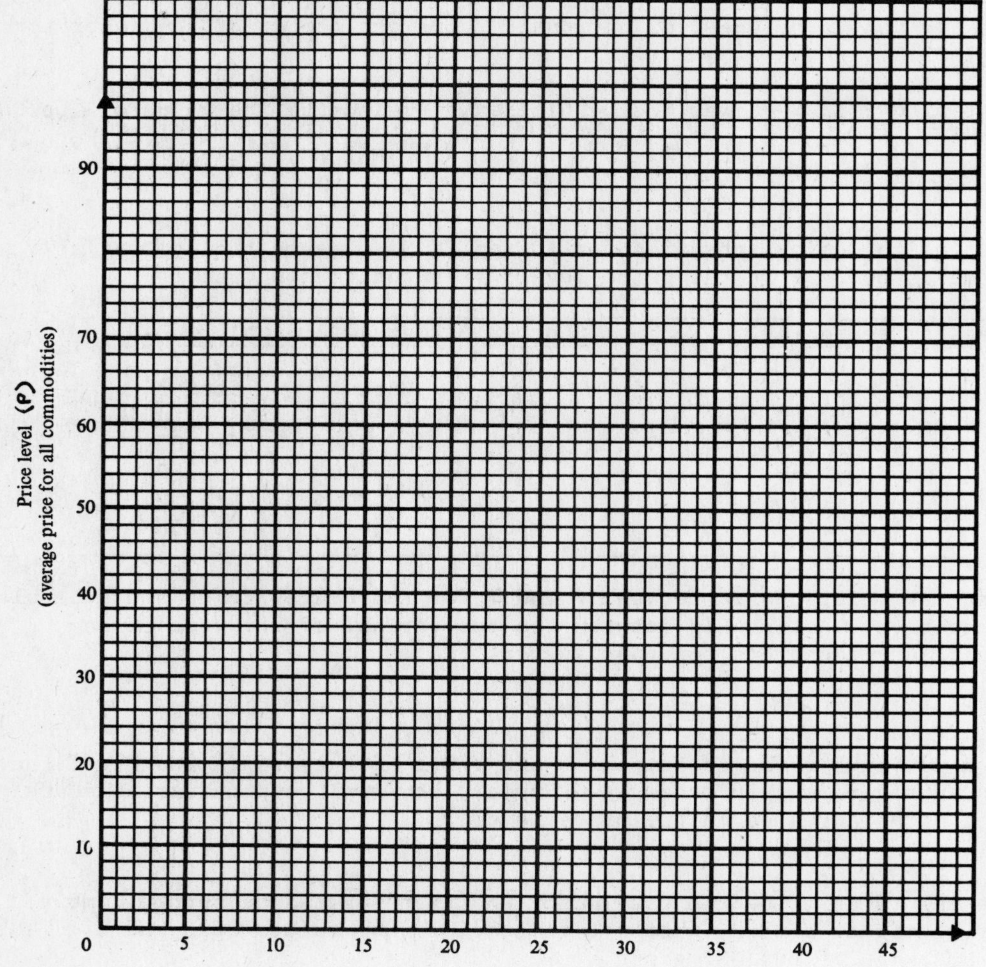

(b) Plot the SRAS curve in the diagram.

(c) Referring to the diagram, what are the equilibrium levels of P and Y? Prove algebraically that the intersection of the two equations yields these equilibrium values.

(d) What is the magnitude of the GNP gap?

(e) Suppose that expression for the AD curve became $P = 70 - 2Y$. Plot this expression in the diagram and discuss the changes that occurred to the levels of P and Y and the size of the GNP gap.

(f) Assuming that the SRAS curve is the expression $P = 10 + Y$ and the expression for the AD curve is $P = X - 2Y$, determine the value of X which is necessary in order that the equilibrium level of real national income is equal to potential real income. What is the equilibrium level of prices at potential real income? What is the size of the GNP gap in this case?

CHAPTER 27

MEASURING NATIONAL INCOME

CHAPTER OBJECTIVES

This chapter defines national income and discusses how national income statisticians measure actual aggregate expenditure and national income for an economy. You should understand the equality between measurements of expenditures on newly produced goods and services and the income generated by their production. Moreover, it's important for you to understand the components of aggregate expenditure: consumption, investment, government expenditures, and net exports.

Exercises and problems are provided to improve your understanding of certain related measures of national income: net vs. gross national product, real vs. nominal national income, and net national income at factor cost vs. net national product at market prices.

The chapter concludes by discussing the shortcomings of using the value of GNP as a measure of economic welfare as well as a measure of all economic activity.

MULTIPLE-CHOICE QUESTIONS

1. Value added in production is equal to
   (a) purchases from other firms
   (b) profits
   (c) total value of output including intermediate goods
   (d) total value of output minus value of inputs purchased from other firms

2. All of the following household expenditures would be included in consumption expenditure except:
   (a) payment to a dentist
   (b) purchase of corporate stock
   (c) purchase of a new car
   (d) purchase of a new fur coat

3. Mass marriages of men to their previously paid housekeepers would
   (a) reduce national income as now measured
   (b) increase national income as now measured
   (c) leave national income the same
   (d) effect GNP, but not national income

4. National income can be measured in all but which of the following ways?
   (a) by the flow of goods and services
   (b) by the payments made to purchase this flow of goods and services
   (c) by adding all money transactions in the economy
   (d) by the value of payments made to factors of production that have been used to produce final goods and services

5. Which of the following is not a part of the total of final goods and services included in GNP as currently measured?
   (a) government transfer payments to households
   (b) goods sold to government and foreign countries
   (c) increases in purchases of business equipment
   (d) additions to inventories

6 The difference between GNP and net national product is
   (a) depreciation or capital consumption allowance
   (b) total taxes paid to governments
   (c) net exports
   (d) personal savings

7. Disposable income is
   (a) the same as personal income
   (b) income that is used only for consumption
   (c) personal income remaining after income taxes
   (d) exclusive of welfare payments

8. Which of the following statements is true?
   (a) "Value added" means profits.
   (b) Transfer payments are included in GNP.
   (c) GNP can be measured by adding up all payments made to domestic factors of production.
   (d) GNP can be measured by adding up all expenditure transactions in the economy.

9. Gross investment is defined as
   (a) net investment plus dividend payments by firms
   (b) net investment minus the capital consumption allowance
   (c) net investment minus replacement investment
   (d) net investment plus depreciation

10. Which of the following is <u>not</u> a component of measured investment expenditure?
   (a) unintended inventory increases
   (b) planned inventory increases
   (c) new residential construction
   (d) purchases of Dome Petroleum stocks

11. Which of the following is <u>not</u> measured as consumption expenditure?
   (a) expenditures on restaurant meals
   (b) purchases of automobiles
   (c) purchases of residential houses
   (d) expenditures on skiing trips to Alberta by Canadian households

12. Which of the following items are included in measures of personal income?
   (a) indirect business taxes
   (b) personal income taxes
   (c) retained business earnings
   (d) corporate income taxes

13. Which of the following is omitted from measured GNP?
   (a) winnings from illegal gambling
   (b) tradespeople who do not report earnings from moonlighting
   (c) volunteer work for the Canadian Cancer Society
   (d) all of the above

14. The GNP deflator (or GNE deflator) is defined as
   (a) GNP in constant dollars divided by GNP in current dollars
   (b) GNP in current dollars divided by GNP in constant dollars
   (c) GNP in current dollars divided by GNP in constant dollars times 100
   (d) the consumer price deflator times GNP in current dollars

15. The difference between net national income at factor cost and net national product at market prices is
    (a) depreciation or the capital consumption allowance
    (b) indirect taxes less subsidies
    (c) indirect taxes plus subsidies
    (d) the payment of income to foreigners

16. Gross Domestic Product (GDP) measures
    (a) total output owned by Canadians
    (b) total income accruing to Canadians
    (c) GNP minus net exports
    (d) total output, at factor cost, produced in Canada

17. The GNP understates the total production of goods and services for all <u>but</u> which one of the following reasons?
    (a) No allowances are included for the services of owner-occupied homes.
    (b) Illegal activities are not included in the GNP estimate.
    (c) Legal production in the "underground economy" is not reported for income tax purposes.
    (d) Nonmarketed services of housewives or househusbands are not included.

EXERCISES

1. Some of the following items represent the expenditures and factor incomes for Canada in 1980. By selecting the appropriate items, calculate the value of GNP at market prices and the value for Gross National Expenditure (GNE). (Figures are in billions of 1980 dollars.)

Government purchases of goods and services	$ 58.5
Indirect taxes less subsidies	29.0
Personal income taxes	41.5
Wages and employee compensation (inc. personal income taxes)	165.5
Interest on the public debt	15.5
Consumption expenditure	168.4
Exports	90.9
Capital consumption allowance	33.5
Imports	93.3
Gross investment	67.2
Net interest income	19.0
Residual error of estimate on GNE	+ 0.2
Corporate profits before taxes	36.5
Rental income plus net farm income plus net income of unincorporated business	8.6
Residual error of estimate on GNP	- 0.2

GNP at Market Prices ________________
GNE ______________

2. You are given the following national income measures for an economy in a particular year. (Figures are in billions of dollars.)

Gross National Product at market prices	$ 290
Capital consumption allowances (depreciation)	32
Retained earnings	12
Government transfers to households	30
Personal income taxes	42
Indirect taxes less subsidies	30
Consumption expenditure	168
Business taxes	12

(a) Calculate Net National Income at factor cost.

(b) Calculate the value for personal income and personal disposable income.

(c) What was the magnitude of personal saving?

3. Assuming that there is no residual error of estimate, calculate the value of the Gross Domestic Product at factor cost from the following information.

-- GNP at market prices	2900
-- Investment income from nonresidents	40
-- Investment income paid to nonresidents	100
-- indirect taxes less subsidies	500

4. From 1950 to 1970, personal disposable income in Canada rose from $12.69 billion to $53.60 billion. Population increased from 13.71 million to 21.41 million in the same period. The consumer price index increased from approximately 100.0 to 142.2. What was the total percentage increase in the per capita standard of living as measured by per capita real personal disposable income from 1950 to 1970?

5. (a) Identify the items in the statements below according to the following code. Some statements have more than one answer.

C	Consumption	S_p	Savings of persons or households
I	Investment (domestic)		
G	Government spending on goods and services	M	Imports
		X	Exports
T	Taxes	N	None of the above
S_b	Saving of business		

_______ (1) A student gets a haircut from a self-employed barber.

_______ (2) The barber buys some clippers from the Short-Cut Clipper Company (Toronto).

_______ (3) Out of each day's revenue, the barber sets aside $5 in his piggybank.

_______ (4) When he has enough set aside, the barber buys a share of Royal Bank of Canada Stock.

_______ (5) The Royal Bank expands its computer facilities in its head office.

_______ (6) The Royal Bank pays municipal taxes to the City of Montreal.

_______ (7) The Royal Bank sets aside some of its income as depreciation reserves.

(8) The Short-Cut Clipper Company has profits of $50,000 after paying provincial and municipal taxes.

_______ (a) It pays $17,500 in corporate profits taxes to the federal government.

_______ (b) It pays dividends of $20,000.

_______ (c) It retains the rest and adds it to its surplus.

_______ (9) Canadians go to London, England, and stay at the Savoy Hotel.

_______ (10) Russia buys beef cattle from Alberta beef-cattle farmers.

_______ (11) Acme Construction Company builds 1,000 new houses to put on the market.

_______ (12) The Province of Saskatchewan builds a new highway.

(b) Which of the above would be included in the output-expenditure approach to measuring GNP?

6. The value of a product in its final form is the sum of the value added by various firms throughout the production process. Using the information below, calculate the value of one loaf of bread which is ultimately sold to a household. In doing so, calculate the value added at each stage of production. [This example demonstrates that the value-added approach avoids double counting.]

	Stage of Production	Selling Price to Next Stage	Value Added
1.	Farmer (production of wheat)	$0.30	$ _______
2	Milling Company. (flour)	0.55	_______
3.	Bakery (production of wholesale bread)	0.90	_______
4.	Retailer (sells to household)	1.00	_______
	TOTAL	2.75	$ _______

7. Each component of GNE has its own implicit deflator. The constant dollar value of a component is calculated by dividing the current dollar value by the implicit deflator for that component and multiplying by 100. The types of goods and services which the household buys may be quite different from those purchased by the various levels of government and hence the inflation rates for goods and services encountered by the household sector may differ from those experienced by the central authorities when they purchase goods and services.

Two components of GNE, consumption and government expenditure on goods and services, are illustrated in the schedule below in both current and constant dollars (1971 is the base year). All values are in millions of dollars.

	Consumption		Government Expenditure	
Year	Current $	Constant $	Current $	Constant $
1980	168,395	81,984	58,538	22,782
1981	191,025	83,535	66,749	22,988

(a) Calculate to the first decimal the implicit deflator for consumption expenditure in 1980. For 1981.

(b) Calculate to the first decimal the implicit deflator for government expenditure in 1980. For 1981.

(c) What was the rate of inflation for goods and services purchased by the household over this period? By the government?

CHAPTER 28

NATIONAL INCOME AND AGGREGATE DEMAND

CHAPTER OBJECTIVES

The focus of this chapter is on the determinants of desired aggregate expenditure (consumption, investment, government expenditure, and net exports) and the determination of equilibrium national income assuming that the price level remains constant.

The chapter concentrates primarily on factors that affect desired consumption expenditure and net exports and illustrates how a consumption function and a net export function are derived and drawn. It is important for you to learn that movements along these curves are caused by changes in real national income while changes in economic factors other than real national income cause shifts in these curves. In addition, you should learn how to calculate certain important ratios such as the average and marginal propensities to consume and the marginal propensity to spend.

Several questions are devoted to improving your understanding of the definition, derivation, and graphing of an aggregate expenditure (AE) curve. Make sure you understand the equilibrium condition for real national income and how the economy adjusts when desired aggregate expenditures are different from actual real national income.

MULTIPLE-CHOICE QUESTIONS

1. A Keynesian short-run aggregate supply curve depicts a situation in which
   (a) national income is varying over the range below potential GNP
   (b) firms respond to cyclical declines in demand by holding their prices constant
   (c) firms will supply whatever they can sell at their existing prices as long as they are producing below their normal capacity
   (d) all of the above are true

2. If an economy has a horizontal SRAS curve, the amount of real national income which is produced is
   (a) by aggregate demand (AD) alone
   (b) by aggregate supply alone
   (c) indeterminate even if the AD curve is specified
   (d) determined by none of the above

3. The aggregate expenditure function is a relationship between the level of
   (a) actual expenditure and real national income
   (b) desired real expenditure and nominal national income
   (c) actual expenditure and nominal national income
   (d) desired real expenditure and real national income

4. The slope of the aggregate expenditure function is most accurately represented by
   (a) the marginal propensity to save
   (b) the marginal propensity to consume
   (c) the marginal propensity to spend
   (d) none of the above

5. The equilibrium level of national income occurs where total output equals
   (a) the desired levels of the components of aggregate expenditure
   (b) the actual levels of the components of aggregate expenditure
   (c) the desired levels of only consumption and investment expenditure
   (d) the actual levels of only investment and net exports

6. Which of the following is not a component of aggregate expenditure?
   (a) investment in plant and equipment
   (b) government expenditure on goods
   (c) personal taxes
   (d) exports

7. The average propensity to consume out of disposable income is defined as
   (a) the ratio of total consumption expenditure to total national income
   (b) the ratio of total consumption expenditure to total disposable income
   (c) the ratio of the change in consumption expenditure to total disposable income
   (d) $\Delta C/\Delta Y_d$

8. If households desire to consume 80¢ out of every additional dollar of disposable income they receive, we can say that
   (a) the marginal propensity to consume is 8
   (b) the marginal propensity to consume is 0.2
   (c) the marginal and average propensities are necessarily both equal to 0.8
   (d) the marginal propensity to consume is 0.8

9. Below the break-even level of disposable income, households
   (a) dissave
   (b) consume less than their disposable income
   (c) save
   (d) spend an amount on goods and services equal to the value of their disposable income

10. For the short-run consumption function depicted in the text, it is likely that as disposable income rises, the APC value
   (a) falls
   (b) rises
   (c) is constant
   (d) is zero

11. Disposable income will be less than national income if
   (a) personal income taxes are less than transfer payments to households
   (b) personal income taxes are greater than transfer payments to households
   (c) business taxes are less than personal income taxes
   (d) personal taxes are equal to transfer payments

12. If the marginal propensity to save out of disposable income is 0.25, then the MPC is
   (a) 0.25
   (b) 0.75
   (c) 1.0
   (d) 0.33

13. If $Y_d = 0.8Y$ and consumption was always 80 percent of disposable income, then the marginal propensity to consume out of total income would be
   (a) 0.8
   (b) 0.2
   (c) 1.0
   (d) 0.64

14. Aggregate expenditure is equal to
   (a) C + I + G + (X - M) + transfers
   (b) C + I + G + (X + M)
   (c) C + I + G + (X - M)
   (d) C + I + G + (M - X)

15. Equilibrium national income occurs when
   (a) Y = C + I + G + (X - M)
   (b) the average propensity to spend is one
   (c) desired aggregate expenditure equals total output
   (d) all of the above

16. If desired aggregate expenditure exceeds real national income, there will be a tendency for
(a) output and real income to contract
(b) output and real income to expand
(c) output and real income to remain constant
(d) an equilibrium to exist in the economy

17. The AE diagram analyzes the determination of equilibrium income on the assumption that firms are able and willing to produce whatever is demanded at
(a) all levels of prices
(b) the existing price level
(c) all levels of wages
(d) a given output level

18. When real national income (Y) is 0, desired aggregate expenditure is
(a) 0
(b) equal to actual output
(c) 200
(d) 300

19. When real national income is 600, desired aggregate expenditure is
(a) 600
(b) less than income
(c) 300
(d) greater than income

20. If actual real national income was 400, desired aggregate expenditure
(a) exceeds income, and hence output and income are likely to contract
(b) is less than income, and hence income is likely to contract
(c) exceeds income, but equilibrium exists
(d) exceeds income, and hence output and income are likely to expand

21. When actual (measured) real national income is equal to 700, desired aggregate expenditure
(a) is less than real income, and hence inventories are likely to fall unintentionally
(b) is less than real income, and hence inventories are likely to rise unintentionally
(c) is less than real income, but no change in inventory occurs
(d) is equal to 700

Questions 18 through 26 refer to the diagram below. The price level is assumed constant.

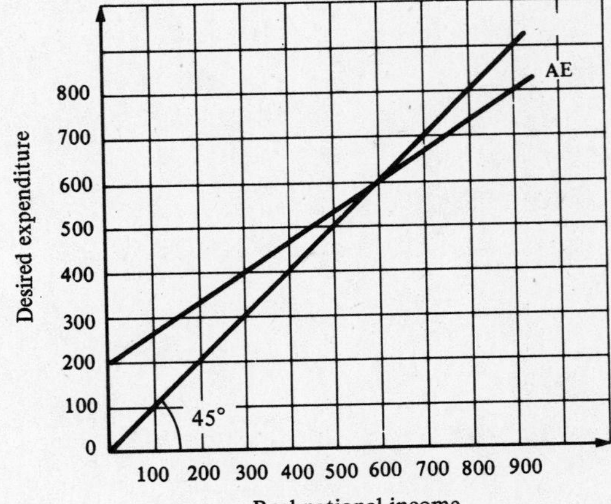

22. According to the diagram, the marginal propensity to spend is
   (a) two-thirds and constant
   (b) less than one but variable according to the level of income
   (c) one-third and constant
   (d) always equal to the average propensity to spend

23. The marginal propensity not to spend in this case is
   (a) two-thirds
   (b) one-third
   (c) equal to one
   (d) a variable fraction

24. The equilibrium level of national income is
   (a) 500
   (b) 700
   (c) in the range 400 to 500
   (d) 600

25. At a real national income level of 300, desired aggregate expenditure equals
   (a) 400 and the average propensity to spend is 0.75
   (b) 400 and the average propensity to spend is two-thirds
   (c) 400 and the average propensity to spend is less than the marginal propensity to spend
   (d) 400 and the average propensity to spend is four-thirds

26. At a real national income level of 600, the value of the average propensity to spend is
   (a) equal to the value of the marginal propensity to spend
   (b) unity
   (c) less than the value of the marginal propensity to spend
   (d) less than unity

27. The net export function is typically
   (a) downward sloping because as Y increases expenditure on imports increases, thereby decreasing net exports
   (b) downward sloping because as Y increases exports fall
   (c) downward sloping because as relative prices rise imports rise and exports fall, thereby reducing net exports
   (d) downward sloping because as Y increases imports fall

EXERCISES

All of the following questions assume that the price level is constant (the economy has a Keynesian short-run aggregate supply curve).

1. The first two columns of the following schedule depict the relationship between desired consumption expenditure (C) and real disposable income (Y_d).

Y_d	C	APC	ΔY_d	ΔC	MPC	S
0	80	N.A.				-80
			100	50	0.50	
100	130	1.30				-30
			60	30	0.50	
160	___	1.00				___
			___	20	0.50	
200	180	___				20
			___	___	0.50	
400	___	0.70				120
			350	___	___	
750	455	___				___

(a) Fill in the missing values for the change in real disposable income (ΔY_d).

(b) Fill in the missing values for C using the formula $C = 80 + 0.5Y_d$.

(c) Using the definition for the average propensity to consume (APC), fill in the missing values for APC. What did you notice happened to the value of APC as the level of Y_d increased?

(d) Fill in the missing values for ΔC.

(e) Using the definition for MPC, calculate it for the income change from 400 to 750.

(f) Using the definition for saving $S = Y_d - C$, fill in the missing values in the table. Using the formula $\Delta S/\Delta Y_d$, prove that the marginal propensity to save is constant and equal to 0.5.

(g) What is the break-even level of real disposable income? What is the amount of saving at this level of Y_d?.

(h) Plot both the desired consumption and desired savings functions in the diagram below. In addition, draw the 45° line in the diagram and prove that this line intersects the consumption function at a level of Y_d for which S = 0.

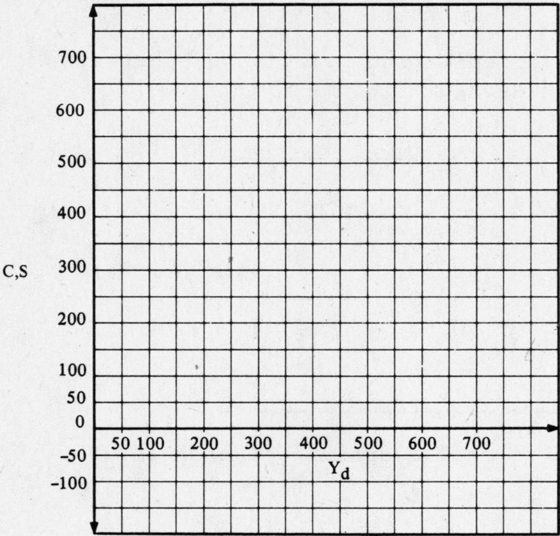

(i) Would you agree that, for this example, desired consumption expenditure is both autonomous and induced. Explain.

2. You are given the following information:

Real Y	Real Y_d	Desired C	APC	$S = Y_d - C$
100	70	100	1.43	-30
200	140	156	____	-16
314.3	220	220	____	0

(a) What relationship exists between Y and Y_d? Why is Y_d less than Y?

(b) Prove that the marginal propensity to consume out of real disposable income is constant and equal to 0.80.

(c) Calculate the marginal propensity to consume out of real income (Y).

(d) Calculate the values for APC out of real disposable income (the fourth column).

(e) What is the marginal propensity to save out of real disposable income?

(f) What is the break-even level of real disposable income? Total real national income?

3. Question 2 is based on specific mathematical relationships. The relationship between real income (Y) and real disposable income (Y_d) is $Y_d = 0.7Y$, and the consumption function is given by $C = 44 + 0.8Y_d$. The coefficient 0.8 is the slope of the consumption function (the MPC out of disposable income). You may wish to recheck your answers to question 2 using these equations.

(a) Suppose Y = 400. Calculate the values for Y_d and C. Do the same for Y = 500 and Y = 600.

(b) Now assume that the relationship between Y and Y_d becomes $Y_d = 0.6Y$, but the consumption function remains the same. What factor might have caused the change? Recalculate the values of C and Y_d for levels of income of 400, 500, and 600. Compare these values with the values in part (a).

(c) Suppose the consumption function becomes $C = 44 + 0.9Y_d$ while the relationship between Y and Y_d given in part (a) still holds ($Y_d = 0.7Y$). What is the value of the MPC out of real disposable income? Out of real total income? Calculate the values for C when Y has values of 400, 500, and 600.

4. <u>Real Wealth and the Consumption Function</u>

Suppose that an economy has a consumption function given by $C = 60 + 0.8Y + 0.1\ (W/p)$. The term W/p is the level of "real" wealth, W is the level of nominal wealth, and p is the price level. C represents desired consumption expenditure and Y represents the level of real national income. Assume that the price level has a value of 1.0 and is constant and that the economy's total nominal wealth is 400. Therefore, in this case real and nominal wealth are both equal to 400. [The distinction between real and nominal wealth will be important for the exercises in the next chapter.]

(a) Given that W/p = 400, rewrite the expression for the consumption function.

(b) Fill in the missing values in columns (2) and (4) in the schedule below.

(1)	(2)	(3)	(4)	(5)
Y	C (W/p = 400)	C (W/p = 2400)	S (W/p = 400)	S (W/p = 2400)
0	100	300	-100	-300
500	___	700	___	-200
1000	900	1100	+100	-100
1500	___	___	___	___
2000	1700	1900	+300	+100

(c) Assume that the economy's real and nominal wealth increases from 400 to 2400 (the price level remains at 1.0). Write the new consumption function and fill in the missing values in columns (3) and (5).

(d) As a result of the wealth increase, what happens to the consumption function? The saving function? Check your answers with the diagram in the textbook.

5. As an economy expands in terms of real income, the balance of trade (or, for our purposes, net exports) typically falls. If (X - M) is negative, a <u>deficit</u> in the balance of trade is said to exist. To understand this we present the following hypothetical schedule, where Y represents levels of real national income, X represents desired exports, and M represents desired imports.

Y	X	M	(X - M)
0	40	0	______
100	40	10	______
200	40	20	______
400	40	40	______
800	40	80	______

(a) Exports are assumed to be autonomous (independent of the level of Y). However, what specific relationship exists between M (imports) and Y? Identify some factors that explain the positive relationship between desired imports and real national income.

(b) Calculate the values for (X - M). Does the balance of trade fall (become smaller) as Y increases?

(c) Plot the net export curve in the diagram below.

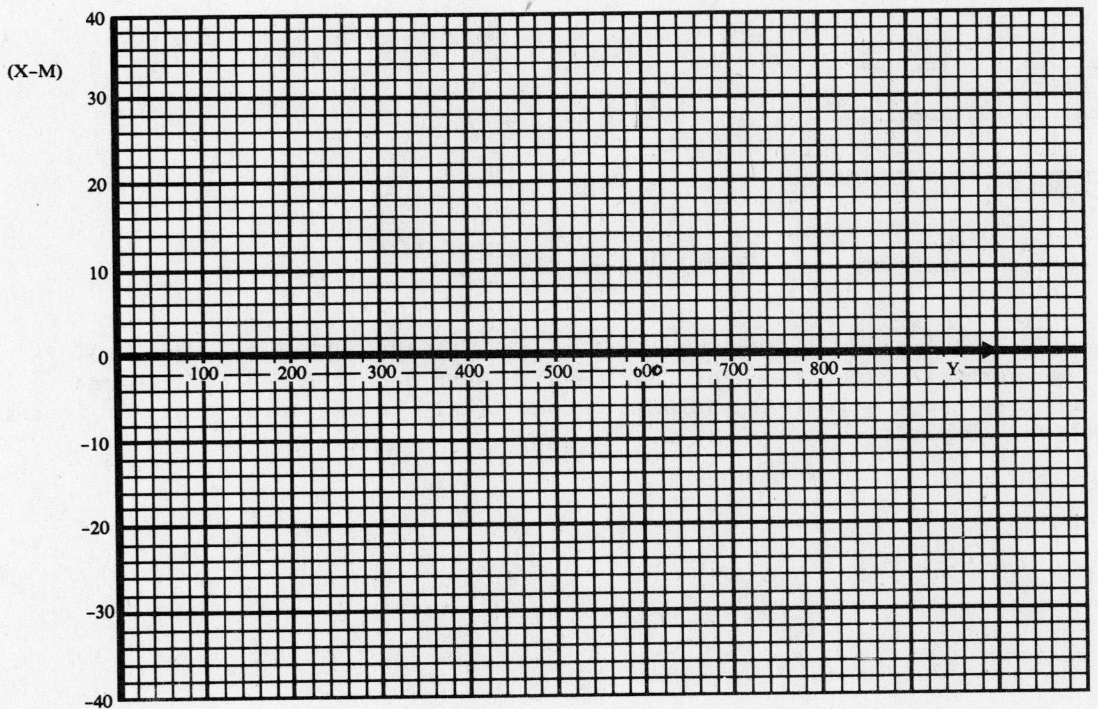

(d) Suppose that exports at each level of Y fell from 40 to 30. Recalculate the value of X - M at each level of Y and plot the new net export curve.

(e) Identify three factors that might have caused exports to decline as in (d).

6. (a) The table below shows the relationship between the various components of desired aggregate expenditure and real national income. Fill in the blanks and plot the values of total aggregate expenditure (AE) associated with levels of Y on the graph.

Y	C	I	G	(X - M)	AE	ΔY	ΔAE
0	90	10	30	20	______	______	______
100	150	10	30	10	______	______	______
200	210	10	30	0	______	______	______
300	270	10	30	-10	______	______	______
400	330	10	30	-20	______	______	______

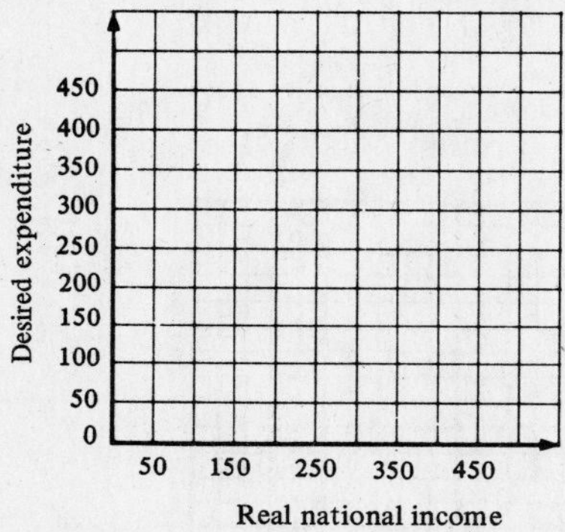

(b) The equilibrium level of national income is __________. Explain.

(c) Suppose actual (measured) real national income was 400. What is the value of desired aggregate expenditure at that level? What does the residual amount (Y - AE) represent? Is real national output likely to expand or contract in this situation? Explain.

(d) Calculate the values for ΔY and ΔAE and fill in the table. Prove that the marginal propensity to spend is constant and equal to 0.50. The slope of the AE function you plotted should be one-half.

(e) The marginal propensity not to spend is ______________.

7. An Algebraic Determination of Equilibrium National Income

You are given the following information about behavior in an economy:

Equation 1: the consumption function

$$C = 100 + 0.7Y_d$$

Equation 2: the relationship between Y and Y_d

$$Y_d = 0.8Y$$

Equation 3: investment expenditures

$$I = 56$$

Equation 4: the net export function

$$(X - M) = 10 - 0.1Y$$

Equation 5: government expenditures

$$G = 50$$

(a) Referring to the consumption function, what does the coefficient 0.7 mean?

(b) What components of aggregate expenditure depend upon national income?

(c) Aggregate expenditure is the algebraic sum of the various components. Derive the algebraic expression for AE.

(d) Equilibrium national income is where Y = AE. This is the expression for the 45° line. Equate your expression for AE in part (c) with Y. Solve for Y.

(e) Derive the marginal propensity to spend. (Hint: substitute values for Y equal to 100 and 200 into the algebraic expression for AE and then calculate ΔY and ΔAE.

CHAPTER 29

CHANGES IN NATIONAL INCOME I:

THE ROLE OF AGGREGATE DEMAND

CHAPTER OBJECTIVES

A change in the equilibrium level of real national income is often caused by changes in autonomous expenditure. A change in autonomous expenditure causes the aggregate expenditure function to shift which in turn causes the aggregate demand curve (AD) to shift. The change in national income is normally larger than the change in the autonomous component of aggregate expenditure. This is referred to as the multiplier analysis.

When a shift in the AD curve generates no change in the price level, the ratio of the change in real national income to the change in the autonomous component which causes the AD curve to shift is called the simple multiplier. Several problems are devoted to calculating the simple multiplier and you will learn that its value depends on the value of the marginal propensity to spend.

If a shift in the AD curve causes the price level to change, then the value of the multiplier is smaller than the value of the simple multiplier.

An exercise is provided to illustrate that an AD curve is downward sloping because price level changes evoke opposite changes in real wealth and desired consumption expenditure.

MULTIPLE-CHOICE QUESTIONS

1. Movement along an aggregate expenditure function
   (a) represents a change in prices at every level of national income
   (b) causes a change in the equilibrium level of national income
   (c) represents induced changes in expenditure caused by changes in national income
   (d) has no effect on the level of national income

2. A change in the equilibrium level of national income is caused by
   (a) a shift in the aggregate expenditure function
   (b) only a movement along the aggregate expenditure function
   (c) an increase in output with aggregate expenditure remaining constant
   (d) a change in taxes caused by a change in national income

3. Increases in national income are predicted to be caused by increases in all but which of the following, other things being equal?
   (a) taxes
   (b) exports
   (c) government expenditure
   (d) investment

4. Decreases in national income are predicted to be caused by increases in all but which of the following, other things being equal?
   (a) the marginal propensity to save
   (b) tax rates
   (c) imports
   (d) exports

5. A decrease in the marginal propensity to spend out of national income will cause the AE function to
   (a) shift upward in a parallel fashion
   (b) shift downward in a parallel fashion
   (c) decrease in slope
   (d) have a steeper slope

6. The effect on national income of a fall in investment could be offset by
(a) a rise in saving at each level of income
(b) a rise in the tax rate
(c) a rise in the government expenditures
(d) a rise in imports at each level of income

7. The <u>simple</u> multiplier measures
(a) the extent to which national income will change in response to a change in autonomous expenditure at a constant price level.
(b) the rise in expenditures caused by a change in national income
(c) the marginal propensity to spend
(d) the extent to which national income will change in response to a change in autonomous expenditure at varying price levels

8. Which of the following formulaes is the correct expression for the simple multiplier?
(a) $K = 1/(1 - z)$, where z is the marginal propensity to spend
(b) $K = 1/(1 + z)$, where z is the marginal propensity to spend
(c) $K = \Delta A/\Delta Y$, where ΔA is the change in autonomous expenditure and Y is real national income
(d) $K = 1/z$, where z is the marginal propensity to spend

9. If expenditure in the economy did not depend upon the level of national income, the value of the simple multiplier would be
(a) zero
(b) unity
(c) infinite or undefined
(d) -1

10. If the marginal propensity not to spend is .2, the simple multiplier is
(a) equal to the marginal propensity to spend
(b) 2.0
(c) 5.0
(d) 1.25

11. Assuming a horizontal aggregate supply curve and a marginal propensity to spend of 0.75, an increase in autonomous expenditure of $1 million should increase equilibrium national income by
(a) $1 million
(b) $250,000
(c) $4 million
(d) $750,000

12. Other things being equal, a rise in the price level will cause
(a) a lower equilibrium level of national income
(b) a lower value of real wealth
(c) increases in saving at every level of national income
(d) all of the above

13. The aggregate demand curve illustrates
(a) levels of equilibrium real national income that correspond with given price levels
(b) all of the price levels corresponding with a constant equilibrium income
(c) all of the equilibrium real income levels corresponding with a particular price level
(d) levels of aggregate expenditure that correspond with given national income levels

14. Movement along an aggregate demand curve
(a) results from a shift in the aggregate expenditure function at a given price level
(b) shows the response of equilibrium real national income to a change in the price level
(c) results from a movement along an aggregate expenditure function
(d) none of the above

15. If an economy is operating on the upward-sloping portion of the short-run aggregate supply curve, an increase in aggregate demand will
(a) increase the price level but not real GNP in the short run
(b) increase real income, but not the price level in the short run
(c) increase neither real income nor the price level
(d) increase both real income and the price level in the short run

Questions 16 through 21 refer to the diagram below. Assume that the price level is constant for all levels of real national income.

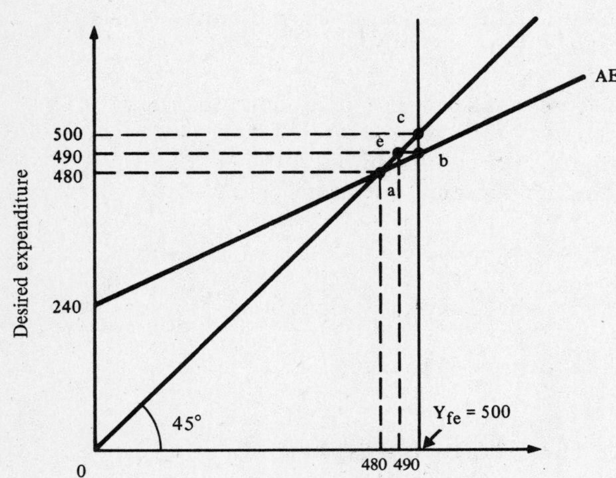

16. The level of autonomous expenditure is
(a) 240 (c) 0
(b) 480 (d) 490

17. With the aggregate expenditure curve labeled AE, the current equilibrium level of real national income is
(a) 500 (c) 490
(b) 480 (d) at point b

18. The AE curve has a slope of
(a) 0.5 (c) 12/25
(b) 2.0 (d) 0.6

19. The value of the simple multiplier is
(a) 2.0 (c) 2.5
(b) 0.5 (d) 1.9

20. Suppose that government expenditure increased by 5 at all levels of real national income. The aggregate expenditure function would
(a) shift upward by 10 and intersect the 45° line at point c
(b) shift upward by 5, have a slope of 0.5 and intersect the 45° line at point e
(c) intersect the 45° line somewhere between e and c
(d) shift upward by 5 and increase in slope

21. The increase in government expenditure of 5 causes equilibrium real national income to
    (a) increase in total by 5
    (b) increase by the autonomous increase of 5 plus another 5 of induced expenditure
    (c) decrease in total by 10
    (d) increase in total by the autonomous increase of 5 plus one-half of the 5 due to induced expenditure

Questions 22 to 27 refer to the following diagrams:

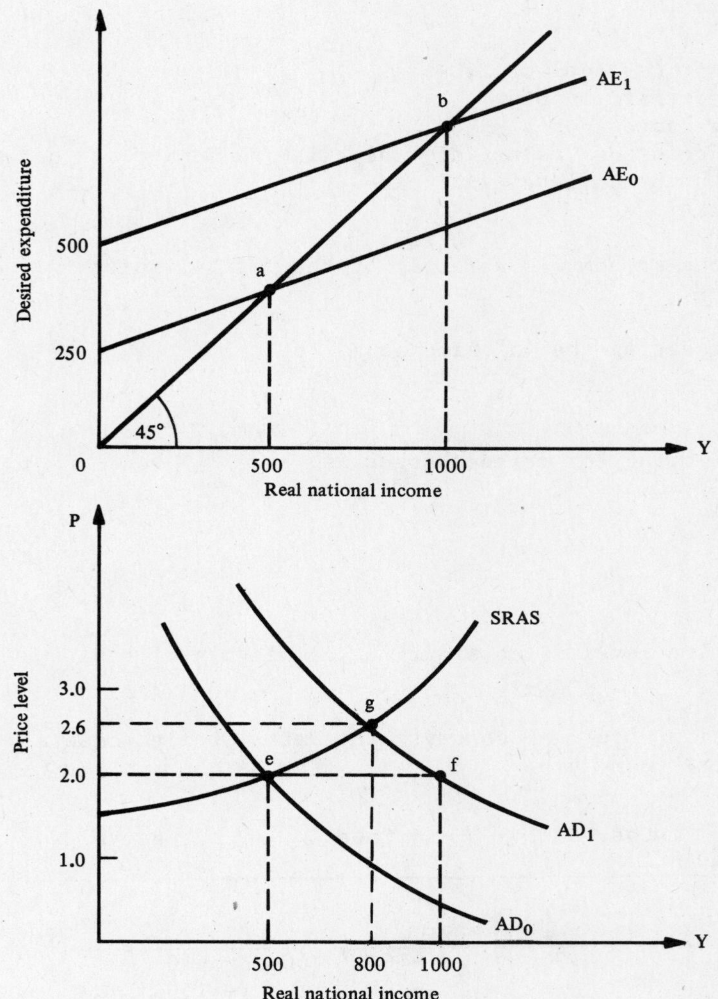

22. According to the curves labeled AE_0 and AD_0, the equilibrium levels of price and real national income are, respectively,
    (a) 2 and 500
    (b) 2.6 and 800
    (c) 2 and 1000
    (d) none of the above

23. Assuming that the AE curve shifts from AE_0 to AE_1 but the price level remains constant at its initial level, we can say that
   (a) autonomous expenditure must have increased by 250
   (b) real national income increases by 500
   (c) the aggregate demand curve shifts to the right so that Y = 1000 at the price level 2.0
   (d) all of the above

24. The value of the simple multiplier is
   (a) 5.0
   (b) 0.5
   (c) 2.0
   (d) 4.0

25. Given the curves SRAS and AD_1 and a price level of 2,
   (a) aggregate demand is less than aggregate supply
   (b) aggregate demand is equal to aggregate supply
   (c) firms will be unwilling to produce enough to satisfy the existing demand at the existing price level and hence the price level will rise
   (d) the price level is likely to fall

26. The final short-run equilibrium in the economy as a result of the initial shift in the AE curve will be
   (a) at point f
   (b) depicted by a new AE curve intersecting the 45° line at Y = 800
   (c) at point g
   (d) both (b) and (c)

27. The value of the multiplier after allowing for price changes is
   (a) 1.2
   (b) 2.0
   (c) 1.0
   (d) 4.0

EXERCISES

Exercises 1 through 4 assume that the price level is constant for all levels of real national income (a Keynesian SRAS curve).

1. You are given the following information about an economy. The data labelled case A represent the initial situation in the economy.

	Case A					Case B		Case C		Case D	
Y	C	I	G	(X - M)	AE	I	AE	(X-M)	AE	C	AE
0	10	50	10	10	80	60	90	-10	60	10	80
200	190	50	10	-10	240	60	___	-30	___	150	___
300	280	50	10	-20	320	60	___	-40	___	220	___
400	370	50	10	-30	400	60	___	-50	___	290	___
450	415	50	10	-35	440	60	___	-55	___	325	___

   (a) For case A, determine the equilibrium level of real national income and the marginal propensity to spend.

(b) Plot the aggregate expenditure curve in the diagram below and indicate the equilibrium level of real national income (Case A).

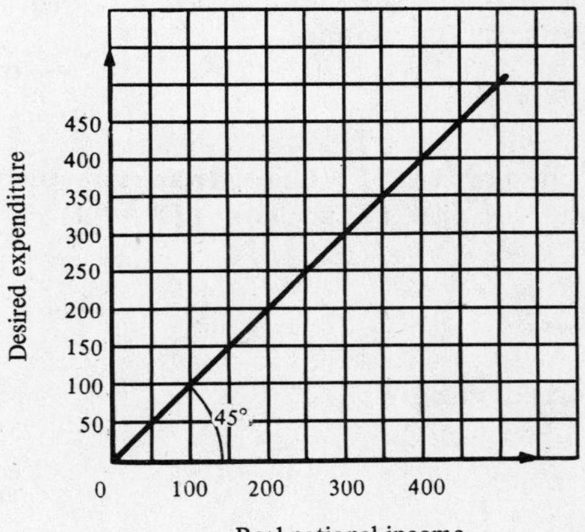

(c) Now assume that a change occurs in the economy such that case B holds. Case B is identical to case A except that investment at every level of Y increases from 50 to 60. Fill in the missing values in the previous table for AE and plot the new aggregate expenditure curve in the diagram above. What has happened to the aggregate expenditure curve? (Compare case A with case B.)

(d) Using the AE curve for case B, what is the value of desired AE at a level of real national income of 400? What do you predict will happen to the equilibrium level of real national income in this situation? Explain.

(e) What is the equilibrium level of real national income for case B? What has been the total change in real national income (ΔY) between case A and B? Calculate the ratio $\Delta Y/\Delta I$ from A to B. What is the value of the simple multiplier?

(f) Calculate the value of the marginal propensity to spend (denoted as z in the text) for case B? Using the formula K = 1(1 - z), confirm your answer for the value of the simple multiplier in part (e).

(g) The total change in income is composed of two parts: the change in the autonomous component of AE (ΔA), which in this case is ΔI, and the induced change in aggregate expenditure (ΔN). What is the value for ΔN? What was the change in consumption? The change in (X - M)?

2. Assume that case A is the initial situation and that exports at every level of income fall such that a new (X - M) has fallen by 20 at every level of Y.

   (a) Fill in the missing values of AE for case C. What is the new equilibrium level of real national income? What is the marginal propensity to spend?

   (b) Comparing case A with case C, what is the total change in Y? Calculate the value of the multiplier. Calculate the change in ΔA and ΔN (in this case $\Delta(X - M)$.

   (c) What happened to the AE curve? (Compare case A with case C.)

3. Assume that case A is the initial situation but that factors in the economy change such that case D applies. Case D is identical to case A except that the consumption function is now quite different.

   (a) Calculate the marginal propensities to consume out of national income for both cases and indicate the nature of the behavioral change between the two cases.

   (b) Fill in the missing values of AE for case D. Plot the new aggregate expenditure curve in the diagram on page 183 and compare it with that for case A.

   (c) Calculate the marginal propensity to spend for case D and compare it with that for case A. Calculate the multiplier value and compare it with the multiplier for case A.

   (d) What is the equilibrium level of real national income for case D?

4. You are given the following equations:

Equation 1: the consumption function

$$C = 30 + 0.9Y_d$$

Equation 2: the relationship between Y_d and Y

$$Y_d = 0.8Y$$

Equation 3: investment expenditures

$$I = 40$$

Equation 4: government expenditures

$$G = 20$$

Equation 5: the net export function

$$(X - M) = 20 - 0.12Y$$

Equation 6: the AE expenditure identity

$$AE = C + I + G + (X - M)$$

Equation 7: the equilibrium condition

$$AE = Y$$

(a) Substitute equation 2 into equation 1 and solve for C in terms of Y. Call this equation 8.

(b) Substitute equations 8, 3, 4, and 5 into the right-hand side of equation 6. What is the value of the slope of the AE function ($\Delta AE/\Delta Y$)? This is the marginal propensity to spend.

(c) Using equation 7, solve for the equilibrium level of Y.

(d) Now suppose that the federal government raised the personal income tax rate such that equation 2 changed to $Y_d = 0.689Y$. Call this equation 9.

(i) Substitute equation 9 into equation 1 and solve for C in terms of Y. Call this equation 10.

(ii) Substitute equations 10, 3, 4, and 5 into the right-hand side of equation 6. What is the slope of this AE function? Compare it with the value you obtained for part (b).

(iii) Using equation 7 and the new expression for the aggregate expenditure function, solve for the equilibrium level of Y. Compare this with your answer to part (c).

(e) Calculate and compare the value of the simple multipliers before and after the tax rate increase.

5. The Derivation of an Aggregate Demand Curve

The consumption function for an economy is $C = 60 + 0.8Y + 0.1\ (W/p)$ where W/p is real wealth. All other components of desired aggregate expenditure are assumed to be autonomous and the sum of these components is 100. The nominal value of wealth (W) is assumed to be 400.

(a) What is the value of real wealth when p = 1.0? When p = 0.5? When p = 2.0? What do you conclude happens to the value of real wealth when the price level increases?

(b) What happens to the value of consumption at each level of real national income when the value of real wealth increases? Decreases? Inspect the values in columns 2, 3, and 4 in the schedule below to confirm your answers.

Real National Income Y	Desired Consumption C			I+G+X-M	Desired Aggregate Expenditure AE		
	p = 1.0	p = 0.5	p = 2.0		p = 1.0	p = 0.5	p=2.0
0	100	140	80	100	200	240	180
800	740	780	720	100	840	880	820
900	820	860	800	100	920	960	900
1000	900	940	880	100	1000	1040	980
1100	980	1020	960	100	1080	1120	1060
1200	1060	1100	1040	100	1160	1200	1140

(c) An aggregate demand curve plots combinations of equilibrium real national income associated with given price levels. What is the equilibrium national income level associated with a price level of 1.0? Plot the AD curve in the diagram below for the three price levels indicated in the table above.

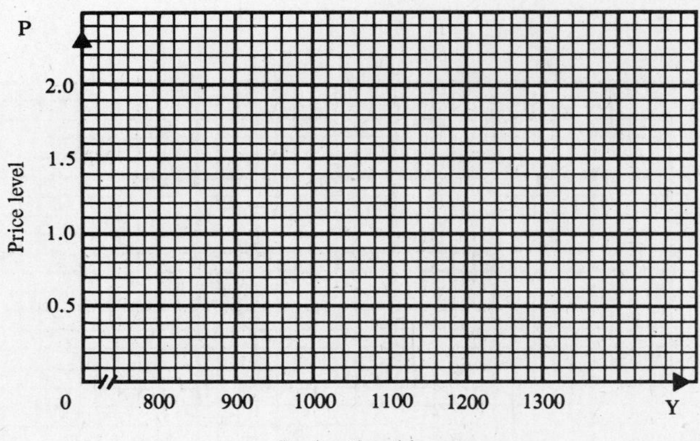

(d) An increase in the price level, <u>other things being equal</u>, causes a movement along the AD curve while shifting the AE curve downward. Do you agree? Explain.

(e) Suppose that the value of I + G + X - M falls from 100 to 80 at all levels of Y. What is the new equilibrium level of Y when p = 1? When p = 0.5? When p = 2.? Plot the new AD curve in the diagram above.

6. The Value of the Multiplier Allowing for Price Changes

You are given the following information about an economy:

The aggregate demand function,

$$p = \frac{60}{(.2Y - 25)}$$

The short-run aggregate supply function: $p = .02Y$

The AE function: $AE = 0.8Y + 25 + 0.1(W/p)$

p represents the price level, Y represents national income, and W is nominal wealth. The marginal propensity to spend is 0.8 and the nominal value of wealth is 600.

(a) Plot the AD and SRAS curves in the diagram below:

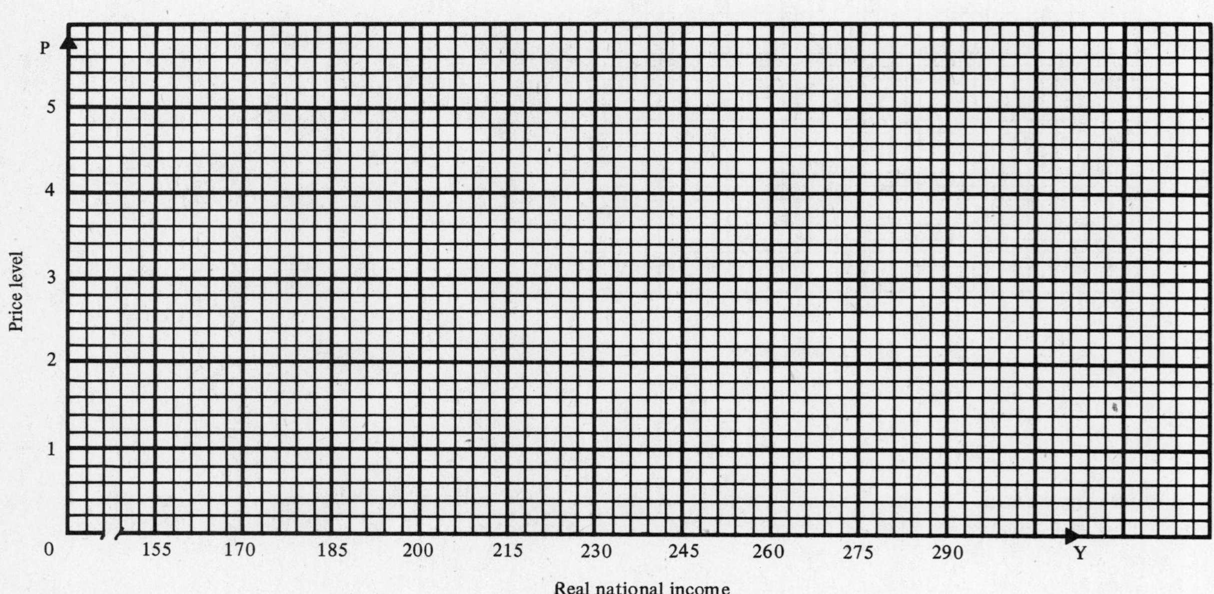

(b) According to your diagram, what are the equilibrium values of p and Y?

(c) Using the equilibrium condition, Y = AE, prove that your answer for the equilibrium value of Y (when p = 4) in part (b) is confirmed.

(d) What is the value of the simple multiplier?

(e) Suppose that the AE function becomes AE = 0.8Y + 10 + .1(W/p) because a component of autonomous expenditure decreases by 15. As a consequence, the AD function becomes

$p = \frac{60}{0.2Y - 10}$. This expression when plotted lies to the left of the initial AD curve.

If the price level remained at 4 for the time being, what is the new equilibrium level of Y according to the new AE function? [Note: This is not a permanent equilibrium value, as the next question points out.]

(f) What is the quantity of output supplied at a price level of 4 according to the SRAS function? What is the quantity demanded at a price level of 4 according to the new AD function?

(g) In the situation depicted in part (f), the price level will fall. Prove that the new AD curve intersects the SRAS curve at a price level of 3 and a real income level of 150.

(h) A fall in autonomous expenditure of 15 triggered a decline in the equilibrium level of Y of 50. What is the value of the multiplier which allows for price level changes? How does this value compare with the value of the simple multiplier?

CHAPTER 30

CHANGES IN NATIONAL INCOME II:

THE ROLE OF AGGREGATE SUPPLY

CHAPTER OBJECTIVES

This chapter begins by discussing the economic factors which explain why a SRAS curve may have a positive and increasing slope. Three possible ranges of a SRAS curve are identified: the Keynesian range, the intermediate range, and the classical range. Several problems are devoted to testing your understanding that the shape of the SRAS curve is crucially important in determining the short-run effects on real national income and the price level of shifts in the AD curve. The causes and effects of shifts in the SRAS curve are also discussed.

The chapter stresses that the long-run aggregate supply curve is drawn vertically at the potential level of real national income. Some problems are designed to enhance your appreciation of the implications of a vertical LRAS curve. Specifically, you will see that shifts in the AD curve affect short-run real national income but have no effect on national income in the long run, and providing that wages and prices are flexible, both inflationary and recessionary gaps may be eliminated without government intervention. However, many economists believe that elimination of a recessionary gap by wage and price adjustments is likely to be very slow, causing unacceptably high levels of unemployment for lengthy periods of time.

MULTIPLE-CHOICE QUESTIONS

1. The positive slope of the short-run aggregate supply (SRAS) curve indicates that
   (a) the price level and real national income are negatively related
   (b) a higher price level is associated with a higher level of real national income
   (c) final output prices and input costs are negatively related
   (d) there is no association between real national income and the price level in the short run

2. The increasing slope of the SRAS curve is meant to reflect which one of the following?
   (a) below potential national income, changes in output are accompanied by only small changes in the price level
   (b) above potential national income, changes in real income are accompanied by only small changes in the price level
   (c) below potential national income, changes in real income are accompanied by large changes in the price level
   (d) above potential national income, changes in output are accompanied by large increases in factor prices

Questions 3 through 6 refer to the diagram below:

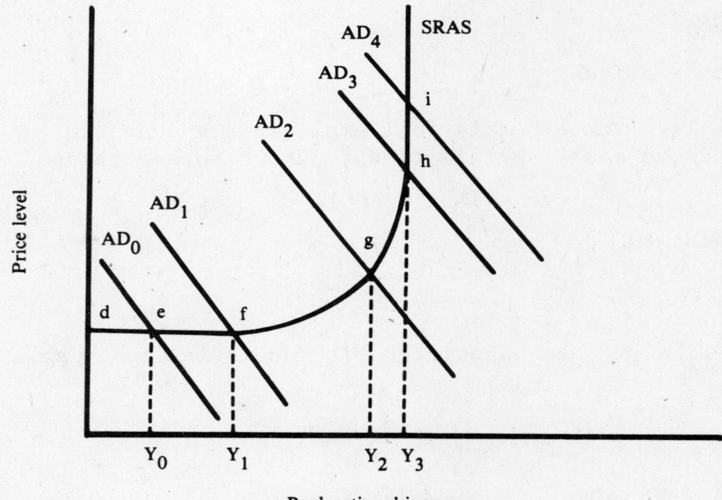

3. The Keynesian range of the SRAS curve is defined by the line segment
   (a) df
   (b) fh
   (c) hi
   (d) fi

4. Point i is in the
   (a) Keynesian range of the SRAS curve
   (b) intermediate range of the SRAS curve
   (c) recessionary gap
   (d) classical range of the SRAS curve

5. Assuming that the aggregate demand curve shifts from AD_1 to AD_2,
   (a) nominal GNP increases in the short run, whereas real GNP is constant
   (b) it is likely that unemployment will increase
   (c) prices and output will both increase at least in the short run
   (d) factor prices will rise

6. Assuming that the aggregate demand curve shifts from AD_3 to AD_4
   (a) the aggregate expenditure curve will shift upward to a permanently higher position
   (b) the aggregate expenditure curve will shift downward to a permanently lower position
   (c) the aggregate expenditure curve will shift upward temporarily but as the price level increases, will shift downward to its original position
   (d) none of the above

7. The SRAS curve will shift in response to a change in all <u>but</u> which one of the following?
   (a) factor prices
   (b) productivity of inputs
   (c) the price level
   (d) factor supplies which change factor prices

8. From an initial real national income level with nearly full employment and a stable price level, which of the following could cause an inflationary shock, other things being equal?
   (a) an increase in taxes
   (b) a sharp rise in investment expenditure
   (c) an increase in imports
   (d) an increase in desired saving

9. Which one of the following is least likely to be associated with an inflationary gap, other things being equal?
   (a) rising output
   (b) increasing employment
   (c) increasing unemployment
   (d) a rising price level

10. If wages were sufficiently flexible downward,
   (a) upward shifts in SRAS could offset recessionary shocks
   (b) downward shifts in SRAS could offset recessionary shocks
   (c) upward shifts in SRAS could offset inflationary shocks
   (d) downward shifts in SRAS could offset inflationary shocks

11. Important lessons learned from the experience of the Great Depression include all <u>but</u> which one of the following?
   (a) Price levels can be very slow to adjust in a downward direction.
   (b) Large recessionary gaps can persist for a relatively long time unless there is sufficient stimulus from the demand side.
   (c) Price levels can either rise or fall even with large GNP gaps.
   (d) Price levels must fall in order to eliminate a recessionary gap.

12. When the long-run aggregate supply curve is vertical,
   (a) aggregate supply determines real national income and aggregate demand determines the price level
   (b) output is determined solely by the level of aggregate demand
   (c) equilibrium real national income is indeterminate
   (d) the price level is determined solely by aggregate supply

13. The primary purpose of the tax incentives recommended by supply-side economists was to
   (a) decrease aggregate demand
   (b) decrease aggregate supply
   (c) decrease both aggregate demand and aggregate supply
   (d) increase potential output

14. The combination of a rising price level and falling real output can be caused by
   (a) aggregate demand shifts along a given SRAS curve
   (b) the automatic adjustment mechanism of a deflationary shock
   (c) rightward shifts in the LRAS curve
   (d) SRAS shifts to the left along a particular AD curve

15. With a vertical LRAS curve, shifts in the AD curve
    (a) have no effects on real national income in the long run
    (b) have no effects on the price level in the long run
    (c) change the level of real national income in the long run
    (d) change the level of potential real national income

EXERCISES

1. Assume that an economy has a downward-sloping AD curve and an upward-sloping SRAS curve. For each of the following changes, indicate the response in terms of a shift in or movement along the AD curve or the SRAS curve and the effect on real GNP and the price level. In all cases, assume a short-run time period and that all other things are equal. Indicate shifts in the curves by "S" and movement along the curves by "A." In the last two columns, indicate increases as "+," decreases as "-," and no change as "0."

Event	Aggregate Demand Curve	Aggregate Short-run Supply Curve	Real National Income	Price Level
(a) An increase in exports				
(b) An increase in the price of imported production inputs				
(c) A major reduction in government expenditure				
(d) An increase in labor productivity due to a technological change				

2. Analyze the long-run effects on the price level and real national income of events (a) and (c) in the preceding question. In both cases assume that the economy was at its potential level of real national income <u>before</u> the change. Make sure you indicate your assumptions concerning the degree of flexibility of wages in the long run.

3. The aggregate demand function is given by the expression $P = 40 - 2Y$, and the SRAS curve is given by the following:

(i) $P = 20$ for $0 \leq Y \leq 30$*;

(ii) $P = 5 + 0.5Y$ for $30 \leq Y \leq 50$, and

(iii) $Y = 50$ for $P \geq 30$

*$0 \leq Y \leq 30$ means that real income has a range greater than or equal to zero but less than or equal to 30.

(a) Plot the AD curve in the diagram below and carefully indicate the intercept values. Label the curve AD_0.

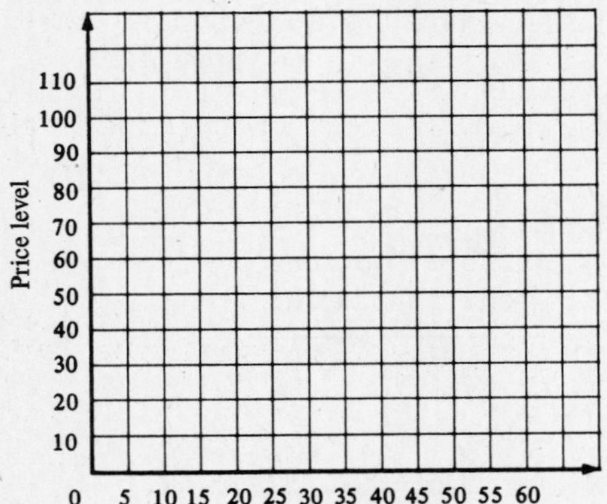

(b) Plot the SRAS curve in the diagram. Indicate the Keynesian, intermediate, and classical ranges.

(c) Referring to the diagram, what are the equilibrium levels of P and Y? Prove algebraically that the intersection of equation (i) and the AD expression yields these equilibrium values.

(d) Suppose the expression for the AD curve became $P = 80 - 2Y$. Plot this expression in the diagram (label it AD_1) and discuss the short-run changes in P and Y that are likely to occur.

(e) Suppose the expression for the AD curve became $P = 105 - 2Y$. Plot this relationship (AD_2) and determine the new short-run equilibrium levels of P and Y. Compare short-run equilibrium price levels and outputs for AD_2 and AD_1.

4. An economy has a SRAS function given by P = 1 + 0.01Y which is presented below in schedule form, where P is the price level and Y is the level of real national income. The long-run aggregate supply curve is vertical at a real national income level of 1000. Two schedules for the AD curve are presented below, with case I being the initial situation.

SRAS		LRAS		AD Case I		AD Case II	
Y	P	Y	P	Y	P	Y	P
0	1.0	1000	1.0	0	111	0	116.5
500	6.0	1000	6.0	500	61	500	66.5
1000	11.0	1000	11.0	1000	11	1000	16.5
1050	11.5	1000	11.5	1050	6	1050	11.5

(a) Taking case I for the AD curve, what are the equilibrium levels of P and Y? What is the value of the GNP gap?

(b) Assume that the AD curve shifts upward, represented by case II. If the SRAS curve does not change immediately, what are the new short-run equilibrium values for P and Y? What type of gap exists and what is its magnitude?

(c) Given the shift to the AD curve, what do you predict will happen in the long-run to the equilibrium levels of P and Y? What will happen to the short run GNP gap?

(d) Explain what is likely to happen to the SRAS curve in the long run and rewrite the algebraic expression for it assuming the slope of the SRAS curve does not change.

CHAPTER 31

BUSINESS CYCLES: THE EBB AND FLOW OF ECONOMIC ACTIVITY

CHAPTER OBJECTIVES

This chapter focuses on factors which cause fluctuations in national income and describes the various phases of a business cycle. The main sources of disturbances are aggregate demand shocks caused by shifts in the four main components of aggregate expenditure. Several problems test your knowledge of the factors that cause changes in these components.

Changes in investment and net exports are two of the most important determinants of business cycles in Canada. One problem demonstrates how a business cycle in a foreign economy may be transmitted to a particular domestic economy. The chapter also outlines the accelerator theory of investment and an exercise illustrates the multiplier accelerator theory of cyclical movements in national income.

MULTIPLE-CHOICE QUESTIONS

1. A trough is characterized by
   (a) high unemployment of labor
   (b) large amounts of unused industrial capacity
   (c) low business profits and pessimistic expectations about future profits
   (d) all of the above

2. There is a consensus among students of economic fluctuations that
   (a) there is a common pattern of variation that pervades most economic series
   (b) there is little difference from cycle to cycle in duration or in amplitude
   (c) there are few, if any, differences among economic series in their particular patterns of fluctuations.
   (d) there are factors at work causing the economy to display continual long-term fluctuations around its short-term rising growth trend

3. The largest component of aggregate expenditure in Canada is
   (a) consumption expenditure
   (b) government expenditure
   (c) net exports
   (d) investment expenditure

4. The upper turning point will <u>not</u> include which one of the following?
   (a) a high degree of utilization of existing capacity
   (b) a high unemployment rate
   (c) shortages of certain key raw materials
   (d) shortages of labor in certain key skill categories

5. Which one of the following would tend to shift the consumption function upward?
   (a) Real interest rates increase
   (b) Prices are expected to fall in the future.
   (c) Government lowers income tax rates.
   (d) Increased uncertainty lowers expectations about future income.

6. You pay $8 interest for a $100 loan for one year, during which the annual rate of inflation is 5 percent. The real rate of interest is
   (a) 8 percent
   (b) 3 percent
   (c) 13 percent
   (d) none of the above

7. Which one of the following will tend to increase Canadian exports?
   (a) a rise in the Canadian dollar's exchange rate
   (b) a decrease in the Canadian price level relative to foreign price levels
   (c) an increase in domestic firms' costs relative to foreign costs
   (d) a recession in the economy of a major trading partner such as the United States

8. If you were measuring the total amount of investment expenditure, which of the following would you not include?
   (a) purchases of stocks and bonds
   (b) changes in inventories
   (c) new residential construction
   (d) business fixed investment

9. Other things being equal, investment in inventories tends to vary
   (a) positively with production and sales; negatively with interest rates
   (b) negatively with production and sales; negatively with interest rates
   (c) positively with production and sales; positively with interest rates
   (d) negatively with production and sales; positively with interest rates

10. The fact that there are many different interest rates rather than a single interest rate for all borrowers is because interest rates reflect
   (a) differences in risk
   (b) differences in maturity dates
   (c) differences in costs of administering credit
   (d) all of the above

11. Other things being equal, which one of the following is likely to increase business fixed investment?
   (a) an increase in interest rates
   (b) an increase in corporate tax rates
   (c) an increase in national income
   (d) expectations of lower future profits

12. According to the accelerator theory, net investment is a function of
   (a) the level of national income
   (b) changes in national income and a constant capital-output ratio
   (c) changes in national income and a variable capital-output ratio
   (d) savings

13. If for every one unit of output produced, three units of capital are required, then
   (a) the capital-output ratio is one-third
   (b) the capital-output ratio is three
   (c) six units of capital are required to produce three units of output
   (d) three units of labor services are necessarily required as well

14. The multiplier and accelerator effects operating together
   (a) tend to cancel out
   (b) help to explain why movements of the economy tend to acquire momentum
   (c) make the amplitude of cycles less than they otherwise would be
   (d) tend to keep economic growth going perpetually

15. Imagine an economy that has been in a recovery following a depression. In its initial stages, it should be characterized by all but which one of the following?
   (a) increases in aggregate demand
   (b) rising incomes
   (c) increased inflation
   (d) favorable business and consumer expectations

16. Today most economists agree that
   (a) most business cycles are politically inspired
   (b) all cycles are characterized by a lengthy period of severe inflation
   (c) most cycles last for a one-year period
   (d) there is not a single cause or class of causes governing business cycles

17. Domestic absorption is defined as
   (a) the difference between exports and imports
   (b) the sum of all aggregate expenditures
   (c) the sum of total expenditure on all goods and services for use within the domestic economy
   (d) national income plus net exports when national income is at its equilibrium level

EXERCISES

1. Illustrating the Accelerator Principle
The table below shows the hypothetical situation for a firm that requires 1 machine for every 1000 units of product it turns out annually. As it increases its output and sales in response to changing demand, show how its investment will be affected. Replacement for depreciation is one machine per year throughout.

Year	Annual Output (units)	Units of Capital Needed	New Machines Required	Replacement Machines	Total Machines to Be Purchased (Desired Investment)
1	10,000	10	0	1	1
2	10,000	______	______	1	______
3	11,000	______	______	1	______
4	12,000	______	______	1	______
5	15,000	______	______	1	______
6	17,000	______	______	1	______
7	18,000	______	______	1	______
8	18,000	______	______	1	______

(a) Between year 2 and year 5, output increased by what percent? ______
(b) In the same period, the firm's desired investment increased by what percent? ______
(c) Plot the cyclical fluctuation in desired investment in the diagram below.

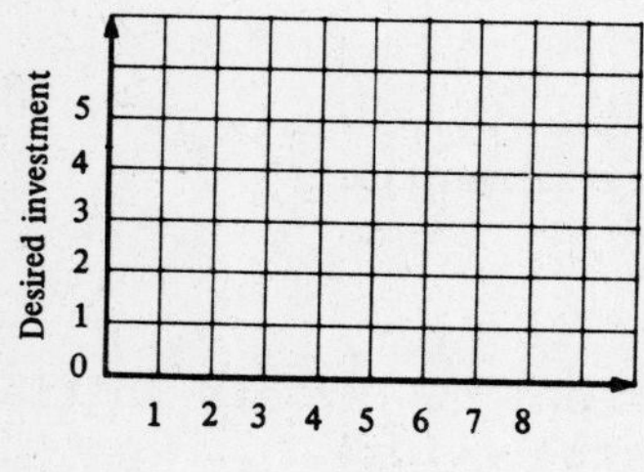

2. A seller of shirts has had weekly sales of 100 and tries to keep inventory in stock equal to twice its weekly sales, adjusting weekly orders from the jobber according to the current week's sales. Complete the following table showing how actual inventory and orders from the store's supplier would change as weekly sales change.

Week	Weekly Sales	Actual Inventory, End of Week	Inventory/ Sales Ratio	Desired Inventory	Desired Inventory Plus Expected Sales	Weekly Orders for Next Week
1	100	200	2	200	300	100
2	100	200	2	200	300	100
3	110	190	1.7	220	330	140
4	110	220	___	___	___	___
5	120	210	___	___	___	___
6	120	240	___	___	___	___
7	110	250	___	___	___	___
8	110	220	___	___	___	___
9	100	230	___	___	___	___

(a) The range of weekly sales was from ____________ to ________________.
(b) The range of weekly orders was from ____________ to ____________.
(c) How do these findings illustrate the accelerator theory?

3. Assume there are two consumers in economy, Tom and Kerry. Their consumption schedules as well as the average aggregate schedule are illustrated below.

Kerry		Tom		Average Aggregate	
C	Y_d	C	Y_d	C	Y_d
80	0	80	0	80	0
980	1000	580	1000	780	1000
1880	2000	1080	2000	1480	2000
2780	3000	1580	3000	2180	3000

(a) Calculate the marginal propensities to consume for Kerry and Tom as well as for the average aggregate schedule.

(b) Suppose that the government increases taxes on Tom and gives all of this tax revenue to Kerry. Assuming that the MPC values do not change for either Tom or Kerry, calculate the new values of C and fill in the table below.

AFTER INCOME DISTRIBUTION

Kerry		Tom		Average Aggregate	
C	Y_d	C	Y_d	C	Y_d
80	0	80	0	80	0
1070	1100	530	900	800	1000
____	2200	____	1800	____	2000
____	3300	____	2700	____	3000

(c) Calculate the MPC for the average aggregate case after the income redistribution program and compare it with the original value.

(d) What has happened to the aggregate consumption function?

4. For some countries such as Canada and the United Kingdom, exports comprise a large share of GNP. For example, approximately 30 percent of Canada's GNP is comprised of exports, making Canada's economy activity critically dependent on foreigners' willingness to buy Canadian goods and services, and allowing cycles in foreign economic activity to be transmitted to Canada. A major determinant of foreign imports is their national income, which itself can display cyclical activity.

You are given the following hypothetical relationship between foreign income and Canadian exports. Assume that the export multiplier on Canadian GNP is 2.

Year	Foreign GNP	Canadian Exports	Δ In Canadian GNP
1	100	10	
2	150	15	+10
3	200	20	____
4	180	18	____
5	100	10	____
6	100	10	____

(a) Deduce the relationship between foreign GNP and Canadian exports. List some factors that explain why foreign income levels might determine Canadian exports.

(b) Assume that exports change between two years, and the multiplier process works itself through by the end of the second year. On this basis, fill in the missing values for the change in the Canadian GNP.

(c) Has a business cycle been transmitted to Canada? Does it have the same basic characteristics of the foreign business cycle?

5. Changes in Desired Capital Stocks

The following two schedules relate desired capital stock to the interest rate.

Schedule A		Schedule B	
Capital Stock	Interest Rate(%)	Capital Stock	Interest Rate (%)
100	20	150	20
200	18	250	18
300	14	350	14
400	8	450	8
500	1	550	1

(a) Inspect both schedules. Does a negative or positive relationship exist between the desired capital stock and the rate of interest? ________________

(b) Assuming schedule A applies, if the current rate of interest rates falls from 20 percent to 18 percent, what is the change in the desired capital stock? Desired investment?

(c) Suppose that the schedule given by A suddenly changed to that given by schedule B. With a current interest rate of 14 percent, what is the new magnitude of the desired capital stock? Does the change in the schedule imply new desired investment activity? Indicate two factors that may have caused the schedule to change.

6. <u>The Multiplier-Accelerator Interaction Theory</u>
The multiplier when combined with the accelerator may generate fluctuations in national income. For this model we have assumed: (1) the marginal propensity to consume is 0.5; (2) consumption in time period t depends on the level of income one period past (t - 1); (3) the capital-output ratio, or what is often referred to as the accelerator coefficient, is constant and equal to 1; and (4) investment in time period t depends on an autonomous amount, 100, plus the difference in income between t - 1 and t - 2.

These assumptions are expressed by the following equations:

$$C_t = 0.5Y_{t-1}$$

and

$$I_t = 100 + 1[(Y_{t-1}) - (Y_{t-2})]$$

Therefore, since Y = C + I,

$$Y_t = 0.5Y_{t-1} + 100 + 1\,[(Y_{t-1}) - (Y_{t-2})]$$

The economy is assumed to be at an equilibrium level of income of 200 in the current time period 0 and has been at that level for two previous periods, -2 and -1. In period 1 autonomous investment increases from 100 to 200 and stays at that level permanently.

The effect of this increase shows up in national income in period 1 as simply an increase of 100. Why? Since consumption depends on the last period's income (period 0), and income is 200, the consumption level remains at a level of 100. Furthermore, there is no accelerator effect in period 1 since the difference between income in period 0 and period -1 (one period and two periods removed from period 1, respectively) is zero.

However, interesting things start to occur to national income thereafter. We have started the process by completing the entries until period 6.

(a) Fill in the missing values for periods 6 through 9 in the chart below.

Period	Consumption $C_t = 0.5Y_{t-1}$	Investment (I_t): Autonomous	Investment (I_t): Accelerator $1(Y_{t-1}-Y_{t-2})$	National Income $Y_t = C_t + I_t$
-2	100	100	0	200
-1	100	100	0	200
0	100	100	0	200
1	100	200	0	300
2	150	200	100	450
3	225	200	150	575
4	287.5	200	125	612.5
5	306.3	200	37.5	543.8
6	_____	200	_____	_____
7	_____	200	_____	_____
8	_____	200	_____	_____
9	_____	200	_____	_____

(b) Identify by period(s) the trough of the cycle, the peak, the expansion phase, and the recession phase.

(c) Did the accelerator process counteract or reinforce the multiplier process during the expansion phase? The recession phase?

(d) Assume that the autonomous element of investment is sensitive to the rate of interest. What changes in the level of the rate of interest might the government of this economy pursue in periods 2 to 4 and periods 5 to 8 to "smooth out" this business cycle?

CHAPTER 32

FISCAL POLICY

CHAPTER OBJECTIVES

Fiscal policy refers to the use of tax policies and public expenditures to achieve specific economic objectives such as a lower rate of inflation or a reduction in the unemployment rate. Tax revenues and public expenditures may change automatically as a consequence of changing economic conditions or as a deliberate result of policy. Regardless of the forces which change government revenues and expenditures, the budget balance will be affected. This chapter tests your understanding of how the budget balance changes as national income changes and the extent to which the budget balance at full employment can be used to monitor fiscal policy. The exercises review the method by which fiscal policy can, theoretically, close the GNP gap and demonstrate the potential impact which deficit financing may have on interest rates and on private sector economic activity.

1. Fiscal policy refers to
   (a) government's attempt to regulate individual prices
   (b) budget results that change procyclically
   (c) the use of tax, expenditure, and debt management policies to reach desired levels of national income
   (d) government's attempt to have revenues exactly equal to expenditures

2. An increase in government spending accompanied by an equal increase in tax revenues
   (a) reduces the size of the public debt
   (b) must be financed by selling Treasury bills or bonds to commercial banks
   (c) has no effect on the relative shares of public and private sector economic activity
   (d) is called a balanced budget change in spending

3. An increase in the government's budget deficit, assuming private expenditure functions do not shift,
   (a) is an example of contractionary fiscal policy
   (b) would be an appropriate policy for closing an inflationary gap
   (c) will shift the aggregate demand curve to the right
   (d) will have no effect on aggregate demand

4. If there is currently an inflationary gap, an appropriate fiscal policy would be to
   (a) increase taxes
   (b) increase government spending
   (c) decrease taxes
   (d) increase transfer payments

5. If the government increases personal income tax revenues by $5 billion and increases purchases of goods and services by the same amount, the most likely effect is
   (a) a net decrease in aggregate expenditures
   (b) a net increase in aggregate expenditures
   (c) aggregate expenditures would remain unchanged
   (d) an increase in the balanced budget multiplier

6. Consider an increase in government purchases of $X, a tax cut of $X, and a balanced budget increase in expenditure of $X as alternative policies. Which will probably yield the largest increase in national income?
   (a) the expenditure increase
   (b) the tax cut
   (c) the balanced budget increase
   (d) They will all increase national income by $X times the multiplier.

7. A recessionary gap may be removed by
   (a) a (slow) downward shift of the SRAS curve
   (b) a policy-induced increase in aggregate demand
   (c) a natural revival of private sector demand
   (d) any of the above

8. An inflationary gap may be removed by
   (a) a downward shift of the SRAS curve
   (b) a natural increase in private sector demand
   (c) a policy-induced reduction in aggregate demand
   (d) none of the above

9. If the MPC out of disposable income is 0.75 and the marginal tax rate is 0.3, then the MPC out of national income is:
   (a) 0.75
   (b) 0.525
   (c) 0.45
   (d) 0.225

10. Fiscal "fine-tuning" calls for
    (a) no change in taxes or expenditure unless actual national income is far from its desired level
    (b) using tax rates only to stabilize the economy
    (c) minor changes in fiscal variables whenever actual national income deviates slightly from its desired level
    (d) a passive role on the part of the government in terms of influencing aggregate expenditures

11. Built-in stabilizers tend to
    (a) stimulate inflations
    (b) prolong recessions
    (c) reduce cyclical fluctuations
    (d) stabilize income but destabilize prices and employment

12. Which one of the following is <u>not</u> a built-in stabilizer?
    (a) a change in tax rates
    (b) unemployment insurance payments
    (c) government expenditures that increase automatically as national income decreases
    (d) agricultural subsidies

13. The aggregate demand curve can be moved to the right by
    (a) an increase in tax rates
    (b) a decrease in government expenditures
    (c) an increase in the federal budget surplus
    (d) an increase in transfer payments

14. The impact of temporary income tax rate changes on consumption expenditures may be small
    (a) when incomes are high
    (b) when consumption is geared to lifetime income rather than current income
    (c) when the change in rates is large
    (d) if the economy is close to full employment

15. The budget surplus function
    (a) relates taxes to income
    (b) shows the size of the surplus when tax revenue exceeds expenditure
    (c) is graphically a straight line for most economies
    (d) relates the budget surplus (tax revenue minus government expenditure) to the level of national income

16. If total government expenditure (goods and services plus transfers) (G) = 20 - 0.05Y and taxes (T) = 0.10Y where Y is national income, then the budget surplus function (B) is equal to
    (a) B = 20 - 0.10Y
    (b) B = -20 + 0.15Y
    (c) B = 20 - 0.05Y
    (d) B = 20 + 0.05Y

17. Which of the following would give the best measure of the stance of current fiscal policy?
    (a) tax rates alone
    (b) changes in the cyclically adjusted budget surplus
    (c) the size of the current budget surplus or deficit
    (d) the rate of inflation

18. A persistent government budget deficit, financed by borrowing from the public is more likely to "crowd out" private investment
    (a) if both the government and the private sector are spending on similar items
    (b) the closer the economy is to full employment
    (c) when there is a large recessionary gap
    (d) if the country experiencing the budget deficit is an "open economy"

19. The primary burden of the public debt in an "open economy"
    (a) results when interest payments and principal repayments are made to foreigners
    (b) is the higher interest rates due to "crowding out" private investments
    (c) is the reduced capital stock for the present generation
    (d) is the higher taxes needed to pay the interest on the debt

20. True economic limitations to the level of the national debt
    (a) do not exist whatever the level of debt
    (b) are imposed by Parliament
    (c) exist in terms of the ability of a nation to finance the interest on the debt out of tax returns
    (d) are measured by the absolute size of the debt

21. The balanced budget multiplier
    (a) is larger than the multiplier for government expenditures
    (b) applies when additional tax receipts are equal to additional government expenditures
    (c) is the same as the multiplier for government expenditures
    (d) is the same as the multiplier for tax changes

22. Endogenous changes in the government's actual budget balance due to changes in national income
    (a) are shown by shifts in the budget surplus function.
    (b) result from policy-induced changes in tax rates or expenditures
    (c) are shown by movements along the budget surplus function.
    (d) cause shifts of the aggregate demand curve.

EXERCISES

1. Point E_0 in the diagram below represents the current equilibrium level of national income for an economy. Full employment real national income is shown by Y* and the long-run aggregate supply schedule (LRAS). Aggregate demand and the short-run aggregate supply are shown as AD_0 and SRAS.

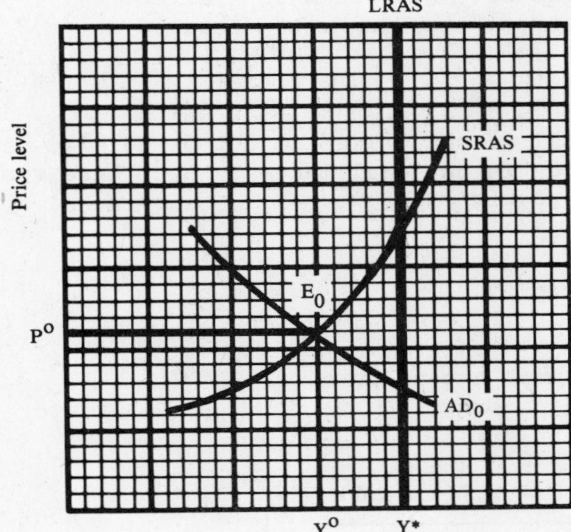

(a) Indicate the magnitude of the GNP gap on the diagram.
(b) Suppose the government closes one-half the gap by an expansionary discretionary fiscal policy. Suggest appropriate policies. What happens to aggregate demand? Illustrate the new aggregate demand curve (AD_1) on the diagram.
(c) What effect on the price level and real national income does the policy in (b) have? Illustrate on the diagram.

2. In the figure below, D_0 represents the demand for funds by the private sector and S_0 represents the supply of funds. Assume that the public sector incurs a deficit and needs to borrow funds. This causes the demand for funds to shift to D_1.

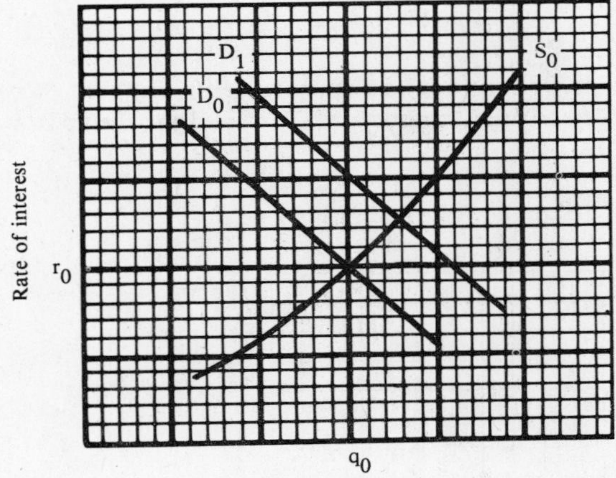

(a) Illustrate on the diagram, what will happen to the interest rate and the quantity of funds borrowed after the shift in the demand for funds, other things being equal.

(b) What happens to private sector borrowing? Illustrate the change in private sector borrowing on the diagram.

(c) Suppose that the extra government expenditure increases national income, thereby raising the amount of saving in the private sector. How would this affect interest rates? How will it affect the amount of "crowding out" compared to (b)?

3. It is possible to set government expenditures equal to some fixed amount or to allow a portion of the expenditure to be related to changes in national income. Let these two options, or expenditure functions, be described as

(1) $G = 10$

(2) $G = 20 - 0.1\ (AE - G)$

where AE is aggregate expenditure and G is government expenditure.

(a) Complete the last column in each table.

(1) G = 10

(AE − G)	G	AE
100	10	____
120	10	____
120	10	____
110	10	____

(2) G = 20 − 0.1(AE − G)

(AE − G)	G	AE
100	10	____
120	8	____
120	8	____
110	9	____

(b) Which of these government expenditure functions provides built-in stability? Explain your answer, relating it to the definition of automatic stabilizers in the text.

4. Assume that the government's tax function is $T = 0.05Y$ and that government expenditure is fixed at G = $100 million. Y is the level of national income. The budget surplus function (B) is defined as $B = T - G$.

(a) For the following levels of Y, calculate and plot B. Label it B_1.

Y($M)	B($M)
1000	____
1500	____
2000	____
2500	____
3000	____

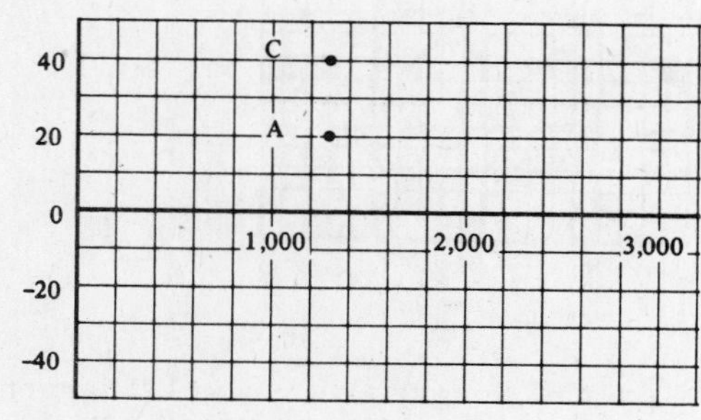

(b) If the tax rate is increased to 7 percent, plot the new budget surplus function (or as much of it as you can) and label it B_2.

(c) If we observed from one year to the next a movement from A to C (at Y = 1300) on the graph, could we conclude that the government has adopted a more restrictive fiscal policy? Explain.

PART NINE

MONEY, BANKING, AND MONETARY POLICY

CHAPTER 33

THE NATURE OF MONEY & MONETARY INSTITUTIONS

CHAPTER OBJECTIVES

The nature, functions, and measurement of the money supply are discussed in the first part of this chapter. The largest component of money is deposits at chartered banks. Therefore, the chapter concentrates on the nature of the banking system and how the money supply is changed by the behavior of chartered banks. Through a series of examples, you learn how banks create money by a multiple amount when they have excess reserves. Learn the various items on the asset and liability sides on a bank's balance sheet and be able to show changes in the balance sheet when banks conduct various transactions.

MULTIPLE-CHOICE QUESTIONS

1. For money to serve as an efficient medium of exchange, it must have all but which one of the following characteristics?
   (a) general acceptability
   (b) convertibility into precious metals
   (c) high value for its weight
   (d) divisibility

2. The value of money depends primarily on
   (a) the gold backing of the currency alone
   (b) the gold backing of both currency and deposits
   (c) its purchasing power
   (d) who issues it

3. To be a satisfactory store of value, money must have
   (a) a relatively stable value
   (b) a direct relationship to national income
   (c) a highly volatile value over time
   (d) no interest payment for holding it

4. "Debasing" the coinage had the effect of
   (a) causing prices to fall in the economy
   (b) causing inflation
   (c) increasing the purchasing power of each coin
   (d) a loss to the person issuing the coins

5. A requirement for the gold standard was that
   (a) the price level be stable
   (b) there be no paper money
   (c) paper money be convertible into gold at a fixed price
   (d) gold coinage be 100 percent of the money supply

6. A fractionally backed paper money system is when claims against banks' reserves
   (a) have 100 percent backing in precious metals
   (b) exceed the value of actual reserves
   (c) have a direct relationship to GNP
   (d) have a fixed relationship to the quantity of coinage

7. Today, paper money in Canada is issued by
   (a) the banks
   (b) the central bank of Canada (the Bank of Canada)
   (c) the Queen
   (d) the Department of Finance

8. Today all Canadian currency (coins plus paper notes) is
   (a) fractionally backed by gold
   (b) fractionally backed by gold and silver
   (c) interest bearing
   (d) fiat money

9. A chartered bank is able to create money by
   (a) printing it
   (b) creating a deposit as it extends a new loan
   (c) maintaining reserves
   (d) issuing checks to its depositors

10. A money substitute is something that serves as a
   (a) store of value
   (b) unit of account
   (c) temporary medium of exchange but not as a store of value
   (d) temporary medium of exchange and also as a store of value

11. The doctrine of the neutrality of money states that the quantity of money influences
   (a) the level of money prices but has no effect on the real part of the economy
   (b) the real part of the economy but has no effect on the money part of the economy
   (c) both the real and money parts of the economy in an identical fashion
   (d) neither the real nor the money part of the economy

12. The M1A measure of the Canadian money supply is defined as
   (a) currency
   (b) currency, demand deposits, and other deposits transferable by check
   (c) currency, demand deposits, and all term deposits
   (d) currency, demand deposits, and near money

13. The key distinguishing feature between a bank and other institutions that offer banking services is that only a bank
   (a) accepts deposits
   (b) has its charter granted from provincial legislation
   (c) accepts demand deposits on which checks may be used to transfer funds
   (d) extends loans to consumers

14. Which one of the following is <u>not</u> an asset of a bank?
   (a) deposits of households
   (b) reserves
   (c) loans
   (d) Government of Canada securities

15. The cash reserve ratio is the fraction of
   (a) a bank's deposits that it must hold in the form of currency
   (b) a bank's deposits that it holds as reserves either in currency or as deposits with the central bank
   (c) a bank's assets that it holds in the form of reserves
   (d) a bank's reserves that it must hold in the form of deposits with the Bank of Canada

16. The process of creating deposit money by chartered banks
   (a) is possible because of the fractional-reserve requirement
   (b) is consciously undertaken by each bank
   (c) must occur if there are excess reserves
   (d) permits only small, gradual changes in the supply of money

17. A reduction in bank reserves by payments of currency to foreigners, will
   (a) always cause a multiple contraction in deposits
   (b) cause a multiple contraction in deposits only if there are no excess reserves
   (c) not affect domestic deposits
   (d) not affect the availability of domestic credit

18. The existence of a cash drain will, other things equal,
   (a) reduce the ability of the banking system to expand or contract the money supply
   (b) have no effect on the ability of the banking system to contract the money supply
   (c) have no effect on the ability of the banking system to expand the money supply
   (d) increase the ability of the banking system to expand or contract the money supply

Questions 19 through 22 refer to the following information about a banking system.

i) There is a banking system in which all deposits must have a cash reserve ratio of 5 percent.

ii) There is no cash drain from the banking system and all banks are assumed to hold no excess reserves for a prolonged period of time.

iii) Banks experiencing excess (deficient) reserves respond by increasing (decreasing) loans.

iv) The current status of the balance sheet of <u>all banks</u> is as follows:

ALL BANKS

Reserves $__________	Deposits $300 million
Loans $270 million	
Securities __________	

Fill in the blanks in the table and answer the following questions.

19. If all banks initially had no excess reserves, the
   (a) reserves of the banks must have been $30 million
   (b) holdings of securities by the banks must have been $15 million
   (c) reserves of the banks must have been 5 percent of loans or $13.5 million
   (d) reserves of the banks must have been $300 million

20. If all banks initially had $16 million of actual reserves then,
    (a) excess reserves are $15 million
    (b) the banks have $1 million in deficient reserves
    (c) excess reserves are $1 million
    (d) the banks have $1.5 million in deficient reserves

21. Assuming that the banking system begins with no excess reserves, a loss of one million dollars of deposits from the system will ultimately lead to
    (a) a reduction in the money supply of $19 million
    (b) a reduction in the money supply of $.5 million
    (c) an increase in the money supply of $20 million
    (d) deposit liabilities of $280 million

22. Assuming that the banking system begins with no excess reserves, a gain of one million dollars of deposits will ultimately lead to
    (a) increased deposits of $20 million
    (b) increased loans of $20 million
    (c) increased loans of $1 million
    (d) a $5 million increase in the money supply

EXERCISES

1. Indicate which of the three functions of money is demonstrated in each of the following transactions. Use the appropriate number: (1) medium of exchange; (2) store of value; (3) unit of account.
    (a) Farmer Brown puts cash in a mattress. ________

    (b) Storekeeper Jones adds up the total sales for the day. ________

    (c) Plumber Smith makes $500 per week. ________

    (d) Traveling salesperson Lee buys $100 of gasoline per week. ________

    (e) The Blacks buy a good oriental rug with the thought that it will keep its value for a long time. ________

2. Which of the following might be regarded as "money," which as "near money," and which as neither? Briefly explain your answers.

    (a) A share of stock in Bell Canada ________

    (b) A $10 Bank of Canada note ________

    (c) A Canada Savings Bond maturing in 1990 ________

    (d) A bank note issued by a Saskatchewan bank in 1897 ________

    (e) An ounce of gold in a Kruggerand (South African coinage provided for hoarders and speculators) ________

    (f) A checking-savings account at a trust company ________

    (g) A demand deposit at the Bank of Nova Scotia ________

3. <u>Olympic Coins</u>

The Olympic Committee announced early in 1973 that they intended to finance the 1976 Olympic Games in Montreal partly by the sale of about $240 million in special Olympic coins.

The federal government agreed to instruct the Mint in Ottawa to produce the coins in various face values. The coins were sold to the Olympic Committee at cost, which was well below the total face value of the coins. The Olympic Committee then sold the coins to the public at their face value. Furthermore, the coins were declared legal tender by the federal government.

(a) If the Olympic Committee sold all of the coins, would the money supply increase? Explain.

(b) According to the details you have been given, does it appear that the value of the coins depended on the value of their metallic content? What did their value depend upon?

(c) Suppose that these coins became valuable collectors' items, doubling their market price (the price determined on the coin collectors' market). Would the money supply double?

(d) Suppose that the price of the metals used to produce these coins increased tenfold so that the metallic price of the coins became greater than their face value. How do you think the holders of these coins would react?

4. From the data pertaining to the Canadian banking system below,* calculate the magnitude of M1, M1A, M2, and M3. (All figures are in millions of dollars as of March 1984).

Currency outside banks	$11,755
Daily interest checkable and nonpersonal notice deposits	9,105
Demand deposits	16,597
Other personal savings deposits and personal fixed-term deposits at the chartered banks	98,615
Nonpersonal fixed-term deposits and foreign currency deposits	48,438

*Source: <u>Bank of Canada Review</u>, April 1984.

M1 = __________ M1A = __________ M2 = __________ M3 = __________

5. Arrange the following items on the proper side of a bank's balance sheet.

(a) Demand deposits	$5,000,000
(b) Savings deposits	1,000,000
(c) Currency in vaults	60,000
(d) Deposits in the Bank of Canada	1,000,000
(e) Loans to public	4,000,000
(f) Security holdings (Canadian government, provincial, municipal, and other)	1,500,000
(g) Bank buildings and fixtures	360,000
(h) Capital and surplus	920,000

Assets	Liabilities

6. We use "T-accounts," abbreviated balance sheets for a bank to show changes in a bank's reserves, loans, and deposits. Make the entries on the T-accounts below, using + and - signs to show increase or decrease, for each of the following independent events. (Remember that all changes must balance.)

Event	Assets	Liabilities
(a) You deposit your pay check of $100 at your bank.	Reserves: Loans and securities:	Deposits:
(b) A bank sells $10,000 of government bonds in the market to replenish its reserves.	Reserves: Loans and securities:	Deposits:
(c) A bank makes a loan of $5,000 to a local business and credits it to its checking account.	Reserves: Loans and securities:	Deposits:
(d) A bank sells $50,000 of securities to the Bank of Canada and receives deposits in the Bank of Canada.	Reserves: Loans and securities:	Deposits:
(e) A business uses $5,000 of its demand deposit to pay off a loan from the same bank.	Reserves: Loans and securities:	Deposits:
(f) A bank orders $5,000 in currency from the bank of Canada.	Reserves: Loans and securities:	Deposits:

7. Suppose that bank A, a Canadian bank, begins with the T-account shown below. The required cash reserve ratio is assumed to be 10 percent. Joe Doe, a holder of a deposit in bank A, withdraws $1,000 and deposits this amount in a commercial bank in a foreign country. Thus $1,000 has been taken out of the Canadian banking system.

Bank A (initial situation)

Assets		Liabilities
Reserves:	$10,000	Deposits: $100,000
Loans:	90,000	

Bank A (after the withdrawal)

Assets	Liabilities
Reserves:	Deposits: $
Loans:	

(a) What were bank A's required reserves? Did it have excess reserves initially?

(b) Show the immediate effect of the withdrawal from bank A.

(c) What is the status of bank A's cash reserves now?

(d) Bank A reacts by calling in a loan that it had made to Mary Smith equal to the amount of its reserve deficiency. Mary repays the loan by writing a cheque on her account in bank B, another Canadian bank. Bank B's initial T-account is shown below. Fill in the T-accounts below for the effects of bank A's receiving the payment from Mary and of bank B's losing Mary's deposit.

Bank B (initial situation)

Assets		Liabilities
Reserves:	$ 5,000	Deposits: $ 50,000
Loans:	45,000	

Bank B (after losing Mary's deposit)

Assets	Liabilities
Reserves: $	Deposits: $
Loans:	

Bank A (after receiving loan repayment)

Assets	Liabilities
Reserves: $	Deposits: $
Loans:	

(e) After this transaction, does Bank A have deficient reserves? Bank B?

(f) In fact, bank B has a deficiency of reserves. It reacts by calling in a loan made to Peter Piper equal to the amount of the deficiency. Peter cashes in a savings deposit that he held in Bank C; that is, Bank C loses a deposit and Peter repays bank B. Bank C's initial situation is shown below. Fill in the T-accounts for the effects of bank B's receiving the loan repayment and bank C's losing Peter's savings deposit.

Bank C (initial situation)	
Reserves: $ 7,000	Deposits: $ 70,000
Loans: 63,000	

Bank C (after losing Peter's deposit	
Reserves: $	Deposits: $
Loans:	

Bank B (after receiving loan repayment)	
Reserves: $	Deposits: $
Loans:	

(g) After this transaction, does bank B have deficient reserves? Bank C?

(h) After this transaction, the reduction in the money supply has been Joe's original withdrawal plus $ ____________ in other deposits. Loans have been reduced by $____________.

(i) The process will continue until the total reduction in the money supply (M1) will be $____________. The total reduction in loans will be $ ____________.

8. Suppose that a foreign company withdraws money from its account in a foreign country, buys $1 million of Canadian currency and deposits this sum into the Canadian banking system. The required cash reserve ratio is assumed to be 8 percent and there is no cash drain. The initial situation in the Canadian banking system is depicted below.

All Banks

Reserves:	$ 72 million	Deposits	$900 million
Loans:	728 million		
Securities:	100 million		

(a) According to the initial scenario, required reserves are $________ and excess reserves are $ ____________.

(b) After the $1 million deposit, required reserves are $ __________ and excess reserves are $ __________.

(c) Assuming that all excess reserves are used to expand loans, the final (increase/decrease) in the money supply will be ________ times the $1 million new deposit, which is equal to ____________.

(d) The final (increase/decrease) in loans will be $ __________.

CHAPTER 34

THE ROLE OF MONEY IN MACROECONOMICS

CHAPTER OBJECTIVES

This chapter discusses the effects of changes in the money supply on macroeconomic variables such as national income and the price level. The analysis runs as follows: Changes in the money supply cause an initial disequilibrium in the money (and bond) market which leads to changes in the equilibrium level of the interest rate. A change in interest rates generates changes in certain components of aggregate expenditure which cause both the AE and AD curves to shift. As a result, real income or prices (or both) are affected. One of the exercises is developed step by step to outline this process.

You should learn that the slopes of the MEI curve and the demand for money curve determine the effectiveness of changes in the money supply to influence real income.

In addition, in order to understand how changes in the money supply lead to changes in the interest rate, you should comprehend the motives for holding money and the economic factors which influence the demand for money. Several questions ask you to discuss the influence of real national income, the price level, and interest rates on the demand for money. Part of this process involves understanding the relationship between the market value (or present value) of a bond and the interest rate on that bond.

MULTIPLE-CHOICE QUESTIONS

1. A bond which pays interest forever and never repays the principal is called a
   (a) perpetuity
   (b) fixed-term bond
   (c) preferred share
   (d) Treasury bill

2. The present value of a bond is
   (a) always the same as its face value at some future maturity date
   (b) the interest rate per period to maturity
   (c) the specified value of the bond at maturity plus the interest in future value terms
   (d) the current value of a future stream of payment(s) to which the bond represents a claim

3. The present value of a bond maturing at some future date
   (a) is negatively related to the interest rate
   (b) is positively related to the interest rate
   (c) depends entirely on the maturity date rather than the interest rate
   (d) will be greater for a later maturity date, other things equal

4. When the interest rate on an annual basis is 7 percent, the present value of a bond which promises to pay $114.49 one year hence is equal to
   (a) $1,635.57
   (b) $122.50
   (c) $107
   (d) $114.49

5. If Sue pays $95.24 for a one-year bond which promises to pay $100 at the end of the year, then the interest rate on this bond if Sue holds it to maturity is
   (a) 5.24%
   (b) 5.00%
   (c) 4.76%
   (d) 9.52%

6. The amount of money held for transactions balances will
   (a) vary in the same direction as national income measured in current prices
   (b) vary in the same direction as interest rates
   (c) vary negatively with savings
   (d) be larger with shorter intervals between paydays

7. Precautionary balances would be expected to increase if, other things being equal,
   (a) business conditions were to become much less certain
   (b) interest rates increased
   (c) people were expecting securities prices to rise
   (d) prices and income fall

8. The speculative motive for holding money balances
   (a) applies to bonds, but not to other interest-earning assets
   (b) is not related to interest rates
   (c) assumes that the opportunity cost of holding money is zero
   (d) suggests that individuals will hold money in order to avoid or reduce the risk associated with fluctuations in the market prices of assets

9. If there is an excess supply of money, households and firms will
   (a) sell bonds and add to their holdings of money, thereby causing the interest rate to fall
   (b) purchase bonds and reduce their holdings of money, thereby causing the interest rate to rise
   (c) purchase bonds and reduce their holdings of money, thereby causing the interest rate to fall and bond prices to rise
   (d) purchase bonds and reduce their holdings to money, thereby causing the price of bonds to fall

10. The marginal efficiency of the investment curve illustrates the
   (a) positive relation between investment and the rate of interest
   (b) negative relation between investment and the rate of interest
   (c) negative relation between the capital stock and the rate of interest
   (d) positive relation between the capital stock and the level of investment

11. Other things being equal, a fall in the interest rate will cause
   (a) a shift in the MEI curve to the left
   (b) a shift in the MEI curve to the right
   (c) a movement down the MEI curve
   (d) the capital stock to decline

12. Changes in interest rates caused by monetary disequilibrium
   (a) are usually of little consequence in influencing economic activity
   (b) provide the link between changes in the money supply and changes in aggregate demand
   (c) cause the liquidity preference curve to shift, thus affecting desired investment expenditures
   (d) cause a change in the money supply, thereby affecting interest-sensitive expenditures

13. If the Bank of Canada increases the money supply, other things being equal, we would expect the
   (a) interest rate to fall, the AE curve to shift upward, and the AD curve to shift to the left
   (b) interest rate to fall, the AE curve to shift downward, and the AD curve to shift to the right
   (c) interest rate to fall, the AE curve to shift upward, and the AD curve to shift to the right
   (d) interest rate to fall, the AE curve to be unaffected, and the AD curve to become flatter

14. A rise in the price level, other things being equal, will tend to shift the aggregate expenditure curve downward because of
    (a) reduced demand for money balances
    (b) a rise in the demand for money balances which increases the interest rate
    (c) an excess supply of money balances which reduces the interest rate
    (d) the fact that interest rates will fall

15. The monetary adjustment mechanism will eliminate an inflationary gap by
    (a) raising interest rates, reducing investment, and increasing aggregate expenditure
    (b) lowering interest rates, increasing investment, and increasing aggregate expenditure
    (c) raising interest rates, reducing investment, and moving leftward along the aggregate demand curve
    (d) raising interest rates, reducing investment, and shifting the aggregate demand curve

16. A given change in the money supply will exert a larger effect on national income
    (a) the flatter the LP curve and the steeper the MEI curve are
    (b) the flatter both the LP and the MEI curves are
    (c) the steeper both the LP and the MEI curves are
    (d) the steeper the LP curve and the flatter the MEI curve are

17. A sufficiently large rise in the price level will eliminate an inflationary gap provided that
    (a) the nominal money supply remains constant
    (b) the nominal money supply increases
    (c) the Bank of Canada validates the inflation
    (d) government expenditures are financed by increases in the money supply

18. An inflation is said to be <u>validated</u> when
    (a) the money supply increases at the same rate as the price level rises
    (b) the nominal money supply remains constant
    (c) the monetary adjustment mechanism is unaffected by Bank of Canada policy
    (d) it receives approval from the House of Commons

19. The neo-Keynesians believe that
    (a) both the LP and MEI curves are relatively flat
    (b) both the LP and MEI curves are relatively steep
    (c) the LP curve is steep whereas the MEI curve is flat
    (d) the LP curve is flat whereas the MEI curve is steep

20. The crowding-out effect is smaller
    (a) the steeper the MEI curve
    (b) the flatter the MEI curve
    (c) the flatter both the LP and MEI curves are
    (d) the steeper both the LP and MEI curves are

EXERCISES:

1. Calculate the present value for each of the following assets:

   (a) a bond that promises to pay $100 3 years from now and which has a constant annual interest rate of 2 percent.

   (b) a bond that promises to pay $100 2 years from now and which has a constant annual interest rate of 6 percent.

   (c) a perpetuity that pays $100 a year and which has an interest rate of 17 percent.

   (d) an investment which pays $100 after 1 year, $150 after 2 years, and $80 after 3 years and which has an annual interest rate of 10 percent.

2. The Relation Between the Present Value and the Interest Rate of a Bond

   If you are not convinced that interest rates and present value are negatively related, perhaps this exercise will eliminate your doubt. The present value of a bond is often called the market price of the bond. Consider two bonds, A and B. Bond A promises to pay $120 one year hence and bond B promises to pay $120 two years from now.

   (a) Calculate the present value for bond A when the interest rate is 8 percent. Calculate the present values for interest rates of 10 percent, 20 percent, and 25 percent. What happened to the market price when interest rates rose?

   (b) If you were told that the market price (present value) of bond A increased, what would you conclude is happening to the interest rate on bond A?

   (c) Calculate the present values for bond B for interest rates of 10%, 20%, and 25%.

   (d) If the current rate of interest on both bonds was 20 percent, which bond would currently be selling for the highest market price? Why?

(e) An individual who insists on receiving a 14 percent return on all assets would be prepared to pay what market price for bond A? Bond B?

3. Suppose that a household is paid $1,000 at the beginning of each month. The household spends all of its income on the purchase of goods and services each month. Furthermore, assume that these purchases are at a constant rate throughout the month. Consequently, payments and receipts are not perfectly synchronized.

(a) What is the value of cash holdings at the beginning of the month? At the end of the first week? At the end of the third week? At the end of the month?

(b) What is the magnitude of the average cash holdings over the month?

(c) Suppose that the household's income increases to $1,200 and purchases of goods and services during a month are equal to this amount. What is the average cash holding?

(d) Suppose that the household is paid $1,000 over the month but in installments of $500 at the beginning of the month and $500 at the beginning of the third week. What is the magnitude of the average cash holdings per month?

4. Two liquidity preference curves are drawn below.

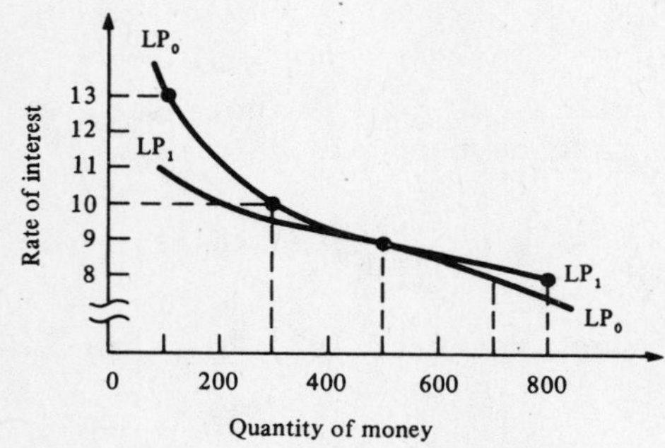

(a) Using your knowledge of the transactions and speculative motives for money, explain why the quantity of money demanded falls when interest rates rise.

(b) If the money supply is 500 and constant at all levels of interest rates, what interest rate is associated with monetary equilibrium? Plot the supply of money function in the above diagram and indicate the monetary-equilibrium interest rate.

(c) Suppose that the monetary authority decreased the money supply from 500 to 300. At an interest rate of 9 percent, what kind of situation exists in the money market? Would households and firms tend to buy or sell bonds? Explain. Predict what is likely to happen to bond prices and interest rates.

(d) As interest rates rise, what happens to the quantity of money demanded? Predict the new equilibrium level of interest rates using LP_0. Using LP_1.

(e) What increase in the money supply would be necessary to achieve an equilibrium interest rate of 8 percent if LP_0 applies? If LP_1 applies? Comment on how the shape of the LP curve affects the effectiveness of monetary policy to achieve an interest rate target.

5. Suppose that the economy is currently experiencing unemployment. The central bank considers potential (full-employment) national income to be the target variable. The economy's liquidity preference curve is that labeled as LP_0 in question 4, and the current money supply is 500. Other information about the economy is described below.

(i) the marginal propensity to spend is 0.50;

(ii) the potential national income is 1,600;

(iii) the MEI function is given by the following schedule:

Investment Expenditure	Interest Rate (%)
160	13
180	11
200	9
210	8

(iv) Aggregate expenditures are depicted by the following schedule:

Y	C	I	G	(X - M)	AE
1,520	912	200	300	138	1,550
1,540	924	200	300	136	1,560
1,560	936	200	300	134	1,570
1,580	948	200	300	132	1,580
1,600	960	200	300	130	1,590

(v) the LP curve is not influenced by changes in the level of national income;

(vi) the AS curve is horizontal at a price level of 2.0 for all levels of national income less than potential national income (1,600), at which level it becomes vertical.

The central bank sets its research department to work in order to establish accurate information about the current situation and to suggest what it should do in order to eliminate unemployment.

(a) Referring to the LP_0 curve in Exercise 4, what is the current equilibrium level of the interest rate?

(b) Given the interest rate, what is the level of desired investment expenditure according to the MEI schedule?

(c) What is the current equilibrium value of real national income? What is the value of the GNP gap?

(d) What is the value of the simple multiplier? What change in autonomous expenditure is required for the economy to achieve the potential national income level without inflation?

With all of the information, the research department is in a position to recommend policy changes for the central bank.

(e) Should the money supply be increased or decreased? Should the interest rate be increased or decreased?

(f) Changes in the money supply and the interest rate will change the level of investment. How much must investment be increased from its current level in order to achieve potential national income?

(g) To achieve this higher level of investment, what is the required level of the interest rate? (Refer to the MEI schedule.)

(h) Given the required level of the interest rate, what must the money supply be in order to achieve equilibrium in the money market at that interest rate? Refer to the LP_0 curve in question 4. What change in the current money supply is necessary?

Policy Evaluation

Suppose that the central bank is successful in lowering the interest rate and increasing investment by the appropriate magnitudes. It follows that real national income should increase by a multiple and attain a level of 1,600.

(i) Calculate the new level of consumption expenditure and calculate the aggregate level of expenditure at Y = 1,600. Is this an equilibrium situation?

(j) Illustrate the change in the AE and AD functions in the diagrams below.

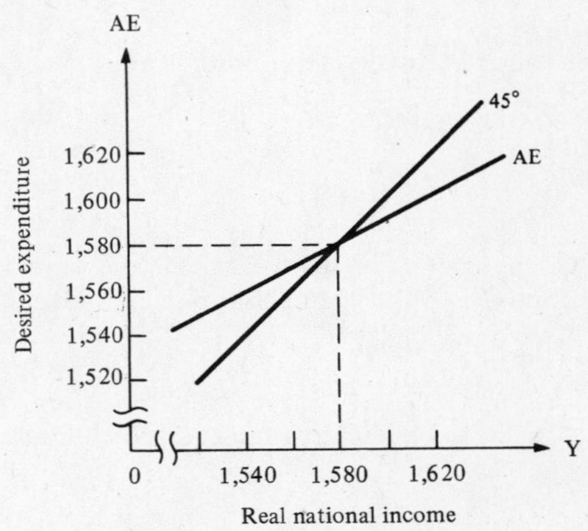

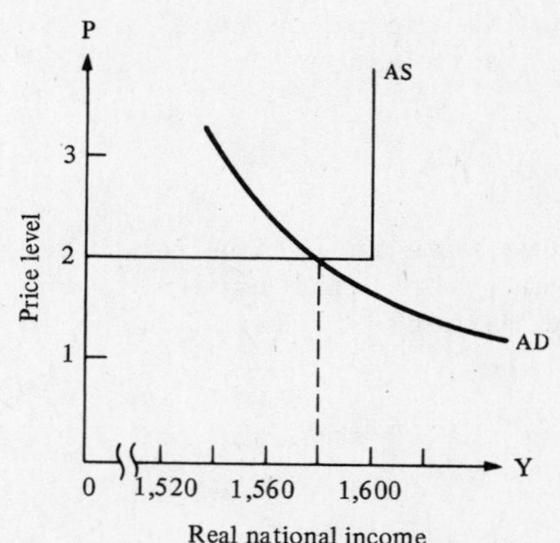

6. The Shape of the Aggregate Demand Curve

(i) The Effects of Changes in the Price Level on Desired Investment

LP SCHEDULE

Rate of Interest	Quantity of Money Demanded	
(%)	P = 1	P = 2
4	80	100
6	70	90
8	60	80
10	50	70
12	40	60
14	30	50

MEI SCHEDULE

Rate of Interest (%)	Desired Investment Expenditure
10	180
11	179
12	177
13	174
14	170

Assume that the supply of money is fixed at a value of 50.

(a) Assuming the price level is 1.0, what is the equilibrium interest rate? Desired investment expenditure?

(b) Assume that the price level becomes 2.0. For a given level of real national income, what will happen to the demand for money? What will happen in the bond market? Explain.

(c) Using the LP schedule for P = 2, determine the new equilibrium interest rate.

(d) Given this change in the interest rate, what is the new level of desired investment expenditure?

(ii) The Effects of Changes in Desired Investment (I) on Real National Income (Y)

Desired Y	C	Desired I (interest = 10%)	AE (r = 10%)	AE (r = 14%)
340	170	180	350	____
350	175	180	355	____
360	180	180	360	____
370	185	180	365	____

(e) What is the equilibrium level of real national income (Y) associated with an interest rate of 10 percent and a price level of 1.0?

(f) Given the interest rate increase because of a doubling of the price level, what is the level of desired investment? Fill in the values for the new level of aggregate expenditure. What is the new equilibrium level of Y?

(iii) Synthesis: The Relationship Between P and Y

(g) Draw the AD curve on the diagram below, Plotting the negative relationship between P and Y for this problem. (Use your answers to parts (e) and (f).)

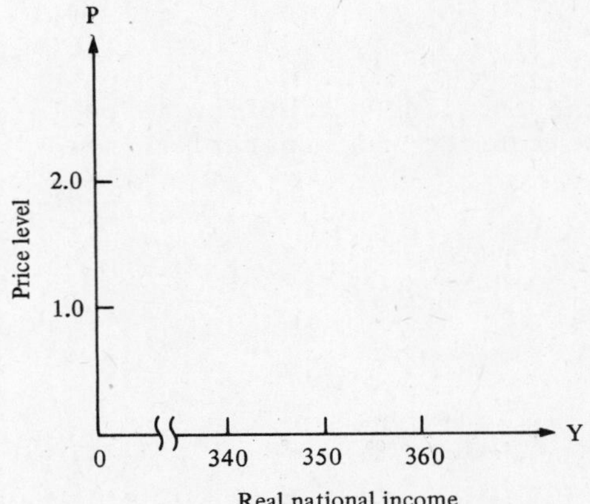

7. The Crowding-out Effect

Suppose that the federal government decides to increase its expenditures by $500 million permanently. The price level and foreign exchange rates are assumed constant. The marginal propensity to spend is 0.5, potential GNP is $151 billion, and current equilibrium GNP is $150 billion.

(a) What is the size of the GNP gap?

(b) The government assumes that the interest rate will not change due to its policy change. If this assumption is correct, will the increase in G eliminate the gap?

(c) In fact, suppose that the demand for money equation is given by the expression $D_M = 0.8Y - 2i$, where Y stands for GNP and i represents the level of the interest rate (in percentage terms.) If the current money supply is $100 billion and Y = 150, solve for the level of i assuming the money market is in equilibrium.

(d) If the government's policy raised real GNP to $151 billion, what would be the effect on the level of the interest rate?

(e) Suppose you know that every increase in the interest rate of 0.1 decreased desired investment expenditures by $125 million. Given your answer to part (d), what is the total effect on desired investment expenditures?

(f) Instead of the relationship given in (e), suppose that for every increase in the interest rate of 0.1, investment expenditure fell by $25 million. Given your answer to part (d), what is the total effect on desired investment expenditure now?

(g) What is the extent of the crowding-out effect in part (e). Part (f)? Which result is most likely to reflect the monetarist view?

CHAPTER 35

MONETARY POLICY

CHAPTER OBJECTIVES

This chapter deals with the functions of a central bank and focuses on the techniques which are available to it in order to affect the money supply and interest rates. In doing so, they seek to influence two major policy variables--real national income and the price level. The major policy instrument used by the Bank of Canada is open-market operations. The questions in this chapter focus on showing you how and why the Bank of Canada purchases and sells government securities in the bond market. The Bank of Canada purchases securities in order to increase the money supply and decrease the interest rate, thereby attempting to eliminate a recessionary gap. During inflationary periods, the Bank of Canada sells government securities in the open market, with the opposite intended effects.

You should also learn the distinctions among policy instruments, policy variables, and intermediate targets.

MULTIPLE-CHOICE QUESTIONS

1. Which one of the following is <u>not</u> a function of the Bank of Canada?
   (a) providing banking services for the federal government
   (b) acting as a lender of last resort to the banks
   (c) controlling the supply of money and credit
   (d) lending to business firms

2. The deposits of chartered banks, which constitute their reserves, appear as
   (a) a liability on the Bank of Canada's balance sheet
   (b) an asset on the Bank of Canada's balance sheet
   (c) a liability on the balance sheet of the chartered banks
   (d) a component of the item "purchase and resale agreements" on the Bank of Canada's balance sheet

3. Purchase and resale agreements (PRA) involve
   (a) sales and purchases of government securities among chartered banks
   (b) sales and purchases of government securities between the Bank of Canada and the chartered banks
   (c) sales of government securities by investment dealers to the Bank of Canada with agreement to repurchase them at a later date
   (d) sales of government securities by investment dealers to the Government of Canada with agreement to repurchase them at a later date

4. A bank that has insufficient reserves may
   (a) borrow from the Bank of Canada
   (b) call in loans
   (c) reduce its holdings of government securities
   (d) do all of the above

5. Open market operations are
   (a) purchases and sales by the Bank of Canada of government securities in financial markets
   (b) sales of government securities by chartered banks to their customers
   (c) total purchases and sales of government securities in the bond market
   (d) changes in the interest rate charged by the Bank of Canada on loans to the banks

6. Which one of the following is not a policy instrument of the Bank of Canada?
   (a) raising the tax rate on interest income
   (b) moral persuasion
   (c) open-market operations
   (d) establishing the secondary reserve requirement

7. If the Bank of Canada purchases bonds on the open market
   (a) chartered bank reserves will be reduced
   (b) chartered bank reserves will be increased
   (c) the money supply will fall by a maximum of 1/r times the value of the purchase
   (d) chartered bank reserves will be unaffected

8. If the Bank of Canada sold $10 million of securities on the open market,
   (a) reserves and securities in chartered banks would each rise by $10 million
   (b) deposits and reserves of chartered banks would fall by $10 million
   (c) the money supply would be increased by $10 million
   (d) deposits in the banking system would rise by $10 million

9. If the Bank of Canada purchases bonds in the open market, it is likely that
   (a) the price of bonds would fall and the interest rate would rise
   (b) the price of bonds and the interest rate would fall
   (c) the price of bonds and the interest rate would rise
   (d) the price of bonds would rise and the interest rate would fall

10. Which one of the following could be considered an example of an intermediate target of the Bank of Canada?
   (a) open-market operations
   (b) the rate of inflation
   (c) interest rates
   (d) the nominal value of national income

11. The bank rate is defined as
   (a) the interest rate charged on loans by the chartered banks
   (b) the cash reserve ratio times the interest rate on three-month Treasury bills
   (c) the interest rate charged by banks for overdrafts
   (d) the interest rate at which the Bank of Canada makes loans to the chartered banks

12. If the Bank of Canada chooses to set the quantity of open-market sales or purchases, thereby letting the interest rate vary, it is said to be following a(n)
   (a) interest rate control policy
   (b) base control policy, with the monetary base as the policy instrument
   (c) neutral monetary base policy
   (d) combined interest rate control and base control policy

13. If the Bank of Canada wishes to pursue an expansionary monetary policy, it should
   (a) buy bonds on the open market, thus contracting reserves of chartered banks and causing interest rates to rise
   (b) sell bonds on the open market, thus expanding reserves of banks and causing interest rates to fall
   (c) buy bonds on the open market, thus expanding reserves of the banks and causing interest rates to fall
   (d) sell bonds on the open market, thus contracting bank reserves and causing interest rates to rise

14. Suppose that the Bank of Canada believes that there is too much inflationary pressure in the economy. Its policy should include
   (a) the purchase of government securities on the open market
   (b) a decrease in the secondary reserve requirement
   (c) a reduction in the bank rate
   (d) the sale of government securities to banks and the public

15. Generally recognized as a sign of a policy favoring tighter money is a
   (a) reduction of the secondary reserve requirement
   (b) rise in government bond purchases by the Bank of Canada
   (c) rise in the monetary base
   (d) rise in the bank rate

16. An important implication of long and variable execution lags associated with monetary policy is that
   (a) national income can be easily fine-tuned open market with operations
   (b) monetary policy is never capable of eliminating an inflationary gap
   (c) discretionary monetary policy may prove to be destabilizing
   (d) the argument for a constant rate monetary rule is less valid

17. If the demand for money falls to a greater degree than the money supply is being restricted, then
   (a) interest rates will fall
   (b) the quantity demanded for money will be greater than the quantity supplied
   (c) interest rates will rise
   (d) money supply expansion is necessary for achieving the initial target interest rate

18. There is general agreement among economists that
   (a) rapid changes in the money supply have significant effects on aggregate demand
   (b) monetary policy should be given a minor role relative to fiscal policy in stabilizing economic activity
   (c) control of the money supply is a sufficient means for controlling inflation
   (d) changes in the money supply are the only cause of inflation

19. A contractionary monetary policy, assuming money demand is unchanged, will cause
   (a) a decrease in interest rates and the money stock
   (b) a decrease in interest rates and increase in the money stock
   (c) an increase in interest rates and decrease in the money stock
   (d) an increase in both interest rates and the money stock

20. A policy of allowing the money supply to grow at a steady rate would be contractionary if
   (a) interest rates fell
   (b) the demand for money increased sharply
   (c) the demand for money decreased sharply
   (d) bank reserves increased

EXERCISES

1. The Bank of Canada decides to purchase $100 million of Canadian government securities from the nonbank public in open-market operations. Show the effect of this first step on the banking system. (Be sure to use + and - to indicate changes, not totals.) Assume that the public holds all their money in bank deposits.

(a)

Bank of Canada		Chartered Banks	
Assets	Liabilities	Assets	Liabilities
Securities:	Bank reserves:	Reserves:	Demand deposits:

(b) If the required reserve ratio is 10 percent, it is now possible for deposits to increase by a total of ______________ (including the original increase).

(c) What is likely to happen to the level of interest rates?

(d) Will the money supply necessarily increase by the full amount in (b)? Explain.

2. Use the graphs below to illustrate the effects of the following Bank of Canada monetary policies and answer the questions.

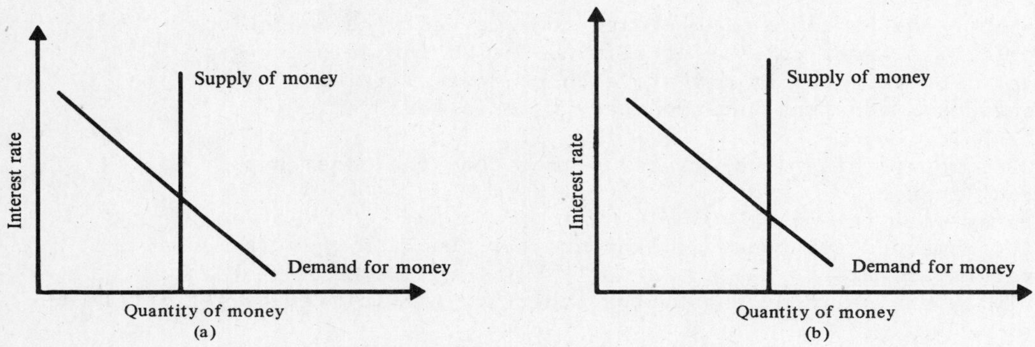

(a) The Bank of Canada sells government securities.

Total reserves will (increase/decrease).
The money supply curve should shift to the ______________.
This policy is (expansionary/contractionary).
The quantity of money demanded will (increase/decrease).
Interest rates will tend to ______________.

(b) The Bank Act changes such that the cash reserve ratio on all types of deposits falls.

Excess reserves will initially (increase/decrease).
The money supply curve should shift to the ______________.
This policy is (expansionary/contractionary).
The quantity of money demanded will (increase/decrease).
Interest rates will tend to ______________.

(c) The demand for money curve shifts farther to the left than does the supply of money curve. (Use the diagram for part (a) for this question).

Interest rates will tend to ______________________.
Investment expenditure will tend to ________________.
National income will tend to ________________________.

3. Suppose that the demand for money function was $D_M = 300 - 20i$, where D_M is the quantity of money demanded and i is the rate of interest in percentage terms. The supply of money is 100.

(a) What is the equilibrium value for the interest rate?

(b) Suppose, because of expansion in the economy, that the demand curve for money becomes $D_M = 400 - 20i$, but the supply of money remains at 100. If the interest remained at 10 percent, what situation exists in the money market? What is likely to happen to the equilibrium level of the interest rate in the future? Be specific.

(c) Given the circumstances described in part (b) and assuming that the Bank of Canada was determined to maintain an interest rate target of 10 percent, what change in the money supply would be required? Be specific.

(d) What type of open-market operations would be appropriate for the change in the money supply discussed in part (c)?

(e) Is this type of open market operation likely to encourage or curtail economic expansion?

4. Suppose the Bank of Canada sells $150 million of Canadian government securities to the chartered banks. Show the immediate effect of this transaction in the balance sheets below. The cash reserve ratio is assumed to be .10.

(a)

Bank of Canada

Assets	Liabilities
Securities:	Bank reserves:

Banking System

Assets	Liabilities
Reserves: Loans: Securities:	Deposits:

(a) Is the money supply immediately changed? Why or why not?

(b) After this transaction, what is the level of deficient reserves in the banking system? What is the total amount of loans that will be called in initially?

(c) What will be the final change in the money supply?

(d) What accompanying change in the bank rate is likely to occur?

PART TEN

MACROECONOMIC PROBLEMS

CHAPTER 36

INFLATION

CHAPTER OBJECTIVES

In the context of the aggregate demand and aggregate supply framework, inflation is the result of continuous upward shifts in either the aggregate supply curve or aggregate demand curve. This chapter reviews the forces which causes shifts in these curves, identifying both demand and supply shocks. The importance of monetary validation and accommodation in sustaining inflation is stressed. Concepts such as the natural rate of unemployment, rational expectations, and the Phillips curve are dealt with in the multiple-choice questions. Exercises require you to manipulate the aggregate supply-demand model to determine how price level changes are initiated.

MULTIPLE-CHOICE QUESTIONS

1. For any increase in the price level to be sustained,
   (a) there must be a supply shock
   (b) supply or demand shocks must be accompanied by increases in the money supply
   (c) both demand and supply shocks must occur simultaneously
   (d) the Bank of Canada must be keeping the money supply growth equal to the growth in real national income

2. Monetary accommodation of an isolated supply shock
   (a) serves to moderate the price level increase
   (b) causes the initial rise in the price level to be followed by another rise
   (c) forces the economy into an extended recession
   (d) moderates inflation rates by increasing unemployment

3. Wage-cost push inflation emanating from labor markets is a type of
   (a) inflation caused by demand shocks
   (b) expectational inflation
   (c) recurring supply shock inflation
   (d) equilibrium inflation

4. The initial consequence of bringing a cost-push inflation to a halt by not increasing the money supply will be
   (a) a rise in output
   (b) to accelerate inflation
   (c) to validate the inflation in the short run
   (d) a fall in output

5. Which one of the following would be the least important part of the process of continuing inflation?
   (a) increases in the money supply
   (b) wage increases
   (c) increasing profit margins
   (d) expectational forces

6. Which one of the following statements is correct?
   (a) An ever-increasing money supply is necessary for an ever-continuing inflation.
   (b) A decrease in the money supply is necessary to halt continuing inflation.
   (c) Monetary accommodation is an effective way to prevent supply shocks from causing a sustained inflation.
   (d) Monetary validation is an effective way to control inflation caused by demand shocks.

7. The phrase monetary accommodation means that
   (a) the money supply is increased in response to a demand shock
   (b) various types of bank deposits have been designed to meet the needs of different types of depositors
   (c) the money supply is increased in response to a supply shock
   (d) people will hold smaller money balances at higher rates of interest

8. The difference between temporary and sustained inflation is that
   (a) the former always occurs when there is full employment
   (b) the latter is the result of monetary accommodation or monetary validation
   (c) the latter occurs only in instances where there is full employment
   (d) the former is induced by a supply shock and the latter by a demand shock

9. All of the following will result with monetary validation of a single demand shock <u>except</u>:
   (a) the AD curve shifts upward, fueled by monetary policy
   (b) wages will rise, causing the SRAS curve to shift upward
   (c) the price level will rise
   (d) real national income will fall

10. The percentage of unemployment that exists when national income is at its potential level is called
    (a) frictional unemployment
    (b) structural unemployment
    (c) inertia unemployment
    (d) the natural rate of unemployment

11. According to the acceleration hypothesis, when there is an inflationary gap and monetary validation,
    (a) inflation expectations will moderate, bringing the inflation under control.
    (b) the rate of inflation will tend to increase
    (c) output will be held below its potential so that a GNP gap occurs
    (d) the rate of inflation will remain unchanged

12. According to the natural rate hypothesis, steady inflation with full employment will result
    (a) when the rates of monetary growth, wage increase, actual inflation, and expected inflation are all equal
    (b) only when the expected inflation rate is zero
    (c) as long as an inflationary gap persists
    (d) as soon as a monetary rule is followed by monetary authorities

Questions 13 and 14 refer to the diagram below.

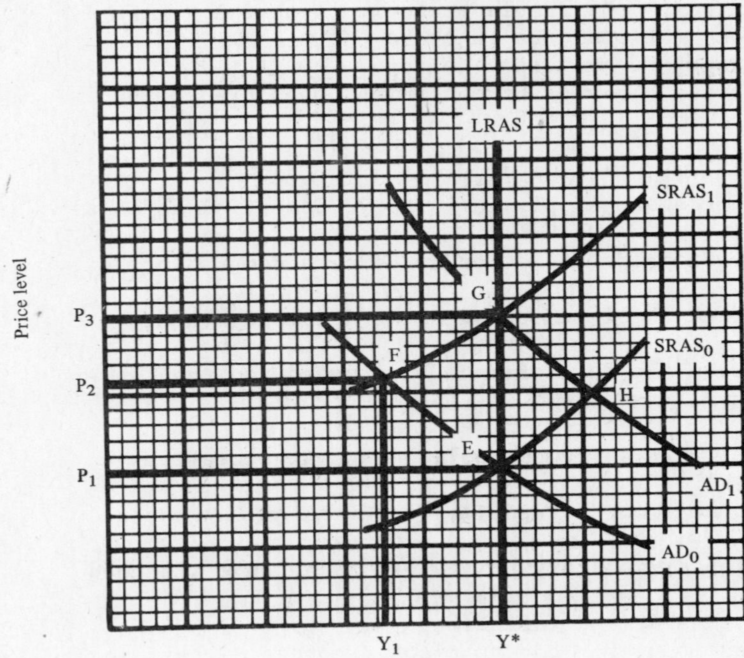

13. Starting from the equilibrium at point E, if the short run aggregate supply curve shifts from $SRAS_0$ to $SRAS_1$, and there is complete monetary accommodation,
   (a) real national income would temporarily fall to Y_1, then be restabilized at Y*
   (b) the aggregate demand curve would shift to the right to pass through point G
   (c) the price level will rise
   (d) all of the above

14. Starting from an equilibrium at point E, if the aggregate demand curve shifts from AD_0 to AD_1 and there is no monetary validation,
   (a) equilibrium will be established at point F
   (b) the price level will remain unchanged, at P_1
   (c) the price level will increase to P_3
   (d) inflation will be sustained, starting from point H

15. The most likely cause of an inflation persisting after the original causes have been removed is
   (a) an inadequate number of jobs in the economy
   (b) a growing GNP gap
   (c) expectations of continuing inflation
   (d) continued increases in imports

16. Neo-Keynesians and monetarists would agree on all <u>but</u> which one of the statements below about inflation?
   (a) Sustained price level increases require monetary accommodation or validation.
   (b) Expectations are an important consideration when devising policies to curb inflation.
   (c) The period of stagflation of an anti-inflationary process (phase 2) will usually be of short duration.
   (d) An entrenched inflation requires demand contraction to remove the inflationary gap.

17. The rational expectations hypothesis implies that
   (a) the future is based entirely on past, observable economic phenomena
   (b) errors can be avoided if everyone rationalizes the past
   (c) inflation can be controlled by long-run monetary policy
   (d) people examine current policies and behavior of government when predicting future inflation

18. The Phillips curve
   (a) is identical to the short-run aggregate supply curve above potential national income
   (b) describes the relationship between price inflation and excess demand in the economy
   (c) describes the relationship between the level of wages and unemployment in the economy
   (d) describes the relationship between the rate of change of wages and the unemployment rate in the economy

19. In which one of the following cases would an income policy be most successful in controlling inflation?
   (a) in conjunction with an expansionary monetary policy, to break an entrenched inflation
   (b) in conjunction with a contractionary monetary policy, to break an entrenched inflation
   (c) alone, as a permanent solution to a demand inflation
   (d) alone, as a well-publicized substitute for contractionary monetary and fiscal policies

20. Which one of the following was not a component of the Canadian authorities' effort to control inflation in the late 1970s?
   (a) monetary gradualism
   (b) wage and price controls administered by the Anti-Inflation Board (AIB)
   (c) actual and high-employment budget deficits
   (d) contractionary fiscal policies

EXERCISES

1. The diagram below illustrates an initial equilibrium at point E with real national income Y_0 and price level P_0.

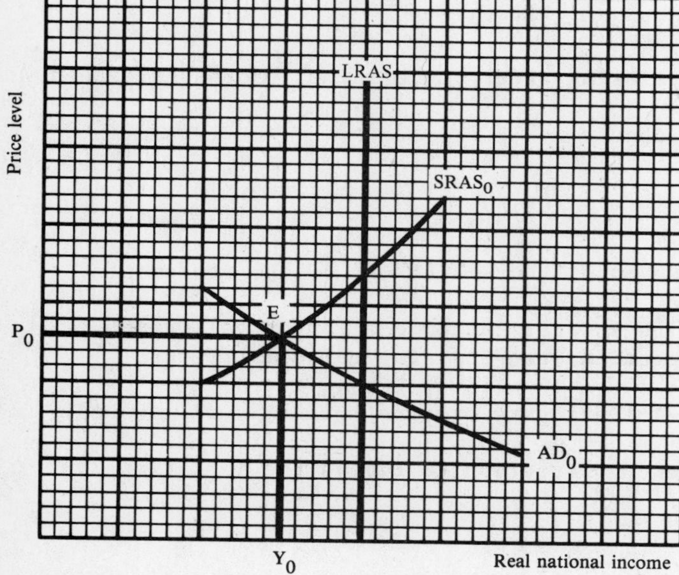

(a) If an increase in the money supply stimulated demand enough to achieve potential GNP, draw the new aggregate demand curve and indicate the new price level.

(b) Suppose the resulting rise in the price level (see (a) above) caused expectations that inflation would occur in the future, and as a result, higher wages throughout the economy occurred. Show on the diagram what would happen to the SRAS curve. What will be the immediate consequence for real national income and the price level?

(c) If the supply shock which occurred in (b) was fully accommodated, what would happen to the aggregate demand curve? Illustrate on the diagram.

2. Briefly explain and also illustrate on the graphs the following:

(a) monetary accommodation of a single supply shock

(b) a single supply shock with no monetary accommodation

(c) a demand shock with no monetary validation

(d) monetary validation of a demand shock

(a)

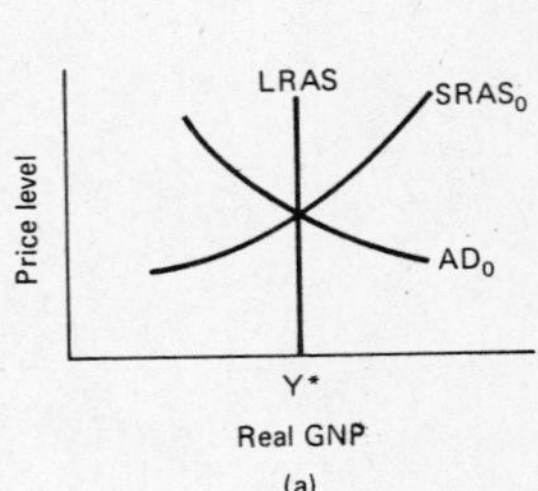

(b)

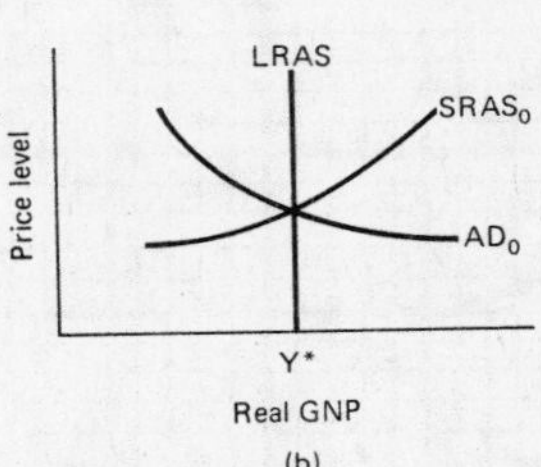

(c)

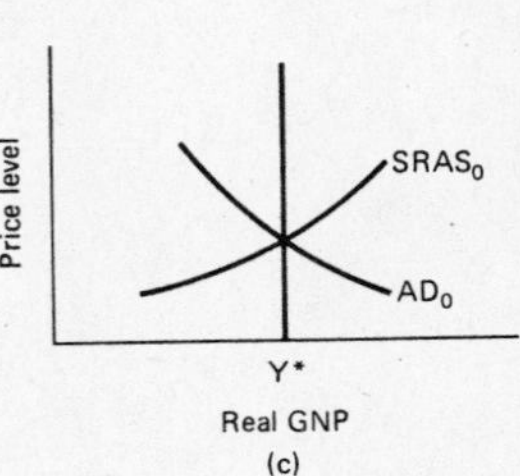

(d)

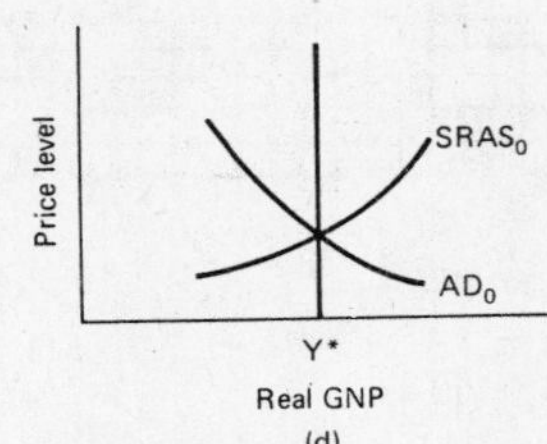

3. The top panel in the diagram below illustrates a version of the Phillips curve (with expectations that there will be no inflation in the future). The bottom panel is an "upside down" illustration of the short-run aggregate supply curve, drawn this way to use a common axis (real national income) for both diagrams.

(a) The economy is initially at E in both panels. We observe in the next period that we are at a point G on the Phillips curve. What is happening to the SRAS curve in the bottom panel?

(b) Some time later, it is observed that while the rate of change in wages is still positive, it is lower than that indicated by point G. What is happening to the SRAS curve now?

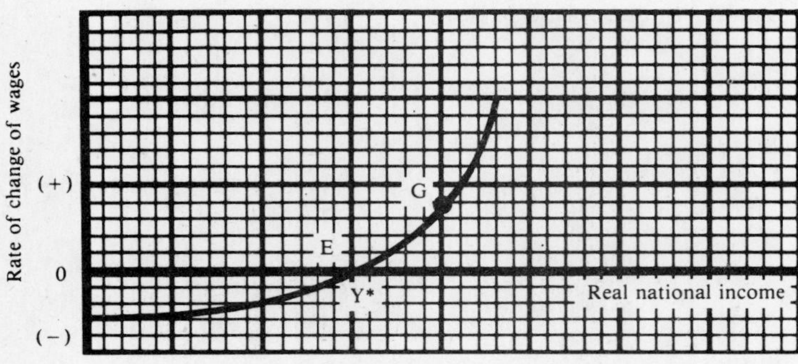

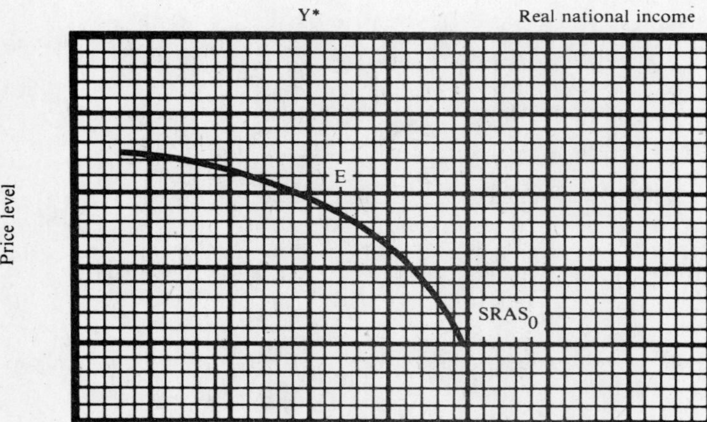

(c) If, again after a period of time, the economy was observed to be back at E on the Phillips curve, where would the SRAS curve be in relation to $SRAS_o$? Why?

CHAPTER 37

EMPLOYMENT AND UNEMPLOYMENT

CHAPTER OBJECTIVES

This chapter discusses the causes of unemployment and explains how measured unemployment may not accurately reflect the actual amount of unemployment in the economy. Make sure you can distinguish deficient demand unemployment from frictional and structural unemployment. Once you have learned the various types of unemployment and the causes of each, try to learn the appropriate policy measures which may be used to reduce each type of unemployment.

1. Voluntary unemployment
   (a) occurs when there is a job available but the unemployed person is unwilling to accept it at the existing wage
   (b) is of more concern to policy-makers than involuntary unemployment
   (c) increases substantially during a deep recession
   (d) occurs when a person is willing to accept a job at the going wage rate but no such job can be found

2. Unemployment that occurs as a result of the normal turnover of labor as people move from job to job is called
   (a) involuntary unemployment
   (b) structural unemployment
   (c) demand-deficient unemployment
   (d) frictional unemployment

3. Structural unemployment means that
   (a) there is an inadequate number of jobs in the economy
   (b) there are not enough employees
   (c) the building trades workers are suffering from high unemployment rates
   (d) the composition of the demand for labor does not match the composition of the available supply

4. Full employment of labor means that
   (a) the unemployment rate is zero
   (b) all unemployment is frictional or structural
   (c) all unemployment is due to deficient demand
   (d) any person who desires a job has one

5. The unemployment rate is defined as
   (a) the percentage of unemployed to employed workers
   (b) the percentage of the adult population who are unemployed
   (c) the percentage of the labor force who are unemployed
   (d) the percentage of the unemployed who are collecting unemployment insurance

6. The real product wage is defined as
   (a) the marginal product of labor times the real wage rate
   (b) the nominal cost of labor to the employer (excluding any taxes or fringe benefits) divided by the CPI
   (c) the nominal cost of labor to the employer (including taxes and fringe benefits) divided by the CPI
   (d) the nominal cost of labor to the employer (including payroll taxes and fringe benefits) divided by the output price of the firm.

7. The measured unemployment figure may underestimate the actual number of unemployed because
   (a) it includes people who have voluntarily withdrawn from the labor force
   (b) part-time workers are not included as members of the labor force
   (c) it does not include discouraged workers who have voluntarily withdrawn from the labor force
   (d) it excludes those who are actively searching for work but who are unable to find work

8. Which one of the following is <u>not</u> correct?
   (a) Unemployment insurance encourages voluntary and search unemployment.
   (b) It is not possible to reduce unemployment to zero.
   (c) Frictional unemployment is inevitable.
   (d) A rise in real product wages will reduce unemployment, other things being equal.

9. Which one of the following has <u>not</u> been an important factor in causing structural unemployment over the past 15 years?
   (a) inappropriate monetary and fiscal policies
   (b) rapidly changing technology
   (c) certain input price shocks
   (d) a changing composition of the labor force

10. Which one of the following would be the most effective policy for reducing structural unemployment in the long run?
   (a) a decrease in personal tax rates
   (b) preservation of jobs in declining industries
   (c) increasing government expenditure on unemployment insurance
   (d) retraining and relocation programs for displaced workers

11. Voluntary frictional unemployment is also known as
   (a) structural unemployment
   (b) deficient-demand unemployment
   (c) search unemployment
   (d) real wage unemployment

12. Deficient-demand unemployment exists because
   (a) frictional and structural unemployment is zero
   (b) real national income exceeds potential income
   (c) the real wage is too high across the whole economy
   (d) there is a recessionary gap

13. Zero unemployment is impossible to attain because, at minimum, there will always be
   (a) deficient-demand unemployment
   (b) frictional unemployment
   (c) classical unemployment
   (d) real wage unemployment

14. A rise in the real product wage will, other things being equal, cause all of the following except
    (a) some firms will no longer be able to cover their variable costs and will shut down
    (b) unemployment to increase
    (c) new labor-intensive plants to be built
    (d) investment in new, more capital-intensive plant and equipment to be undertaken in the long run

EXERCISES

1. Classify the following situations as frictional unemployment, structural unemployment, search unemployment, real wage unemployment, or demand-deficient unemployment, and briefly explain your choice:
    (a) An auto assembly worker is laid off because auto sales decrease with a slowdown in economic activity.

    (b) Firms lay off workers when real wage costs increase because of costlier fringe benefit payments.

    (c) A chartered accountant refuses a job offer and decides to look for another job which has a higher rate of remuneration.

    (d) A social worker is laid off because the government has canceled the Local Initiatives Program (LIP).

    (e) A mechanic in London, Ontario, is laid off when a bus manufacturing firm relocates in Montreal.

    (f) Stenographers are laid off as firms in Calgary introduce word-processing equipment into their offices.

2. The following diagram depicts the demand and supply curves of labor in a particular industry. We assume that both curves depend on the real product wage rate. The current real product wage is RPW_0.

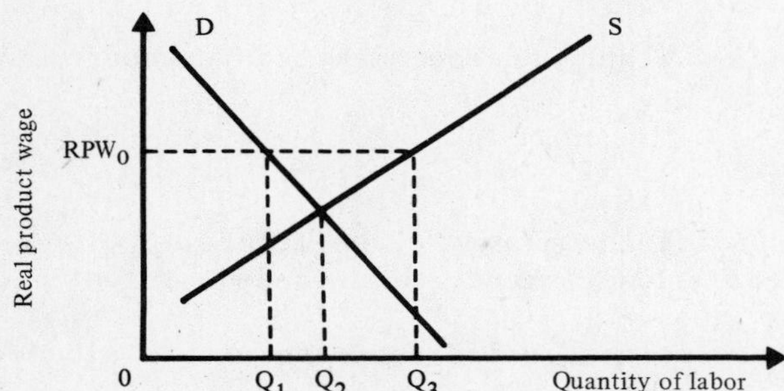

(a) What factors (elements) are included in the real product wage?

(b) Given the current real product wage, what situation exists in the labor market of this industry?

(c) What policy recommendations might you make?

3. What specific government policy would you recommend for each of the following causes of unemployment? Explain.

(a) structural unemployment

(b) deficient-demand unemployment

(c) frictional unemployment

(d) real wage unemployment

CHAPTER 38

ECONOMIC GROWTH

CHAPTER OBJECTIVES

Economic growth is defined as a rise in potential national income due to increases in factor supplies or in the productivity of factors. This chapter discusses some theories of economic growth, most of which focus on investment as the source of growth. The contemporary view of economic growth emphasizes the creation of new investment opportunities rather than the exploitation of existing investment opportunities.

The chapter also discusses the costs and benefits of economic growth. One exercise is designed to illustrate the opportunity costs of higher economic growth while another tests your understanding of the effects of certain events on current and future real consumption per capita.

MULTIPLE-CHOICE QUESTIONS

1. Economic growth is best defined as
   (a) a rise in real national income as unemployment is reduced
   (b) an increase in the current level of real national income
   (c) a rise in potential national income due to increases in factor supplies or in the productivity of factors
   (d) an increase in investment and the capital stock

2. Output per man-hour is likely to increase if, other things being equal,
   (a) the size of the labor force increases
   (b) health improvements increase longevity for (only) the nonworking aged population
   (c) better machinery and training are available for workers
   (d) wages increase

3. Theories of economic growth concentrate on
   (a) the effects of investment on raising potential real national income
   (b) the effects of investment on aggregate demand in the short run
   (c) cyclical fluctuations in national income around some given level of potential national income
   (d) reductions in structural unemployment over time

4. In the long run, an increase in saving, other things being equal, is likely to
   (a) cause the aggregate demand curve to shift to the left
   (b) cause real national income to fall
   (c) increase economic growth because more investment expenditure can be financed from these funds
   (d) demonstrate the "paradox of thrift" phenomenon

5. According to the "rule of 72," a growth in the population of 2 percent per year means that population will be double in approximately
   (a) 2 years (c) 36 years
   (b) 72 years (d) 50 years

6. The marginal efficiency of capital curve
   (a) relates the stock of capital to the productivity of an additional unit of capital
   (b) is generally assumed to be downward sloping as a consequence of the law of diminishing returns
   (c) relates the stock of capital to the efficiency of investment
   (d) both (a) and (b) are correct

7. Economic growth models which assume "no learning" predict that
   (a) the capital-output ratio will be falling through time
   (b) the marginal efficiency of capital increases for successive increments in the capital stock
   (c) more and more investment opportunities appear through time
   (d) the output per unit of capital falls through time

8. With technical change and new knowledge,
   (a) diminishing returns to additional investment will cause the capital-output ratio to fall
   (b) the marginal efficiency of the capital curve will become horizontal
   (c) the marginal efficiency of the capital curve will shift to the left
   (d) the marginal efficiency of the capital curve will shift outward over time

9. The classical view of economic growth assumed that
   (a) investment opportunities are created but at a slower rate than they are used up
   (b) the capital-output ratio was likely to fall through time
   (c) investment opportunities are created at a faster rate than they are used up
   (d) the rate of return increased as the capital stock increased

10. The major difference between the earlier classical theory of economic growth and the contemporary view is that
   (a) contemporary economists place much more importance on the quantity of labor than do classical economists
   (b) classical economists ignored the role of capital accumulation
   (c) contemporary economists emphasize the creation of investment opportunities rather than simply the exploitation of existing opportunities
   (d) classical economists emphasized the role of international trade in economic growth

11. An embodied technical change is one that
   (a) improves the quality of labor
   (b) involves changes in the form of capital goods in use
   (c) is concerned with techniques of managerial control
   (d) is exogeneous to the economic system

12. Suppose two countries have the same per capita output. Country A has an annual economic growth rate of 6 percent while Country B grows at 3% per year. Country A will have a per capita output four times as large as Country B's in
   (a) 12 years   (c) 36 years
   (b) 24 years   (d) 48 years

13. An increase in the rate of economic growth
   (a) will usually require a reduction in the proportion of current national income consumed
   (b) will usually result from an increase in consumption
   (c) is often the result of increased investment in physical capital alone
   (d) will be aided by high interest rates

14. The most important benefit of economic growth historically has been its role in
    (a) redistributing income among people
    (b) raising living standards
    (c) helping countries defend themselves
    (d) providing for the employment of scarce resources

15. Which one of the following has played the largest role in the economic growth of North America since 1900, according to recent studies?
    (a) increases in the quantity of raw materials
    (b) increases in the size of the labor force due to population growth
    (c) improvements in the quality of capital, human as well as physical
    (d) increases in the quantity of capital

16. For the economy as a whole, the primary opportunity cost of economic growth is
    (a) borne by future generations whose living standards will be reduced
    (b) the natural resource shortages that result from economic growth
    (c) the reduction in living standards for the current generation of consumers
    (d) the increased poverty that inevitably results from economic growth

EXERCISES

1. Assume that the productivity of labor increases by 2.5 percent a year, the labor force increases by 1.75 percent a year, hours worked per member of the work force decline by 0.25 percent a year, and population increases by 1 percent a year. Predict:

    (a) the annual increase in real GNP

    (b) the annual increase in GNP per capita

    (c) the number of years to double real GNP

    (d) the number of years to double GNP per capita

2. Designate how each of the following factors would probably affect standards of living as measured by real consumption per capita, now and a few years from now. Use a (+) for an increase, a (-) for a decrease, and (U) for no change or too uncertain to call (first dash is for current effect, second dash for future effect). Assume other things remain constant and full employment of resources.

(a) an increase in the birthrate ________ ________

(b) a decrease in current saving ________ ________

(c) a technological innovation reducing inputs ________ ________

(d) an increase in current expenditures for technical education financed by increased taxes ________ ________

(e) a decrease in the working life span of the labor force ________ ________

(f) an increase in labor force participation ________ ________

3. <u>The Opportunity Costs of Growth</u>

Suppose that the national income of an economy was 100 in year 0 and consumption expenditure was 85 and investment expenditure was 15. The growth of real national income on an annual basis is expected to be 2 percent. The current government urges the citizens of this nation to pursue policies to increase the growth rate to 4 percent on an annual basis. Its economic forecasters suggest that by reducing consumption to 70 (increasing saving by 15), and increasing investment expenditure to a level of 30 that: (1) consumption expenditure 7 years hence will be equal to that level of consumption without these policies (with the economy growing at 2 percent) and (2) the aggregate level of consumption in 20 years would be double the level associated with a 2 percent growth.

Annual Level of Consumption

In year	2% Growth	4% Growth	Cumulative Loss or Gain
0	85.0	70.0	(15.0)
1	86.7	72.9	(28.8)
2	88.5	75.8	(41.5)
3	90.3	78.9	(52.9)
4	92.1	82.1	(62.9)
7	97.8	92.6	(83.3)
8	99.7	96.4	(86.6)
9	101.8	100.3	(88.1)
10	103.8	104.4	(87.5)
17	119.4	138.2	(14.9)
18	121.8	143.8	7.1
20	126.8	155.8	61.5
30	154.9	232.4	
40	189.2	346.7	
50	231.1	517.2	

*Parentheses denote a loss.

Your task is to confirm the accuracy of the government's economic forecasts by answering the following questions:

(a) What is the loss in consumption in year 4 because of the government's growth policy? What is the cumulative loss after 4 years?

(b) In what year will the level of consumption with a 4 percent growth rate equal the level of consumption with a 2 percent growth rate? Compare your answer with the government's assertion.

(c) In what year does this economy recoup all of the cumulative losses in foregone consumption?

(d) Is the government's assertion that this society will double its consumption level in 20 years correct?

PART ELEVEN

INTERNATIONAL MACROECONOMICS

CHAPTER 39

FOREIGN EXCHANGE, EXCHANGE RATES, AND THE BALANCE OF PAYMENTS

CHAPTER OBJECTIVES

This chapter analyzes the relation between various international transactions which are recorded in the balance of payments accounts and the value of the exchange rate between two currencies. Certain questions emphasize the notion that an exchange rate is a relative price; the quantity of one currency that must be given up in order to obtain one unit of another currency. Hence, there are two ways of expressing an exchange rate between two currencies.

Learn that the demand curve for a particular currency is downward sloping and that the supply curve is upward sloping. Current account receipts and capital inflows create a demand for a country's currency while current account payments and capital outflows create a supply. It is important that you learn those factors which cause the curves to shift thereby changing the equilibrium value of the exchange rate.

Some questions test your knowledge of balance of payments accounting, the various subaccounts, and debits and credits. Remember that although the balance of payments must balance in an accounting sense, a country may experience either a deficit or a surplus on the balance of payments. A loss in a country's foreign exchange reserves will signal a balance of payments deficit while an increase in official reserves will signal a balance of payments surplus.

MULTIPLE-CHOICE QUESTIONS

1. An economy which is described as a small open economy (SOE)
   (a) engages in no international trade
   (b) can influence the prices of traded goods by changing the supplies of these goods
   (c) allows free exchange of factors of production such as labor
   (d) is a price taker for goods it trades on the world market

2. The exchange rate refers to
   (a) the ratio of exports to imports
   (b) the rate at which one country exchanges gold with another
   (c) the amount of home currency that must be given up in order to obtain one unit of foreign currency
   (d) the volume of trading of one currency in terms of all others

3. If $1 U.S. trades for $1.32 Canadian, then
   (a) the volume of trade must be in the ratio 1.00 to 1.32
   (b) the price of U.S. dollars in terms of Canadian dollars is $0.758
   (c) one Canadian dollar exchanges for 75.8 U.S. cents
   (d) Canada will always have an excess of imports over exports as far as trade with the United States is concerned

4. If the Canadian dollar price of the U.S. dollar rises from $1.30 to $1.32, then
   (a) the Canadian dollar has depreciated
   (b) the U.S. dollar has appreciated
   (c) the Canadian dollar has appreciated
   (d) both (a) and (b) are correct

5. If a skiing trip to Aspen Colorado costs $3,000 (U.S.) and the Canadian dollar price of one U.S. dollar is $1.40, then
   (a) Canadians must pay $2,142.86 in Canadian funds for this trip
   (b) Americans pay $4,200 in American funds for this trip
   (c) Canadians must pay $4,200 in Canadian funds for this trip
   (d) Americans must pay $2,142.86 in American dollars for this trip

6. An appreciation of the foreign currency, other things being equal,
   (a) lowers the domestic prices of traded (foreign) goods
   (b) raises the domestic prices of traded goods
   (c) has no effect on the domestic prices of traded goods
   (d) raises the relative value of the home currency

7. An appreciation of the home (domestic) currency, other things being equal,
   (a) increases the domestic prices of traded goods
   (b) leads to a reduction in the quantity supplied and an increase in the quantity demanded for traded goods
   (c) is likely to increase the volume of exports and decrease the volume of imports
   (d) does not affect the prices of traded goods relative to domestic goods

Questions 8 through 14 refer to the following diagram. The two countries are Canada (the domestic country) and Japan. The currency of Japan is the yen.

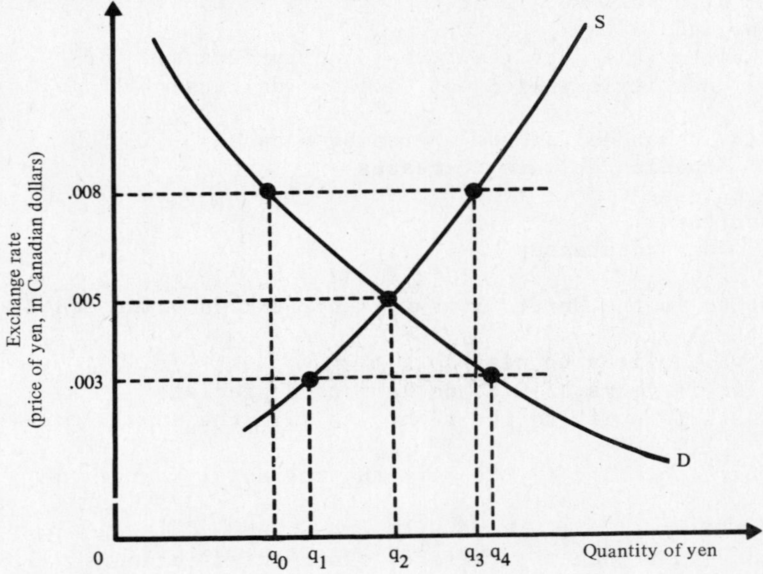

8. A movement down the vertical scale means that
   (a) the yen becomes more expensive
   (b) the Canadian dollar is depreciating relative to the yen
   (c) the yen is depreciating
   (d) Canadian exports to Japan are falling

9. If the exchange rate is 0.005, then
   (a) $200 trades for one yen
   (b) 0.005 yen trades for one Canadian dollar
   (c) one yen trades for 0.005 Canadian dollars
   (d) the quantity demanded of yen is less than the quantity supplied

10. At an exchange rate of 0.008,
   (a) there is an excess demand of yen
   (b) there is an excess supply of yen
   (c) there is an excess supply of Canadian dollars
   (d) there is an equilibrium exchange rate providing that the exchange rate is determined in a free market

11. At an exchange rate of 0.003
   (a) the quantity demanded for yen is $0q_4$ and the quantity supplied is $0q_1$
   (b) the quantity demanded for yen is $0q_3$ and the quantity supplied is $0q_1$
   (c) there is an excess supply of yen of $q_4 - q_1$
   (d) there is an excess demand for Canadian dollars of $q_4 - q_1$

12. Given the demand and supply curves for yen, the equilibrium exchange rate assuming a free market for exchange is
   (a) 0.003
   (b) 0.008
   (c) 0.005
   (d) between 0.005 and 0.008

13. Assuming that the initial exchange rate is 0.008, then forces in a free market for exchange are likely to cause
   (a) the Canadian dollar price of yen to rise
   (b) the Canadian dollar price of yen to remain at 0.008
   (c) the Canadian dollar price of yen to fall such that the quantity demanded for yen increases and the quantity supplied falls
   (d) the Canadian dollar price of yen to fall such that the quantity demanded for Canadian dollars rises and the quantity supplied (of Canadian dollars) falls

14. As the yen depreciates, the quantity demanded for yen increases because
   (a) the price of Japanese goods in Canadian dollars decreases
   (b) Japanese imports from Canada increase
   (c) Canadian imports from Japan decrease
   (d) the price of Canadian goods in Japan decreases

15. A lower inflation rate in Canada than in the United States, other things being equal, is predicted to cause
   (a) the Canadian dollar price of U.S. dollars to rise
   (b) the price of the Canadian dollar in terms of U.S. dollars to depreciate
   (c) the demand curve for U.S. dollars to shift to the right, as will the supply curve for U.S. dollars
   (d) the demand curve for U.S. dollars to shift to the left and the supply curve to shift to the right

16. A desire by Canadians to invest more in France than before, other things being equal, will cause
   (a) the French franc price of Canadian dollars to rise
   (b) the demand curve for francs to shift to the right
   (c) the supply curve for Canadian dollars to shift to the left
   (d) the supply curve for francs to shift to the right

17. If short-term interest rates in Canada increase relative to short-term U.S. interest rates, other things equal, then
   (a) capital flows from the United States to Canada are likely to increase and the U.S. dollar price of Canadian dollars is likely to rise
   (b) it is likely that the price of the Canadian dollar will depreciate
   (c) the demand curve for U.S. dollars will shift to the right
   (d) the Canadian dollar price of U.S. dollars will rise

18. Which of the following is <u>not</u> likely to cause an appreciation of the Canadian dollar?
   (a) an increase in interest rates in Canada relative to rates elsewhere
   (b) a lower inflation rate in Canada relative to foreign inflation rates
   (c) lower earnings expectations in Canada relative to those elsewhere
   (d) expectations of an appreciation of the Canadian dollar

19. If there is a current-account deficit in Canada, the sale of Canadian government bonds to U.S. citizens will
   (a) guarantee a balance on the balance of payments
   (b) increase the likelihood of a balance-of-payments deficit
   (c) be recorded as a payment on the capital account
   (d) offset totally or in part the deficit on the current account

20. The current account includes all <u>but</u> which of the following transactions?
   (a) merchandise exports and imports
   (b) unilateral transfers
   (c) short-run capital transfers
   (d) invisibles

21. Which of the following statements about the balance of payments is true?
   (a) Current-account debits must equal current-account credits.
   (b) Visibles must equal invisibles
   (c) Total debts must equal total credits
   (d) Desired payments must equal actual payments

Questions 22 through 29 refer to the balance-of-payments items listed below:

(a) Long-term capital receipts	$ + 1,305
(b) Merchandise exports	+ 17,785
(c) Freight and shipping receipts	+ 1,170
(d) Freight and shipping payments	- 1,147
(e) Short-term capital receipts	+ 1,182
(f) Use of official reserves	- 777
(g) Merchandise imports	- 15,556
(h) Long-term capital payments	- 814
(i) Short-term capital receipts	- 1,158
(j) Interest and dividend receipts	+ 545
(k) Interest and dividend payments	- 1,613
(l) Other current-account payments	- 721
(m) Net travel payments	- 201

22. The value of merchandise net exports is
   (a) 33,341
   (c) 2,229
   (b) -2,229
   (d) 1,307

23. Which of the following is <u>not</u> an item in the current account?
   (a) item (m)
   (c) item (e)
   (d) item (c)
   (b) item (b)

24. The value of the current-account balance is a
    (a) deficit of 262 (c) surplus of 1,508
    (b) surplus of 262 (d) surplus of 380

25. A surplus in the current account must be matched by
    (a) a deficit in the capital account (c) either (a) or (b) or both
    (b) an increase in official reserves (d) always (b) but never (a)

26. Which of the following is not a capital account item?
    (a) item (f) (c) item (e)
    (b) item (i) (d) item (h)

27. The value of the capital-account balance is a
    (a) deficit of 515 (c) deficit of 262
    (b) surplus of 515 (d) surplus of 262

28. In the situation shown in the information above, the sum of the current and capital accounts indicates that the balance of payments is in a
    (a) surplus position of 777 (c) surplus position of 253
    (b) deficit position of 777 (d) deficit position of 530

29. The value of the balance-of-payments position in the last question is reflected by the fact that official reserves
    (a) increased by 777 (c) decreased by 530
    (b) decreased by 777 (d) did not change

EXERCISES

1. Suppose that the exchange rate between Canadian dollars and American dollars is established in a free exchange market without any intervention by the Bank of Canada. For each of the following events, indicate whether the Canadian dollar price of the U.S. dollar will tend to appreciate, depreciate, or remain unchanged. Explain your answer briefly and indicate whether the event is likely to affect the demand curve for U.S. dollars (denoted as D) or the supply curve for U.S. dollars (denoted as S), or both.

    (a) Los Angeles hosts the 1984 Summer Olympics.

    (b) The rate of inflation in Canada increases relative to the U.S. inflation rate.

    (c) Short-term interest rates rise in the United States relative to those in Canada.

    (d) Prolonged U.S. economic expansion causes Canadian exports to the United States to increase from previous levels.

    (e) A Brian Mulroney Conservative government announces new policies designed to encourage more investment by Americans in Canada.

    (f) Speculators anticipate a depreciation of the U.S. dollar relative to the Canadian dollar.

2. Suppose a small country produces soybeans. It imports manufactured goods but these are not considered in this question. The price/ton of soybeans is established in world markets at $60 (U.S.) per ton. The current exchange rate is 10 units of this country's currency for every U.S. dollar. The domestic demand curve for soybeans is $Q_D = 10,000 - 5P$ and the domestic supply curve is $Q_S = 400 + 11P$, where P is the domestic price of soybeans per ton. The demand and supply curves are drawn below.

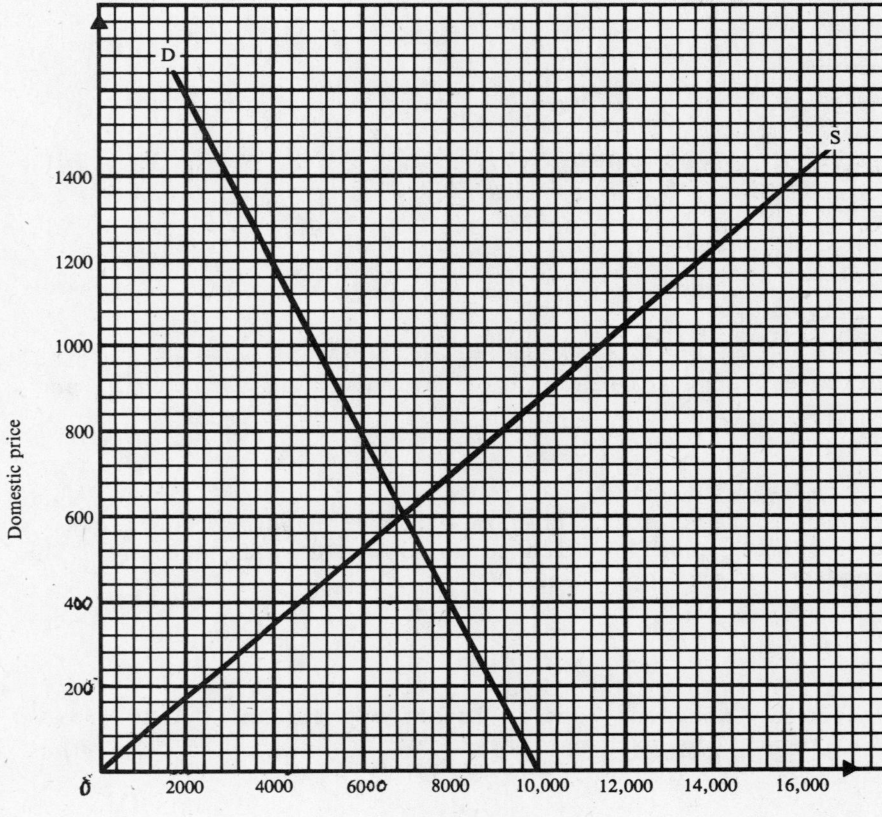

(a) What is the current domestic price of soybeans? How much is produced domestically? What quantity of soybeans would be exported (assuming domestic price $\leq$ the world price)

(b) Suppose the world price of soybeans rises to $100 (U.S.) per ton. What happens to the price of soybeans in this country? At this price, what is the domestic quantity demanded? Quantity supplied? Does this country export or import soybeans? What quantity?

(c) Now suppose that the exchange rate changes such that six units of domestic currency trade for one U.S. dollar. What has happened to the price of the dollar? The price of the domestic currency?

(d) At this new exchange rate, what is the new domestic price of soybeans? What is the domestic quantity demanded at this new price? Quantity supplied? Quantity of exports? Explain your answers.

3. You are given the demand for and the supply of Canadian dollars at alternative prices in terms of U.S. dollars. Assume that the Canadian dollar is floating.

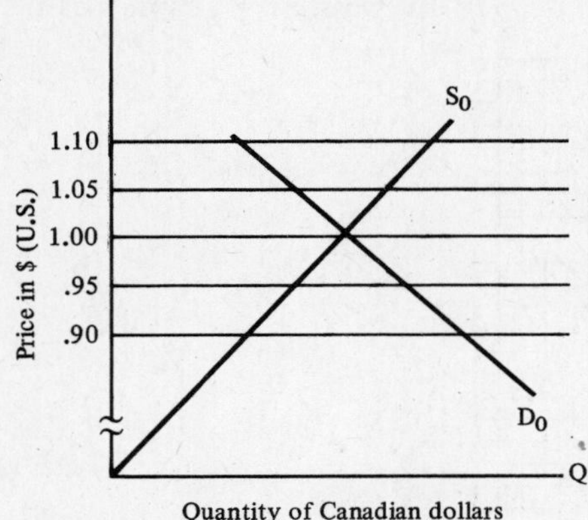

(a) Determine the equilibrium exchange rate for the Canadian dollar assuming D_0 and S_0 apply.

(b) Suppose there is a sizable increase in short-term capital investment outflows from Canada, other things being equal. Which curve(s) would shift and why? What will happen to the exchange rate?

(c) Which curve(s) will shift if Canadians were to import significantly less from the U.S.? What will happen to the exchange rate?

(d) Suppose Canadian exports to the United States were to significantly increase, other things being equal. Predict the effect on the Canadian dollar.

CHAPTER 40

ALTERNATIVE EXCHANGE RATE REGIMES

CHAPTER OBJECTIVES

This chapter distinguishes between three types of exchange rate regimes: pegged (or fixed), flexible (or floating or free), and managed (or dirty) float.

A pegged exchange rate may not represent an equilibrium value or a value which would hold under a flexible exchange rate regime. Some questions illustrate how this can occur and what actions a central bank must undertake in order to maintain the pegged value.

The chapter also discusses the purchasing power parity hypothesis. Exercises are provided to demonstrate that over the long run exchange rates reflect relative rates of national inflation.

MULTIPLE-CHOICE QUESTIONS

1. Under the Bretton Woods agreement
   (a) most countries returned to the gold standard
   (b) countries were given almost complete freedom to let their currencies float
   (c) exchange rates were tied to the U.S. dollar
   (d) gold was completely abandoned as an international means of payment

2. Among postwar international developments were all of the following except
   (a) the dollar shortage confronting war-torn countries that needed U.S. goods
   (b) the dollar surplus Europe and Japan accumulated as they recovered
   (c) prompt upward adjustments of undervalued currencies
   (d) considerable international cooperation to maintain stable exchange rates

3. The International Monetary Fund
   (a) is a fund for long-term development projects
   (b) was designed to assist in making exchange rates more readily flexible
   (c) was designed to help maintain fixed exchange rates in the face of short-term fluctuations
   (d) was abandoned after the dollar shortage of the early 1950s

4. Special Drawing Rights are
   (a) supplementary reserves with the IMF, which member countries can use to finance balance-of-payments deficits
   (b) demand deposits that central banks hold in the World Bank
   (c) special credits given to importers in the IMF countries
   (d) long-term reserves available to member countries in return for gold

5. A floating or flexible exchange rate is
   (a) the same as a fixed exchange rate
   (b) a rate which fluctuates around some fixed rate permitted by IMF rules
   (c) necessarily unstable
   (d) determined in international exchange markets by demand and supply conditions

6. If there is excess demand for a currency at some fixed exchange rate, then the central bank, to maintain this pegged rate, must
   (a) buy its currency in the exchange market
   (b) wait until the demand and supply curves for this currency change such that no excess demand exists
   (c) sell its currency in the exchange market and therefore increase its holdings of official reserves
   (d) increase interest rates by selling government bonds

7. If there is an excess supply of a country's currency at some fixed exchange rate, then
   (a) it is likely that this country has a balance-of-payments deficit
   (b) the central bank of this country will buy its currency in the foreign exchange market to maintain the fixed exchange rate
   (c) the country's official reserves will fall
   (d) all of the above are correct

8. The "dirty" or managed float of currencies means that
   (a) currencies are officially pegged but a large black market exists
   (b) the official price at which gold is being sold is allowed to fluctuate
   (c) currencies are officially floating but are being influenced from time to time by central bank policies
   (d) currency speculation and monetary crises are even worse than under a fixed exchange rate regime

9. According to the purchasing power parity hypothesis, if domestic inflation in country A exceeded that in country B by 10 percent, the price of B's currency expressed in A's currency
   (a) should increase by about 10 percent
   (b) should decrease by about 10 percent
   (c) should not change since inflation rates are calculated on the basis of domestically produced goods
   (d) cannot be predicted because the PPP hypothesis applies only in special circumstances

Questions 10 through 14 refer to the diagram below.

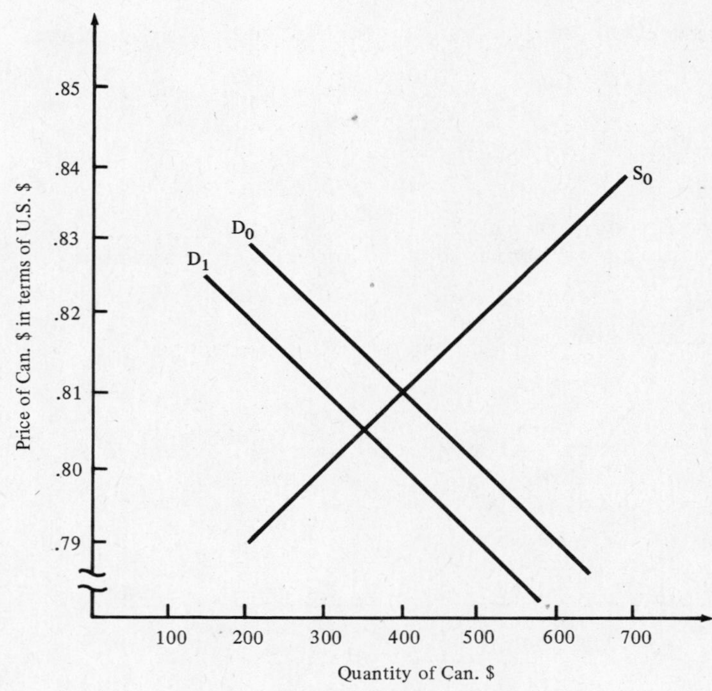

10. Referring to the curves D_0 and S_0 and assuming a floating exchange rate system existed, the price of the Canadian dollar in terms of U.S. dollars would be
    (a) 400
    (b) 0.81
    (c) 1.81
    (d) 1.23

11. If the demand curve shifted downward to D_1, this might be explained by the fact that, other things being equal,
    (a) Canadian export sales fell
    (b) Canadian export sales rose
    (c) imports to Canada rose
    (d) imports to Canada fell

12. Because of the decrease in demand, the price of the Canadian dollar is likely to
    (a) fall to $0.80 U.S.
    (b) fall to $0.805 U.S.
    (c) stay at $.81 U.S.
    (d) rise to $.805 U.S.

13. Assuming that the demand curve was D_1, the Bank of Canada (pursuing a "dirty float" policy) might try to maintain a price of $0.81 for a short period of time by
    (a) selling 100 Canadian dollars
    (b) selling 50 Canadian dollars
    (c) buying 100 Canadian dollars
    (d) buying 50 Canadian dollars

14. The decrease in demand for Canadian dollars might also cause speculators to forecast
   (a) a further decline in the Canadian dollar, and hence they would buy Canadian dollars now
   (b) a further decline in the Canadian dollar, and hence they would sell U.S. dollars now
   (c) a further decline in the Canadian dollar, and hence they would sell Canadian dollars now
   (d) a further decline in the price of the U.S. dollar.

15. Petrodollars refer to
   (a) dollars spent by OPEC countries exploring for oil
   (b) excess purchasing power in oil-producing countries due to balance of payments surpluses
   (c) purchases of SDR's by OPEC countries
   (d) taxes paid by Canadians on oil purchased from OPEC countries

EXERCISES

1. The purchasing power parity hypothesis predicts that over the long run exchange rates will reflect relative rates of domestic inflation. Test this hypothesis for the period 1967-1982 for the following five countries.

	U.S.	Canada	United Kingdom	W. Germany	Japan
1982 CPI (1967 = 100)	290.0	304.0	517.8	196.5	304.2
Exchange rate (U.S. cents)					
1967	--	92.69	275.0	25.08	0.2763
1982	--	80.18	175.2	41.48	0.3981

(a) Predicted (PPP) 1982 exchange rate
   Canada ______________
   United Kingdom ______________
   W. Germany ______________
   Japan ______________

[Hint: Use the formula (U.S. CPI/foreign CPI)(1967 exchange rate).]

(b) For which countries does the PPP hypothesis predict the exchange rate reasonably correctly?

2. During the late 1977 and early 1978 period, the U.S. price of the Canadian dollar fell dramatically, reaching a low of 80.8 cents. This low had not been experienced since September 1931. (Through much of 1984, it sold for 75 or 76 cents U.S.) Several factors contributed to this decline, including increased unemployment, the national unity crisis, poor domestic inflation experience, low forecasts of domestic investment in 1978, adverse speculation, and a poor trade sale performance.

(a) As a Canadian who was engaged in importing goods from abroad, what guarantees might you try to obtain concerning the goods that you were planning to buy during 1978 and early 1979? Why might you wish such guarantees?

(b) As a speculator in the foreign-exchange market, what activity might you become engaged in if you anticipated a worsening in Canadian economic activity and export sales and a growing dependence on foreign oil? If your behavior was a general tendency, what would happen to the price of the Canadian dollar?

3. Assume that the bank of England is trying to maintain a fixed rate of about £1 = \$2.40 U.S. Given demand and supply curves as on the graph below, will it have to be prepared to buy or to sell pounds to maintain the price? ________ About how many? ________ What is the equilibrium exchange rate? ________ Expressed as pounds per dollar? ________

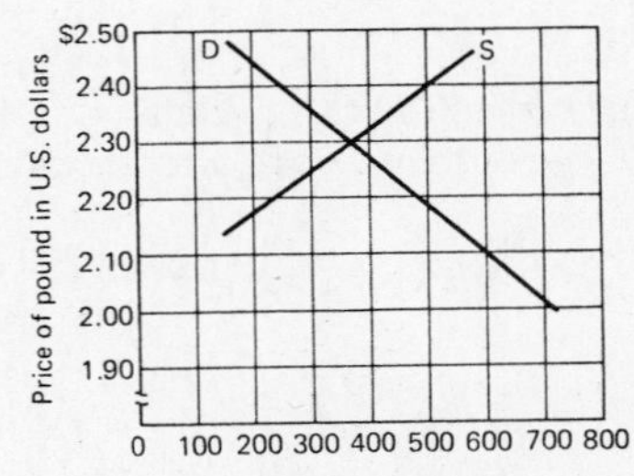

4. (Refer to Exercise 3.)
   (a) Show the same situation with the quantity expressed as U.S. dollars and the price as pounds per dollar.

   (b) Would the Bank have to be prepared to buy or sell dollars to maintain the specified exchange rate? ____________ About how many? ________ What would eventually limit the ability of the Bank of England to maintain the rate of approximately £0.4167 per dollar? ______________________________

   (c) The last time the equilibrium rate was about £.435 per dollar ($2.30 per pound) was in 1980. In the first half of 1983 the rate varied from $1.49 to $1.58 per pound or £________ to £________ per dollar. A special factor was the drop in oil prices in 1982-1983 (Britain was an exporter of North Sea oil). How would this change the exchange rate? ______________.

5. Oil Price Increases and Recycling Petrodollars
   The foreign-exchange reserve positions of a number of countries are shown below. (Figures are in billions of U.S. dollars.)

	1973	1974	1975
Canada	$ 5.8	$ 5.8	$ 5.3
United States	14.4	16.1	15.9
United Kingdom	6.5	6.9	5.3
Japan	12.2	13.5	12.8
Oil-exporting countries (mostly OPEC countries)	14.5	46.4	55.4

   (a) Explain why the rise in the price of oil by the OPEC countries during this period contributed to the significant difference in the reserve positions of the first four countries in the table and the OPEC countries.

   (b) Describe the adjustment process that would have occurred over this period if the world had operated under the gold standard, with the free convertibility of currencies into gold and fixed rates with each other.

(c) In the text, the authors point out that these reserves or petrodollars will eventually be recycled by trade and investment between the OPEC and other countries. Some OPEC countries are interested in investing substantial amounts in Canada. If this were to occur, how might it affect:

(i) Canada's employment situation?

(ii) Canada's foreign-reserve position?

(d) Some of the petrodollar investments in Canada may be in the form of short-term capital, including deposits in Canadian banks. If this were to occur and the OPEC countries suddenly withdrew their OPEC dollar investments from Canada, what would happen to the price of Canadian dollars under the current international monetary system? What type of foreign-exchange speculation might occur as a result of the withdrawal of OPEC dollars?

CHAPTER 41

MACROECONOMIC POLICY IN AN OPEN ECONOMY

CHAPTER OBJECTIVES

Macroeconomic policy in an open economy is far more complicated than in a closed economy. The response of the economy to various policies is different and policy targets may conflict with policy targets arising from domestic considerations alone.

An important distinction is made between expenditure-changing and expenditure-switching policies. Several questions demonstrate that a conflict exists when an expenditure-changing policy involves a situation in which real national income must be changed in one direction to achieve internal balance whereas real national income must be changed in the opposite direction to achieve external balance.

It is important for you to learn that expenditure-changing policies cause movements along a given net-export curve while expenditure-switching policies lead to shifts in this curve. Therefore, it is possible that a combination of these two policies may achieve internal-external balance.

The chapter analyzes the potential effects of balance-of-payments deficits and surpluses on the domestic money supply assuming fixed exchange rates. In addition, you are required to answer questions concerning the effectiveness of monetary and fiscal policy under alternative exchange rate regimes.

MULTIPLE-CHOICE QUESTIONS

1. A country that has a trade-account deficit and an inflationary gap may solve both problems if
   (a) government expenditure increases
   (b) taxes are increased
   (c) taxes are decreased
   (d) government expenditure is financed by an increase in the money supply

2. An example of an expenditure-switching policy is
   (a) a reduction in the money supply
   (b) a cut in the personal income tax rate
   (c) an increase in defense expenditure
   (d) a commercial policy, such as a tariff on imported goods

3. An expenditure-changing policy
   (a) causes movement along a given net export curve
   (b) causes a shift in a net export curve
   (c) has no effect on net exports
   (d) includes such measures as currency devaluation and import tariffs

4. A conflict arises when an expenditure-changing policy involves reduction of both
   (a) a recessionary gap and a trade account deficit
   (b) an inflationary gap and a trade account deficit
   (c) an inflationary gap and a trade account surplus
   (d) both (a) and (c)

5. If an economy has an inflationary gap and a trade account surplus, both internal and external balance may be attained by
   (a) an expenditure-switching policy that involves devaluation of the domestic currency
   (b) policies to induce a switch of expenditure from domestic to foreign goods thereby shifting the net export curve leftward
   (c) a contractionary monetary policy combined with a contractionary fiscal policy
   (d) an expenditure-switching policy that involves export subsidies

6. The capital account is affected by an expansion in government expenditures (taxes constant) because
   (a) foreign-produced defense equipment is purchased by the federal government
   (b) national income will increase and domestic households will travel abroad more frequently
   (c) a current-account surplus that is generated by the fiscal policy change must necessarily affect the capital account since the balance of payments must balance
   (d) an increase in the rate of interest, assuming a fixed money supply, will trigger additional capital inflows.

7. To solve a capital-account deficit in the balance of payments, the central bank should
   (a) buy bonds in the open market
   (b) increase bank reserves
   (c) sell bonds in the open market
   (d) reduce interest rates when foreign central banks raise their interest rates

8. Sale of foreign currencies by the central bank to maintain a fixed exchange rate will, other things being equal,
   (a) have no impact on the money supply
   (b) reduce the money supply
   (c) cause an inflationary gap
   (d) cause interest rates to fall

9. The effectiveness of monetary policy to reduce a large recessionary gap when the country is committed to maintain a fixed exchange rate is
   (a) severely reduced because capital outflows will counteract the expansionary monetary policies
   (b) significantly increased because capital inflows will increase, thereby adding to the monetary expansion
   (c) as effective as monetary expansion under flexible exchange rates
   (d) powerful because a central bank can indefinitely sterilize any balance-of-payments deficit that may result from an expansion in the money supply

10. The effectiveness of expansionary fiscal policy is enhanced under a fixed exchange rate if
   (a) international capital flows are interest-sensitive
   (b) international capital flows are perfectly interest-inelastic
   (c) the money supply is not allowed to change
   (d) the money supply is simultaneously reduced

11. Suppose a country is operating under a flexible exchange rate and is experiencing a recessionary gap. An expansionary monetary policy, assuming that capital flows are interest-sensitive, will cause
    (a) imports to rise initially, capital to flow into the country, and the exchange rate to depreciate
    (b) a capital-account deficit and the exchange rate to appreciate
    (c) a capital-account deficit, the exchange rate to depreciate, and hence the balance of payments to ultimately be restored
    (d) a capital account surplus, exchange rate appreciation, and then a current account deficit

12. Under a flexible exchange rate regime, monetary policy
    (a) is unlikely to be as effective as under fixed exchange rates
    (b) exerts an important crowding-out effect on exports
    (c) is very effective because the initial monetary stimulus can be reinforced by changes in the exchange rate
    (d) requires the use of foreign exchange reserves

13. In order to counteract the influence of the crowding-out effect, an expansionary fiscal policy should be accompanied by
    (a) a contractionary monetary policy
    (b) a purchase of bonds by the central bank on the open market
    (c) an increase in the secondary-reserve requirement
    (d) a monetary-base rule that increases the interest rate

14. The fact that Canada was on a fixed exchange rate from 1962 to 1970
    (a) insulated Canada from the high rates of inflation elsewhere in the world
    (b) prevented authorities from avoiding the rising inflation rates experienced by other countries
    (c) caused massive unemployment
    (d) caused balance-of-payments deficits to increase with a contractionary monetary policy

15. Which one of the following factors has caused the most difficulty for Canadian monetary and exchange rate management in the early 1980s?
    (a) higher real interest rates in the United States than in Canada
    (b) expansionary monetary policy in the United States
    (c) higher inflation rates in the United Kingdom than in Canada
    (d) lower inflation rates in Canada than in the United States

EXERCISES

1. Assume that Canada, which is hypothetically considered to be on a fixed exchange system, experiences a balance-of-payments surplus because of increased sales of natural gas to the United States. Americans are assumed to pay Canadians in U.S. dollars, and the Canadian exporting firms wish to convert U.S. dollars into Canadian dollars. Suppose the sale of natural gas is the equivalent of $40 million Canadian dollars. Fill in the blanks in accordance with the following transactions.

Public:

Assets		Liabilities	
Foreign currency	________		
Deposits	________		

Chartered Banks

Assets		Liabilities	
Reserves with Bank of Canada	________	Deposits	________

Bank of Canada

Assets		Liabilities	
Foreign currency	________	Chartered bank Deposits	________

(a) Americans pay Canadian exporting firms in U.S. dollars assumed to be the equivalent of $40 million (Canadian). Canadian firms wish to convert this amount into deposits at Canadian banks. Show the effect of this transaction in the balance sheet of the public.

(b) Banks, having purchased the U.S. dollars from firms, wish to sell the $40 million to the Bank of Canada. How does the Bank of Canada pay for these U.S. dollars? Show this transaction in the Bank of Canada's balance sheet.

(c) Finally, after the Bank of Canada has purchased the U.S. dollars from the banks, show the effect on the chartered banks' balance sheet.

(d) What do you predict will finally happen to the level of deposits in the banking system if the cash reserve ratio is 0.1 and there is no cash drain?

(e) You should have concluded that the money supply (deposits) increases by a multiple. If the Bank of Canada wishes to sterilize this increase, what should it do--buy or sell bonds to the banks? Explain.

2. The economy of Can trades with other nations but no international capital flows into or out of Can. The current price levels of goods produced in Can and in other countries are 2.0 and 1.0 (in foreign currency), respectively. The exchange rate is fixed at two units of Can's currency per unit of foreign currency. Hence the current terms of trade, (R), is 1.0. The behavioral relationships in Can are:

(i) $C = 80 + 0.6Y$
(ii) $I + G = 40$
(iii) $X = 80 - 20R$
(iv) $M = 0.1Y + 30R$
(v) $Y_P = 310$ (Potential real national income)

(a) Formulate the equation for AE. For domestic absorption (A). What is the marginal propensity to spend?

(b) Using the equilibrium condition Y = AE, calculate the equilibrium value of real national income (Y). At this level of Y, calculate the values of A and net exports.

(c) A recessionary gap of ____________ exists in Can although the balance of trade is balanced (X - M = 0). What specific expenditure-increasing policy with respect to G would you recommend in order to eliminate unemployment? (You may assume that Can's price level doesn't change.)

(d) Your expenditure-increasing policy has generated a trade-balance deficit of ________________ when national income is at its potential level. At Y_P, domestic absorption is ________________________.

(e) To achieve both internal balance ($Y = Y_P$) and external balance (X - M = 0), an expenditure-switching policy must complement an expenditure-increasing policy. Specifically, since X - M is negative at Y_P, the net-export curve must be shifted (upward/downward) so that X - M = 0 at Y_P. To achieve external balance it is clear that the value of R must be (increased/decreased). This may be accomplished by (devaluing/revaluing) Can's currency in the foreign exchange market.

(f) Suppose that the government of Can devalues its currency so that the exchange rate rises from 2.0 to 2.04 and at the same time increases government expenditures by 4 (I + G = 44). Will this combined policy achieve internal and external balance? What is the value of domestic absorption at the new equilibrium level of real national income?

3. You are given the following information about the economy of Oz:
   (a) The SRAS curve is horizontal at P = 2 for Y (real national income) values equal to and less than 180.
   (b) The exchange rate is fixed at a given level.
   (c) Potential real national income equals 180.
   (d) The schedule of Y and desired expenditures are shown below.

Y	C	I + G	X	M	(X - M)	AE	Absorption (A)
0	40	23	22	5	17	80	63
100	100	23	22	15	7	130	123
120	112	23	22	17	5	140	135
160	136	23	22	21	1	160	____
170	142	23	22	22	____	165	____
180	148	23	22	23	____	170	171

(a) <u>Coming to Grips with the Current Situation</u>
Calculate the following information for Oz:

(i) Equilibrium real national income is ________________.
(ii) Domestic absorption at the equilibrium level of Y is ______________.
(iii) The marginal propensity to spend is ________________
(iv) The multiplier value is ________________.
(v) The marginal propensity to consume is ______________.
(vi) The balance of trade at the equilibrium level of Y is ____________.
(vii) For every 10 increase in Y, net exports (<u>increase/decrease</u>) by _______.
(viii) Domestic absorption is ________________ at Y = 170.
(ix) (X - M) is ________________ at Y = 180.
(x) The recessionary gap is ____________.

(b) Plot the net-export curve in the diagram below.

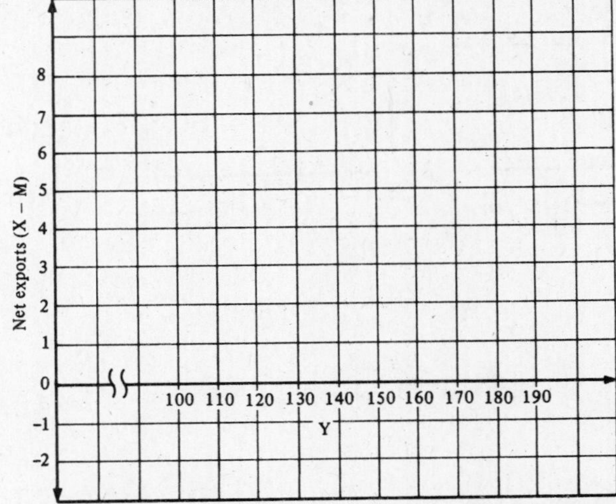

(c) Suppose that exports increased from 22 to 25 at every level of real national income. Calculate the following:
   (i) the new equilibrium level of Y ______________
   (ii) domestic absorption at the new equilibrium Y ______________
   (iii) net exports at the new equilibrium Y ______________

(d) Plot the net-export curve in the diagram above. Demonstrate that at the new level of equilibrium Y, net exports increased less than exports increased. Explain.

(e) What increase in (I + G) from the initial level of 23 (X = 22) is necessary to achieve potential national income (Y_P)? What is the value of (X - M) at Y_P? You should have noticed that the achievement of internal balance (elimination of the GNP gap) created an external imbalance (a trade-balance deficit).

4. [This is an advanced problem.] A country which operates under a flexible exchange rate regime has a recessionary gap situation. The initial conditions in the economy are an interest rate of r_0, a balance in both the trade account and the capital account, and an exchange rate (the foreign price of its currency) of π_0. The government increases its expenditure in order to eliminate the recessionary gap without increasing the domestic price level. The effects on the economy are as follows: (1) the demand curve for money shifts to the right such that the interest rate increases to r_1; (2) although capital outflows are assumed unaffected, capital flows into this economy from other nations will increase; and (3) the external value of this country's currency appreciates to π_1.

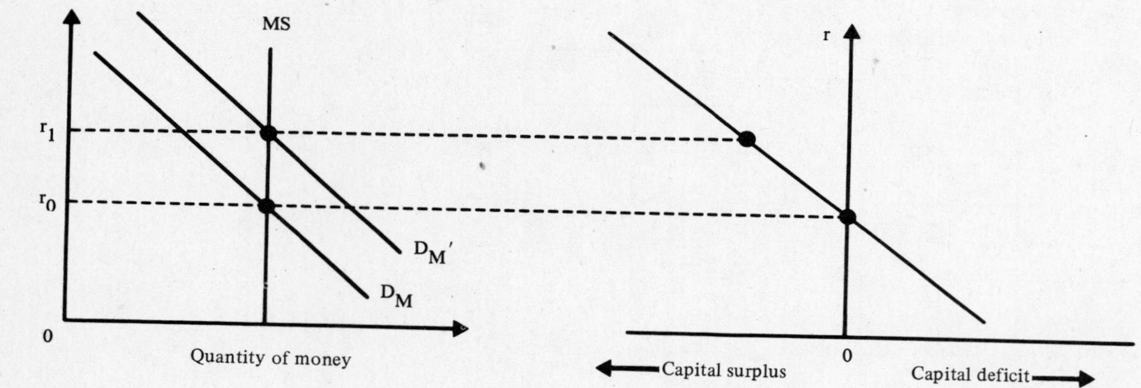

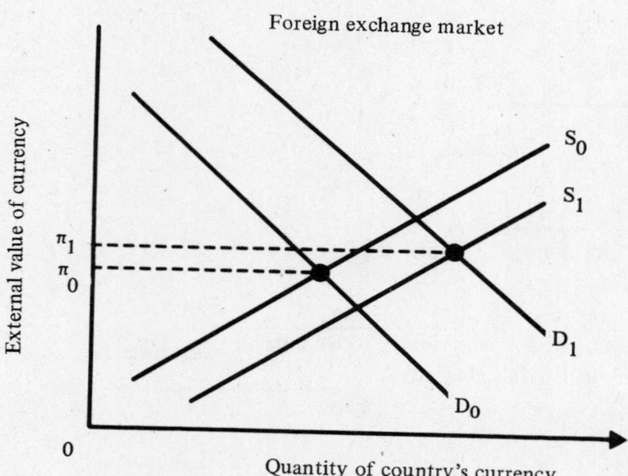

(a) Explain why the government's fiscal policy caused the demand curve for money to shift and the interest rate to increase.

(b) Why is the curve relating the interest rate and the capital-account balance downward-sloping?

(c) Why is a capital-account surplus generated by the government's action?

(d) Why did the supply curve for this country's currency in international markets shift to the right? Why did the demand curve for its currency shift to the right?

(e) At an exchange rate of π_0, with the demand and supply curves in the exchange market labeled D_1 and S_1, what situation exists for this country's balance of payments? What will happen to the external value of the currency?

(f) Outline some of the effects of the fiscal policy on the country's net-export curve.

PART TWELVE

MACROECONOMIC CONTROVERSIES

CHAPTER 42

MACROECONOMIC CONTROVERSIES

CHAPTER OBJECTIVES

In recent years, there has been considerable debate concerning the appropriate role of fiscal and monetary policies as tools to achieve economic objectives. The basic purpose of this chapter is to consolidate your understanding of the arguments put forward by both monetarists (often identified as conservatives with regard to government intervention) and Keynesians or neo-Keynesians (often identified as interventionists). The questions and problems in this chapter review the important links between the money supply, inflation, and aggregate demand as seen by both the neo-Keynesians and monetarists.

MULTIPLE-CHOICE QUESTIONS

1. Those who advocate that macroeconomic goals can be achieved satisfactorily if the free market is left on its own are known as
   (a) neo-Keynesians
   (b) conservatives
   (c) rationalists
   (d) neo-mercantilists

2. In the view of the monetarist group of economists,
   (a) changes in the money supply should be used often as a countercyclical tool
   (b) interest rates have very little effect on spending
   (c) the economy will not recover by itself from recessions
   (d) fluctuations in the money supply cause fluctuations in national income

3. Neo-Keynesians argue that most cyclical fluctuations result from
   (a) variations in the rate of growth of the money supply
   (b) changes in government expenditures
   (c) variations in investment expenditure
   (d) fluctuations in the stock market

4. Which of the following does not represent a monetarist's view of the causes of cyclical fluctuations in the economy?
   (a) A major cause of the severity of the depression of the 1930s was a large decline in the money supply between 1929 and 1933.
   (b) Inflationary gaps and rapid inflation are the result of excessive expansion of the money supply.
   (c) Fluctuations in the money supply cause fluctuations in national income.
   (d) Inflationary gaps created by excess demand will automatically cause an increase in the money supply.

5. The economists called neo-Keynesians in this chapter
   (a) do not agree with Keynes that investment spending is important in causing fluctuations in national income
   (b) believe that fiscal policy is always a more effective stabilization tool than monetary policy
   (c) are opposed entirely to the use of monetary policy
   (d) generally have less faith in the economy's self-correcting mechanisms than do monetarists

6. Neo-Keynesians
   (a) believe that a GNP gap cannot be eliminated in the short run because prices do not adjust downward very rapidly
   (b) do not believe there is any correlation between changes in the money supply and changes in national income
   (c) do not believe that fluctuations in national income can cause fluctuations in the money supply
   (d) all of the above

7. In the stable fiscal and monetary environment sought by conservatives
   (a) the k percent rule is unsuitable
   (b) economic growth will take care of itself
   (c) the goal of an annually balanced budget is stressed
   (d) protection and subsidy for declining industries is vital

8. With reference to the causes of inflation, a major difference between monetarists and neo-Keynesians is that
   (a) monetarists emphasize that short run, supply shock-induced inflation requires active government intervention to arrest the inflation
   (b) monetarists believe that all inflations are caused by excessive monetary expansion and would not occur without it
   (c) neo-Keynesians accept the need for a stable growth in the money supply and argue against government intervention to curb inflation
   (d) neo-Keynesians believe that inflation is largely due to excessive growth in the money supply

9. According to the theory of the Lucas aggregate supply curve, if the ratio of actual to expected inflation declines,
   (a) national output will fall
   (b) the aggregate supply curve will shift left
   (c) the aggregate supply curve will shift right
   (d) an inflationary gap will be created

10. The k percent rule
   (a) is supported by both monetarists and neo-Keynesians
   (b) calls for money supply to grow at a constant rate even when there are short-run fluctuations in aggregate demand
   (c) calls for the money supply to expand and contract as the GNP expands and contracts, respectively
   (d) is equivalent to the central bank following an interest rate target policy

11. The k percent rule as advocated by conservatives usually provides that the money supply should be increased steadily at the same rate of increase as
   (a) the price level
   (b) aggregate demand
   (c) potential real national income
   (d) interest rates

12. Stable, preannounced money supply targets
    (a) are the best approach to interest rate stability
    (b) are consistent with discretionary monetary policy
    (c) permit the use of once-and-for-all monetary expansion
    (d) can induce speculative behavior by bondholders

13. The micro model on which neo-Keynesian economics is based consists of
    (a) perfectly competitive markets and an excess supply of labor
    (b) perfectly competitive markets through which changes in demand are transmitted rapidly
    (c) imperfect markets but flexible prices
    (d) imperfect markets and fairly rigid prices

14. A major source of the divergence between monetarists and neo-Keynesians concerning the potency of fiscal and monetary policy is
    (a) a difference in views on the influence of interest rates on aggregate expenditures
    (b) neo-Keynesians argue that inflation caused by nonmonetary factors can go on indefinitely even without being validated
    (c) monetarists assume that the supply of money is relatively interest-elastic except in periods of major crisis
    (d) neo-Keynesians believe that private investment by firms is relatively responsive to changes in interest rates

15. An important component of the micro model of monetarists is that
    (a) unemployment is involuntary
    (b) firms respond to changes in demand mainly by changing output and employment rather than prices
    (c) prices are inflexible
    (d) the automatic adjustment mechanism of markets works efficiently

EXERCISES

1. Insert an M for monetarist or a K for neo-Keynesian after the statements below.
    (a) The demand for money is quite sensitive to interest rates. __________

    (b) Changes in the money supply are the primary cause of fluctuations in the level of national income. __________

    (c) National income can be influenced strongly by monetary policy, but only weakly by fiscal policy. __________

    (d) Investment spending is much more responsive to profit expectations than to changes in interest rates. ______

    (e) Changes in the money supply may be a response to, rather than the cause of, changes in GNP and the price level. __________

    (f) Fiscal policy works only to the extent that it affects the supply of money. ________

    (g) An activist countercyclical government policy is needed to achieve economic stability. ________

(h) Contraction of the money supply raises interest rates, but the small rise in interest rates only moderately affects expenditures on plant and equipment.

____

(i) Monetary policy is uncertain, variable, powerful, and lagged in its effects; therefore it should be as neutral as possible. ________

(j) Fiscal policy has very general effects on the economy, whereas monetary policy affects primarily interest rates and therefore has its major effect on housing and small businesses. ________

(k) Private sector expenditures would be relatively stable without the interference of erratic fiscal and monetary policy. _______

(i) Cyclical fluctuations in economic activity are largely due to fluctuations in private sector expenditures. ________

2. The data below pertain to the Canadian economy for the 1970-1983 period.

	Percentage Change In:		
Year	Money Supply (M_1)	Consumer Price Index	Nominal GNP
1970	2.4	3.3	7.4
1971	12.7	2.9	10.2
1972	14.3	4.8	11.4
1973	14.5	7.6	17.4
1974	9.3	10.9	19.4
1975	13.8	10.8	12.1
1976	8.0	7.5	15.5
1977	8.4	8.0	9.3
1978	10.0	8.9	10.3
1979	6.9	9.1	13.7
1980	6.4	10.2	12.2
1981	3.8	12.5	14.3
1982	0.6	10.8	5.2
1983	10.2	5.2	9.0

(a) (i) In graph (i) below, plot the percentage change in the money supply as a solid line and the percentage change in the consumer price index as a broken line.

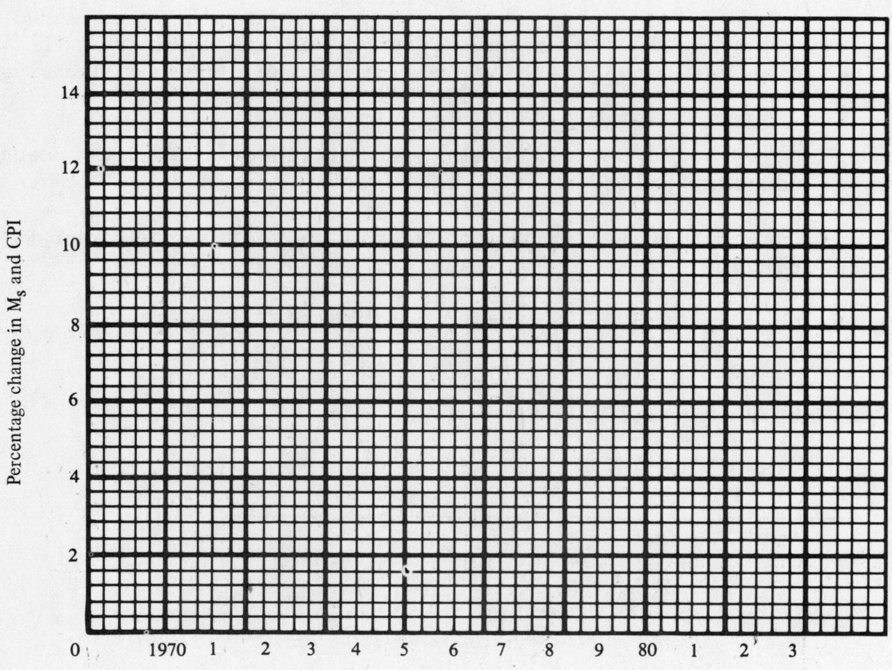

(ii) In graph (ii) below, plot the percentage change in the money supply as a solid line and the percentage change in nominal GNP as a broken line.

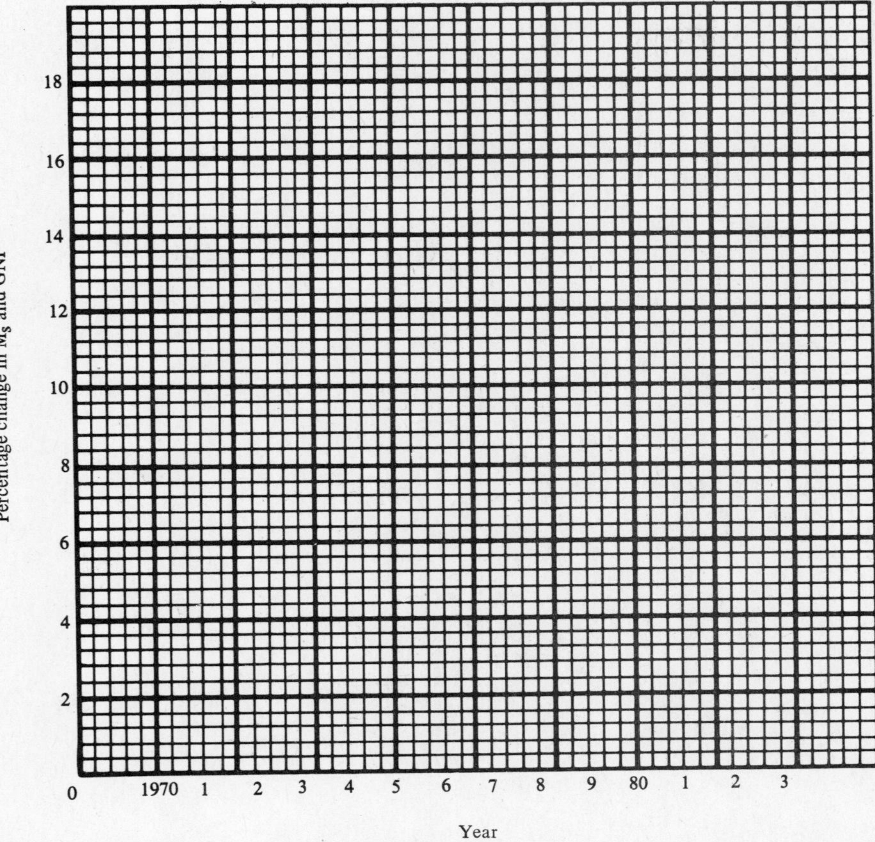

(b) Would it be possible to argue the monetarists position or the neo-Keynesian position on the basis of the data you have plotted? Explain.

3. <u>The Association Between the Money Supply and National Income: The Neo-Keynesian View</u>

Most economists agree that the money supply and national income move together through time, but the direction of casuality is a matter of considerable debate. Suppose that the demand for money equation is $D_M = 0.8Y - 2i$, where i is the interest rate. The current money supply is 60 and real national income (Y) is 100.

(a) What is the current rate of interest? (Assume that the central bank is committed to this level regardless of the level of real national income.)

(b) Suppose that net exports increase such that real national income rises from 100 to 101. If interest rates are allowed to change, what is the new equilibrium level of the interest rate?

(c) However, given the central bank's policy, what change in the money supply is necessary? As you have seen, the money supply change is caused by an interest-rate target policy and an increase in real national income.

ANSWERS

CHAPTER 1

MULTIPLE-CHOICE QUESTIONS

1. (b) 2. (a) 3. (b) 4. (d) 5. (c) 6. (a) 7. (c) 8. (d) 9. (a) 10. (c)
11. (b) 12. (d) 13. (c) 14. (d) 15. (a)

EXERCISES

1. (a)

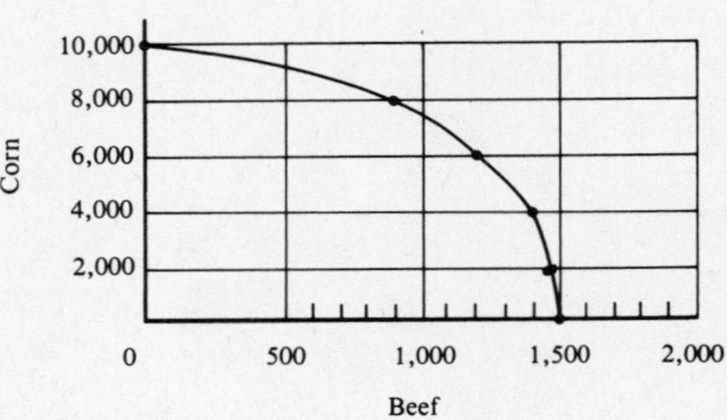

(b) Yes; in fact this combination lies inside the production possibility boundary.
(c) No; this combination lies outside the production possibility boundary.
(d) 2000 bushels of corn are lost (or for every pound of additional beef the loss in corn is 6.67 bushels).
(e) This combination lies inside the production possibility boundary. Therefore resources are underutilized or unemployed.
(f) The opportunity cost increases. The opportunity cost of increasing beef production from 900 to 1200 is 6.67 bushels of corn per unit increase in beef. If beef production is increased from 1,200 to 1,400, the opportunity cost per unit increase in beef is 10.0.

2. (a)

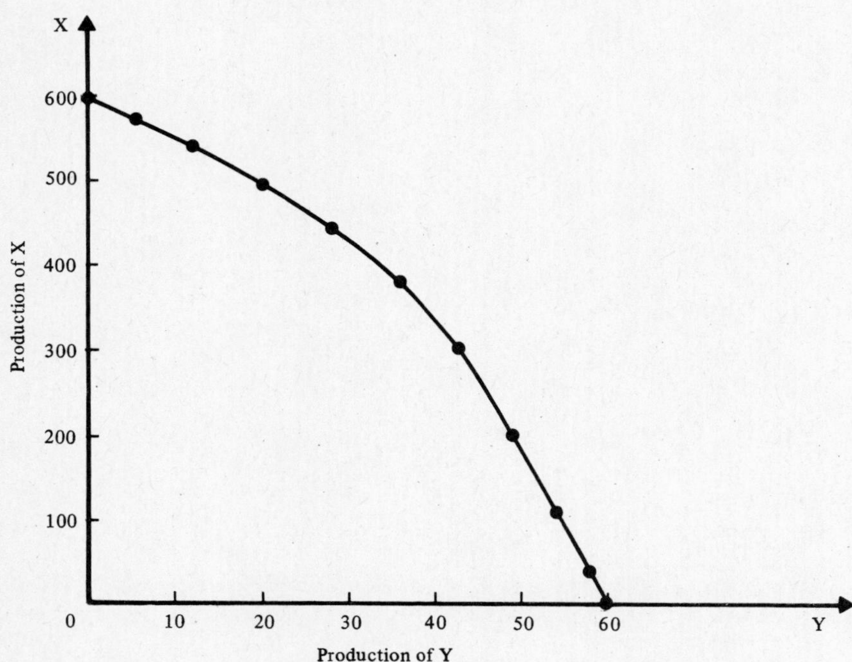

(b) Increasing production of X from 200 to 300 requires 10 more workers. These workers leave the production of Y such that the production of Y falls from 49 to 43. Thus, the opportunity cost is 6 units of Y. Another way of expressing this is to say that each additional unit of X costs .06 units of Y.
When production of X increases from 500 to 600, 30 additional workers are required (100 - 70). These workers leave the production of Y such that the production of Y falls from 20 to 0. Thus, the opportunity cost is 20 units of Y. Thus, each additional unit of X has cost .2 units of Y. We can see that the opportunity costs are increasing.

(c) There are unemployed or inefficiently used workers. This combination lies inside the production possibility boundary.

(d) This combination cannot be achieved in the present situation; it lies outside the production possibility boundary.

(e) The production possibility boundary shifts to the right as is shown below. The planner's aspirations are still not fulfilled. Because of the productivity increase in X, 50 workers can now produce 415 units and 60 workers can now produce 480 units of X. Therefore, approximately 55 workers can produce 450 units of X. Previously, 60 workers were required to produce 450 units of X and so five workers can be reallocated to the production of Y which in turn increases the production of Y somewhere in the range 28 to 36. This falls short of the desired output level of 48.

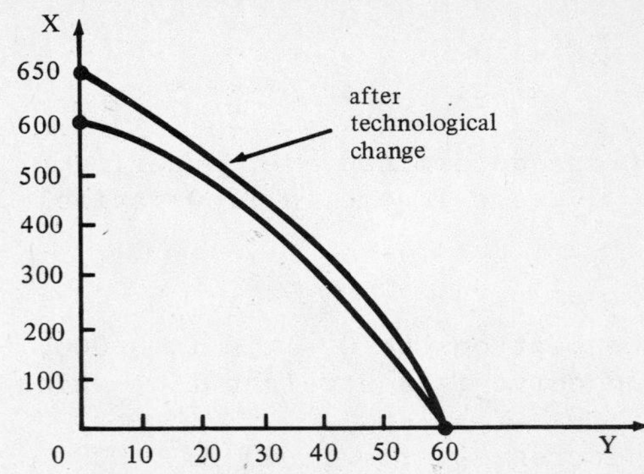

(f) Sixty workers are required to produce 450 units of X. Thus, 40 workers are required to produce 48 units of Y. Given the current technology, 40 workers produce 28 units of Y. Thus, productivity must increase in total by 20 units or ½ unit per worker.

3. (a) If all resources were allocated to the production of good 'a' then there is no production of good b. Hence, according to the mathematical expression, the maximum production of good 'a' is 5 units. If all resources were used to produce good b then B = 20 and the production of good 'a' is zero.
   (b) The increase from 12 to 16 requires a loss in production of good 'a' of 1 (from 2 to 1). An increase in b from 16 to 20 requires a loss in production of good 'a' of 1 (from 1 to 0).
   (c) The opportunity cost is constant whereas it was increasing for both questions 1 and 2.
   (d) According to the equation, 4 units of 'a' and 4 units of b are possible. The combination of 4 of 'a' and 5 units of b is not feasible and indicates that more resources are required than are currently available.

CHAPTER 2

MULTIPLE-CHOICE QUESTIONS

1. (d) 2. (c) 3. (c) 4. (d) 5. (a) 6. (d) 7. (a) 8. (a) 9. (d)
10. (d) 11. (c)

EXERCISES

1. (a) P (b) N (c) P (d) N (e) P
2. (a) F (b) S (c) F (d) S (e) F (f) F (g) S
3. (b) They are positively related; as Y_d increases, so does C.
   (c) The increase in C between 1950-1960 was 293. The increase in Y_d in this time period was 280. Hence $\Delta C/\Delta Y_d = 1.05$. This ratio is the slope of the consumption function.
   For 1960 to 1970, $\Delta C/\Delta Y_d = (1{,}858 - 1{,}435)/(1{,}994 - 1{,}496) = 0.85$.
   (d) Slightly below. The distance is Y_d-C, which you will discover is <u>saving</u>.
   (e) The slope of the <u>consumption function</u>. The sign is positive because C and Y_d are directly or positively related.
4. (a) Q_d and P are determined in the market for television sets. They are endogenous variables.
   (b) Average income, which is determined in many other markets, is not influenced to any significant extent by the market for televisions. It is exogenous to the market for televisions.

(c) Q_d and P are negatively related; as P increases, Q_d falls. Q_d and Y are positively related; as Y increases, Q_d increases.
(d) All three variables are flow variables. Q_d and P are determined over a period of time in the television market. To be consistent, average income, a flow variable, is measured over the same time period.
(e) The equation becomes, $Q_d = 8000 - 4P$.
(f) Q_d = 6,000, 4,000, 0, and 8,000.
(g) The intercept on the P-axis is 2,000, and the intercept on the Q_d-axis is 8,000. Your plotting should also indicate that the demand curve is a straight line which is downward sloping.
(h) The change in quantity demanded is -4,000 when P increases from 1,000 to 2,000. When P increases from 500 to 2,000, quantity demanded falls by 6,000. In both cases the ratio $\Delta Q_d/\Delta P$ is equal to -4.
(i) The intercept on the P-axis is 2,250 and the intercept on the Q_d-axis is 9,000. The slope remains at -4. The demand curve shifted rightward in a parallel fashion. It is likely that average income increased over the two periods from 8,000 to 9,000.

CHAPTER 3

MULTIPLE-CHOICE QUESTIONS

1. (b) 2. (d) 3. (d) 4. (b) 5. (b) 6. (d) 7. (d) 8. (a) 9. (d) 10. (c)
11. (d) 12. (b) 13. (d) 14. (c)

EXERCISES

1. (a), (c), (e), (g)
2. (a) III; (b) IV; (c) II; (d) I; (e) V
3. (a) NM, P
   (b) NM, R
   (c) M, R
   (d) M, P
   (e) M, R
   (f) NM, P

4. (a) GO-HH; injection
   (b) HH-FM
   (c) FM-GO; withdrawal
   (d) BA-FM; injection
   (e) FM-HH;
   (f) HH-BA; withdrawal
   (g) GO-FM; injection
   (h) FM-BA; withdrawal

CHAPTER 4

MULTIPLE-CHOICE QUESTIONS

1. (b) 2. (a) 3. (b) 4. (b) 5. (c) 6. (a) 7. (a) 8. (c) 9. (c) 10. (a)
11. (c) 12. (a) 13. (c) 14. (c) 15. (a) 16. (c)

EXERCISES

1. (a)

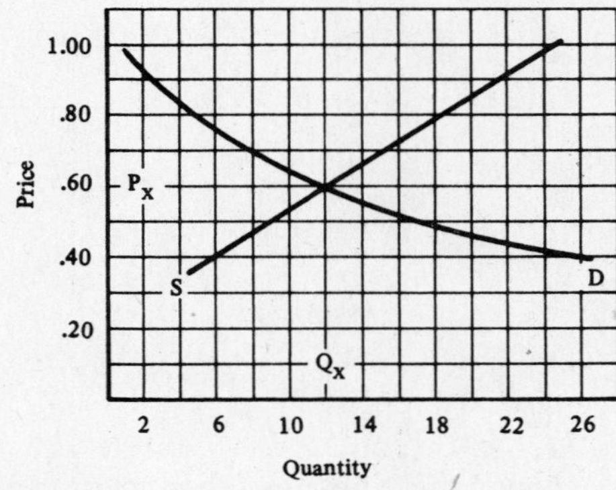

(b) It is zero.

Price	Excess Demand (+) Excess Supply (-)
$1.00	-24
.90	-18
.80	-14
.70	- 7
.60	0
.50	+ 9
.40	+20

(c) If excess demand exists, price is likely to rise; in the event of excess supply, price is likely to fall.

2.

	D	S	P	Q
(a)	0	–	+	–
(b)	+	0	+	+
(c)	+	0	+	+
(d)	+	+	U	+
(e)	–	0	–	–
(f)	0	–	+	–
(g)	+	0	+	+

3. (a) The demand curve would shift rightward and the equilibrium price and output would be higher.
(b) In effect the supply curve becomes vertical at 20,000 and the price would rise to the point indicated by T because, if the output is fixed at 20,000 cases, only at a higher price T would excess demand be eliminated.
(c) Supply curve shifts leftward, price rises, and output falls.

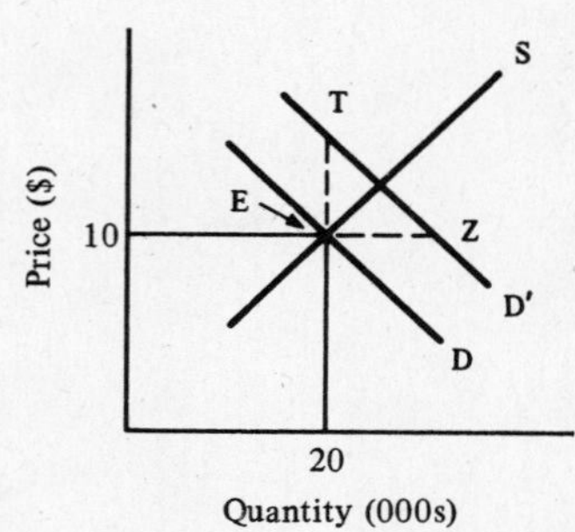

4. (a)

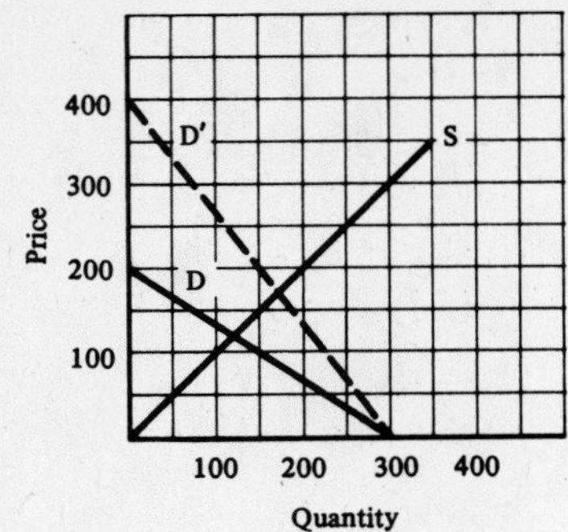

(b) At equilibrium, $Q_S = Q_D$; therefore 300 - 1.5P = 1.0P, and P = 120 and Q = 120.
(c) The demand curve has shifted rightward. Equating the new demand and original supply, P = 171.43 = Q.

5. (a) $Q_D = Q_S$: equilibrium price is 2 and equilibrium quantity is 20.
(b)

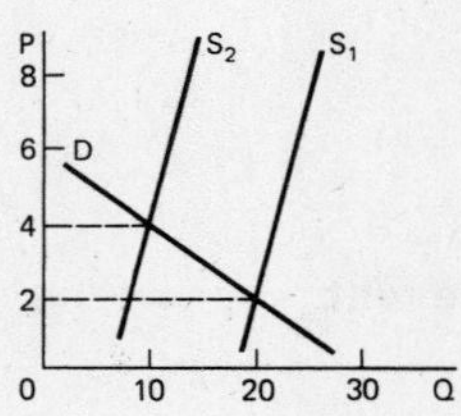

(c) $Q_D = Q_S$; equilibrium price is 4 and equilibrium quantity is 12.
(d) A shortage of 10 would result from the price control. At p = 2, only 10 would be supplied ($Q_S = 8 + p$), whereas 20 would be demanded ($Q_D = 28 - 4p$).

CHAPTER 5

MULTIPLE-CHOICE QUESTIONS

1. (a) 2. (c) 3. (d) 4. (a) 5. (b) 6. (c) 7. (a) 8. (a) 9. (d) 10. (d)
11. (c) 12. (d) 13. (a) 14. (d) 15. (b) 16. (c) 17. (d) 18. (b) 19. (b)

EXERCISES

1. (a) Pork: .68; .89; .55
Eggs: .02; .10; .12
The formula is the percentage change in quantity $[\Delta Q/(Q_1 + Q_2)/2]$ divided by the percentage change in price, where Q_1 and Q_2 are the quantities sold.
(b) Eggs are more important in the "basic" food pattern during these time periods (and in this price range).
(c) They do in the sense that pork does have a number of close substitutes while eggs do not, especially when it comes to the use of eggs in baking and making other foods.

2. (a) Elasticity measures are $\frac{\frac{100}{50}}{\frac{10}{65}} = 13.0$ $\frac{\frac{200}{200}}{\frac{20}{50}} = 2.5;$ $\frac{\frac{200}{400}}{\frac{20}{30}} = .75$

(b) $\frac{\frac{100}{350}}{\frac{10}{35}} = 1.0;$

At this point total revenue is constant. With further declines in price, total revenue will decline as we move into the inelastic portion of the demand curve.

3. (a) A rightward shift in the demand curve with a vertical supply curve. Elasticity of supply is very inelastic (close to zero).
(b) They would probably try to stockpile lumber by buying it now in anticipation of higher prices. This would shift the demand curve schedule again to the right, further raising prices.

4. (a) (i) income elasticity is +.75 (normal good, but income inelastic)
(ii) price elasticity of demand is .45 (inelastic)
(iii) Cannot state price elasticity of demand because both price and income have changed over this period.

5. (a)

Price Elasticity of Demand for X	Price Elasticity of Demand for Y	Income Elasticity of Demand for X	Income Elasticity of Demand for Y	Cross Elasticity of Demand for X
--	--	--	--	--
0.93	--	--	--	--
--	0.33	--	--	-0.29
--	--	+1.24	+0.30	--
--	--	--	--	--

(b) The condition of other things equal does not apply. Not only has income changed, but the price of Y has also changed.

6. (a)

P	Q	TR	Elasticities Point	Arc
$11	1	$11	11	
				5
9	3	27	3	
				2.0
7	5	35	1.4	
				1.0
5	7	35	.7	
				.5
3	9	27	.3	
				.2
1	11	11	.1	

[Note the relationship between the two elasticity measures.]

(b) Demand is elastic when TR rises with falling price, is unitary at peak of TR, and is inelastic when TR falls with decreasing price.

7. (a) = 1 and 6 (b) = 4 (c) = 5 (d) = 2 (e) = 3 (f) = 6

8. Starting from the origin for S_1, the elasticities are $\frac{2/3}{2/3} = \frac{2/5}{2/5} = 1.0$; and for S_2, the elasticities are $\frac{2/3}{2/3} = \frac{2/5}{2/5} = 1.0$

CHAPTER 6

MULTIPLE-CHOICE QUESTIONS

1. (d) 2. (d) 3. (c) 4. (c) 5. (a) 6. (c) 7. (d) 8. (c) 9. (a) 10. (a)
11. (b) 12. (c) 13. (c) 14. (b) 15. (d) 16. (b) 17. (b) 18. (b) 19. (a) 20. (c)
21. (a) 22. (b) 23. (c)

EXERCISES

1. (a) and (b)

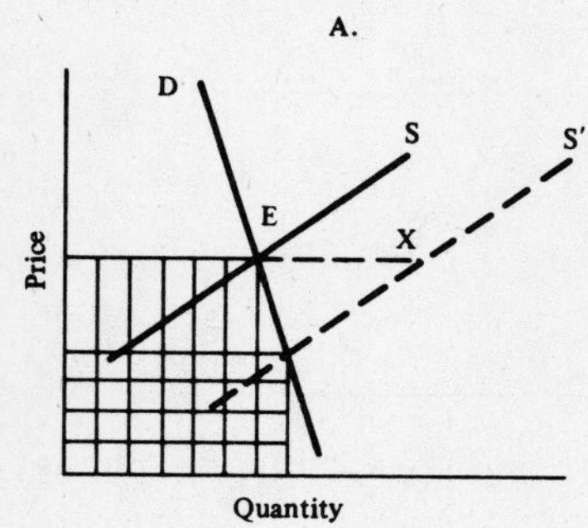

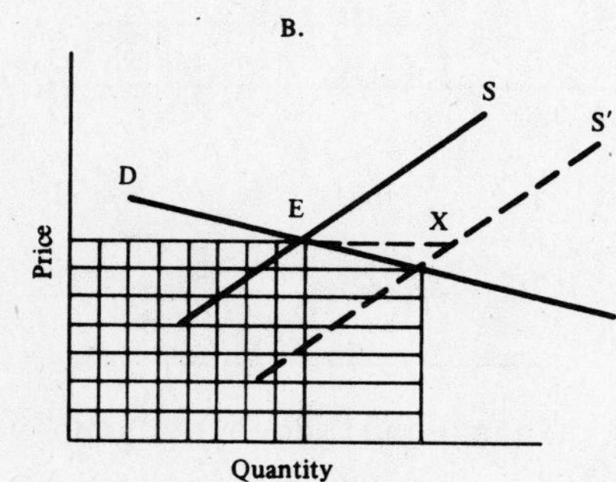

(c) Market A. The demand is inelastic compared to market B.
(d) No. The shift in supply is identical, and at a price equal to original equilibrium price, the quantity of unsold goods (EX in both markets) is the same.

2.

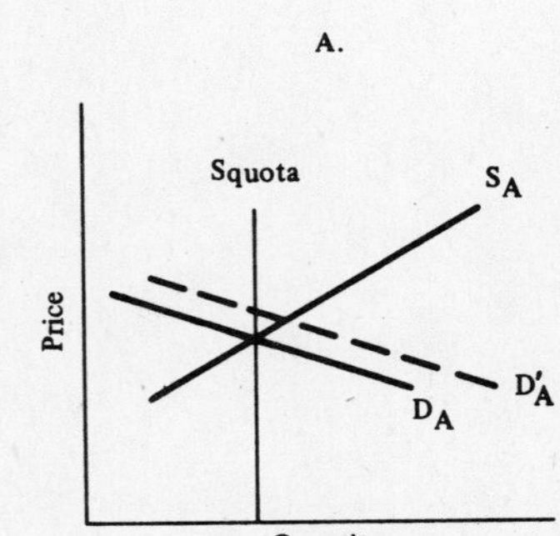

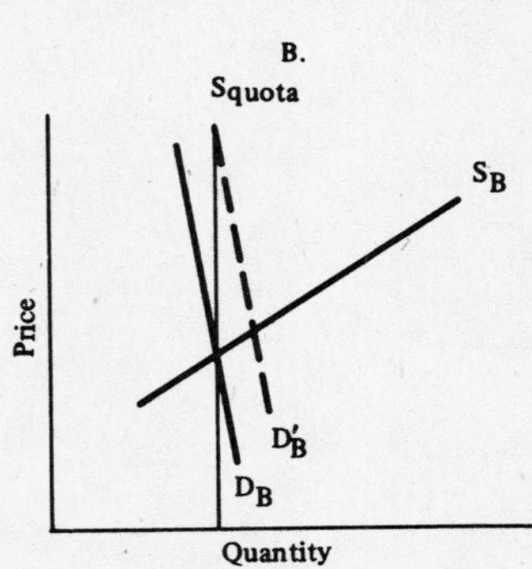

Fix quota at S_{quota}. Shift demand to D_A' and D_B'. Price rises much more in market where there is an inelastic demand.

3. (a) Stock would remain the same in the short run. In the short run, very little new construction of rental apartments can occur.
(b) The short-run supply would, if it could, have to shift out to where D_3 intersects P_2 in order to clear the market.
(c) (i) Quantity demanded will occur at intersection of D_3 and P_2, while producers will be willing to supply an amount where P_2 intersects S_{LR}.
(ii) Price will rise from P_2 to equilibrium price at intersection of S_{LR} and D_3. Quantity supplied will increase along S_{LR} (and quantity demanded will decrease along D_3) to the quantity equilibrium at intersection of S_{LR} and D_3.
(iii) With a temporary increase in demand and no rent controls, rents would rise temporarily then fall. Landlords would get windfall profits due to the inelastic supply. With rent controls, there would be excess demand, but rent control would not affect the supply of units available (as it would in the long run).

4.

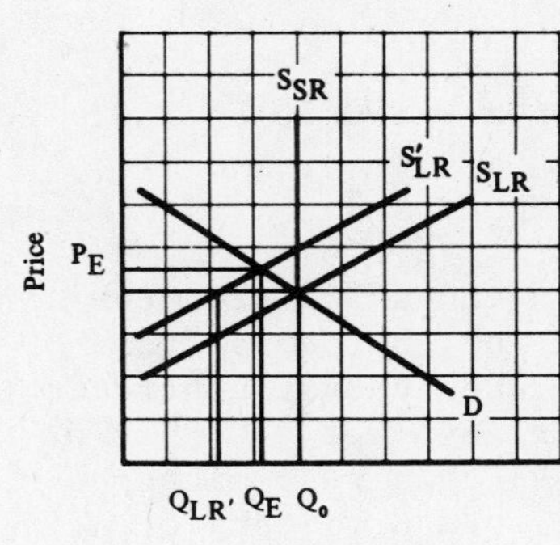

5. (a) $5.25 million (b) $9 million (c) falls by 1 million units (d) 2 million
(e) $4 million

6. The quota would result in a new price of $1.75 and 40,000 units sold for a revenue of $70,000. A fixed price of $1.50 would result in 45,000 units sold for a revenue of $67,500. The quota would maximize income.

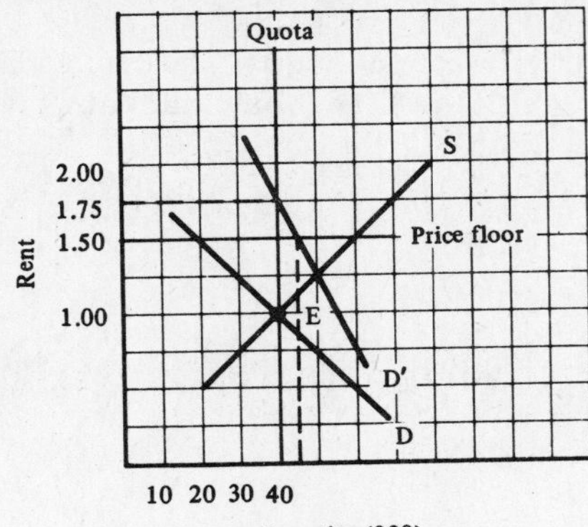

7. (a)

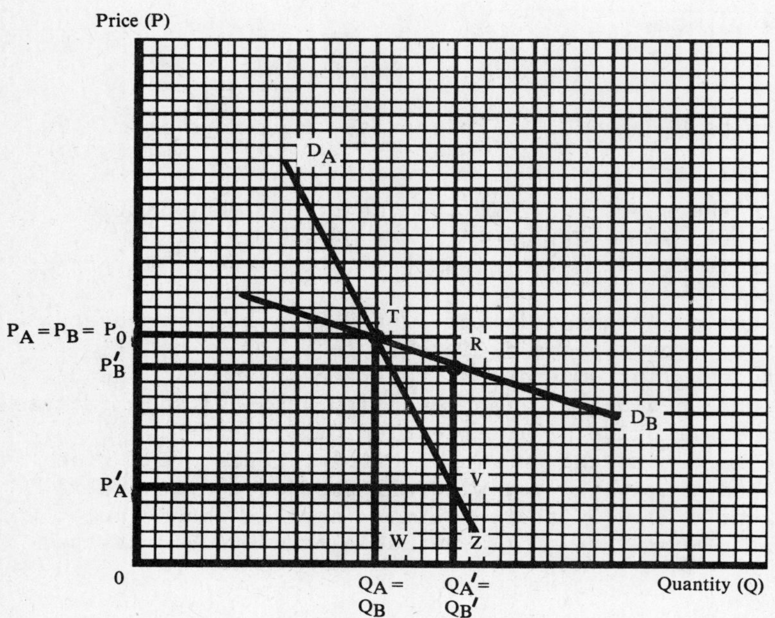

(b) For consumers of B, total expenditures have increased from P_0TWO to P'_BRZO. For consumers, of A, expenditures have declined from P_0TWO to P'_AVZO.

(c) Total expenditures of consumers correspond with total revenues for producers. Thus producers would perhaps desire some form of regulation, but only from producers of commodity A and only when output expands. When output contracts, the inelastic demand curve will produce significantly higher revenues. Output or price controls which would keep prices and revenue higher than what might be expected on average over the long run would be demanded from producers of A. Information on total costs would be necessary to make a more definite answer.

CHAPTER 7

MULTIPLE CHOICE QUESTIONS

1. (b) 2. (c) 3. (b) 4. (c) 5. (d) 6. (a) 7. (b) 8. (b) 9. (b) 10. (a)
11. (d) 12. (b) 13. (b)

EXERCISES

1. (a) The graph should show the following points (marginal utility is given in parentheses next to number of milkshakes consumed): 1(50), 2(40), 3(30), 4(10,) 5(0), 6(-10).
   (b) After the fifth milkshake.

2. (a) 3 hours on tennis, 2 hours on fishing.
   (b) Utility maximization requires that $MU_T/P_T = MU_F/P_F$. When tennis and fishing are priced the same, (e.g. \$1.00 each), the condition is met when 18/1 = 18/1. With the price of tennis increased to \$1.19 (19 percent), the condition is met when 19/1.19 = 16/1 (approximately).

3. Case 1: increase X and decrease Y.
   Case 2: increase X and decrease Y.
   Case 3: decrease X and increase Y.
   Case 4: decrease X and increase Y.
   (Note that as you increase the consumption of one good, its MU falls, and as you decrease the consumption of a good, the MU rises.)

4. Commodity A: low elasticity; a small reduction in quantity demanded will raise the MU significantly.
   Commodity B: high elasticity since it will take a large reduction in quantity demanded to generate a rise in the MU.
   Commodity C: very inelastic because a very small reduction in quantity raises the MU significantly.

5. (a) 5 bottles per week
   (b) \$2.20
   (c) demanded quantity reduced to 3 bottles per week and consumer surplus reduced to \$.90.

CHAPTER 8

MULTIPLE CHOICE QUESTIONS

1. (d)	2. (d)	3. (a)	4. (d)	5. (c)	6. (b)	7. (c)	8. (b)	9. (b)	10. (b)
11. (d)	12. (a)	13. (c)	14. (d)	15. (b)	16. (b)	17. (b)			

EXERCISES

1. (a) The straight line would start at 40 units on the vertical axis and go to 50 units on the horizontal axis.
   (b) No.
   (c) 25 units of movie-going
   (d) There would be a parallel shift in the budget line to the right and the new line would intersect the vertical axis at 60 units.

2. (a) The budget line starts at 40 units on the vertical axis and goes to 75 units on the horizontal axis.
   (b) 37.5.
   (c) The line starts at 40 units on the vertical axis and goes to 50 units on the horizontal axis. It is the same because although the money value of the budget has risen 50 percent so have all absolute prices.

3. (a)

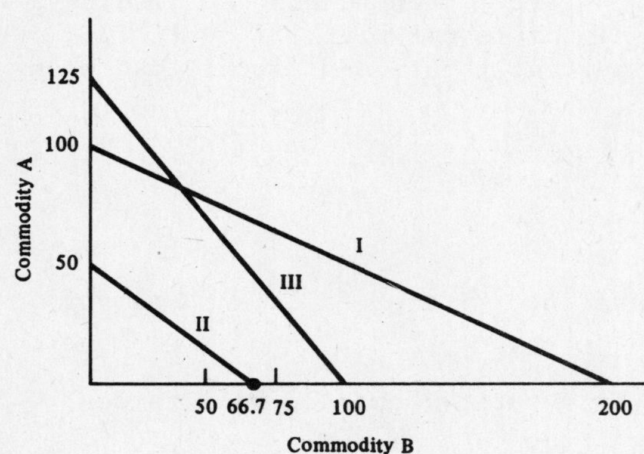

   (b) I: - .5
   II: - .75
   III: - 1.25
   (c) A = 100 - .5B
   (d) 1/3 unit of A

4. (a)

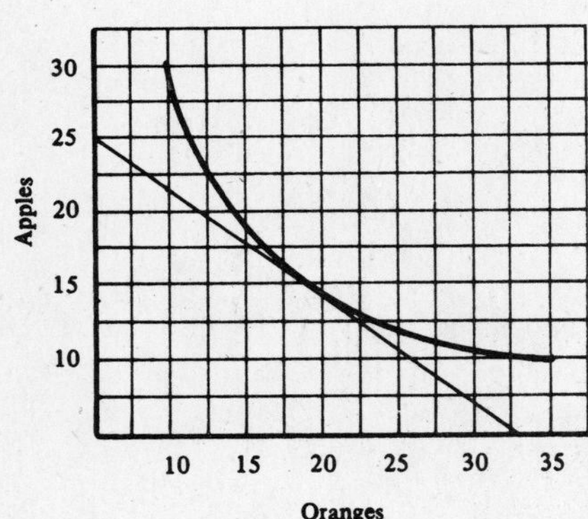

   (b) Yes; 15 oranges and 19 apples would give the same utility as 19 oranges and 15 apples. One more apple (15 oranges and 20 apples) would put the consumer on a higher indifference curve.
   (c) In the range .75 to .85.

5. (a) and (b)

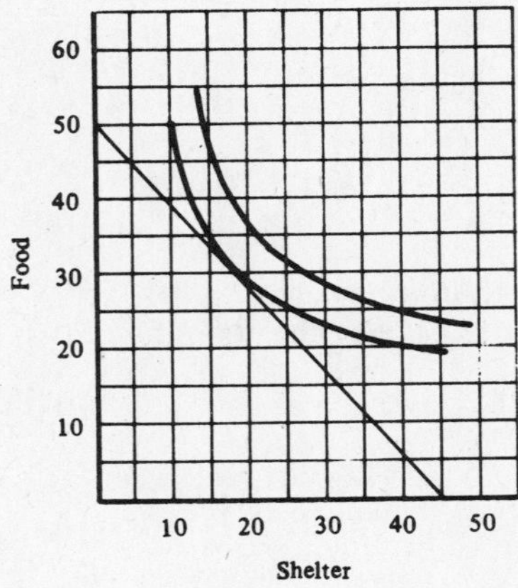

(c) 30 food and 18 shelter. Given the budget constraint, this is the maximum utility attainable. The budget is exhausted at this point of tangency.

6. (a) $12043/1.313 = $9172 (1974 income in 1969 dollars)
9172/7761 = 1.182, thus increase in real constant dollar income is 18.2 percent.
(b) Food: $2442/1.483 = $1647. 1647/1605 = 1.0259.
Percent increase = 2.59.
Clothing: $988/1.219 = $810. 810/727 = 1.115.
Percent increase = 11.5.
Transportation: $1708/1.253 = $1363. 1363/1111 = 1.226.
Percent increase = 22.7.
Alcohol/Tobacco: $482/1.151 = $418. 418/341 = 1.227.
Percent increase = 22.7.
(c) Relative price of food and clothing was increased from 1:1 to 1.2 : 1.
(1.483/1.219 = 1.22)
For alcohol/tobacco to transportation, relative price fell from 1:1 to .9:1
(1.151/1.253 = .92)

7. (a) The substitution effect is AB in the diagram below
(b) The income effect is BC in the diagram below
(c) No. If X were an inferior good, there would have to be a negative income effect.

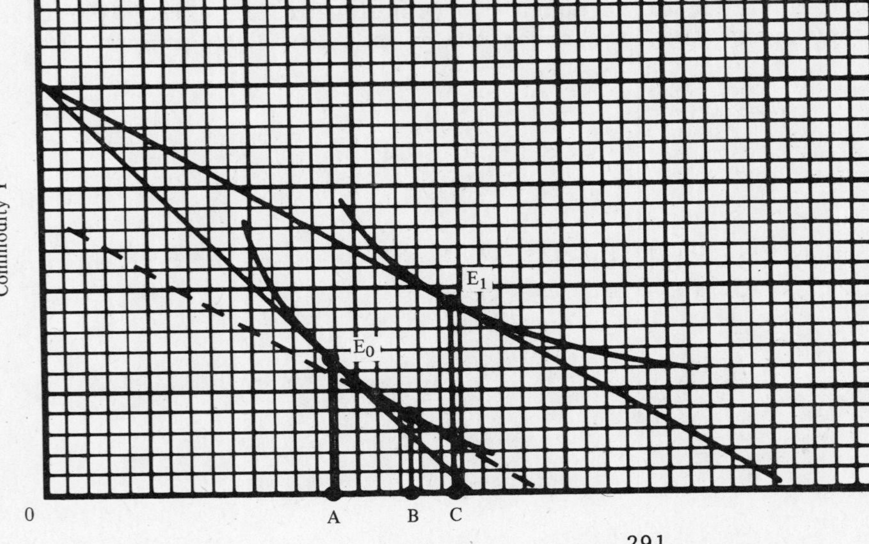

CHAPTER 9

MULTIPLE-CHOICE QUESTIONS

1. (b) 2. (c) 3. (d) 4. (c) 5. (c) 6. (b) 7. (a) 8. (c) 9. (a) 10. (c)
11. (d) 12. (c) 13. (c)

EXERCISES

1. (a) No. Neither method A nor B uses more of both factors than the other.
   (b) Method A, since it is the least-cost method given the price of the two factors.
   (c) Yes. Both methods become the same in terms of this total cost.

2.

Revenue from sales	=	\$ 5.0 million	
less salaries, etc.	=	\$ 3.0 million	
less depreciation	=	\$ 0.5 million	
Net profit before tax	=	\$ 1.5 million	Answer (a)
less cost of capital	=	\$ 0.5 million	
Economic profit	=	\$ 1.0 million	Answer (b)
less taxes	=	\$ 0.75 million	(.5 times \$1.5 million)
Economic profit after tax	=	\$ 0.25 million	Answer (c)

3. (a) Approximately 500 square feet. The answer is derived by computing the cost of production at each garden size, which is the hours of labor times the wage rate plus the depreciation on the tools. At 200 square feet, the total cost of using hand tools is less than using power tools. At 500 square feet and over, the total cost of power tool farming is less than farming with hand tools.
   (b) The answer would change because it would not be economical to use power tools until the size of the garden reached 1,000 square feet.

4. (a) It is a legitimate expense since the value of the capital is being used up. If the firm did not own the truck, it would have to rent one.
   (b) \$250. No payment for services rendered by the owner has been included. Whatever his opportunity cost, it would be necessary to include it to obtain a true profit figure. He also should have imputed foregone interest on his savings used to start the business.
   (c) If profit was regarded as a payment to the owner, it would represent approximately \$1.50 per hour (\$250/160). This hardly seems excessive.
   (d) The decision to return to university occurred after the price of newsprint fell to \$30 per ton. This meant a reduction in monthly accounting profits from \$250 to \$10. In terms of the business then, the opportunity cost was \$10 per month.

CHAPTER 10

MULTIPLE-CHOICE QUESTIONS

1. (b) 2. (b) 3. (b) 4. (a) 5. (d) 6. (b) 7. (c) 8. (c) 9. (a) 10. (a)
11. (a) 12. (b) 13. (c) 14. (c) 15. (d) 16. (c) 17. (a)

EXERCISES

1. (a)

Average Product	Marginal Product
20	
	40
30	
	60
40	
	80
50	
	70
54	
	54
54	
	40
52	
	20
48	
	12
44	
	8
40.4	

(b) Check the data in (a) against your graph.

(c)

Output	TFC	TVC	TC	AFC	AVC	ATC	MC
20	168	80	248	8.40	4.00	12.40	
							2.00
60	168	160	328	2.80	2.67	5.47	
							1.33
120	168	240	408	1.40	2.00	3.40	
							1.00
200	168	320	488	.84	1.60	2.44	
							1.14
270	168	400	568	.62	1.48	2.10	
							1.48
324	168	480	648	.52	1.48	2.00	
							2.00
364	168	560	728	.46	1.54	2.00	
							4.00
384	168	640	808	.44	1.67	2.11	
							6.67
396	168	720	888	.42	1.82	2.24	
							10.00
404	168	800	968	.42	1.98	2.40	

(d)

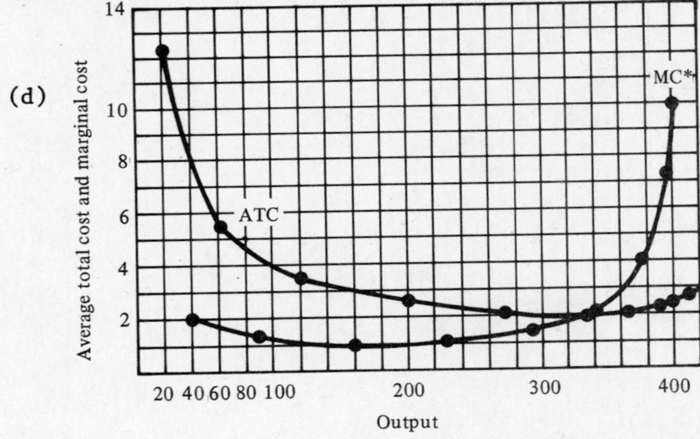

2. (a)

Output	Total Cost	Average Total Cost
1	\$ 3.50	\$ 3.50
2	5.00	2.50
3	6.00	2.00
4	7.25	1.81
5	9.00	1.80
6	11.50	1.92

(b)

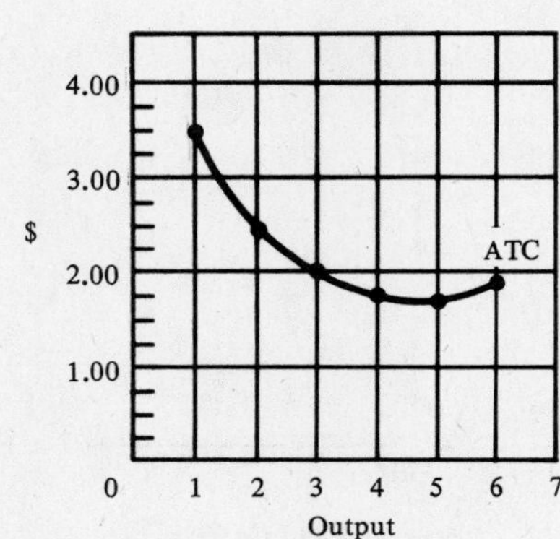

(c) The capacity is where short-run average total cost is at a minimum, or 5 units of output.

3. (a) AFC = (\$2,400 + 4000 + 2000 + 4000 + 6000)/180 = \$102.22; AVC = \$72.22.
(b) \$18,400/90 = \$204.44
(c) Close to zero; the only additional cost might be a meal.
(d) Yes, as it is only necessary to cover variable costs of \$13,000 in the short run.

4. (a)

Q	TFC	TVC	TC	MC	AFC	AVC	ATC
0	50	0	50				
				4			
1	50	4	54		50	4	54
				6			
2	50	10	60		25	5	30
				8			
3	50	18	68		16.67	6	22.67
				10			
4	50	28	78		12.50	7	19.50
				12			
5	50	40	90		10	8	18
				14			
6	50	54	104		8.33	9	17.33
				16			
7	50	70	120		7.14	10	17.14
				18			
8	50	88	138		6.25	11	17.25
				20			
9	50	108	158		5.56	12	17.56
				22			
10	50	130	180		5	13	18
.	.	.	.		.	.	.
.	.	.	.		.	.	.
.	.	.	.		.	.	.
20	50	460	510		2.50	23	25.50

(b) 7
(c) 16
(d) No.
(e) Although average fixed costs are declining because of the 50 (TFC) being spread over more and more units of output, average variable costs are rising and at some point (output level of 8) they offset the falling average fixed costs.

5. (a) 8 (b) 6 to 7 (c) 8

6. (a)

Output 000 (kgms.)	TVC ($000's)	TFC ($000's)	TC ($000's)	ATC ($)	MC ($)
0	0	250	250	00	
					.50
200	100	250	350	1.75	
					.57
375	200	250	450	1.20	
					.67
525	300	250	550	1.05	
					.80
650	400	250	650	1.00	
					1.42
720	500	250	750	1.03	
					1.67
780	600	250	850	1.09	

(b)

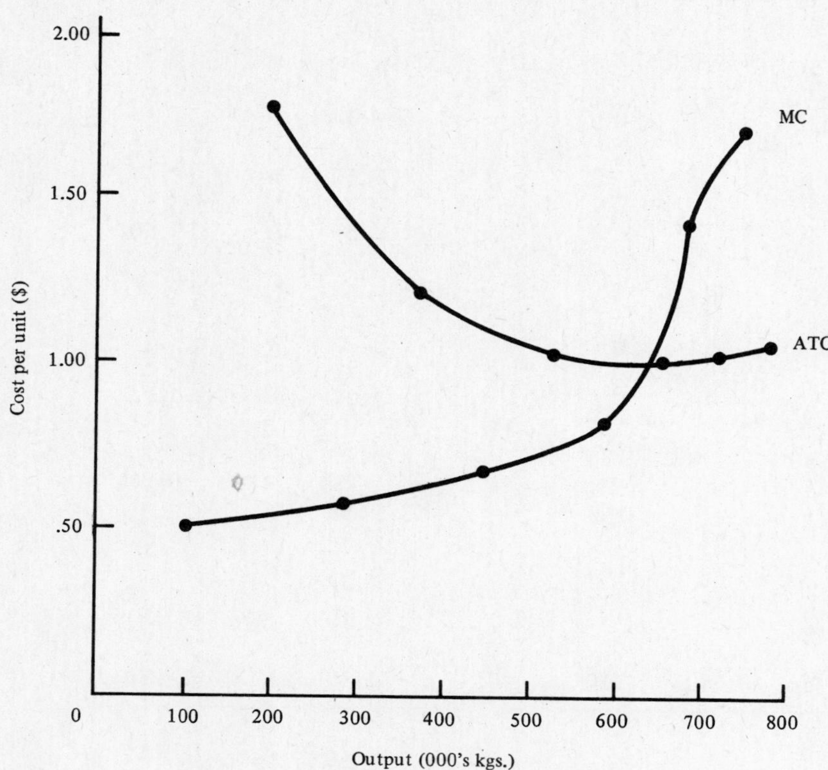

(c) At approximately 650,000 kgms.
(d) The marginal cost schedule intersects the short-run average total cost schedule exactly at the minimum average total cost.

CHAPTER 11

MULTIPLE-CHOICE QUESTIONS

1. (b) 2. (b) 3. (a) 4. (a) 5. (a) 6. (a) 7. (c) 8. (c) 9. (c) 10. (b)
11. (d) 12. (d) 13. (b) 14. (c) 15. (d) 16. (d) 17. (d) 18. (c) 19. (c) 20. (a)
21. (b) 22. (d)

EXERCISES

1. (a) Firm A is minimizing costs since, with combination 3, the ratio of the marginal productivities of capital and labor are equal to the ratio of their cost per unit of the factor employed (6/3 = 10/5).
(b) Firm B would have to move to combination 1 by using less capital, and thereby raise the MP_K, and more labor, thereby reducing the MP_L. Firm C would have to move to combination 3, increasing MP_K and decreasing MP_L.

2. (a) The firm will operate along the SRAC. To move along the LRAC requires a change in fixed factors and a new SRAC. While this would result in a lower cost (if the change could be made quickly), a decline in output back to q_o would put the firm on a new SRAC which would not be optimal for a sustained output at q_o.
(b) If q_2 is to be the new long-run output, it would be efficient for the firm to move along the LRAC to operate on a different SRAC and adjust the mix of factors of production. To remain on the original SRAC, which is coincident with q_o, would see the firm sustaining, in the long run, average costs that are above what is attainable by altering the mix of factors and moving along the LRAC.

3. (a) At the 6 output levels (including 10,000), the LRAC are: \$.50; \$.46; \$.39; \$.35; \$.46; \$.52.
(b) 60,000
(c) It varies slightly, which, given no change in factor prices, might be expected according to the theory in the text.

4. (a)

Method	ΔCapital	ΔLabor	Marginal Rate of Substitution
A			
B	+ 5	-22	-4.40
C	+10	-18	-1.80
D	+15	-16	-1.07
E	+18	- 9	-0.50
F	+22	- 6	-0.27

(b)

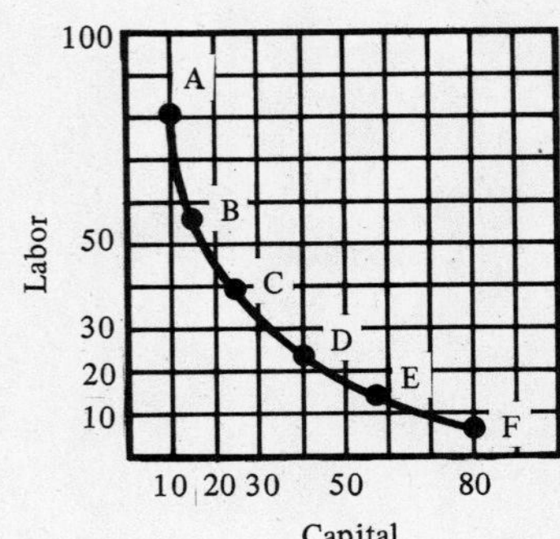

5. (a)

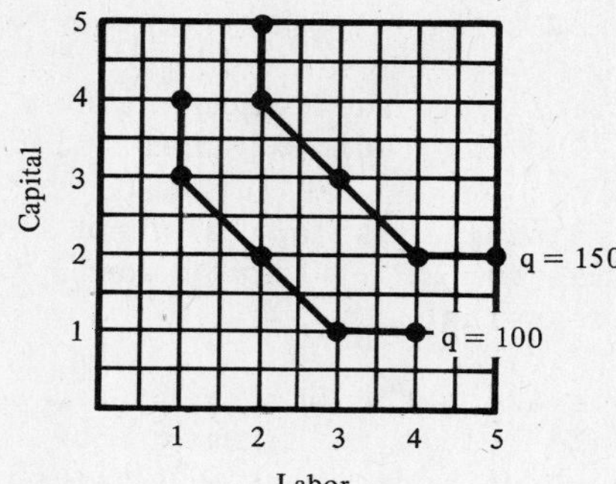

(b) one unit of capital and three units of labor

(c) No. The isocost line would be a straight line tangent to not only the original combination of capital and labor (1 and 3 units, respectively) but also through two other combinations of capital and labor that produce 100 units of output. Thus, in this "unusual" configuration of inputs, the new relative price is compatible with three combinations of factors.

6. (a) one unit of capital and two units of labor

(b) 2.5 units of capital and 1.8 units of labor; the slope of the isocost line is now -2. Optimal mix of capital and labor is at the point of tangency with this isocost with isoquant for 200 units of output.

CHAPTER 12

MULTIPLE-CHOICE QUESTIONS

1. (d) 2. (c) 3. (b) 4. (d) 5. (d) 6. (a) 7. (d) 8. (d) 9. (c) 10. (c) 11. (d) 12. (a) 13. (d) 14. (a) 15. (a) 16. (a) 17. (b) 18. (a) 19. (a).

EXERCISES

1. (a) The market elasticity of demand (E_M) is given by the formula

$$E_M = \frac{\text{\% change in world output}}{\text{\% change in world price}} \quad \text{or}$$

$$\text{\% change in world price} = \frac{\text{\% change in world output}}{E_M}$$

$$= \frac{\frac{4}{(2{,}000 + 1{,}996)/2}}{0.20} = .01$$

(b) The firm's elasticity of demand is the percentage change in the output of the firm divided by the percentage change in world price (calculated above). This is equal to

$$\frac{\frac{(8-4)}{(4+8)/2}}{0.01} = 66.7$$

2.

	$ 12	$ 8	$ 5
(a)	100	80	60
(b)	1,200	640	300
(c)	825 (approx)	640	510
(d)	375	0	-210
(e)	3.75	0	-3.50

3. (a)

Output	TC	AVC	ATC	MC
0	20	--	--	
				15
1	35	15	35	
				9
2	44	12	22	
				6
3	50	10	$16\frac{2}{3}$	
				18
4	68	12	17	
				27
5	95	15	19	
				45
6	140	20	$23\frac{1}{3}$	

(b) The firm should discontinue production since a price of $8 does not cover AVC.
(c) It should produce 3 units a month at this output. Price approximately equals MC, thus maximizing profits (note also that MC=ATC at this output).
(d) Short-run economic profits. New entrants would be attracted to the market, increasing market supply and putting downward pressure on price.

4. (a) and (b): The ATC at an output level of 5,000 is $.90, so economic profits are being made, given a market price of $1. However, the firm's MC exceeds price and thus a reduction to an output level where P = MC would be profit-maximizing.

5. (a) Economic profits (earning profits in excess of all opportunity costs, including the opportunity cost of capital).
(b) No, not in a perfectly competitive industry, because the profits will attract firms into the industry, increasing supply and lowering market price. New firms will continue to enter until all firms are just covering their total costs (that is, breaking even, at a zero-profit equilibrium).

6. (a) Price and output will rise and firms will be enjoying short-run profits, (revenue over and above that sufficient to cover total costs).
   (b) The market supply curve would shift to the right because of the entry of new firms until price is lowered to a level where all firms in the industry are just covering their total costs. This firm will have adjusted its output to the level where P=MC as market price changed.

7.

Firm A		Firm B		Firm C	
Output	MC	Output	MC	Output	MC
30		25		36	
	4		.5*		4*
40		30		40	
	5		2.5*		5
50		35		44	
	7		8		7
60		40		48	
	10		12		10
70		45		52	
	14		18		14
80		50		56	

*Not part of industry supply schedule.

The industry supply curve is derived by selecting a given price and adding together what each firm would offer at that price according to its MC, as follows:

	Approximate Industry Supply			
	Output from			
Price	A	B	C	Total
$ 3	--	35	--	35
4	35	36	--	71
5	45	36	42	123
7	55	37	46	138
10	65	40	50	155
12	70	43	52	165
14	75	44	54	173

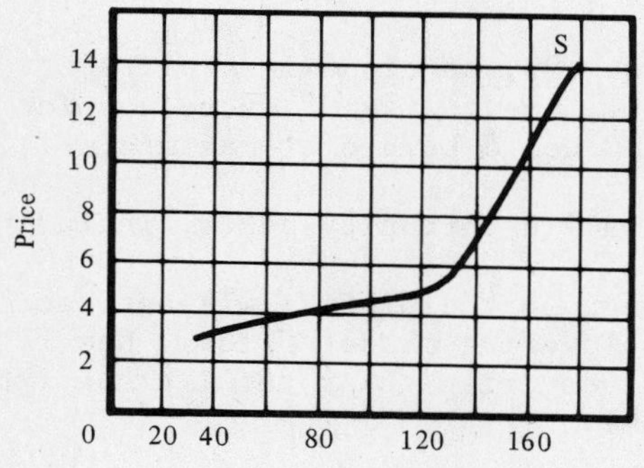

CHAPTER 13

MULTIPLE-CHOICE QUESTIONS

1. (b) 2. (c) 3. (c) 4. (a) 5. (d) 6. (c) 7. (c) 8. (b) 9. (b) 10. (a)
11. (d) 12. (d) 13. (c) 14. (c) 15. (d) 16. (b)

EXERCISES

1. (a) 60 (b) $11 (c) $660 (d) $480 (e) $180 (f) 25 and 90; $14.50 and $7.50 (g) $7.50

2. (a) Marginal and average cost and marginal and total revenue

TR	MR	MC	ATC	Output	Profit
0			0	0	-20
	18	4			
18			24	1	- 6
	14	3			
32			13.50	2	5
	10	5			
42			10.67	3	10
	6	7			
48			9.75	4	9
	2	9			
50			9.60	5	2
	- 2	11			
48			9.83	6	-11

(b) 3 units
(c) $14
(d) At 3 units of output, total revenue is $42, total cost is $32, and profits would be $10.

3. (a) and (b)

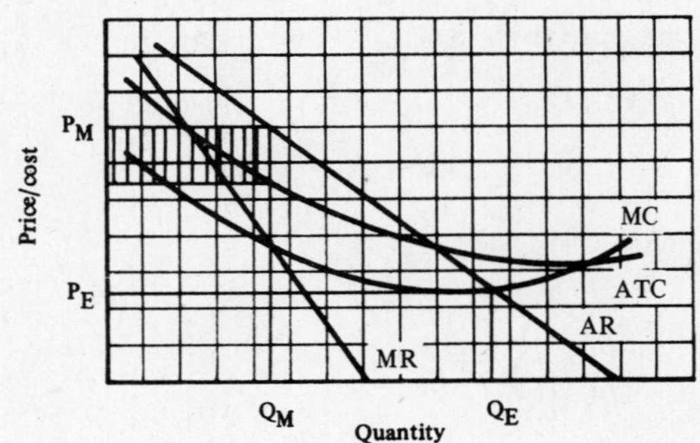

(c) No, it would not, because the ATC exceeds the price and business could not be sustained for long.

4. (a) and (b)

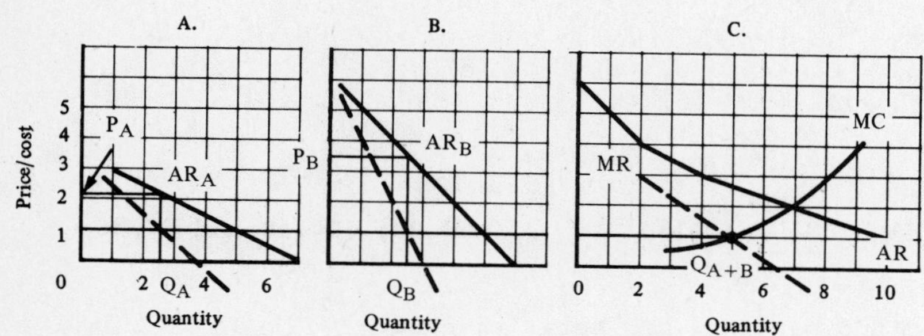

The horizontal summation of AR_A and AR_B will produce AR, as shown in C. The MR for the market is the broken line in C. Next it is necessary to calculate the MR schedules for the individual demand schedules, and these are shown as broken lines in A and B. Relating MC = MR in C to the MR's in A and B produces Q_A and Q_B with the different prices P_A and P_B.

5. (a)

Output	ATC	MC
0		
		2
5	10	
		3
10	6.5	
		5
15	6.0	
		8
20	6.5	
		12
25	7.6	
		17
30	9.2	

(b)

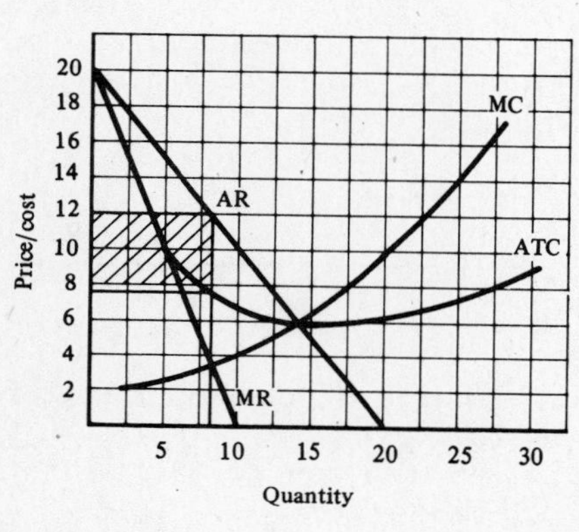

(c) Yes. Output would be reduced and price increased because the tax would raise the MC schedule by $4 and intersect the MR at a new point, indicating that price should rise and output be cut.

CHAPTER 14

MULTIPLE-CHOICE QUESTIONS

1. (d) 2. (d) 3. (b) 4. (b) 5. (b) 6. (c) 7. (c) 8. (b) 9. (c) 10. (c)
11. (a) 12. (d) 13. (a) 14. (c) 15. (a) 16. (b) 17. (d) 18. (d) 19. (b)

EXERCISES

1. (a) \$6
   (b) \$100 [(\$6.00 - \$3.50)x.40 = \$100.00]
   (c) No. New firms will reduce profits.
   (d) ATC curve rises; D curve will shift rightward, with MR curve shifting accordingly. MC curve will be unchanged since, in this case, advertising is a fixed amount.
   (e) The average revenue (demand) and marginal revenue curves for this firm would shift leftward and profits would be reduced.
   (f) As the firm's D curve shifts left to a tangency point on the ATC curve (at an output less than that at minimum ATC).

2. (a)

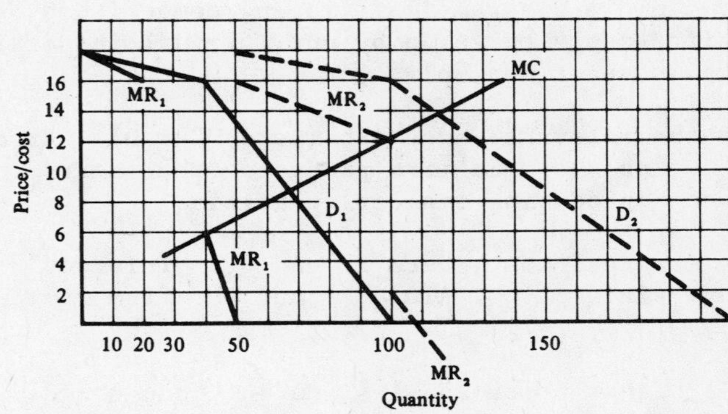

   (b) \$16; \$16   (c) fall; be unchanged   (d) be unchanged; be higher
   (e) oligopoly

3. (a) Set MR = MC to find output: 50 - .02q = 10; q = 2000. Since TR = p x q, price can be found by dividing total revenue by quantity:

   $(50q - .01q^2)/q = 50 - .01q$. At q = 2000, price = \$30.

   (b) Price will be constant; output will vary. High costs of changing administered prices account for their stickiness.
   (c) Profits will be less than "sticky prices" (see calculation below). Note, however, that price changes in response to demand changes can be costly <u>and</u> rivals may well choose not to follow higher price. This explains why stickiness is often observed. For P = 60 - .01q,

	Maximizing	Sticky
P	35	30
Q	2,500	3,000
TR	87,500	90,000
TC	50,000	55,000
Profit	37,500	35,000

   [Note: find Q for "sticky price" by solving P = 60 - .01q, with P = \$30; find profit-maximizing price and quantity in the usual way.]

4. (a) The firm would likely choose the plant with ATC_1. If demand were to vary considerably, the average cost of producing various quantities would not vary considerably whereas with a plant characterized by ATC_2 costs, on average could rise considerably if demand increased or decreased noticeably.
   (b) It suggests that the fixed factors are such that their rate of utilization can be varied so as to keep the variable to fixed factor ratio constant or close to constant.

CHAPTER 15

MULTIPLE-CHOICE QUESTIONS

1. (c) 2. (c) 3. (b) 4. (c) 5. (d) 6. (c) 7. (d) 8. (c) 9. (d) 10. (b) 11. (c) 12. (b) 13. (a)

EXERCISES

1. (a) EO,OK; (b) AEG; (c) Zero; (d) OB,OJ; (e) ABD; (f) BDEF; (g) DFG

2. In the diagram illustrating monopoly, draw in MR and equate to MC to set price and output. Shift MC curve up by one. In the diagram illustrating competition, equate S = D to get price and output. Shift supply curve up by one. Visual inspection should show smaller responses in the case of monopoly.

3. (a) ATC declines continuously over the relevant range (to where MC = D). Productive efficiency would be served by having a single firm producing the entire output rather than having more firms each producing smaller quantities.
   (b) q_2; P_2
   (c) The goal would be price equals marginal cost, here P_0 and Q_0. This would be unattainable (without a subsidy) since at Q_0, ATC > P_0 and the firm would suffer losses
   (d) P_1 and q_1
   (e) Average cost pricing results in higher price and less output than would result from pricing for allocative efficiency (P = MC). The firm would be at a zero-profit equilibrium (covering all costs, including the opportunity cost of capital). However, average cost pricing output will not achieve all of the cost advantages of larger-scale output.
4. (a) \$10; 200 units (b) \$13; 125 units (c) \$3

CHAPTER 16

MULTIPLE-CHOICE QUESTIONS

1. (c) 2. (b) 3. (d) 4. (b) 5. (b) 6. (d) 7. (b) 8. (c) 9. (b) 10. (a) 11. (b)

EXERCISES

1. (a) p_2 and q_1
   (b) from p_1 and q_2 to p_3 and q
   (c) p and q_3

2. (a) Per unit tax = \$.50 shifts up MC and ATC by \$.50. Profit maximizer reduces output and raises price by less than amount of tax. Full-cost pricing requires the tax be shifted to price completely. Sales maximizer was earning profits of about \$1.50 x 4,000 = \$6,000 before tax. A tax of \$.50 per unit would cut this profit to \$4,000, the minimum, and hence no change in price.
   (b) The profit maximizer does not adjust price. Neither does the full cost firm, which will have no excess profit to be taxed. The sales maximizer sees profit cut to \$3,000 so he will raise price to generate, if possible, \$8,000 in pre-tax profits.

3. (a)

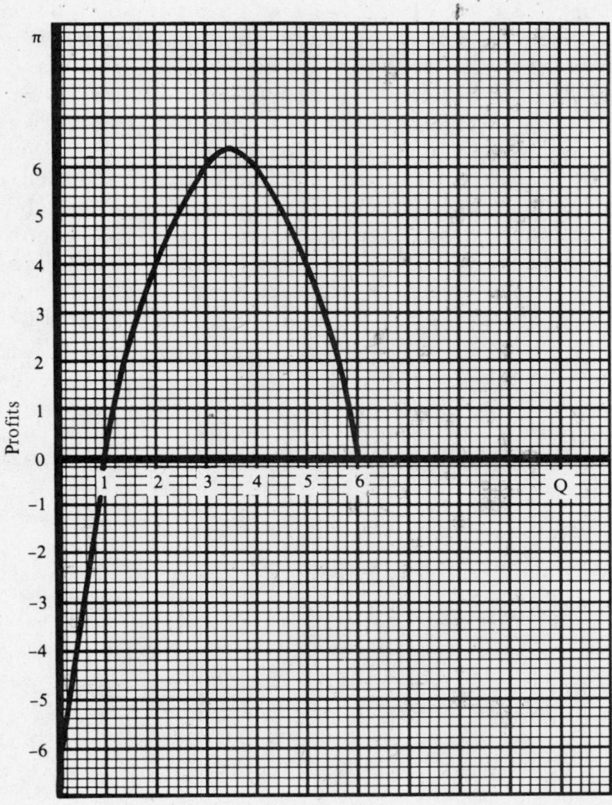

(b) Q = 2 to Q = 5
(c) 3 1/2
(d) Between Q = 5 and Q = 6

CHAPTER 17

MULTIPLE-CHOICE QUESTIONS

1. (b) 2. (b) 3. (c) 4. (c) 5. (a) 6. (c) 7. (a) 8. (a) 9. (c) 10. (a)
11. (a) 12. (b)

EXERCISES

1. (a) The demand curve for labor has an intercept of 95 on the quantity axis and a slope of -4. Case A supply curve of labor has an intercept of 20 on the wage axis and a slope of 2. Case B supply curve of labor is vertical at 60 units of labor.
(b) Cases A and B have equilibrium values of W = 140 and L = 60.
(c) The total economic rents in Case A are given by the area above the supply curve, equal to and below the horizontal line at W = 140, and the equilibrium point W = 140 and L = 60; this is a triangle. All earnings for Case B are economic rents since the supply curve of labor is perfectly inelastic. The transfer earnings of the 60th worker in Case A are equal to the market wage of 140.
(d) W = 160 and L = 70. The total economic rents of the workers who were already in this labor market are 1,200 (60 times (160 - 140).
(e) W = 140 and L = 75. Since the wage rate is the same before and after the policy change, no additional economic rents have been created by this policy.

2.

	Cumulative Percent of income
Lowest fifth	5.8
Second fifth	18.7
Middle fifth	37.3
Fourth fifth	61.8
Highest fifth	100.0

3. (a) Since labor is mobile, there will be no net advantage to being in one particular market. Hence, the wage rate in market A will be equal to that in market B or in this case W*. Employment in market A is OL* and employment in market B is KL*.
   (b) The wage in market B will rise. For example, at KL* employment, the wage is now $\hat{W}$. A dynamic differential between the two markets has been created and thus labor will leave market A and migrate to market B. As this process occurs, the supply curve for labor in market A will shift leftward causing wages in this market to rise and the supply curve for labor in market B will shift rightward causing the wage increase to be less than $\hat{W}$. That is, labor mobility will eliminate the dynamic differential. The final equilibrium will be a wage rate of $\overline{W}$ in both markets. Employment in market B will have increased from KL* to a level of $K\overline{L}$ and employment in market A will have fallen from OL* to a level of $O\overline{L}$.

4. (a) horizontal supply curve at W
   (b) vertical supply curve at E
   (c) any of a number of supply curves dividing rectangle OWEF into two equal areas; diagonal from the origin to F would be one possibility

CHAPTER 18

MULTIPLE-CHOICE QUESTIONS

1. (b) 2. (d) 3. (b) 4. (d) 5. (d) 6. (c) 7. (a) 8. (d) 9. (a) 10. (c)
11. (b) 12. (a) 13. (c) 14. (c)

EXERCISES

1. (a) (i) Medical care services: increased demand for medical care personnel and nonhuman factors, such as medical devices and drugs.
   (ii) Personal computers: increased demand for labor with appropriate training and skills to design, produce, service, and use computers (including) computer engineers, scientists, and programmers to develop software). Increased demand for nonhuman resources also.
   (iii) Outdoor recreation: increased demand for factors used to produce fishing and camping gear (including labor and capital); Increased demand for hiking trails, facilities at provincial parks and other campgrounds, etc.

   (b) (i) Medical personnel must have proper training, thus there may be significant economic rents in the short run to existing trained personnel as earnings rise. Nonhuman factors' earnings will also rise, but to a lesser degree because of their relatively greater mobility. In the long run, economic rents will be reduced because of greater supply elasticity.
   (ii) Much the same as (i) (above).
   (iii) Factors of production (both labor and nonhuman) are likely to be real-tively mobile, in comparison with (i) and (ii). Resources will shift from similar types of employment in response to higher earnings in this sector.

2\. (a) MPP - 0, 11, 12, 13, 14, 13, 11, 10, 9, 5

Case A MRP - 0, 330, 360, 390, 420, 390, 330, 300, 270, 150

Case B MRP - 0, 297, 324, 351, 378, 351, 297, 270, 243, 135

MRP declines in each case as additional labor is employed. This results from the law of diminishing returns.

(b) The MRP for Case B is to the left of the MRP in Case A; fewer units will be employed.
(c) 8 workers in Case A; 7 in Case B
(d) The number employed would decline. Firms would hire fewer since the MRP schedule is unchanged but factor price is higher.

3\. MRP for 8 workers is 300 = (10 times 30) and for 9 workers is 180 = (6 times 30). The MRP curve with production function #2 lies to the right of the MRP curve with production function #1. Employment will increase when the production function changes. Employment with production function #1 is 7 workers while employment with production function #2 is 8 workers.

4\. (a) At a wage of w_0 the total supply is $h_1 + h_2$. At a wage of w_1, individuals A and B increase their hours and individual A is now prepared to supply some hours. In the range w_1 w_2, the total labor supply curve is upward sloping.
(b) Hours have increased because the participation rate has increased and individuals C and B have also increased hours supplied to the market.
(c) Only individual B is prepared to work at a wage of w_2. Hence the participation rate is one-third.

CHAPTER 19

MULTIPLE-CHOICE QUESTIONS

1\. (d) 2. (b) 3. (a) 4. (c) 5. (c) 6. (a) 7. (d) 8. (d) 9. (b) 10. (d)
11\. (d) 12. (d) 13. (c) 14. (d) 15. (a) 16. (b) 17. (b) 18. (c) 19. (a) 20. (b)

EXERCISES

1\. Total cost: $80.00; 94.50; 110.00; 126.50; 144.00; 162.50; 182.00
Marginal cost: $14.50; 15.50; 16.50; 17.50; 18.50; 19.50

2\. (a) w_3; q_4

(b) q_2; q_5-q_2; horizontal at w_4 to q_5 on supply curve and corresponding with the supply curve thereafter.

(c) w; w_2; w_5; q_2; w_1; w_4; w_4; employment is less and the amount of wages are lower than in (a).

(d) q_4

(e) The supply curve shifts leftward. All wage predictions are raised, and employment levels lowered.

3. (a) For market X, equilibrium Q is found by equating 360 - 3Q to 40 + 2Q. Hence, Q = 64 and W = 168. For market Z, Q = 68 and W = 156.
(b) At the minimum wage, the quantity of labor demanded is 66 while the quantity of labor supplied is 71. Unemployment is therefore 5, and employment in market Z would be two fewer than under competitive conditions.
(c) The supply curve in X now becomes W = 30 + 2Q [or Q = .5W-15 instead of Q = .5 W -10]. Setting D = S and solving, Q = 66 and W = 162. Thus, 2 of the unemployed workers from Z are now employed in X and the wage in X falls to 162 from 168.

CHAPTER 20

MULTIPLE-CHOICE QUESTIONS

1. (d) 2. (c) 3. (a) 4. (a) 5. (c) 6. (a) 7. (d) 8. (c)

EXERCISE

1. (a) Largest investments in formal education are likely to have been made by individuals whose occupations are managerial, professional, and clerical in nature. Craftsmen are likely to have undergone the greatest degree of on-the-job training. All of these occupations are characterized by low probabilities of poverty.
(b) Farmers and farm workers, loggers and fishermen, and recreation workers are likely to be subject to large seasonal demands. Services and general laborers are likely to be low-skilled workers. These workers tend to be laid off first if cutbacks in production are necessary. For all of these occupations, the incidence of poverty tends to be high relative to others.

CHAPTER 21

MULTIPLE-CHOICE QUESTIONS

1. (c) 2. (d) 3. (b) 4. (b) 5. (b) 6. (a) 7. (c) 8. (a) 9. (d) 10. (a)
11. (c) 12. (c)

EXERCISES

1. (a) Canada 2.0; 0.5
Argentina 0.33; 3.0
Canada should specialize in the production of beef; Argentina should specialize in the production of wheat.
(b) Canada 2.0; 0.5
Argentina 3.0; 0.33
Canada should specialize in the production of wheat; Argentina should specialize in the production of beef.
(c) Canada 2.0; 0.5
Argentina 2.0; 0.5
Canada should produce both and Argentina should produce both. There are no gains from trade.

2. (a) .2 (Canada) and .5 (Australia)
   (b) Comparative advantage exists for Canada in wheat production.
   (c) Yes; the opportunity costs differ between the two countries.
   (d)

	Wheat	Wool
Canada	+5	-1
Australia	-3	+1½
World	+2	+½

   (e) Yes, each Canadian resource unit is worth $30 in wheat output and $16 in wool so it should specialize in wheat and trade for wool; the reverse for Australia, with values of $36 and $48, respectively.

3. (a) Terms of trade: 102.0; 100; 101.0; 107.4; 115.9; 110.6; 111.8; 107.0; 102.3; 108.5
   (b) 1970-1975: F   1972-1973: F   1975-1979; U   1971-1979: F   1974-1978: U
   (c) 49.5 (This is obtained by multiplying 50 by 100.0/101.0)

4. First of all, draw in a line to represent the terms of trade, 2:1, as shown by tt below.

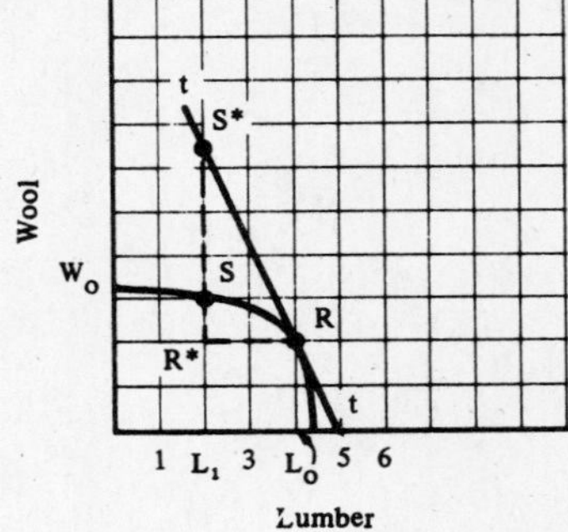

   (a) With "no trade," the country would have to move to a point on the production frontier above L_1 (shown here as S). More wool would be produced.
   (b) Instead, the country could continue to produce at R and export L_0L_1 of lumber in exchange for R*S* of wool, which would make them better off than in the "no trade" situation. Exports = RR* and imports = R*S*.

CHAPTER 22

MULTIPLE-CHOICE QUESTIONS

1. (a) 2. (d) 3. (d) 4. (c) 5. (b) 6. (b) 7. (b) 8. (b) 9. (d) 10. (b)
11. (c) 12. (b) 13. (d) 14. (c)

EXERCISES

1. (a)

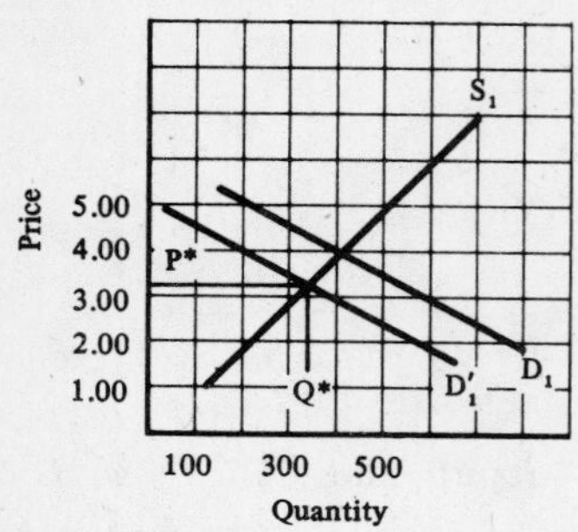

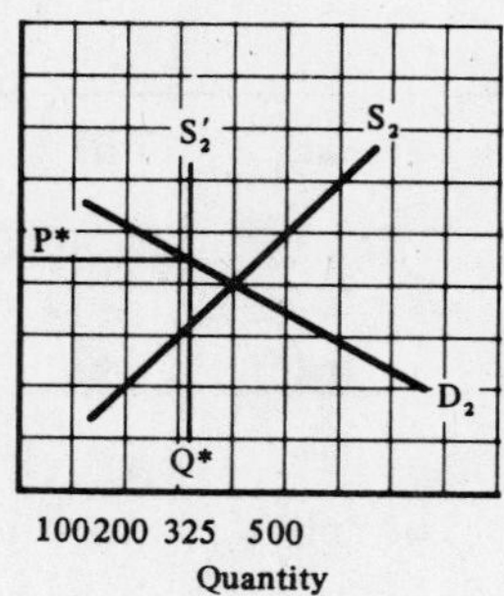

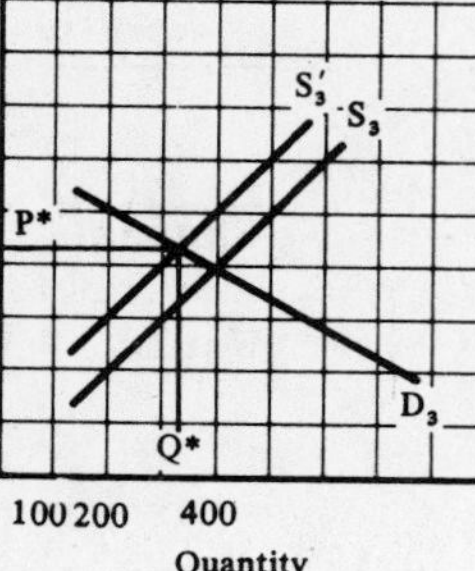

(b) It would not choose the tariff policy. The price might rise by almost the amount of the tariff, but there would be little reduction in imports.

(c) Policy 1, a restriction on demand, not only reduces the amount of imports but also lowers the price.

2. (a)

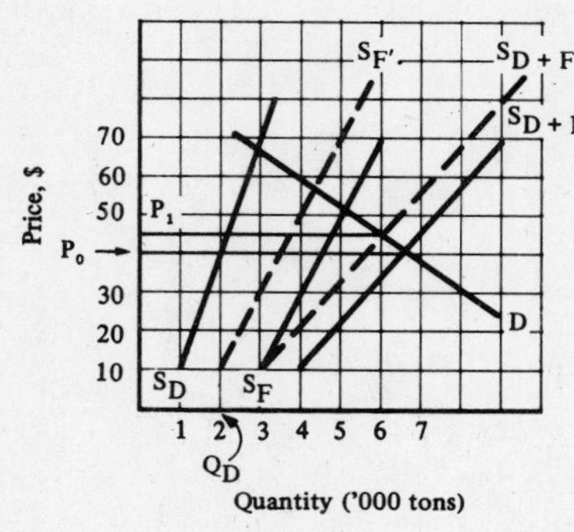

(b) See diagram above.

3. (a) Possibly not, in the long run. Higher tariffs may reduce real income and even raise the overall unemployment rate.

(b) Yes, the particular industry would ordinarily be helped by increased sales and/or higher prices as competing imported products are reduced.

(c) It could. Real income of consumers should decrease, causing cutbacks in expenditures affecting all sectors of the economy. Under a fluctuating exchange rate regime, the foreign exchange value of the domestic currency would be higher, and exports reduced.

CHAPTER 23

MULTIPLE-CHOICE QUESTIONS

1. (b) 2. (b) 3. (c) 4. (d) 5. (b) 6. (a) 7. (c) 8. (a) 9. (c) 10. (c)

EXERCISES

1.

	Country A	Country B	Difference
Year X	$2,000	$100	$1,900
Year X + 1	2,060	103	1,957
Year X + 24	4,000	200	3,800

2. (a) 18; 24; 72
   (b) 3 percent
   (c) 30 years

3. (a) Opportunity costs are increasing in both countries. For example, in country A, to obtain an increase in 10 bushels of wheat from 20 to 30, the loss in production in peanuts is 3. However, to increase wheat from 30 to 40, a loss of 4 is required. For country B, an increase of wheat from 20 to 40 requires a loss of 10. An increase of wheat from 40 to 60 requires a loss of 11 bushels of peanuts.

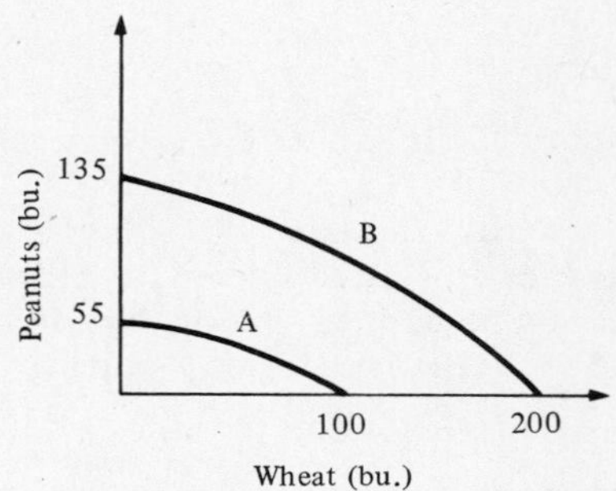

   (b) A combination of 80 wheat and 16 peanuts represents a point inside the production possibility boundary in country A. It is technically possible for country A to produce 80 and 19. Country B is operating on its production-possibility boundary, but there may be allocative inefficiency.
   (c) GNP in country A is $2 x 80 plus $.5 x 16, which equals $168. GNP in country B is $2 x 160 plus $.5 x 35, which equals $337.50. Per capita GNP in country A is $168 divided by 8, which equals $21. Per capita GNP in country B is $337.50 divided by 10, which equals $33.75.
   (d) Country B has avoided X-inefficiency. Although country A and country B have the same number of <u>units</u> of labor, land, and capital, these resources are more productive in country B than in country A. In a sense, all of country A's resources are being used less efficiently than in country B. This may be due to differences in social and cultural attitudes, differences in market organization, or differences in labor skills and productivity. Land quality might also differ.
   (e) The objectives should be to assist country A to attain a point on the production-possibility boundary and also to shift the boundary itself to the right. Aid might come in many forms: retraining labor and improving land cultivation by various Canadian experts from agricultural schools in Canada; increasing the capital intensity of production by giving country A more tractors and other farm equipment; introducing better peanut and wheat seed. Hopefully, the production-possibility boundary would shift to the right in time.

   Alternatively, living standards in country A could be improved by simply giving country A more wheat or peanuts as an outright gift. This would allow consumption to be greater than production, but it is hard to believe that this is an appropriate long-run solution to country A's problems.

CHAPTER 24

MULTIPLE-CHOICE QUESTIONS

1. (b) 2. (b) 3. (c) 4. (d) 5. (b) 6. (d) 7. (d) 8. (c) 9. (d) 10. (c)
11. (a) 12. (c) 13. (a) 14. (b) 15. (d)

EXERCISES

1. (a) Where the demand and S(= MC) schedules intersect for Mr. Maple.
   (b) Add the demand schedules vertically; that is, find out the total willingness to pay for each level of quality from 0 to Q*.

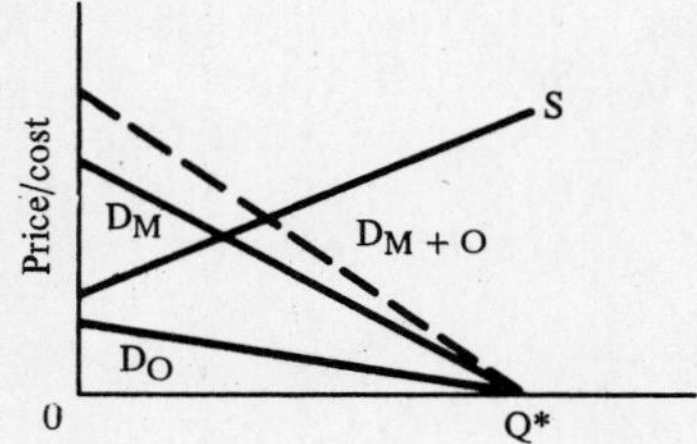

   (c) Yes. The S = MC would intersect the D_{M+O} to the right of the D_M intersection with S, indicating an improvement in road quality.
   (d) It depends on how the costs are "shared." If both Mr. Oak and Mr. Maple pay one-half, then Mr. Maple would pay less. The new cost would be only slightly above what Mr. Maple paid before, but half the cost would be borne by Mr. Oak. Other cost-sharing arrangements are certainly possible.

2. (a) trucking down; railroads up
   (b) private gasoline consumption down; trucking unaffected
   (c) airlines down; railroads up
   (d) foreign publishers down; Canadian publishers up

3. (a)

Output (tons/wh)	APC	MPC	ASC	MSC
0		500		600
1	500		600	
		50		175
2	275		387.50	
		70		210
3	206.67		328.33	
		90		240
4	177.50		306.25	
		110		270
5	164		299	
		230		400
6	175		315.83	
		300		480
7	192.86		339.29	

   (b) \$177.50 and \$306.25, respectively
   (c) \$164; 5 tons/week
   (d) higher; less; \$299 (the lowest average social cost); low

4. (a) The producer would choose OA_1 since that would maximize net private benefits. Every unit less than OA_1 results in NPB > 0; every unit beyond OA_1 results in NPB < 0.
(b) Where the MNPB and MSD schedules intersect. Beyond this point the additional costs to society exceed the additional benefits. To the left of this point, marginal benefits exceed marginal damages and output should expand.
(c) Worse off. By restricting output to A*, the net benefit foregone by society (compared to the firm's optimal output level) is ZTQ (that is, the loss in net benefits to the producer, A^*TQA_1, minus the reduction in marginal social damages, A^*ZQA_1).

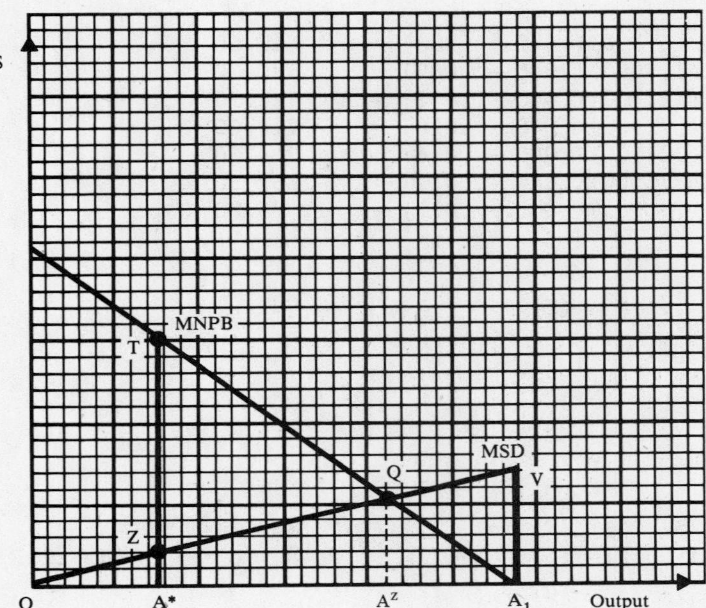

CHAPTER 25

MULTIPLE-CHOICE QUESTIONS

1. (b) 2. (c) 3. (c) 4. (c) 5. (d) 6. (b) 7. (a) 8. (d) 9. (c) 10. (c)
11. (b) 12. (b) 13. (c) 14. (b) 15. (c)

EXERCISES

1. (a) Situation C. Demand is very elastic, and quantity of accommodation would decline significantly with little rise in price.
(b) Situation A. Demand is inelastic and does not respond significantly to the higher price.
(c) In the short run the landlord would shoulder all the tax.

2. (a) Tax A is proportional.
Tax B is regressive.
Tax C is progressive.
(b) For each income group the tax rates are: 22 percent for \$5,000, 23 percent for \$10,000, 24 percent for \$20,000, and 24.3 percent for \$30,000. The tax system is progressive.

3. (a) The ratio of tax paid to income for the nine income classes shown are, from lowest to highest income groups, 7.3, 4.7, 3.8, 3.2, 3.1, 2.8, 2.6, 1.7 and 1.1 percent, suggesting a regressive tax.

(b) Taking again the mid-points of these income ranges, such a scheme suggests reduced taxes for the first two income groups of ($3,750)(.073 - .040) = $123.75 and ($6,000)(.047 - .040) = $42. All other groups would pay an additional tax as follows:

Income Group	Additional Tax	
$ 7,000- 9,999	(8,500)(.040 - .038) = $	17.00
10,000-11,999	(11,000)(.040 - .032) =	88.00
12,000-14,999	(13,500)(.040 - .031) =	121.50
15,000-19,999	(17,500)(.040 - .028) =	210.00
20,000-24,999	(22,500)(.040 - .026) =	315.00
25,000-49,999	(37,500)(.040 - .017) =	862.50
50,000-99,999	(75,000)(.040 - .011) =	2,175.00

4. (a) IR (b) G (c) N (d) R (e) N (f) G (g) R

CHAPTER 26

MULTIPLE-CHOICE QUESTIONS

1. (d) 2. (b) 3. (b) 4. (b) 5. (b) 6. (a) 7. (d) 8. (c) 9. (a) 10. (d)
11. (b) 12. (c) 13. (c) 14. (a) 15. (b) 16. (b) 17. (c) 18. (d) 19. (d) 20. (d)
21. (c)

EXERCISES

1. (a) Base year: (3,000 x .3) + (2,500 x .25) + (5,000 x .15) + (100 x .1) + (60 x .1) + (300 x .1) = 2,321

Next year: (3,300 x .3) + (2,500 x .25) + (5,000 x .15) + (110 x .1) + (60 x .1) + (330 x .1) = 2,415

(b) Index = (2,415/2,321) x 100 = 104.0

(c) No; the prices increased by approximately 4 percent. This is because shelter, clothing, and other goods are only 50 percent of total expenditures.

(d) The price increase from the base year for this group of households (using their fixed weights) is 5.5 percent. Hence, the overall price increase reflected by the overall price index underestimates the cost-of-living increase of this group.

(e) Most likely shelter and transportation. Weights of shelter and transportation might increase and hence other components (food, clothing, entertainment, and other) might fall.

2. (a)

Yr.	Nominal Value of Output in A	In B	In Economy
1	80,000	100,000	180,000
2	132,000	84,000	216,000
3	144,000	108,000	252,000

(b) Industry A:
real value in yr. 1 = 4,000 times 20 = 80,000
in yr. 2 = 6,000 times 20 = 120,000
in yr. 3 = 6,000 times 20 = 120,000

Industry B:
real value in yr. 1 = 20,000 times 5 = 100,000
in yr. 2 = 21,000 times 5 = 105,000
in yr. 3 = 18,000 times 5 = 90,000

Real Output in Economy:
yr. 1 = 80,000 + 100,000 = 180,000
yr. 2 = 120,000 + 105,000 = 225,000
yr. 3 = 120,000 + 90,000 = 210,000

(c) yr. 1: 180,000 divided by 180,000 times 100 = 100.0
yr. 2: 216,000 divided by 225,000 times 100 = 96.0
yr. 3: 252,000 divided by 210,000 times 100 = 120.0

3. (a) 3.2 percent and 2.6 percent
(b) 25.1 percent
(c) 126.5

4. (a) 1971: 94.45 1972: 105.0 1974: 111.68 1975: 165.4
(b) 1971, since the GNP deflator was 100; 1971
(c) 102.7 percent increase in current dollar GNP; 26.4 percent increase in constant dollar GNP

5. (a) Labor force: 1977: 10,498 = (850 ÷ .08097); 1981: 11,831 = (898 + 10,933)

Unemployed: 1976 = 727; 1978: 910 = (10,882 x .08362)

Employed: 1977: 9,648; 1978: 9,972; 1979: 10,369

Unemployment rate: 1979: 7.477 percent; 1982: 10.986 percent

(b) 1978-79: Percentage change in real GNP = 2.93; percentage change in employment = 3.98

1981-82: Percentage change in real GNP = -4.83; percentage change in employment = -3.28

(c) Positive relationship; they change in the same direction.

(d) The labor force increased more in percentage terms that did employment. That is, more of those who entered the labor force became unemployed than employed.

(e) 1979: $11,582; 1982: $10,775
(f) Value of the GNP gap = + $2.3 billion = ($121.4 - $119.1)

6. (a) Negative relationship. The three theoretical reasons given in the text are the substitution of foreign goods effect, the wealth effect on expenditure, and the interest rate effects on expenditure.
   (b) Since real output increases are associated with rising unit costs, firms will increase prices.
   (c) Equilibrium occurs when, at a given price, aggregate quantity demanded equals aggregate quantity supplied. Hence, P = 20, Y = 800. Since potential real GNP is 800, it follows that there is no GNP gap.
   (d) The SRAS curve associated with Case B is to the left of that for Case A. For example, when P = 10, quantity supplied is 400 for Case A but is only 250 for case B. In fact for all price levels, the quantity supplied for Case B is less than that for Case A. The equilibrium is now P = 30 and Y = 750. Hence, compared with your answers to part (c), real output has fallen and the price level has increased. The size of the GNP gap is now +50 = (800 - 750)

7. Answers for (a), (b), (e), and (f) are on the graph below:

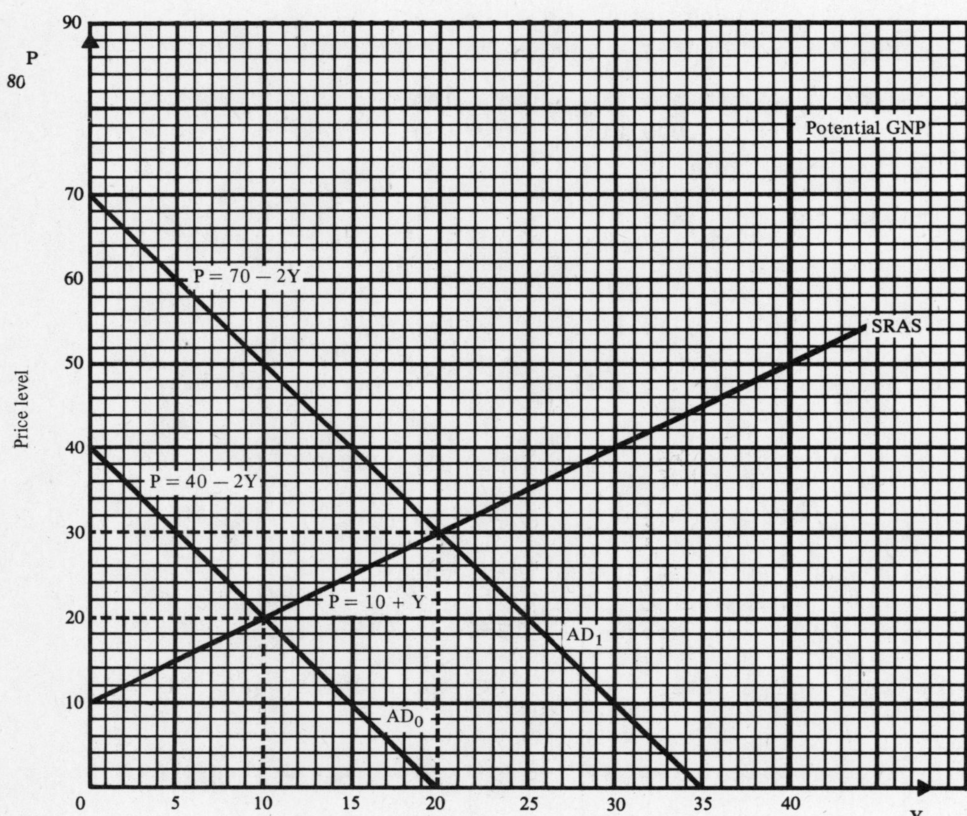

7. (c) Equilibrium is P = 20 and Y = 10. This can be solved algebraically by 40 - 2Y = 10 + Y which gives Y = 10. Substituting Y = 10 into either equation gives P = 20.
(d) The GNP gap is +30 = (40 - 10)
(e) The new equilibrium is P = 30 and Y = 20. The size of the GNP gap is + 20.
(f) For equilibrium SRAS must equal AD or 10 + Y = χ - 2Y. Since Y = 40, then 50 = χ - 80 or χ = 130. Price at potential GNP is 50, as illustrated on the graph. Since equilibrium income is at its potential level, then the GNP gap is 0.

CHAPTER 27

MULTIPLE-CHOICE QUESTIONS

1. (d) 2. (b) 3. (a) 4. (c) 5. (a) 6. (a) 7. (c) 8. (c) 9. (d) 10. (d)
11. (c) 12. (b) 13. (d) 14. (c) 15. (b) 16. (d) 17. (a)

EXERCISES

1. (See Figure 27-1) GNP = 29.0 + 165.5 + 33.5 + 19.0 + 36.5 + 8.6 - 0.2 = 291.9.

GNE = 58.5 + 168.4 + 67.2 + 90.9 - 93.3 + 0.2 = 291.9.

2. (See Table 27-2)
(a) NNI at factor cost = GNP minus capital consumption allowances minus indirect taxes less subsidies. In this case, NNI = 290 - 32 - 30 = 228.

(b) Personal Income = NNI - retained earnings - business taxes + government transfers 228 - 12- 12 + 30 = 234.

Personal disposable income = 234 - 42 = 192.

(c) Personal saving = Personal disposable income minus consumption expenditure. In this case, S = 192 - 168 = 24.

3. GDP at factor cost is found by: GNP - indirect taxes + investment income paid to non-residents - investment income received from non-residents. In this case, GDP = 2900 - 500 + 100 - 40 = 2460. Notice that GNP = GDP + indirect taxes + investment income received from non-residents - investment income paid to non-residents or 2460 + 500 + 40 - 100 = 2900.

4. Real disposable per capita income was 925.60 and 1760.55 in 1950 and 1970, respectively. The percentage increase was 90.2 percent.

5. (a) (1) C (2) I for barber (3) S_b (4) N (5) I (6) T (7) S_b
(8) (a) T (b) N (c) S_b (9) M and C (10) X (11) I (12) G
(b) 1, 2, 5, 9, (as a deduction) 10, 11, 12

6. The market value of one loaf of bread is $1.00. This is found by the sum of the value-added (0.30 from the first stage plus 0.25 from the second stage plus 0.35 from the third stage plus 0.10 from the fourth stage). Thus, the sum of the values added at each stage equal the value of the final product.

7. (a) 1980 = (168,395 divided by 81,984) times 100 = 205.4
1981 = (191,025 divided by 83,535) times 100 = 228.7

(b) 1980 = 256.9
1981 = 290.4

(c) 11.3% for consumption expenditure and 13.0% for government expenditure.

CHAPTER 28

MULTIPLE-CHOICE QUESTIONS

1. (d)	2. (a)	3. (d)	4. (c)	5. (a)	6. (c)	7. (b)	8. (d)	9. (a)	10. (a)
11. (b)	12. (b)	13. (d)	14. (c)	15. (d)	16. (b)	17. (b)	18. (c)	19. (a)	20. (d)
21. (b)	22. (a)	23. (b)	24. (d)	25. (d)	26. (b)	27. (a)			

EXERCISES

1. (a) 40, 200
(b) 160, 280
(c) .90, .61; the value of APC progressively fell.
(d) 100, 175
(e) .50 = 175 ÷ 350
(f) 0, 295. The marginal propensity to save is .50 and is constant. For an increase in Y_d from 0 to 100, saving increases from -80 to -30. The ratio of the changes is .50.
(g) 160, at which S = 0.
(h)

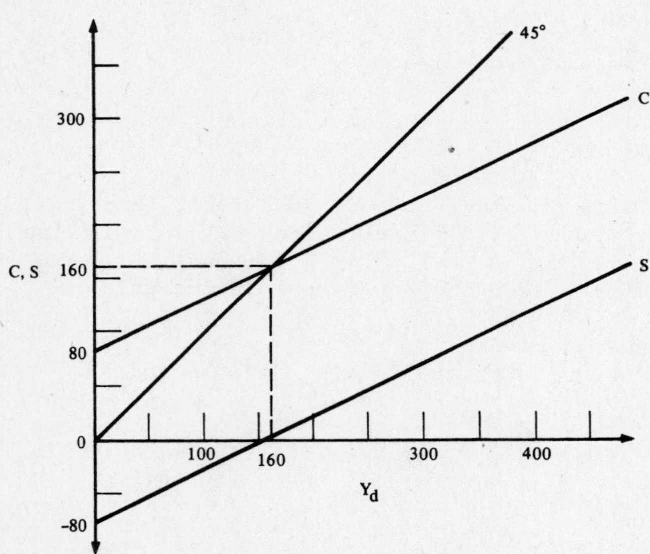

(i) Consumption expenditure is both autonomous and induced. It has an autonomous component because consumption is 80 when disposable income is zero. Since the marginal propensity to consume is 0.50, consumption is therefore induced as well.

2. (a) There is a positive relationship given by the expression $Y_d = .7Y$. It is less because taxes outweigh transfer payments.
(b) $\Delta C/\Delta Y_d = 56/70$ and $64/80$
(c) $\Delta C/\Delta Y^d = 56/100 = 64/114.3 = .56$
(d) APC = 156/140 = 1.11; APC = 220/220 = 1.00
(e) .2 = 1 - .8
(f) When $C = Y_d$, which is 220; when C = Y, which is 100

3. (a) When Y = 400, Y_d = 280 and C = 268; when Y = 500, Y_d = 350 and C = 324; when Y = 600, Y_d = 420 and C = 380

(b) The amount of income going to personal income taxes has likely increased. When Y = 400, Y_d = 240 and C = 236. When Y = 500, Y_d 300 and C = 284. When Y = 600, Y_d = 360 and C = 332. For a given level of Y, both Y_d and C have fallen.

(c) MPC out of Y_d is .9, while the MPC out of total income is .63 (= .9 times .7). When Y = 400, 500, and 600, C values are 296, 359, and 422, respectively.

4. (a) When W/p = 400, the consumption function becomes C = 60 + .8Y + .1(400) or C = 100 + .8Y

(b) C (when W/p = 400) is 500, 1300.

S (when W/p = 400) is 0, +200.

(c) The consumption function becomes C = 60 + .8Y + .1(2400) or C = 300 + .8Y.

C (when W/p = 2400) is 1500.

S (when W/p = 2400) is 0.

(d) The consumption function shifted up in a parallel fashion (an increase of 200 at every level of real national income). The saving function shifted down in a parallel fashion (a decrease of 200 at every level of real national income.

5. (a) Imports are positively related to national income by the expression M = .1Y. As national income rises, households buy more imported goods; business firms, in order to produce more goods, require more imported inputs; and it is possible for governments and firms to import various imported machines, goods, and services as part of their investment and expenditure programs.
(b) 40, 30, 20, 0, -40. Yes, because imports rise as income rises.

(c)

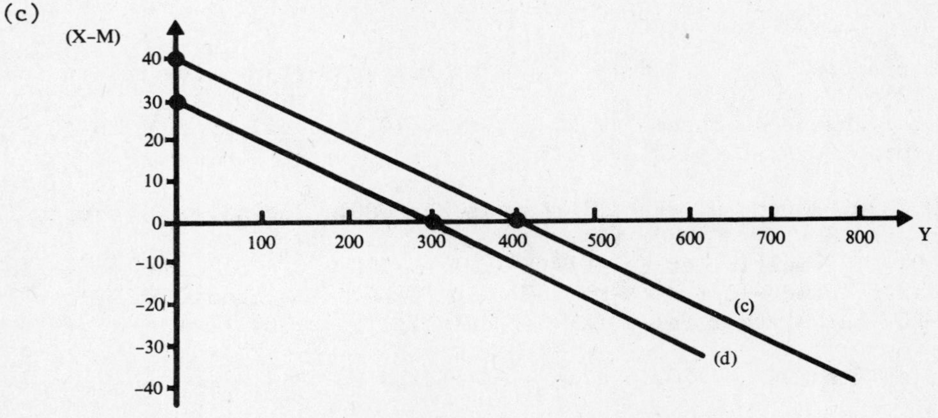

(d) Y = 0, (X-M) = 30; Y = 100, (X-M) = 20; Y = 200, (X-M) = 10; Y = 300, (X-M) = 0; Y = 400, (X-M) = -10; Y = 800, (X-M)= -50.

(e) The domestic currency appreciated; foreign income fell; domestic inflation was higher than foreign inflation.

6. (a) AE values are 150, 200, 250, 300, 350.
   (b) Equilibrium is 300 because AE(C + I + G + X - M) = Y.
   (c) AE = 350 (330 + 10 + 30 - 20). Y - AE = 50 is the amount of unintended inventory accumulation. Since there are costs associated with holding high levels of unplanned inventory, firms are likely to reduce production and lay off factors of production. As a consequence, real income falls.
   (d) ΔY = 100, 100, 100, 100; ΔAE = 50, 50, 50, 50; marginal propensity to spend = 50/100 = 0.5.
   (e) The marginal propensity not to spend is equal to (1 - .5) = .5.

7. (a) The coefficient .7 is the marginal propensity to consume out of real disposable income.
   (b) Net exports (because of imports) and consumption (through disposable income) depend on national income.
   (c) AE = 100 + .7 (.8Y) + 56 + 50 + 10 - .1Y, or AE = 216 + .46Y
   (d) 216 + .46Y = Y, or Y = 400.
   (e) When Y = 100, AE = 262; when Y = 200, AE = 308. Hence, ΔAE/ΔY = 46/100 = .46.

CHAPTER 29

MULTIPLE-CHOICE QUESTIONS

1. (c)	2. (a)	3. (a)	4. (d)	5. (c)	6. (c)	7. (a)	8. (a)	9. (b)	10. (c)
11. (c)	12. (d)	13. (a)	14. (b)	15. (d)	16. (a)	17. (b)	18. (a)	19. (a)	20. (b)
21. (b)	22. (a)	23. (d)	24. (c)	25. (c)	26. (d)	27. (a)			

EXERCISES

1. (a) AE = Y at 400. The marginal propensity to spend is .80 and is constant (ΔAE = 160, ΔY = 200, ΔAE/ΔY = .80).
   (b) The AE curve has an intercept value of 80 on the vertical axis, a slope of .80, and intersects the 45° line at an income level of 400.
   (c) AE : 90, 250, 330, 410, 450. The AE curve shifts vertically upward by 10 in a parallel fashion.
   (d) AE = 410 when Y = 400. Since AE is greater than national income, real income and employment will rise.
   (e) AE = Y at 450. The change in income is 50 and ΔY/ΔI = 5. The value of the simple multiplier is 5.
   (f) The marginal propensity to spend is .80. The marginal propensity not to spend is .20. K = 1/.2 = 5.
   (g) Since the total change in income is 50 and ΔI = 10, the value of ΔN is 40. The value 40 is composed of ΔC = 45 and Δ(X - M) = -5.

2. (a) AE : 60, 220, 300, 380, 420. Equilibrium is Y = 300. The marginal propensity to spend remains at .80.
   (b) Y fell by 100. The multiplier is ΔY/Δ(X - M) = -100/-20 = 5. The change in income was distributed -10 for (X-M) and -90 for C. The change in autonomous (X -M) was -20, but since Y fell, (X - M) only fell by -10. The rest of ΔN is consumption.
   (c) The AE curve shifts down by 20 in a parallel fashion.

3. (a) Case A: MPC = .90; Case D: MPC = .70. Consumers have become more frugal; they are saving a higher proportion of national income.

(b) AE : 80, 200, 260, 320, 350. The new AE has an intercept of 80 on the vertical axis, a slope of .60, and intersects the 45° line at Y = 200. The AE curve for case D is flatter than that for case A.

(c) The marginal propensity to spend for case D is .60, which is lower than .80 for case A. The multiplier for case D is therefore 1/(1 - .60) = 2.5.

(d) AE = Y when Y = 200.

4. (a) C = 30 + .9(.8Y)
= 30 + .72Y : Equation 8

(b) AE = 30 + .72Y + 40 + 20 + 20 - .12Y
= 110 + .60Y
The slope of the AE function is .60

(c) 110 + .6Y = Y or Y = 275

(d) (i) C = 30 + .9(.689Y)
= 30 + .62Y (approximately): Equation 10

(ii) AE = 30 + .62Y + 40 + 20 + 20 - .12Y
= 110 + .50Y
The slope is .50 and hence the AE curve is flatter.

(iii) Y = 110 + .50Y or Y = 220. National income has fallen from 275 to 220.

(e) The multipliers before and after the tax rate increase are 2.5 and 2.0, respectively.

5. (a) 400; 800; 200. The value of real wealth falls when the price level increases.

(b) Since consumption and real wealth are directly related, it follows that when real wealth increases consumption expenditures increase. The schedule indicates that consumption increases at every level of real national income when the value of real wealth increases.

(c) At p = 1, AE = Y when Y = 1000.

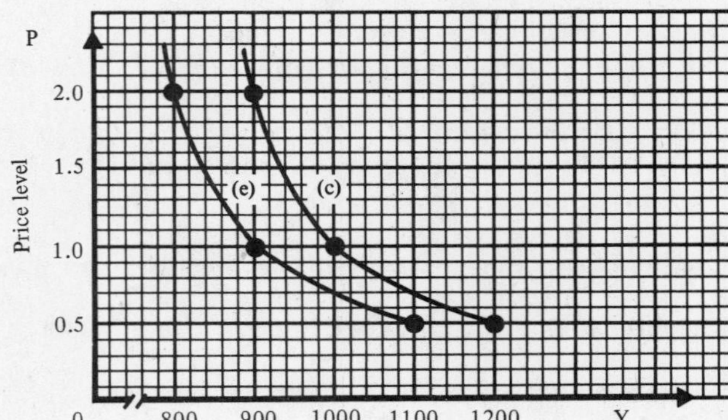

(d) This statement is correct. When the price level increases, AE decreases at every level of national income. For example, when the price level increases from 1.0 to 2.0, the equilibrium level of national income decreases from 1000 to 900. The AE curve has shifted down by 20 at every level of national income. This change is shown by a movement up the AD curve from a combination of p = 1.0 and Y = 1000 to p = 2.0 and Y = 900.

(e) When p = 1, the new equilibrium is 900. When p = 0.5, Y = 1100. When p = 2.0, Y = 800. The AD curve has shifted down or to the left.

6. (a)

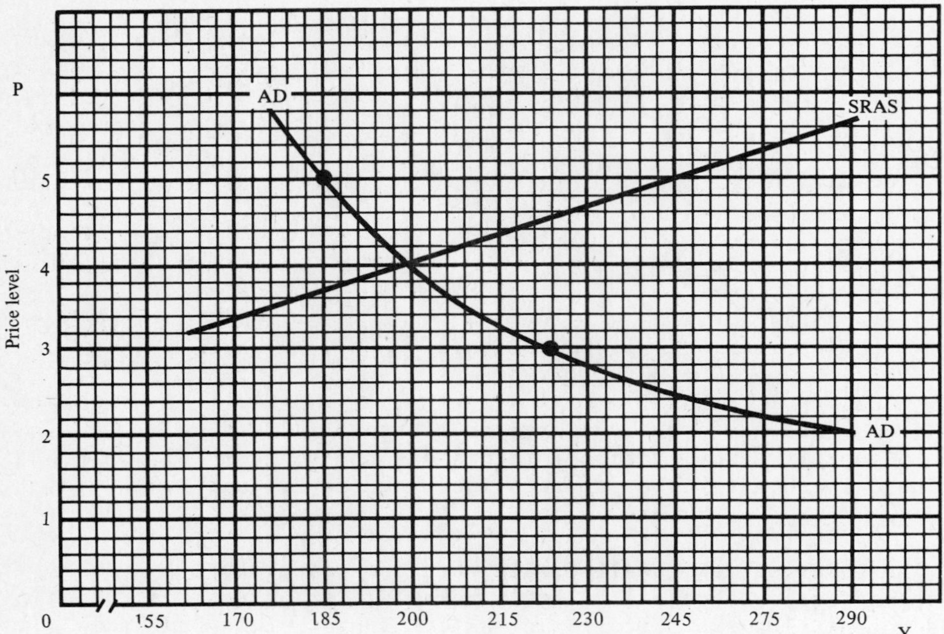

(b) The equilibrium levels are p = 4 and Y = 200

(c) When p = 4, the value of real wealth is 150. Hence, consumption expenditure plus the autonomous components of AE are 40 + .8Y. AE = Y at Y = 200.

(d) Since the marginal propensity to spend is 0.8, the value of the simple multiplier is 5.0.

(e) Equilibrium is given by Y = .8Y + 10 + 15 or Y = 125.

(f) At p = 4, the quantity of aggregate supply is 200. At p = 4, the quantity of aggregate demand is 125.

(g) For equilibrium, aggregate supply equals aggregate demand or $.02Y = \dfrac{60}{.2Y - 10}$.

According to the SRAS function, p = 3 when Y = 150. According to the AD function, when Y = 150, p = 3.

(h) The value of the multiplier is 50 divided by 15 or 3.33. This is smaller than the value of the simple multiplier which in this case is 5.0.

CHAPTER 30

MULTIPLE-CHOICE QUESTIONS

1. (b) 2. (a) 3. (a) 4. (d) 5. (c) 6. (c) 7. (c) 8. (b) 9. (c) 10. (b)
11. (d) 12. (a) 13. (d) 14. (d) 15. (a)

EXERCISES

1. (a) S, A, +, +. (c) S, A, -, -.
   (b) A, S, -, +. (d) A, S, +, -.

2. For the increase in exports, there will be increases in real GNP and the price level in the short-run (because of the inflationary gap). Wages are likely to rise and hence firms will increase their prices. This causes the SRAS curve to shift upward. Eventually, real income will be restored at potential GNP. However, the price level will be higher than before.

   For the reduction in government expenditure, real national income and the price level will fall in the short-run. <u>If wages fall</u>, then firms will reduce price levels of their goods and services and hence the SRAS curve will shift down. Real income will be restored at potential GNP and the price level will be at a lower level than before. If wages do not fall and hence prices are rigid downward, then the recessionary gap will not be eliminated and unemployment may persist for a prolonged period of time.

3. (a) The AD curve (AD_o) has the following intercept values: when Y = 0, P = 40; when P = 0, Y = 20. The slope is -2.

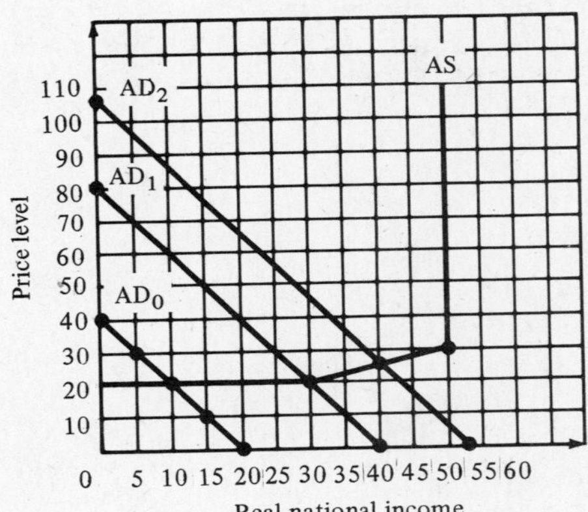

(b) The Keynesian range is a horizontal line at P = 20 for Y values from zero to 30. The intermediate range is an upward sloping line (slope of .5) from Y = 30 to Y = 50. The classical range is a vertical line at Y = 50.

(c) Y = 10 and P = 20; The equilibrium values are in the Keynesian range. Notice, 20 = 40 - 2Y means Y = 10.

(d) The AD_1 curve has the following intercept values: when Y = 0, P = 80; when P = 0, Y = 40. The slope is -2. This AD curve lies to the right of that in part (b). The equilibrium values are Y = 30 and P = 20. Hence real income has increased but the price level has remained constant.

(e) The AD_2 curve has the following intercept values: when Y = 0, P = 105; when P = 0, Y = 52.5. The slope is -2. The new equilibrium values are Y = 40 and P = 25. AD_2 lies to the right of AD_1. Hence, both output and prices have increased. The new equilibrium point lies in the intermediate range.

4. (a) The equilibrium levels are P = 11 and Y = 1000. The GNP gap is 0.

(b) The new equilibrium levels are P = 11.5 and Y = 1050. The GNP gap is a negative value (-50). This is known as an inflationary gap of 50.

(c) In the long-run, potential GNP will be restored at Y=1000. According to the AD curve (case II), Y = 1000 is associated with a price level of 16.5. Since the LRAS curve is vertical at Y = 1000, the SRAS curve will intersect the new AD curve at Y = 1000 and P = 16.5. The short-run inflationary gap will be eliminated in the long run with a rise in the price level.

(d) The SRAS curve shifts upward and intersects the AD curve and the LRAS curve at P = 16.5 and Y = 1000. The new algebraic expression for the SRAS function is P = 6.5 + .01Y. Notice that when Y = 1000, P = 16.5, which are the equilibrium values in the long run.

CHAPTER 31

MULTIPLE-CHOICE QUESTIONS

1. (d) 2. (a) 3. (a) 4. (b) 5. (c) 6. (b) 7. (b) 8. (a) 9. (a) 10. (d)
11. (c) 12. (b) 13. (b) 14. (b) 15. (c) 16. (d) 17. (c)

EXERCISES

1.

Year	Units of capital needed	New Machines required	Replacement machines	Total machines to be purchased
1	10	0	1	1
2	10	0	1	1
3	11	1	1	2
4	12	1	1	2
5	15	3	1	4
6	17	2	1	3
7	18	1	1	2
8	18	0	1	1

(a) 50 percent; (b) 300 percent

(c)

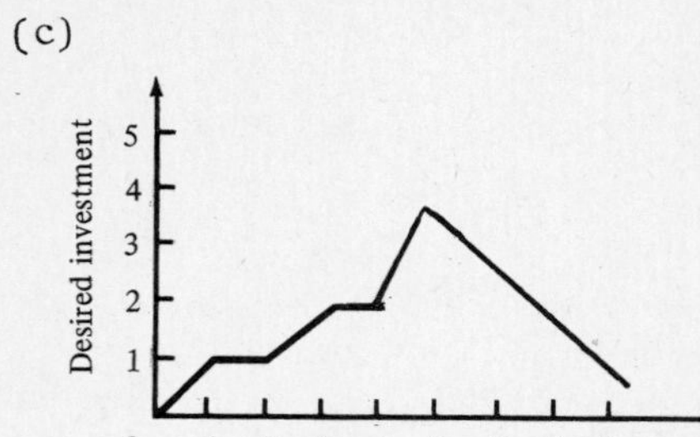

2.

Week	End of week	Inventory/ sales ratio	Desired inventory	Desired inventory plus expected sales	Weekly orders for next week
1	200	2	200	300	100
2	200	2	200	300	100
3	190	1.7	220	330	140
4	220	2	220	330	110
5	210	1.8	240	360	150
6	240	2	240	360	120
7	250	2.3	220	330	80
8	220	2	220	330	110
9	230	2.3	200	300	70

(a) 100; 130
(b) 70; 150
(c) Orders for inventory (a form of investment) fluctuate more widely than sales. This variation in investment spending is a major factor behind economic fluctuations.

3. (a) Kerry: .90 Tom: .50 average aggregate: .70

(b)

Kerry		Tom		Average Aggregate	
C	Y_d	C	Y_d	C	Y_d
80	0	80	0	80	0
1,070	1,100	530	900	800	1,000
2,060	2,200	980	1,800	1,520	2,000
3,050	3,300	1,430	2,700	2,240	3,000

(c) the MPC increases from .70 to .72.
(d) The consumption function has a steeper slope

4. (a) Canadian exports are positively related to foreign GNP. It appears that exports are 10 percent of foreign income. Foreign households will tend to buy more Canadian products when their incomes rise; foreign firms require more Canadian-produced inputs in order to expand their production.
(b) Year 3: Δ in Can. GNP = 2 x 5 = 10
Year 4: Δ in Can. GNP = 2 x (-2) = -4
Year 5: Δ in Can. GNP = 2 x (-8) = -16
Year 6: Δ in Can. GNP = 0
(c) Clearly, a business cycle has been transmitted from abroad. The cycles of both economies are similar; they peak and trough in similar fashions.

5. (a) Negative
(b) Capital stock increases from 100 to 200. Desired investment is 100.
(c) Desired capital is 350. Yes, desired investment increases by 50. Profit expectations may have improved because of new innovations and/or there are more optimistic forecasts about future sales.

6. (a)

Period	C_t	Autonomous	Accelerator	Y_t
6	271.90	200	- 68.70	403.20
7	201.60	200	-140.60	261.00
8	130.50	200	-142.20	188.30
9	94.15	200	- 72.70	221.45

(b) Trough: period 8; peak: period 4; expansion phase: periods 1, 2 and 3; recession phase: periods 5, 6, and 7.
(c) Without the accelerator, the multiplier process would have increased Y by 200 (i.e., 100/(1-.50). The accelerator process reinforced the multiplier during the expansion phase but caused a recessionary phase later on.
(d) During periods 2 to 4, the government should increase the interest rate to dampen investment. During periods 5 to 8, it should reduce the interest rate to increase investment.

CHAPTER 32

MULTIPLE CHOICE QUESTIONS

1. (c) 2. (d) 3. (c) 4. (a) 5. (b) 6. (a) 7. (d) 8. (c) 9. (b) 10. (c)
11. (c) 12. (a) 13. (d) 14. (b) 15. (d) 16. (b) 17. (b) 18. (b) 19. (a) 20. (c)
21. (b) 22. (c)

EXERCISES

1. (a) The GNP gap is the horizontal distance $Y^* - Y_0$.

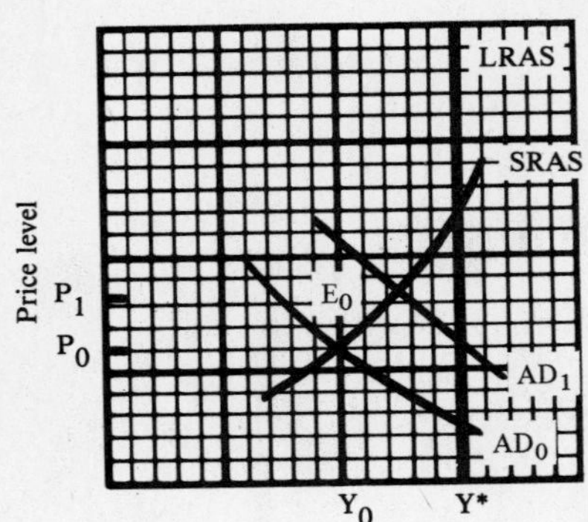

(b) Policies include tax cuts, expenditure increases, or a balanced budget increase. Aggregate demand will shift to the right to intersect the SRAS as shown above.

(c) The price level will rise from P_o to P_1, real national income will also rise.

2. (a) As shown on the diagram, the interest rate will rise and quantity of funds borrowed will rise.

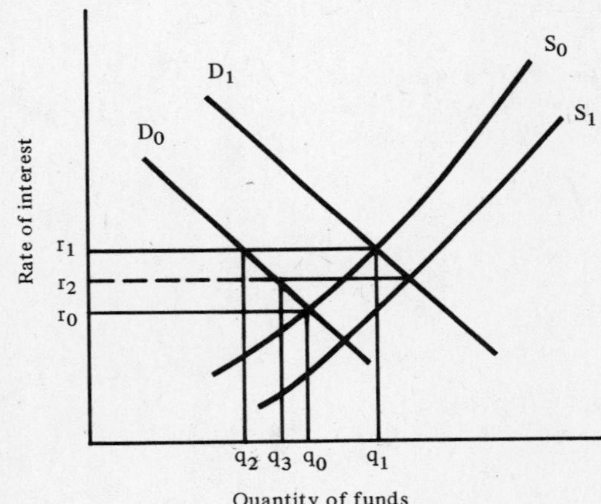

(b) With the increase in demand, government borrows an additional amount of q_2q_1, so private sector borrowing must decrease by q_2q_0. This is "crowded-out" private sector borrowing.

(c) The shift in savings curve from s_0 to s_1 will change the interest rate to r_2. Compared to (b) interest rate will be lower and private sector borrowing crowded-out is less, and equals q_3q_0

3. (a)

(1) AE	(2) AE
110	110
130	128
130	128
120	119

(b) Function 2 provides built-in stability since government expenditure responds inversely to change in private spending. Looking at the completed column above, function 2 reduces the fluctuations in total aggregate expenditure.

4. (a)

B ($M)
- 50
- 25
0
+ 25
+ 50

(b)

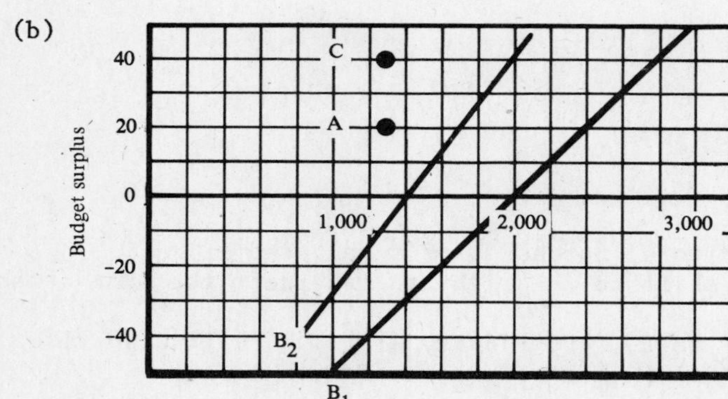

(c) A move A to C could only occur if either expenditure was cut, tax increased, or some combination of both to raise the surplus at Y = 1,300. The move would be a restrictive policy.

CHAPTER 33

MULTIPLE-CHOICE QUESTIONS

1. (b) 2. (c) 3. (a) 4. (b) 5. (c) 6. (b) 7. (b) 8. (d) 9. (b) 10. (c)
11. (a) 12. (b) 13. (c) 14. (a) 15. (b) 16. (a) 17. (b) 18. (a) 19. (b)
20. (c) 21. (d) 22. (a)

EXERCISES

1. (a) 2; (b) 1 and 3; (c) 3; (d) 1; (e) 1; and the rug serves as function 2

2. (a) neither
(b) money
(c) near money; it is easily convertible to money
(d) neither; once money, but now a collector's item
(e) neither; but readily convertible into money and considered by some to be a good store of value
(f) near money
(g) money

3. (a) Yes, initially by $240 million, because the coins were declared legal tender.
   (b) No; their value is determined by the monetary unit ascribed to them, which exceeds the value of the metal content.
   (c) No; their nominal value was fixed by the government.
   (d) If the metal content value exceeds the nominal value and/or the collectors' price, holders of these coins would be tempted to melt down the coins and sell them for their metal value. (This is an illegal act!)

4. M1 = 28,352 (11,755 + 16,597)
   M1A = 37,457 (28,352 + 9,105)
   M2 = 136,072 (37,457 + 98,615)
   M3 = 184,510 (136,072 + 48,438)

5.

Assets		Liabilities	
Currency in vaults	$ 60,000	Demand deposits	$5,000,000
Deposits in Bank of Canada	1,000,000	Savings deposits	1,000,000
Loans to public	4,000,000		
Security holdings	1,500,000		
Banking building and fixtures	360,000	Capital and surplus	920,000
	$ 6,920,000		$ 6,920,000

6. (a) Reserves +100; deposits +100
   (b) Reserves +10,000; securities -10,000
   (c) Loans +5000; deposits +5,000
   (d) Reserves +50,000; securities -50,000
   (e) Loans - 5,000; deposits -5,000
   (f) Total reserves unchanged; currency +5,000 and reserve deposits with the Bank of Canada, -5,000

7. (a) Required reserves = $10,000. No
   (b) Deposits -1,000 to 99,000 and reserves -1,000 to 9,000
   (c) Required reserves = 9,900; actual reserves = 9,000; hence its reserves are deficient by 900.
   (d) Bank A: reserves +900; loans -900. Bank B: reserves -900 to 4,100; deposits -900 to 49,100.
   (e) Bank A does not, but Bank B has a deficiency of 810.
   (f) Bank B: reserves +810; loans -810. Bank C: reserves -810 to 6,190; deposits -810 to 69,190.
   (g) No, but Bank C has a deficiency of 729.
   (h) (-900, + -810 + -729) = -2,439. Loans down by 1,710.
   (i) 10,000; 9,000

8. (a) $72 million (.08 times $900 million); 0
   (b) $72.08 million (.08 times $901 million); $.92 million
   (c) increase; 12.5 (1/.08); $12.5 million.
   (d) increase; $11.5 million (12.5 minus 1).

CHAPTER 34

MULTIPLE-CHOICE QUESTIONS

1. (a)	2. (d)	3. (a)	4. (c)	5. (b)	6. (a)	7. (a)	8. (d)	9. (c)	10. (b)
11. (c)	12. (b)	13. (c)	14. (b)	15. (c)	16. (d)	17. (a)	18. (a)	19. (d)	20. (a)

EXERCISES

1. (a) $PV = \$100/(1 + .02)^3 = \$94.23$

   (b) $PV = \$100/(1 + .06)^2 = \$89.00$

   (c) $PV = \$100/.17 = \$588.24$.

   (d) $PV = \$100/(1.10) + \$150/(1.10)^2 + \$80/(1.10)^3$

   $PV = \$90.91 + \$123.97 + \$60.11 = \$274.99$

2. (a) PV at 8% is \$120/(1.08) = \$111.11;
   PV at 10% is \$120/(1.10) = \$109.09;
   PV at 20% is \$120/(1.20) = \$100.00;
   PV at 25% is \$120/(1.25) = \$ 96.00.

   As the interest rate increased, the market price (present value) of bond A fell.

   (b) Other things being equal, the interest rate must have been falling.

   (c) PV at 10% is $\$120/(1.10)^2 = \$99.17$;

   PV at 20% is $\$120/(1.20)^2 = \$83.33$;

   PV at 25% is $\$120/(1.25)^2 = \$76.80$.

   (d) Bond A has the highest market price (compare \$100 with \$83.33). The farther in the future that dollars are received, the lower the present value of those dollars, other things equal. For bond A, \$120 was received one year from now whereas bond B paid \$120 two years from now.

   (e) He/she should be prepared to pay \$105.26 for Bond A; \$92.34 for B.

3. (a) \$1000, \$750, \$250, \$0
   (b) \$1000/2 = \$500
   (c) \$1,200/2 = \$600
   (d) \$500/2 = \$250

4. (a) As the opportunity cost of money rises, people will tend to economize on their transactions demand for money. In addition, they are prepared to take more risk (and therefore buy more bonds) since the return on bonds has risen.
   (b) Demand (either LP_1 or LP_0) equals supply at 9 percent.
   (c) At r = 9 percent, an excess demand for money exists. Households and firms would sell bonds to satisfy their increased demand for money. Hence bond prices would fall and interest rates would rise.
   (d) As interest rates rise, the quantity demanded falls until demand equals the lower value of the money supply. Interest rates would equal 10 percent and 9.5 percent for LP_0 and LP_1, respectively.
   (e) If LP_0 applies, the money supply must be 700. If LP_1 applies, the money supply must be 800. Monetary policy aimed at lowering interest rates would be more effective if LP_0 applied since it takes only an increase in the money supply of 200 (700 - 500) rather than 300 (800 - 500).

5. (a) 9 percent, at which demand is equal to supply.
   (b) 200
   (c) When Y = 1,580, AE = Y. The GNP gap is 1,600 - 1,580 = +20.
   (d) K = 1/(1 - .5) = 2. Autonomous expenditure must increase by 10 to achieve an increase in Y of 20.
   (e) Since AE must increase, the interest rate must fall and hence the money supply must rise.
   (f) 10
   (g) The interest rate must fall from 9 percent to 8 percent.
   (h) According to the diagram in exercise 4, the money supply must increase from 500 to 700: an increase of 200.
   (i) Consumption now equals 960, an increase of 12 (20 x MPC of .6). When Y = 1,600, C = 960 and AE = Y. This is equilibrium.
   (j)

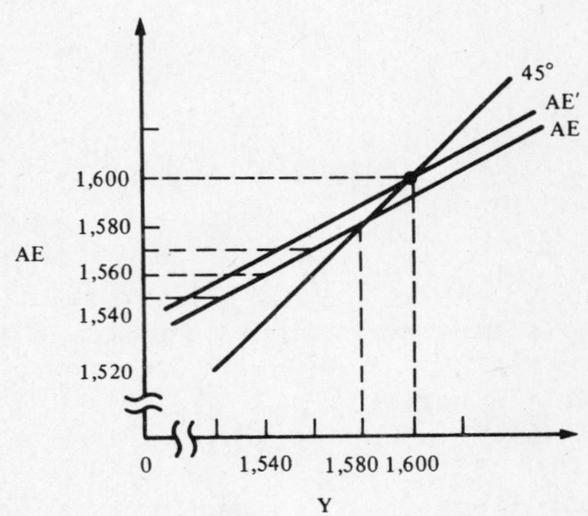

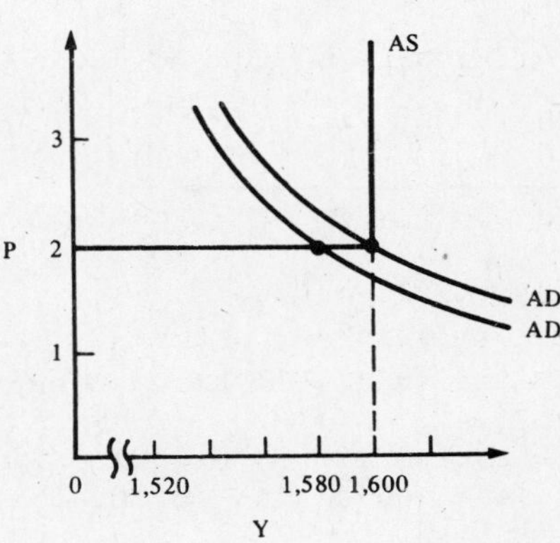

6. (a) Demand equals supply (50) at an interest rate of 10 percent. Desired investment expenditure is therefore 180.
   (b) If price increases, the LP shifts upward (the demand for money increases at every interest rate). Hence, bonds will be sold, lowering their price. As a consequence, the interest rate increases.
   (c) The new equilibrium interest rate is 14 percent.
   (d) The new level of investment is 170.
   (e) Y = AE at 360 (10 percent interest rate and P = 1.0).
   (f) Investment is now 170. AE: 340, 345, 350, 355. AE = Y at 340. National income has fallen by 20.
   (g) 

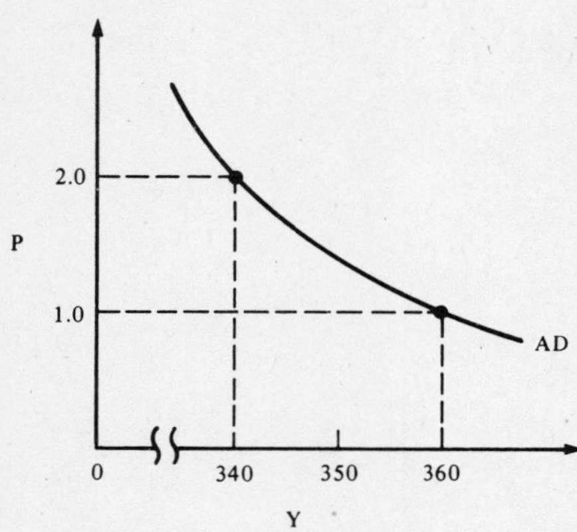

7. (a) The GNP gap is $1 billion.
   (b) Yes; the increase in G will have an expansionary effect on national income of $1 billion (.5 times 2).
   (c) Since in equilibrium 100 = .8(150) - 2i, i equals 10 percent.
   (d) The interest rate would rise to 10.4 percent. This is shown by the expression 100 = .8(151) - 2i.
   (e) Since the interest rate has increased by .4, it follows that desired investment expenditure falls by $500 million.
   (f) The interest rate increases by .4, but investment expenditure falls by only 4 x $25 million, or $.1 billion.
   (g) The crowding-out effect for part (e) is 100 percent or $.5 billion. The crowding-out effect for part (f) is $.1 billion. The result of part (e) reflects the monetarist view.

CHAPTER 35

MULTIPLE-CHOICE QUESTIONS

1. (d) 2. (a) 3. (c) 4. (d) 5. (a) 6. (a) 7. (b) 8. (b) 9. (d) 10. (c)
11. (d) 12. (b) 13. (c) 14. (d) 15. (d) 16. (c) 17. (a) 18. (a) 19. (c) 20. (b)

EXERCISES

1. (a)

Bank of Canada		All Banks	
Securities: +100	Bank reserves +100	Reserves: +100	Deposits +100

(b) $1 billion (10 x $100 million).
(c) Other things equal, interest rates are likely to fall because banks wish to make new loans and hence reduce the loan rate. All interest rates will fall because other institutions will want to be competitive with the banks.
(d) Excess reserves make money (demand deposit) creation possible. However, the actual effects on the money supply depend on the willingness and ability of banks to lend their excess reserves, and whether there are any leakages.

2. (a) decrease; left; contractionary; decrease; rise
(b) increase; right; expansionary; increase; fall
(c) fall; increase; increase

3. (a) Equating demand with supply, we obtain an equilibrium level of interest rates of 10%.
(b) At an interest rate of 10%, there would be an excess demand for money. Firms and households would sell their bonds, thereby reducing their prices and increasing the interest rate on bonds. Equating the new demand function with the money supply, we find that the new equilibrium level of the interest rate is 15%.
(c) Since an excess demand for money exists at i = 10% with the new demand for money function, it follows that the Bank of Canada must increase the money supply in order to prevent interest rates from rising. Using the function $D_M = 400 - 20i$ and the fact that i must be equal to 10 (percent), then D_M must equal 200. Since the demand for money must equal to the supply of money, and since the demand for money with a 10 (percent) rate of interest is 200, it follows that the supply of money must be increased from 100 to 200, an increase of 100.
(d) The Bank of Canada should buy bonds in the open market to provide additional reserves for banks.
(e) Given the increase in the demand for money with a fixed supply of money, the resulting interest rate increase would have reduced some investment expenditure thereby curtailing some of the economic expansion. However, with the Bank of Canada's interest rate target policy and the expansionary open market operation, economic expansion would be sustained or perhaps increased.

4. Bank of Canada: Securities, -$150 million; Bank Reserves, -$150 million
Banking System: Securities, +$150 million; Reserves, -$150 million
(a) No; deposits have not been affected.
(b) Deficient reserves are equal to 150 million. Loans will be reduced by this amount.
(c) Final decrease in the money supply is 10 times 150, or 1,500 million.
(d) The Bank of Canada is likely to increase the bank rate as a signal that it wishes the financial market to contract credit.

CHAPTER 36

MULTIPLE-CHOICE QUESTIONS

1. (b) 2. (b) 3. (c) 4. (d) 5. (c) 6. (a) 7. (c) 8. (b) 9. (d) 10. (d)
11. (b) 12. (a) 13. (d) 14. (c) 15. (c) 16. (c) 17. (d) 18. (d) 19. (b) 20. (d)

EXERCISES

1. (a) The new AD curve is AD_1 and the price level is P_1 (See diagram below.)
   (b) The SRAS would shift to the left, for example $SRAS_1$ in the diagram below, and the price level would rise further (along AD_1) to P_2. Real national income would decline to Y_1.
   (c) The aggregate demand curve would shift to AD_2 (See diagram).

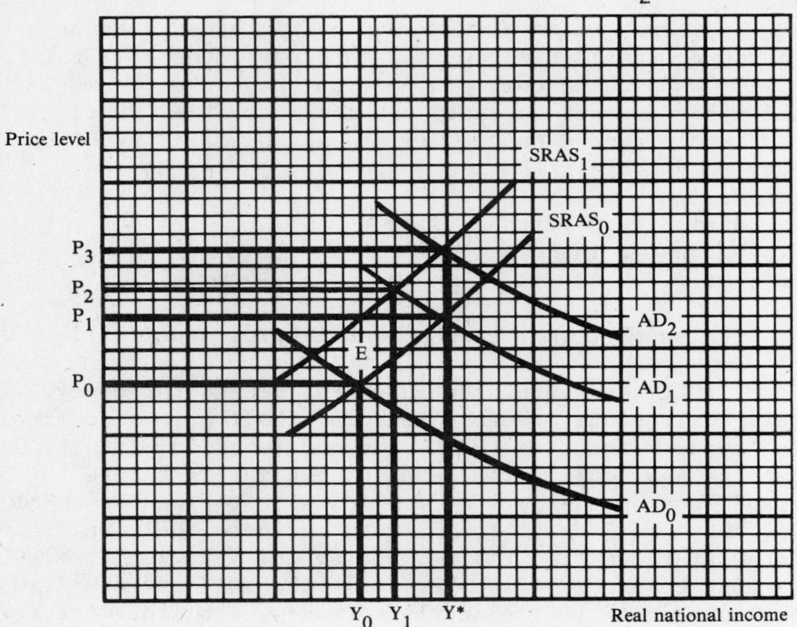

2. (a) Monetary accommodation of a single supply shock causes costs, the price level, and the money supply all to move in the same direction. The supply shock is represented in the leftward shift of the SRAS curve; monetary accommodation shifts the AD curve upward also. Equilibrium shifts from E_0 to E_2.

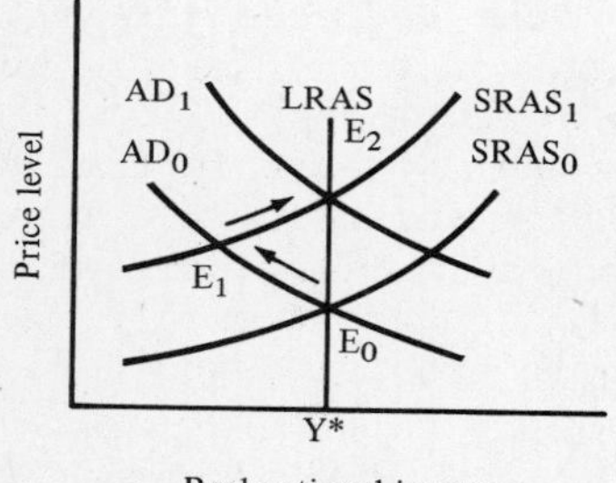

(a)

   (b) The supply curve shifts to the left as a result of the supply shock, but without monetary accommodation, unemployment puts downward pressure on wages and costs, shifting the SRAS curve back to $SRAS_0$.

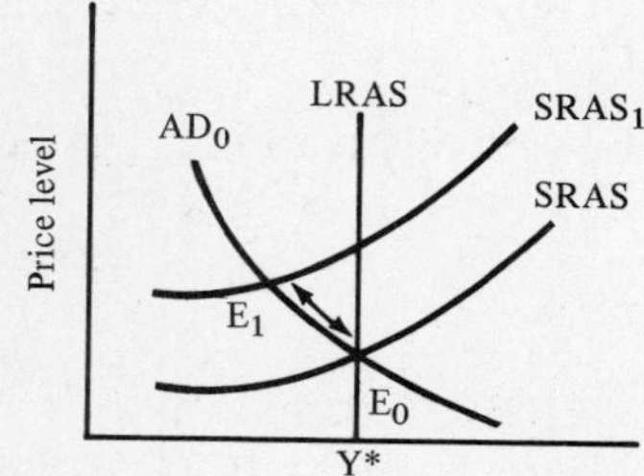

(b)

(c) The demand shock shifts the AD curve and creates an inflationary gap; this causes wages to rise, shifting the SRAS curve to the left. The monetary adjustment mechanism causes movement along the AD curve with the rise in price level eliminating the inflationary gap (at E_2).

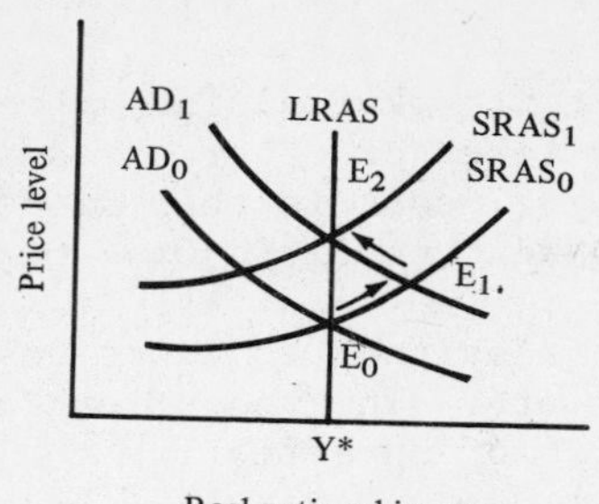

(c)

(d) The adjustment process in (c) is frustrated with monetary validation; increase in the money supply shift the AD curve to the right and the inflation is sustained.

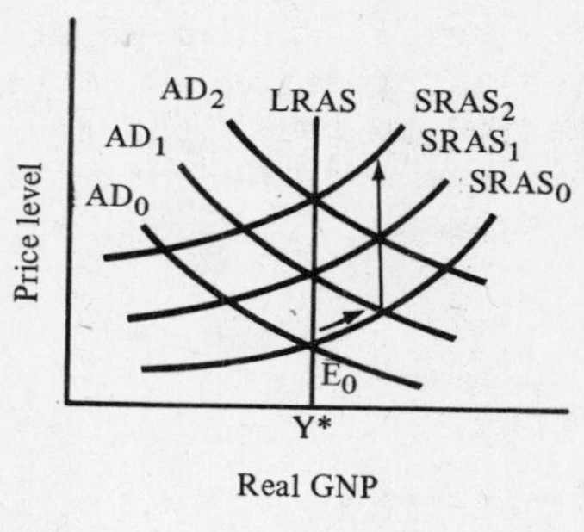

(d)

3. (a) The SRAS curve will be shifting, in this case, down to the left continuously.
   (b) It is still shifting, but not as rapidly as before.
   (c) The SRAS curve would stop shifting, but be to the left and down from $SRAS_0$. Once the rate of change of wages is zero at potential national income, and there are no further inflationary expectations, there is no force operating on the short run supply curve to cause it to shift.

CHAPTER 37

MULTIPLE-CHOICE QUESTIONS

1. (a) 2. (d) 3. (d) 4. (b) 5. (c) 6. (d) 7. (c) 8. (d) 9. (a) 10. (d)
11. (c) 12. (c) 13. (b) 14. (c) 15. (c)

EXERCISES

1. (a) Demand-deficient because of the slowdown in economic activity.
   (b) Real wage unemployment. Increased real wage costs have forced firms to lay off workers, perhaps through plant shutdowns.
   (c) Search or voluntary frictional unemployment. The accountant refused a job because of the expectation of finding another job with a higher rate of remuneration.
   (d) Frictional if short-term; structural if the social worker is unable to find work after a prolonged search.
   (e) Frictional if short term; structural if the mechanic cannot find work in London or refused to move to Montreal.
   (f) Structural; stenographers may have to undergo retraining in order to acquire skills required by word-processing equipment or other types of occupations. It would be frictional if the stenographers could find office work elsewhere.

2. (a) As the textbook explains, the nominal costs include wages, fringe benefits, and payroll taxes or other taxes (firm's contributions to UI, Canada Pension, etc). The nominal cost is then divided by the firm's product price.
   (b) Unemployment equal to $Q_3 - Q_1$ exists in this industry.
   (c) A policy designed to lower costs such as a decrease in nominal wages might be appropriate. The reduction in the purchasing power of workers is not likely to have much of an effect on the demand curve for this industry's product.

3. (a) Retraining and relocation grants to make movement of labor easier; policies to improve information about existing and (possibly) future employment opportunities
   (b) expansionary fiscal and monetary policies
   (c) increased information about employment opportunities; decrease unemployment compensation to raise the cost of staying unemployed
   (d) The real wage must be cut while aggregate demand is increased; an incomes policy may be necessary.

CHAPTER 38

MULTIPLE-CHOICE QUESTIONS

1. (c) 2. (c) 3. (a) 4. (c) 5. (c) 6. (d) 7. (d) 8. (d) 9. (a) 10. (c)
11. (b) 12. (d) 13. (a) 14. (b) 15. (c) 16. (c)

EXERCISES

1. (a) 4 percent (2.5 + 1.75 - .25)
   (b) 3 percent (4% - 1%)
   (c) 18 = 72/4
   (d) 24 = 72/3 [use the rule of 72 for (c) and (d)]

2. (a) - U increases number of nonworking dependents in population now
   (b) + - current increase in consumption; reduction in future output
   (c) - + current effect depends on investment required if "embodied"
   (d) - + contribution to intangible capital, increasing production in future
   (e) - - reduces proportion of productive population; immediate effect may be negligible so "U" could be entered.
   (f) + + more producers for given population

3. (a) The loss in consumption is 10 (92.1 - 82.1); 62.9 is the cumulative loss.
   (b) According to the schedule, C (4% growth) will equal C (2% growth) sometime in years 9 and 10. This is substantially longer than suggested by the government.
   (c) Sometime between the 17th and 18th year.
   (d) No; it is much later. According to the schedule, C (growth 4%) is double C (growth 2%) in approximately 45 years.

CHAPTER 39

MULTIPLE-CHOICE QUESTIONS

1. (d) 2. (c) 3. (c) 4. (d) 5. (c) 6. (b) 7. (b) 8. (c) 9. (c) 10. (b)
11. (a) 12. (c) 13. (c) 14. (a) 15. (d) 16. (b) 17. (a) 18. (c) 19. (d) 20. (c)
21. (c) 22. (c) 23. (c) 24. (b) 25. (c) 26. (a) 27. (b) 28. (a) 29. (a)

EXERCISES

1. (a) Assuming Canadians visit Los Angeles, the (Canadian) demand curve for U.S. dollars should shift to the right and hence the U.S. dollar is likely to appreciate.
   (b) A greater inflation rate in Canada will cause Canadian exports to the US to fall and imports from the U.S. to increase. The demand curve for U.S. dollars will shift to the right and the supply curve for U.S. dollars will shift to the left. Both are likely to cause the Canadian price of the U.S. dollar to appreciate (that is, the price of the Canadian dollar to depreciate).
   (c) The U.S. is likely to experience more capital inflows from Canada and less international capital will flow from the U.S. to Canada. Hence, both the demand and supply curves of U.S. dollars are affected such that the U.S. dollar will appreciate.
   (d) The supply curve of U.S. dollars will shift to the right and hence the U.S. dollar will depreciate.
   (e) The same answer as part (d).
   (f) The U.S. dollar will depreciate. Both the demand and supply curves of U.S. dollars will be affected.

2. (a) The domestic price is 600 per ton. Production is 7000 tons. No soybeans would be exported.
   (b) The price of soybeans now rises to 1000 units per ton. Quantity demanded is now 5000 tons and quantity supplied is about 11,400 tons. This country now exports 6,400 tons.
   (c) The U.S. dollar has depreciated and the domestic currency has appreciated.
   (d) The domestic price of soybeans is again 600. Quantity demanded and quantity supplied are both 7000 tons. Therefore, the country no longer exports soybeans.

3. (a) $1
   (b) The supply curve of Canadian dollars will shift right. The Canadian dollar will depreciate.
   (c) The supply curve shifts leftward. The Canadian dollar will appreciate.
   (d) The demand curve shifts rightward. The increased exports cause greater demand for the Canadian dollar, other things equal. The Canadian dollar will appreciate.

CHAPTER 40

MULTIPLE-CHOICE QUESTIONS

1. (c) 2. (c) 3. (c) 4. (a) 5. (d) 6. (c) 7. (d) 8. (c) 9. (a) 10. (b)
11. (a) 12. (b) 13. (c) 14. (c) 15. (b)

EXERCISES

1. (a) Canada: 88.3
United Kingdom: 154.0
W. Germany: 37.0
Japan: .2634
(b) Canada and W. Germany. Canada's actual change in the exchange rate was 13.5%, the predicted change was 4.7%. West Germany's actual change in its exchange rate was 65.4% (appreciation) whereas the predicted change is 47.5%.

2. (a) If you anticipated a further decline in the price of the Canadian dollar, you might try to negotiate a fixed price of imports in terms of Canadian dollars. Hence, if the price of the Canadian dollar declines even further, you have protected yourself. The importer bears the risk of the exchange rate change. Of course, if you anticipate that the price of the Canadian dollar is going to rise, there is no need to protect yourself. You gain!
(b) You would be selling your Canadian dollars and buying foreign currencies that are either going to appreciate or maintain their value. If you are typical of all speculators, the price of the Canadian dollar would fall in the absence of Bank of Canada policy to maintain the current price.

3. Buy; ≈ £250 million (QS - QD at $2.40); $2.30 (U.S); £.435

4. (a) The corresponding prices and quantities would be:

£ price of $	($/£)	≈ Demand for $'s (Supply of pounds)	≈ Supply of $'s (Demand for pounds)
.4565	($2.20)	505	1080
.4347	($2.30)	860	860
.4167	($2.40)	1220	600

(b) Would sell about 600 million dollars (for £250 million); limited reserves of $'s.
(c) £.671 to £.637; by reducing demand for the pound, its price in dollars would fall (that is, the price of the dollar in pounds would rise).

5. (a) Since the demand for oil tends to be fairly inelastic, importers had to pay more for the same amount of oil. <u>Ceteris paribus</u>, this caused greater balance-of-payment deficits and hence the reserve position of the oil-importing countries fell over the period 1974-1975. Of course, the reserve position of the oil-exporting countries rose substantially.
(b) Under the gold standard, the deficits of the oil-importing countries should generate a decrease in their money supplies and hence a reduction in the prices of their products. Exports to the oil-producing countries should rise and exports of oil should fall. The money supply in the oil-producing countries should be increased, generating inflation in those countries.
(c) If the petrodollars were recycled into investment projects in Canada, (i) employment in Canada should rise by the multiplier process, and (ii) Canada's reserves should increase.

(d) The price of the Canadian dollar would surely fall, ceteris paribus. The Bank of Canada, under a dirty-float system, might attempt to maintain the price of the Canadian dollar by buying Canadian dollars in the world exchange market. This means, however, that the reserve holdings of foreign currencies would fall. Speculators might pick up this piece of information and speculate that the Canadian authorities will not be able to protect the price of the Canadian dollar continually. Hence, they will sell Canadian dollars and buy other currencies. The Bank of Canada will have a much more difficult time protecting the price of the Canadian dollar.

CHAPTER 41

MULTIPLE-CHOICE QUESTIONS

1. (b) 2. (d) 3. (a) 4. (d) 5. (b) 6. (d) 7. (c) 8. (b) 9. (a) 10. (a)
11. (c) 12. (c) 13. (b) 14. (b) 15. (a)

EXERCISES

1. Public: (Canadian)

Assets		Liabilities	
Foreign currency	-40		
Deposits	+40		

Chartered Banks:

Assets		Liabilities	
Reserves with Bank of Canada	+40	Deposits	+40

Bank of Canada:

Assets		Liabilities	
Foreign currency	+40	Chartered bank deposits	+40

(a) Once the public has sold the foreign currency to the banks, their holdings of foreign currency fall by $40 million and their holdings of deposits rise by $40 million. Hence, the public has converted one asset into another.

(b) The Bank of Canada simply increases the reserves of the banks by $40 million. Recall that reserves are deposits with the Bank of Canada. The Bank of Canada's holdings of foreign exchange increase by $40 million and the deposits of the banks in the Bank of Canada increase by $40 million.

(c) The reserves of the banks increase by $40 million and the deposits of the public in the banks also increase by $40 million.

(d) The banks now have excess reserves. Required reserves (additional) are $4 million and hence excess reserves are $36 million. The money supply will increase by $400 million ($40 million x 1/.1).

(e) To prevent the money supply from increasing, the Bank of Canada should sell bonds to the banks or the public.

2. (a) AE = .5Y + 80 + 40 + (60 - 30). A = (C + I + G) = 120 + .6Y. The marginal propensity to spend is .5.

   (b) AE = Y; or .5Y + 80 + 40 + (60 - 30) = Y; Y = 150 /.5 = 300. Absorption (A) equals 300 and therefore net exports are zero.

   (c) Recessionary gap is 10. Increase in G is necessary. With a multiplier of 2, the needed change is equal to one-half the value of the recessionary gap, or 5.

   (d) X still equals 60, but imports are now .1(310) + 30, or 61. Hence net exports are -1, a trade deficit. Domestic absorption is 311, which is equal to [125 + .6 (310)].

   (e) upward; decreased; devaluing

   (f) Yes; exports will increase from 60 to 60.4. This is because the new terms of trade are 2/(2.04 x 1), which equals .98. Imports also increase from 60 to 60.4. This is because national income is 310 and the terms of trade are .98. Domestic absorption is also 310.

3. (a) (i) 160 because Y = AE.
   (ii) 159 = C + I + G
   (iii) .5 and constant
   (iv) 2 = 1/(1 - .5)
   (v) .6
   (vi) surplus of 1
   (vii) decrease by 1
   (viii) 165 = C + I + G
   (ix) deficit of 1 (-1 surplus)
   (x) 20(180 - 160)

(b) and (c) (i) Y = 166; ΔY = 6 = (3 x 2)
   (ii) C = 139.6 at Y = 166 and (I + G) = 23. Hence A = 162.6
   (iii) (X - M) = 166 - 162.6 = 3.4

   (d) Although exports rose by 3, additional imports of .6 were induced by the multiplied increase in Y. Since ΔY = 6, imports rose by .6. Net exports increased by only 2.4.

   (e) An increase in (I + G) of 10 is required to increase Y from 160 to 180. (X - M) at Y = 180 is -1.

4. (a) An expansionary fiscal policy increases real national income which in turn increases the transactions demand for money. This causes the demand curve for money to shift to the right. An excess demand for money is created and hence decision makers will sell bonds in order to obtain the additional money. This will lower the price of bonds and increase the interest rate.

   (b) For high interest rates (relative to foreign rates), capital inflows should be large and capital outflows small thereby creating a capital account surplus. For low interest rates, capital inflows will be small and capital outflows will be large thus creating a deficit on the capital account.

   (c) Since the interest rate has risen, more capital will flow into this country from other nations thus creating a capital account surplus

   (d) Increased real national income will induce more imports (a movement along the net-export function) and shift the supply curve for this country's currency to the right. Since capital outflows are assumed to be unaffected, increased capital flows will cause the demand curve to shift to the right.

   (e) An excess demand for this country's currency exists; the external value of the currency will therefore appreciate.

   (f) The increase in real national income causes a movement down the net-export function; the appreciation of the currency causes the net-export function to shift down (or to the left).

CHAPTER 42

MULTIPLE-CHOICE QUESTIONS

1. (b) 2. (d) 3. (c) 4. (d) 5. (d) 6. (a) 7. (b) 8. (b) 9. (a) 10. (b)
11. (c) 12. (d) 13. (d) 14. (a) 15. (d)

EXERCISES

1. (a) K (b) M (c) M (d) K (e) K (f) M (g) K (h) K (i) M
(j) K (k) M (l) K

2. (a) See graph 2 a) i) and 2 a) ii below.

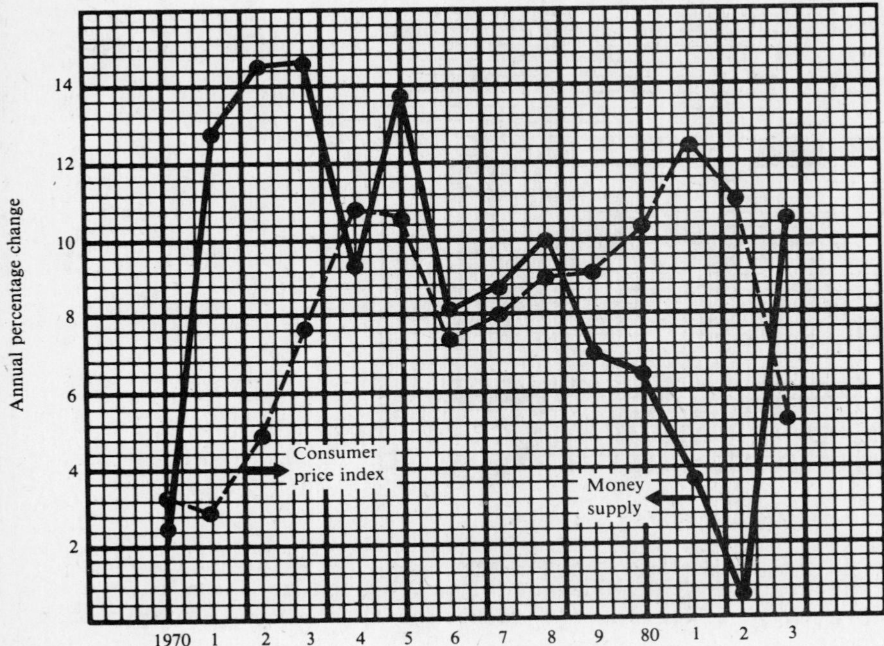

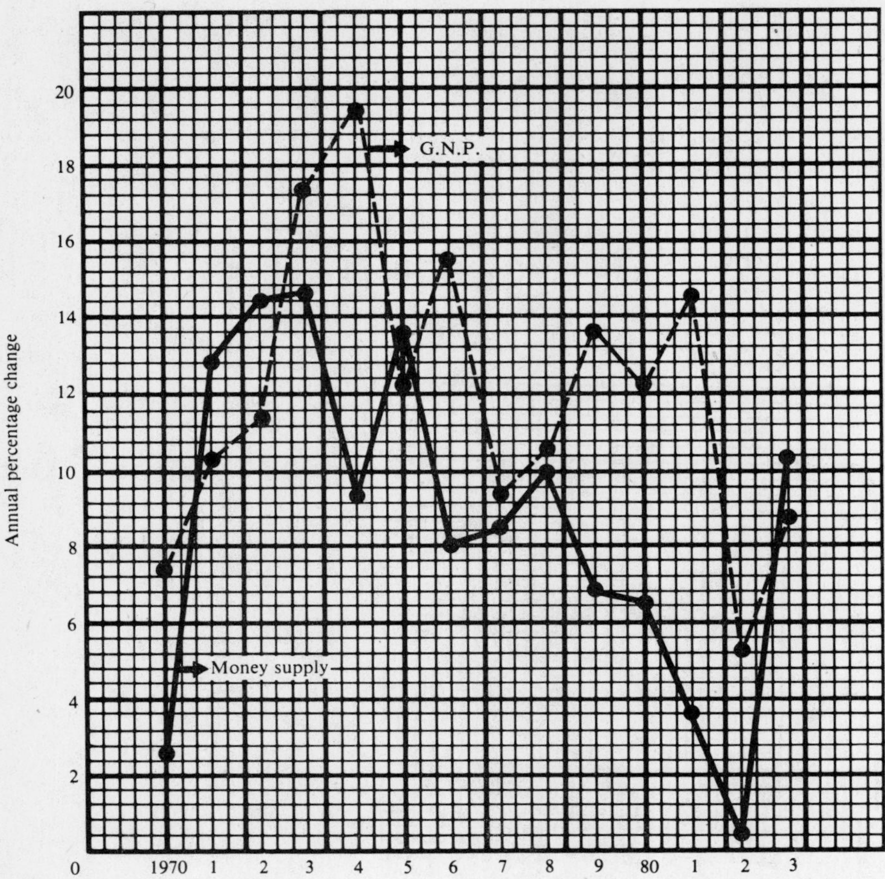

(b) With reference to graph (i), monetarists would point to the period 1970-74 and argue that the rapid expansion in the money supply gave rise to the rising inflation, albeit with a lag. Likewise, the reduction in the money supply from 1978 to 1982 reduced inflation, again with a lag. Neo-Keynesians would argue that the association between the two series is really only valid between 1975 and 1978 which was a period of mandatory wage and profits control.
In graph (ii) it is clear that the two series do move together in a rough way. However, a simple graphical description of this sort cannot be used to say anything meaningful about the cause and effect between money supply growth and GNP growth.

3. (a) Interest rate is currently 10 percent according to the equation.
   (b) The interest rate increases from 10 to 10.4 percent.
   (c) The money supply would have to increase from 60 to 60.8 in order to maintain an interest rate of 10 percent.

85 86 87 88 9 8 7 6 5 4 3 2 1